The Bounty
OF EAST TEXAS

Proceeds from the sale of **The Bounty of East Texas** cookbooks will be used for Community Service Projects sponsored by The Junior League of Longview, Inc.

Additional copies may be obtained by sending $9.95 plus $1.50 postage for each copy to the following address. (Texas residents add 5% tax.)

Junior League of Longview, Inc.
Box 866
Longview, Texas 75606

First Printing	October 1977	15,000
Second Printing	July 1981	10,000

ISBN 0-9605422-0-5
Copyright © 1977
The Junior League of Longview, Inc.
Longview, Texas

Printed by
Hart Graphics, Inc.
8000 Shoal Creek Blvd.
Austin, Texas 78758

Foreword

East Texas truly abounds in natural resources, beauty, and (as you'll soon discover) good food! We present **The Bounty of East Texas** in appreciation for the natural resources of our region as well as for the good cooks of our area. It is a pleasure to share this bounty of delicious recipes from the past and the present.

Longview is nestled in the pine forests and gently rolling hills of northeastern Texas. Many of the basic ingredients for the recipes collected here are native to this region. Lakes and rivers abound with freshwater fish, while seafood is easily accessible from the nearby Gulf Coast. During the long growing season, farmers' markets provide farm-to-home produce, and in this jet age, our supermarkets make the exotic and out-of-season within everybody's reach. This fertile land assured a prosperous agricultural region long before the oil boom of the 1930's.

The discovery of oil revolutionalized Longview and East Texas. Since that time industry has been attracted to the area's petroleum reserves as well as to its adequate water supply and appealing tax structure. Northerners who migrate to our comfortably warm climate often stay permanently. Lignite, often called "the fuel of tomorrow" may well be found in vast reserves all over this region.

Longview, thriving in a prosperous present, also promises a bright tomorrow. It is our hope that **The Bounty of East Texas** will enable us to share our East Texas hospitality and delicious food with each and every one of you!

Original Woodcuts by Vera Mitchell Garlough

Contents

Appetizers 7
Soups 41
Salads and Dressings 61
Meats 109
Seafoods 147
Poultry and Game 171
Eggs and Cheese 193
Vegetables 205
Breads and Sandwiches 231
Desserts 251
Accompaniments 295
Men's Fare 303
Wine and Beverages 315
Index and Charts 332

cIc This symbol is used throughout the book to designate recipes that were originally printed in the **Charity League Cookery**, 1953.

ARTICHOKE DIP

1 (6 oz.) jar marinated
  artichokes, drain and
  save liquid
1 C. sour cream
½ t. onion salt
Dash cayenne pepper

Place artichokes in blender and blend. Transfer to a bowl and add sour cream, onion salt, cayenne and some of the reserved liquid if needed to thin. Serve with crackers or fresh vegetables.

Cookbook Committee

ARTICHOKE NIBBLES

2 (6 oz.) jars marinated
  artichoke hearts
1 large onion, finely chopped
1 clove garlic, minced
4 eggs
¼ cup fine dry seasoned
  bread crumbs
½ t. salt
1/8 t. pepper
1/8 t. orégano
1/8 t. Tabasco sauce
½ lb. sharp Cheddar cheese,
  grated
2 T. minced parsley

Drain marinade from 1 jar of artichokes into a skillet. (Drain other jar of artichokes, discarding marinade.) Chop artichokes and set aside. Sauté onion and garlic in marinade until onion is limp, about 5 minutes. Beat eggs until fluffy, then add bread crumbs, salt, pepper, orégano and Tabasco sauce. Stir in cheese, parsley, artichokes and onion mixture. Mix well and pour into a greased 11" x 7" baking pan. Bake in a preheated 325° oven 30 minutes. Let cool in pan and cut into 1 inch squares.
Serve warm or cold. Good either way! (These can be reheated in oven 10 to 12 minutes.)

YIELD: 6 dozen

Cookbook Committee

HOT ARTICHOKE DIP

1 C. Hellmann's mayonnaise
1 C. Parmesan cheese
1 (14 oz.) can artichoke hearts,
  drained and chopped

Mix all together. Place in baking dish and bake at 325° for 20-30 minutes or until lightly browned. Serve with Melba Rounds, Garlic Melba Rounds or homemade bread rounds. Easily doubled or tripled.

SERVES 6

Mrs. Tommy Fugua
Texarkana, Texas

Donor. Martha Hoss Whitehead
  (Mrs. R. Laughton, Jr.)

ANTIPASTO
"Serve as a salad or a dip"

1 (8 oz.) jar mushrooms, drained
1 (14 oz.) can artichokes, drained
1 (5 oz.) jar Spanish olives, drained
1 can pitted ripe olives, drained
¼ C. bell pepper
½ C. celery

MARINADE :
¾ C. oil (½ olive oil and ½ salad oil)
¾ C. white vinegar
¼ C. minced dry onions
2 t. Italian seasoning
1 t. salt
1 t. seasoned salt
1 t. garlic salt
1 t. onion salt
1 t. Accent
1 t. sugar
½ t. seasoned pepper

Mince all vegetables fine. Combine marinade ingredients and bring to a boil. Pour over minced vegetables and chill overnight. Will keep two weeks or longer in refrigerator. Serve on crackers.

YIELD: 1⅓ quarts

Mrs. Gay Gene Glover

ARKANSAS HOT PEPPER PECANS

¼ C. butter
2 C. pecan halves
4 t. soy sauce
1 t. salt
12 dashes Tabasco

Melt butter in baking pan. Spread pecans evenly in pan and bake at 300° for 30 minutes. Combine soy sauce, salt and Tabasco and toss with pecans. Spread on paper towel to cool.

Mrs. Jack Williams
San Antonio, Texas

BROCCOLI TURNOVERS

3 (10 oz.) pkgs. frozen broccoli spears OR chopped spinach
6 oz. cream cheese
3 T. fresh lemon juice
¼ t. salt (or to taste)
Flaky pastry (See Index)
¼ C. butter, melted
Parmesan cheese
1 C. sour cream

Cook broccoli or spinach in salted water. Drain well. In mixer, cream the cheese and add lemon juice and salt. Blend well. Cut coarse stems off broccoli and add to mixer. Make a flaky pastry and cut 3 or 4 inches rounds. Place a teaspoon of the broccoli mixture in the center of each round and fold over. Crimp the edges with a floured fork. May be frozen at this point. Just before baking, brush with melted butter and sprinkle with Parmesan cheese. Bake at 350° for 15-20 minutes. Serve while hot with a teaspoon of sour cream on top.

Dorothy Robbins Kennedy
(Mrs. George E., Jr.)

CAPONATA
(Eggplant Relish)

1½ lbs. eggplant, peeled and cut into ½ inch cubes
1 C. olive oil
1½ C. chopped celery
2 green peppers, sliced
1 onion, chopped
2 cloves garlic, chopped
2½ C. plum tomatoes, drained
⅓ C. wine vinegar
2½ T. salt
2 T. sugar
2 T. capers
1 T. tomato paste
1 T. chopped parsley
10 pitted green olives, coarsely chopped
Freshly ground pepper
1 T. olive oil, optional
2 T. pine nuts, optional
1 T. parsley, chopped

Sauté eggplant in olive oil for 10 minutes. Remove the eggplant with a slotted spoon, drain on paper towels, and reserve it. In the remaining oil, sauté chopped celery and green peppers for 10 minutes, or until the vegetables are soft. Add chopped onion and garlic and cook until soft. Add the reserved eggplant, canned plum tomatoes, vinegar, salt, sugar, capers, tomato paste, parsley, green olives, and pepper to taste. Simmer the mixture for 15-20 minutes. Sauté pine nuts in 1 T. olive oil until they are lightly colored. Add the nuts to the eggplant mixture and add 1 T. chopped parsley. Transfer the caponata to small jars, seal them, and store them in the refrigerator. Keeps for at least 2 or 3 weeks. Serve on wheat crackers or crusty Italian bread.

YIELD: 8 cups

Eleanor Croxton Lawrence
(Mrs. Thomas W.)

CAVIAR MOLD

1 (8 oz.) pkg. cream cheese
1 T. mayonnaise
3 green onions with tops, finely chopped
3 oz. caviar
3 hard cooked eggs, finely chopped or grated

Soften cream cheese. Beat in mayonnaise and green onions with electric mixer. Mold in small bowl lined with plastic wrap. Refrigerate. Before serving, invert on plate, ice with caviar and surround with egg. Serve with buttered home-made Melba toast.

Eleanor Croxton Lawrence
(Mrs. Thomas W.)

SOUR CREAM AND CAVIAR CRÊPES

12 crêpes
2 cartons sour cream
½ onion, grated fine
¼ t. salt
3 jars black or grey caviar
Juice of 1 lemon
3 hard boiled eggs, grated fine

Mix together the sour cream, grated onion, and salt. Set aside. To assemble crêpes, fill each crêpe with 2 T. sour cream mixture, then layer over the sour cream about 2 t. caviar, sprinkle a few drops of lemon juice, and about 2 t. grated egg.
Fold the crêpe and place on a decorative platter or silver tray. Garnish by adding more sour cream to top of crêpes, then more grated egg. Serve cold. Note: This makes a pretty cake-like crêpe. If served round, just layer flat crêpes and filling, ice with additional sour cream and grated egg. To serve cut in wedges.

SERVES 12

Dorothy Robbins Kennedy
(Mrs. George. E., Jr.)

CAVIAR SUPREME

2 (4 oz.) jars caviar
Juice of 1 lemon (or lime)
1 C. sour cream
1 onion, grated
1 hard-boiled egg, grated

Place caviar in serving bowl or icer and pour the lemon juice (or lime) over and stir. Spread the sour cream over the top. Sprinkle the grated onion and finally the grated egg.

Curtain Call Cookbook

Appetizers 13

MOLDED CAVIAR

1 envelope gelatine
¼ C. milk
1 C. mayonnaise
1 (3½ oz.) jar inexpensive caviar
Juice of 1 lemon
1 C. heavy cream, whipped

Dissolve gelatine in milk and heat to melt. Cool. Mix mayonnaise, caviar and lemon juice. Add cooled gelatine. Fold in whipped cream. Pour into a greased 2 C. mold. Chill until firm. Serve with Melba toast or crackers. May be garnished with grated hard-boiled eggs or additional caviar.

Carmen Huggins Hilliard
(Mrs. George M., III)

CANTONESE EGG ROLLS

1 C. cooked diced shrimp
1 C. minced cooked pork
1 C. minced celery
1 C. finely chopped green onion
1 (8 oz.) can water chestnuts, diced and drained
1 T. oil
1 T. smooth peanut butter
2 t. salt
1 t. sugar
1/8 t. ground black pepper
1/8 t. five spice powder
2 eggs, well beaten
8 egg roll wrappers

Mix together. Place about 2 T. on center of wrapper and roll up, carefully tucking in the ends. Fry in deep fat until golden. Cut into quarters.

Mrs. John Ferrell

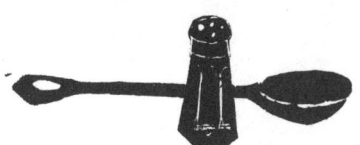

DILL DIP

1 (8 oz.) pkg. cream cheese
⅔ C. mayonnaise
1 T. dill seed
1 T. dry onion
1 T. dried parsley flakes
1 t. Beau Monde
Dash Tabasco

Soften cream cheese and blend in other ingredients. Serve as a dip with raw vegetables or chips.
YIELD: 2 cups

Normand Dufilho Wilkinson
(Mrs. Jacques)

CANAPÉS

BACON-CHEESE
Grind half-cooked bacon with onion, grated sharp Cheddar Cheese, and Worcestershire sauce. Spread on bacon crackers. Put under broiler until bubbly.

CRAB
Mix a can of Geisha crabmeat (drained) with Hollandaise sauce, lemon juice and chives to taste. Spread on toast rounds and heat under broiler.

MUSHROOM
Spread toasted bread rounds with mayonnaise. Spread chopped onion and mushroom mixture which has been sautéed in butter on squares and sprinkle with Parmesan Cheese. Run under broiler until bubbly and golden.

ONION
Spread toasted bread rounds with mayonnaise. Place a tissue paper thin onion slice sprinkled with Parmesan cheese on top of round and run under broiler until golden and bubbling.

CHERRY TOMATOES
Spread toasted bread rounds with butter, sliced tomatoes, salt and pepper, Parmesan cheese, orégano and grated onion. Dot with butter and run under broiler for 5—6 minutes.

HOT CHEESE BALLS

1½ C. grated American cheese
1 T. flour
¼ t. salt
1/8 t. cayenne pepper
3 stiffly beaten egg whites
Cracker crumbs

Mix cheese with flour and seasonings. Add egg whites and shape into small balls. Roll balls in cracker crumbs and fry in deep fat until brown. Drain on absorbent paper. Serve while hot as an appetizer or with salad course.

Virginia Elms MoRoo
(Mrs. J. T.), Dallas, Texas

CHEESE WAFERS

2 C. sharp cheese, grated
1 C. margarine
2 C. flour
Salt
Dash red pepper
2 C. Rice Krispies

Cream cheese and margarine. Add sifted dry ingredients. Fold in Rice Krispies. Pinch dough and roll into small balls. Place on ungreased cookie sheet and press flat with fork. Bake at 350° about 8 minutes or until done. May be frozen.

Mrs. George M. Hilliard, Jr.
Jacksonville, Texas

CHEESE SQUARES
"Drop in company? Freezer to guests in a few minutes."

1 (1 lb.) pkg. Old English cheese
1 C. butter or margarine
Pinch salt
2 loaves bread (day-old)

VARIATION: To basic recipe Substitute:
4 loaves Pepperidge Farm Cracked Wheat Bread
Add:
1 t. Tabasco
1 t. onion powder
1½ t. Worcestershire sauce
Dash cayenne
2 T. dill weed
1 T. dry onion
1 can jalapeño peppers, sliced
Sesame seeds

Soften cheese. Add butter and salt and mix well. Cut the crusts off bread. Ice with cheese mixture between slices of three slices of bread. Then ice the four sides of stacked bread like a cake. Slice into fourths. Place on cookie sheet and freeze. These must be cooked frozen. Bake at 350° for about 15 minutes or until golden brown.

Marguerite Swearingen Harrington (Mrs. H. M.)

Put four slices of jalapeño peppers between layers of bread. Sprinkle iced layers with sesame seeds.

YIELD: 20 per loaf or 80 total

Maud Norton Bivins
(Mrs. James K., III)

ELEGANT CHEESE DIP

2 Camembert cheese
1 Liederkrantz cheese
¼ lb. Roquefort cheese
¼ lb. unsalted butter
2 T. flour
2 T. butter
1 pt. heavy cream
1 (4¼ oz.) can chopped ripe olives
1 (2 oz.) jar chopped pimiento
Cayenne pepper

Melt cheese and butter slowly in top of double boiler. Make a cream sauce of flour, butter and cream. Cook slowly. When done, fold in cheese mixture. Add olives, pimiento and pepper.

Mrs. Kurt Borris

SAUSAGE CHEESE MOLD

1 lb. Velveeta cheese
1 lb. Cheddar cheese
1 lb. extra sharp N. Y. State cheese
2 lbs. hot bulk sausage
6 jalapeños, seeded and Chopped
1 C. finely chopped onions

Melt cheese in top of double boiler. Crumble sausage in skillet and sauté until done. Drain on paper towels. Fold in sausage, jalapeños and onions. Pack into a well-oiled bundt pan lined with Saran wrap. Chill. Serve with assorted crackers.

SERVES 60—70

Mrs. Kurt Borris

WALNUT SWISS CHEESE SPREAD

8 oz. Swiss cheese, grated
½ C. butter, softened
3 T. milk
2 T. dry Sherry
¼ t. salt
1/8 t. cayenne pepper
1 C. finely chopped walnuts

Beat until creamy all ingredients except the walnuts. Pack into a 2 cup non-metal container. Cover tightly. Refrigerate at least 24 hours. Remove from refrigerator 1 hour before serving. Garnish with walnuts. Serve with crackers. Will keep for 2 weeks.

YIELD: 2 cups

Sharon Wildstein Bindler
(Mrs. Donn)

Appetizers 17

CHEESE MOLD

1 (5 oz.) jar Kraft Old English cheese spread
1 (8 oz.) pkg. cream cheese
¼ C. Bleu cheese
1 T. Worcestershire sauce
½ t. Accent
1 small glass dried chipped beef

Have cheeses at room temperature. Mix cheeses, Worcestershire sauce and Accent together with an electric mixer until light and fluffy. Shape mixture into a ball. Place in bowl lined with foil. Chill overnight. About one hour before serving, roll ball in finely chopped chipped beef. Place on platter and surround with crisp crackers. Very good and freezes well.

VARIATION: To basic recipe Substitute:
½ lb. natural Cheddar cheese, grated
1 (3 oz.) pkg. cream cheese, softened
Omit: Bleu cheese
Add:
¼ C. pitted ripe olives, chopped
3 T. Sherry
Dash each onion, garlic and celery salts

Faye Jeter Lewis
(Mrs. Harry, Jr.)

Variation
Joanie Marvel Abbott
(Mrs. Frank)

ROQUEFORT RING

1 envelope gelatine
¼ C. cold water
6 oz. Roquefort cheese
6 oz. cream cheese, softened
½ C. heavy cream
1½—2 T. grated onion
4 or 5 stuffed green olives, chopped
Salt and white pepper to taste

Sprinkle gelatine over cold water and let soften ten minutes. Stir in a double boiler over hot water until it is dissolved, then cool. Press Roquefort cheese through a sieve into a bowl and blend with cream cheese. Stir in cream, gelatine, onion, green olives and salt and pepper. Pour into a 3 C. ring mold and chill, stirring gently once or twice until it is set. Unmold and serve with **unsalted** crackers.

SERVES 15

Carolyn Smith Russell
(Mrs. Ralph H.)

CHUTNEY ROLL

¼ lb. Bleu cheese
8 oz. cream cheese
¼ C. chopped chutney
½ C. chopped toasted almonds

Mix the Bleu cheese, cream cheese and chutney. Form into a large roll and roll in chopped almonds. Chill or freeze. Serve with crackers.

Patsy Lacy Griffith
(Mrs. J. W.), Sante Fe, New Mex.

APPETIZER CHEESE CAKE

1 box Nabisco small square aged Cheddar cheese crackers
½ C. stuffed green olives, finely chopped
½ C. celery, finely chopped
1 medium green pepper, finely chopped
1 small onion, finely chopped
2 T. lemon juice
1 t. salt
1 t. Worcestershire sauce
¼ t. paprika
Dash Tabasco
2 C. sour cream

Crush ⅔ box of crackers; cover sides and bottom of a 9" pie pan with ½ crumbs. Combine vegetables and other ingredients and pour over crust. Spread evenly and top with rest of the crumbs. Cover with wax paper and refrigerate at least 24 hours. Serve on Melba Rounds.

Celeste Davis

Donor: Cookbook Committee

HOT GALA PEPPER DIP

1 (8 oz.) pkg. cream cheese
2 T. milk
1 (2½ oz.) jar dried beef, diced
2 T. finely chopped onion
½ t. garlic salt
½ t. pepper
¼ C. finely chopped green pepper
½ C. sour cream
½ C. chopped pecans

Melt cream cheese and milk in top of double boiler. Add remaining ingredients. Serve hot in chafing dish with Melba Rounds or toast points. Also good served on English muffins for brunch. This recipe is easily doubled.

VARIATION:
Combine cream cheese and milk until well blended, add other ingredients except pecans and put into a 9" pie plate. Top with pecans which have been toasted in 2 T. margarine and ½ t. salt. Bake at 350° for 20 minutes.

SERVES 8-10
Betty Ruth Curtis Gray
(Mrs. Charles)

CURRIED CHICKEN DIP

1 (8 oz.) pkg. cream cheese
2-3 T. mayonnaise
½ t. curry powder
Dash salt
1 (5 oz.) can boned chicken or turkey

Smooth cream cheese with mayonnaise. Add curry powder, salt and chicken or turkey. If needed, add more mayonnaise. Refrigerate. Serve with dip size Fritos.

Susie Moore French
(Mrs. Paul E.)

CHICKEN TURNOVERS

PASTRY:
1½ C. margarine
3 C. sifted flour
3 (3 oz.) pkgs. cream cheese

FILLING:
1 small can Swanson boned chicken
1 (10¾ oz.) can cream of mushroom soup
Paprika

VARIATION: Add
½ t. curry powder
Parmesan cheese to filling and sprinkle on top

Prepare pastry by mixing together margarine, flour and cream cheese. Chill. Roll thin and cut into 2" rounds.

FILLING:
Combine chicken and soup. Place 1 t. of filling on rounds and fold over. Press edges with a fork and prick pastry. Sprinkle with paprika. Bake at 400° for 20 minutes. May be frozen before or after baking.

YIELD: 200

Dorothy Robbins Kennedy
(Mrs. George E., Jr.)

CHILI CHEESE DIP

1 lb. ground meat
1 onion, chopped
1 C. celery, chopped
2 lbs. Velveeta cheese, melted
1 (10 oz.) cans Rotel tomatoes, drained
1 (8 oz.) can mushroom pieces
Salt
Pepper
Garlic

Sauté ground meat, onion and celery. Drain. Melt Velveeta in double boiler with Rotel tomatoes and combine all ingredients together. Serve warm.

Kathie Gorman Russell
(Mrs. E. O., Jr.)

CHILI DIP

2 lbs. ground round
½ lb. bulk sausage (hot or regular)
1 (12 oz.) can V-8 juice
1 pkg. William's Chili Mix
1 (15 oz.) can hot chili
2 T. cumin
Salt
Garlic
Worcestershire sauce
Tabasco sauce
Seasoned salt
Finely chopped onions
Finely chopped stuffed olives
1 lb. grated sharp cheese

Brown meat and sausage. Add V-8 juice, chili mix, chili, cumin and seasonings to taste. Simmer for several hours. Serve hot garnished with chopped onions, olives and cheese. Serve with chips.

SERVES 20

Mrs. Robert A. Bruyere

PICADILLO DIP

1 lb. venison or lean beef, ground
1 onion, chopped
1 (16 oz.) can solid pack tomatoes
1 (16 oz.) can stewed tomatoes
3 T. vinegar
1½ t. sugar
1 clove garlic (or more)
¼ t. orégano
1½ t. cinnamon
1 pinch cloves
½ t. ground comino
1 t. salt (or more)
1 C. raisins
1 t. chili powder
Tabasco to taste
½ C. slivered almonds, blanched & toasted

Brown meat; drain well. Add onion; sauté until clear. Add other ingredients, except almonds, and bring to a boil. Simmer 20 minutes. Serve warm in a chafing dish with toasted almonds on top. Serve with tortilla chips to dunk, or may be spread on crackers.

SERVES 24

Nancy Rogers Smith
(Mrs. Robert H.)

CHILI SOUR CREAM BISCUITS

1 can top grade chili (no beans)
16 oz. sour cream (divided)
3 pkg. Hungry Jack Buttermilk canned biscuits
Parmesan cheese

Remove any gristle from the chili and mix the chili with 1 cup of the sour cream. Use a sharp knife and slice through the center of the uncooked biscuits so that you have two complete thin circles from the one biscuit. Place the cut biscuits on a buttered cookie sheet and make a depression on the center of each with your thumb. Put a heaping teaspoon of the mixture in the indention and top with sour cream; then sprinkle with Parmesan cheese liberally. Bake in 350° oven for about 12 minutes.

YIELD: 60
Dorothy Robbins Kennedy
(Mrs. George E., Jr.)

HOT CLAM DIP

8 oz. Old English cheese
2 (8 oz.) pkgs. cream cheese
1 large onion, chopped
5 (6½ oz.) cans minced clams, drained and rinsed in cold water
¼ C. catsup
¼ C. lemon juice
¼ C. Worcestershire sauce
½ t. cayenne pepper
½ t. salt
4 dashes Tabasco
¼ C. dry white wine

Melt cheeses together and add remaining ingredients. May add more wine if needed to thin Serve hot from a chafing dish with Melba Rounds.

Eleanor Croxton Lawrence
(Mrs. Thomas W.)

CORNED BEEF CAPERS

1 (15½ oz.) can corned beef
7 T. real mayonnaise
5 T. prepared mustard
¼ t. pepper
½ t. garlic salt
5 (or more) dashes Tabasco
1 loaf thin sandwich bread (fresh that day)
½ C. melted butter
Parmesan cheese

Flake the corned beef. Mix in mayonnaise, mustard and seasonings. Mix well. Trim crusts from bread. Spread corned beef mixture on bread slices. Roll up tightly and place side by side on cookie sheet. (Rolls may be frozen at this point.) Brush on all sides with melted butter, and roll in grated Parmesan cheese. Cut each roll into thirds and bake on ungreased cookie sheet at 400° for 8-10 minutes.

Martha Hess Whitehead
(Mrs. R. Laughton, Jr.)

HARRIETTE BRIGGS CEVICHE

2 lbs. white fish fillets (flounder is best)
1 C. fresh lime juice
Stuffed olives
½ C. white wine vinegar
6 T. salad or olive oil
1 medium tomato, diced
2 T. parsley
1 t. salt
¼ t. orégano
¼ t. pepper
½ bottle Picante sauce
Seasoned salt

Cut up fish before completely thawed. Put lime juice over fish and refrigerate overnight. Squeeze out lime juice and add all other ingredients. Serve with crackers.

Jo Ruth Edwards Maness
(Mrs. Bob)

CRABMEAT APPETIZER

1 (8 oz.) pkg. cream cheese
1 T. milk
1 lb. fresh crabmeat (or canned)
2 T. finely chopped onion
½ t. cream style horseradish (or more)
¼ t. salt
Dash pepper
⅓ C. toasted sliced almonds

Soften cream cheese with milk. Add all other ingredients except almonds. Spoon into an ovenproof dish. Sprinkle with toasted almonds. Bake at 375° for 15 minutes. Serve piping hot with crackers or icebox rye for guests to spread themselves. (This can also be served cold. Add lots of horseradish and more pepper.)

Carolyn Smith Russell
(Mrs. Ralph H.)

CRABMEAT AND BROCCOLI DIP

2 pkgs. frozen chopped broccoli
1 onion, chopped
½ C. butter
2 (10¾ oz.) cans mushroom soup
1 (6 oz.) roll Kraft garlic cheese
Tabasco to taste
2 lbs. lump crabmeat

Cook and drain broccoli. Sauté onion in butter. Add cooked broccoli, mushroom soup, cheese and Tabasco. Add crabmeat. Heat and serve from a chafing dish.

Mrs. Kurt Borris

AVOCADO-CRAB DIP

1 large avocado, peeled and cubed
1 T. lemon juice
1 T. grated onion
1 t. Worcestershire sauce
1 (8 oz.) pkg. cream cheese, softened
¼ C. sour cream
¼ t. Accent
¼ t. salt
1 (7½ oz.) can crabmeat, drained and flaked

In blender container or small mixer bowl, combine avocado, lemon juice, onion and Worcestershire sauce; blend until smooth. Add cream cheese, sour cream, Accent and salt; blend well. Stir in crabmeat. Chill.

Mrs. Jonas Silberstein,
Austin, Texas

Donor: Sharon Wildstein Bindler
    (Mrs. Donn)

CRABMEAT DIP

1 bunch green onions, chopped
1 bell pepper, chopped
1 C. diced celery
½ C. butter
1 (10¾ oz.) can cream of mushroom soup
2 (7½ oz.) cans King crabmeat
1 (8 oz.) can water chestnuts, sliced
Salt and pepper to taste

Sauté onions, pepper and celery in butter. Add other ingredients and cook for 20 minutes over low heat. Serve in chafing dish with Melba toast.

Mrs. Mack Williams,
Gainesville, Fla.

Donor: Katy Hall Painter
    (Mrs. Paul)

CHAFING DISH CRABMEAT

3 (8 oz.) pkgs. cream cheese
1 lb. fresh crabmeat
½ t. garlic salt
½ C. mayonnaise
2 t. prepared mustard
¼ C. dry white wine
½ t. seasoned salt
4 green onions with tops, finely chopped

Melt cream cheese in double boiler. Add remaining ingredients, mixing well. Serve warm from chafing dish. May be prepared ahead of time by softening cream cheese, adding other ingredients, and placing in a pyrex dish. Bake at 350° until just warm, about 20—30 minutes.

SERVES 50

Mrs. Joseph H. Croxton

MARINATED CRAB CLAWS

⅓ C. minced green onion
⅓ C. minced parsley
1 stalk celery, minced
1 clove garlic, minced
⅓ C. olive oil
⅓ C. Wishbone salad dressing
2 T. tarragon vinegar
¼ C. fresh lemon juice
½ C. water
Dash orégano
A-1 Steak Sauce to taste
Worcestershire to taste
1 lb. crab claws

Mix all ingredients except crab claws in a bowl and let chill for several hours. Add a container of crab claws and marinate several more hours.

Curtain Call Cookbook

CRAB HAM ROLLS

1 (7½ oz.) can King crab
1 T. lemon juice
1 (8 oz.) pkg. cream cheese, softened
¼ C. finely chopped celery
2 T. chopped parsley
¼ C. chopped, toasted almonds
Thin-sliced, lean, boiled ham
Salt and pepper to taste

Drain crabmeat, place on chopping board and slice fine with a sharp knife. Sprinkle with lemon juice. Blend cream cheese with crab, celery, parsley, almonds, salt and pepper. Spread mixture on the thin slice of ham and roll. Chill well. Slice into ½" thick slices.

Curtain Call Cookbook

CRAB RANGOON

½ lb. crabmeat (canned is fine)
1 (8 oz.) pkg. cream cheese
½ t. A-1 sauce
¼ t. garlic powder
1 egg yolk, beaten
Won Ton squares
Peanut oil

Shred crabmeat and blend with cheese and seasonings. Put a half-teaspoon of the mixture in the center of a won ton square and fold into triangle. Moisten the edges slightly with beaten egg and twist bottom corners toward center. Fry in a deep fat fryer in peanut oil until golden. Serve hot with sweet and sour sauce and hot mustard.

YIELD: 150 squares

**Carmen Huggins Hilliard
(Mrs. George M., III)**

SWISS CRABMEAT DIP

1 C. butter
12 green onions and tops, chopped
1 bunch parsley, chopped
4 T. flour
1 pt. light cream
1 lb. Swiss cheese, grated fine
1 lb. lump crabmeat
Salt
Cayenne
4 T. Sherry, optional

Sauté chopped green onions and parsley in butter. Add flour and cream, and stir until smooth. Add cheese and stir until it melts. Add crabmeat, salt and cayenne. Add Sherry if desired. Serve hot in chafing dish with toast rounds.

Vivienne Johnson Calk
(Mrs. Earl, Jr.)

DEVILED HAM PUFFS

36 bread rounds
½ lb. cream cheese
1 t. onion juice
½ t. baking powder
1 egg yolk
2 (2¼ oz.) cans deviled ham
Salt to taste

VARIATION:
Substitute 2 cans well-drained clams for deviled ham.

With biscuit cutter, cut 4 rounds from each slice of bread and toast on one side. Blend baking powder with egg yolk and add to softened cheese, onion juice and salt. Spread untoasted sides with ham and cover each with a mound of cheese mixture. Bake at 375° until puffed and brown. (about 10-12 minutes).

Curtain Call Cookbook

EMPANADAS

2 T. oil
½ C. chopped onion
½ C. chopped green pepper
1 clove garlic, crushed
1½ C. ground cooked roast
⅔ C. tomatoes
2 T. flour
½ t. chili powder
Salt and pepper
Rich pie pastry (See Index)
9 stuffed olives, thickly sliced
3 hard cooked eggs, thinly sliced
Cream

Sauté onion, pepper and garlic in oil until soft. Add meat, tomatoes, flour, chili powder, salt and pepper to taste. Cook and stir 2 minutes. Roll out pastry and cut into 4 inch rounds. Put a tablespoon of the meat mixture on each. Then press in a thick slice of olive and a thin slice of egg. Top the pies with a pastry round and crimp edges. Brush with cream, prick twice with fork. Bake at 425° for 10 minutes.

Etta Remer Sosland
(Mrs. Morris)

EYE OF ROUND ROAST WITH BUNS

Eye of Round roast
Garlic
Soy sauce
Worcestershire sauce
Wishbone Italian dressing
Lemon Pepper Marinade
Cocktail buns
Horseradish mayonnaise

Make slits along the fat side of a roast and place garlic bits in them. Sprinkle soy sauce, Worcestershire sauce and Italian dressing over the roast. Dust heavily with lemon pepper marinade. Marinate for at least 24 hours, turning several times. Cook over a charcoal fire or smoker. When brown all around, insert meat thermometer in and cook to desired doneness. Slice very thin and serve on cocktail buns with horseradish mayonnaise.

Curtain Call Cookbook

SOUR CREAM BEEF MOLD

1 pkg. instant onion soup mix
1 C. sour cream
Lean roast beef, medium cooked, thinly sliced in 2" x 3" pieces

Mix soup mix and sour cream together and dip both sides of roast beef in this mixture. Place, layer after layer, of roast in rounded mold. (A plastic lettuce keeper is fine, and easy to remove.) Place in refrigerator until firm, overnight. Remove from mold and place on lettuce leaves and serve with biscuits. Serve on a large tray with a fork to pick up pieces.

**Mrs. Ben Barnes,
Brownwood, Texas**

GOURMET BEEF AND ARTICHOKE DIP

¼ C. butter or margarine
2 (2½ oz.) jars dried beef
3 T. flour
2 pts. sour cream
2 (14 oz.) cans artichokes OR 2 pkgs. frozen, cooked
3 T. grated Parmesan cheese
½ C. dry white wine
1 (4 oz.) can mushrooms
Dash Worcestershire sauce
Dash pepper
Dash Tabasco

Sauté beef in butter and sprinkle with flour. Stir well and add sour cream. (Milk may be added if mixture is too thick.) Add other ingredients and stir. Serve in chafing dish with miniature pastry shells.

Shreveport Junior League

Appetizers

STEAK TIDBITS

3 (10½ oz.) cans consommé
3 (10½ oz.) cans beef bouillon
Juice of 1½ lemons
1 (8 oz.) bottle Wishbone Italian Dressing
4 T. Worcestershire sauce
4 garlic pods, pressed
Cracked pepper (quite a bit)
1 (12 oz.) bottle red wine
Sirloin steaks
½ C. butter

Combine first 8 ingredients and marinate sirloin steaks for 24 hours. Reserve marinade. Cook over a charcoal fire. Leave quite rare. Cut into bite-sized pieces. Add butter to marinade, heat and pour over steak tidbits. Serve in a chafing dish. This is enough marinade for 10 large sirloin steaks.

SERVES 250

Curtain Call Cookbook

GUACAMOLE

"A dip today—A soup tomorrow"

1 C. diced, peeled tomatoes
2 avocados, peeled and mashed
¼ C. chopped onion
⅓ C. Miracle Whip salad dressing
1 t. salt
4 slices crisply cooked bacon, crumbled

Combine the tomato, avocado, onion, salad dressing and salt. Mix well until smooth. Stir in bacon just before serving. Note: Stir heavy cream into leftover guacamole dip immediately for a delicious cold soup.

Jane Weeks Johnston
(Mrs. J. Glenn)

CHEESE STUFFED MUSHROOMS

3 pints fresh mushrooms
10 slices crisp bacon, crumbled
¾ C. mayonnaise
Seasoned salt to taste
1 medium onion, finely chopped
1½ C. grated sharp cheese

Wash mushrooms in salted water. Remove stems. Mix other ingredients except cheese, and stuff mushrooms with mixture. Place in oblong baking dish. Sprinkle cheese all over. Cover with foil and bake at 325° for 15—20 minutes.

SERVES 16

Barbara York Richardson
(Mrs. Kenneth C.)

Appetizers

SWEDISH MEATBALLS

MEATBALLS:
1 lb. ground round
½ lb. fresh pork, ground
¼ lb. salt pork, ground
1 egg
1 C. bread or cracker crumbs
¾ C. chopped onion
1¼ t. sweet basil
¾ t. marjoram
1½ t. salt
⅓ C. cream
Pepper
Accent

SAUCE:
1 T. flour
1 T. drippings
2 bouillon cubes
 (cooked 3 minutes in
 1 C. water)
1 C. sour cream

Have meat ground three times. Combine all meatball ingredients and roll into small balls. Brown in salad oil.
SAUCE:
Add the flour to the tablespoon of drippings from the meatballs. Cook until bubbly and add bouillon. Let simmer a few minutes and add sour cream. Pour this sauce over the meatballs. The sauce and the meatballs may be cooked a day ahead, but the sauce should not be added until just before serving.

YIELD: 125 meatballs

Aliece McHenry Mucher
(Mrs. Joseph)

FRIED MUSHROOMS

Raw mushrooms
Flour
Egg
Milk
Toasted bread crumbs

Wash mushrooms well, cut into bite-size pieces, and drain. Dip in a batter of seasoned flour, egg and milk. Cover with toasted bread crumbs and let set until firm. Fry in deep fat. Serve with tartar sauce.
Verne Monday Smith
(Mrs. W. Bruner)

MUSHROOM WON TONS

½ lb. mushrooms
1 onion, chopped
¼ C. butter
1 (8 oz.) pkg. cream cheese
Won Ton wrappers

Sauté mushrooms and onion in butter. Drain off juice. With heat off, add cream cheese. Season heavily with all kinds of salt. Put ½ t. mixture in each won ton square. Fold and seal with egg white. Deep fry in oil; or spread on bread squares dip in egg and milk batter. Deepfry in oil.

Mary Loomis

COCKTAIL MEATBALLS

MEATBALLS:
2½ lbs. ground chuck
2 eggs
3 t. brown sugar
2 t. salt
½ t. pepper
1 large onion, chopped fine
½ C. cracker meal
Water to moisten

SAUCE:
4 large onions, chopped and
   browned
1 (12 oz.) bottle chili sauce
1 (12 oz.) bottle water
1 t. Worcestershire sauce
Juice of 2 lemons
2 cloves of garlic
1 t. brown sugar
½ t. pepper

MEATBALLS: Mix all ingredients well. Form into small balls and brown in oil.
SAUCE: Combine ingredients and cook 30 minutes. Place meatballs in sauce and simmer another 30 minutes. Serve in chafing dish.

YIELD: 100 small meatballs

Mrs. Kurt Borris

MUSHROOM CANAPÉ DIP

1 lb. fresh mushrooms, chopped
¼ C. butter
½ C. sour cream
½ C. Parmesan cheese
¼ C. parsley, chopped
Dash of Tabasco
Salt and pepper to taste
Dry wine to taste
Toast rounds

Sauté mushrooms in butter until tender. Add remaining ingredients, heat and serve from a chafing dish on toast rounds.

Susanne Sandberg Northcutt
(Mrs. W. D., III)

OYSTERS ERNIE

1 qt. oysters
Flour
Salt and pepper
3 T. melted butter
⅓ C. fresh lemon juice
1 C. A-1 Steak sauce
⅓ C. Worcestershire sauce
2 jiggers Sherry

Flour, salt and pepper the oysters. Fry in Crisco shortening. Place in a chafing dish after draining on paper towels. Make a sauce from the butter, lemon juice, A-1 and Worcestershire sauces and Sherry Heat the sauce and pour over the oysters.

Curtain Call Cookbook

Appetizers

MINIATURE QUICHES

PASTRY:
½ C. butter, softened
1 (3 oz.) pkg. cream cheese, softened
1 C. flour, unsifted

FILLING:
1 large egg, slightly beaten
½ C. milk
¼ t. salt
1 C. grated (medium-fine) Swiss or Cheddar cheese, not packed down

FILLING II:
1 pkg. cream of leek soup
2 C. milk
1 C. cream
4 eggs
½ lb. Swiss cheese, grated
1 t. dry mustard
1 t. salt
¼ t. pepper

VARIATION To filling II recipe Substitute 2 cans crabmeat or 1 cup ground ham for part of the cheese in the filling.

Cream butter and cheese and work in the flour. Chill if very soft. Roll into 24 balls and press each over the bottom and up the sides of small muffin pan cups, each 1¾" across the top.

Combine egg, milk and salt. Pat cheese into unbaked pastry shells. Slowly dribble egg mixture over cheese. Bake in a preheated 350° oven 30 minutes.

YIELD: 24

Curtain Call Cookbook

Bring soup and milk to a boil. Cool slightly and stir in cream. Cool. Beat eggs with remaining ingredients and add to soup. Fill pastry cups and bake at 375° until brown. May be frozen and reheated in foil.

YIELD: 4 dozen

Curtain Call Cookbook

MUSHROOMS STUFFED WITH SNAILS

12 small bread rounds, toasted
12 mushrooms
12 snails
¼ lb. butter
1 clove garlic, minced
Bread crumbs
Parsley

Remove stems from mushrooms. Sauté caps in butter. Drain. Melt butter and add garlic. Stuff mushrooms with snail. Cover with ½ t. bread crumbs. Put stuffed mushroom on toast. Pour garlic butter over canapé. Bake at 350° 8—10 minutes. Sprinkle with parsley.

Cookbook Committee

STUFFED MUSHROOMS

1 lb. mushrooms
½ lb. ground raw pork
1 (8 oz.) can water chestnuts, chopped
¼ C. minced green onions
1 egg
1 t. shoyu sauce
1 t. salt
Freshly ground pepper
Melted butter
Sesame seeds

Remove stems from mushrooms. Chop stems and mix with pork, water chestnuts, green onions, egg, shoyu sauce, salt and a little freshly ground pepper. Mix well and stuff mushroom caps with mixture. Dip in melted butter, dip stuffed part in sesame seeds, and arrange in a baking dish, stuffed side up. Bake at 350° for 35 minutes. Serve hot. DO NOT OVERBAKE.

Dorothy Robbins Kennedy
(Mrs. George E., Jr.)

EASY MUSHROOM HORS D'OEUVRES

1 loaf sandwich bread
1 (10¾ oz.) can cream of mushroom soup
½ lb. bacon, cut in half

Slice crusts off bread. Spoon a little mushroom soup on bread right from the can. Fold diagonally place ½ slice bacon on top and fold ends under. Place on cookie sheet and bake at 350° 30 minutes. Can be prepared ahead. Serve as hors d'oeuvres or as compliment to salad luncheon.

YIELD: 24

Mrs. Fred Souerbry III

OYSTER ROLL

1 (8 oz.) pkg. cream cheese
2 T. mayonnaise
2 T. milk
Worcestershire sauce to taste
½ t. powdered garlic
Lemon juice to taste
Salt and pepper to taste
Tabasco to taste
1 can smoked oysters, drained and chopped
1 pkg. slivered almonds, toasted
Paprika, chives OR parsley to garnish

Cream cheese with mayonaise, milk, garlic and seasonings. Spread mayonnaise on wax paper. Spread between two pieces of wax paper and roll flat. Chill for better rolling. Remove top paper. Sprinkle with oysters and almonds. Roll like a jelly roll. Garnish. Serve with assorted crackers.

Ernestine Fountain

Donor: Cookbook Committee

ITALIAN OYSTERS

1 qt. oysters
½ C. butter
2 pods garlic, pressed or minced
1½ C. bread crumbs
1½ C. Parmesan cheese
1 T. dried parsley flakes

Drain oysters. Butter a 9 x 13" casserole. Melt half of the butter in a skillet. Press the garlic pods into the butter and add the bread crumbs and Parmesan cheese. Spread half of the bread crumb mixture in the casserole and add a layer of oysters. Cover with the remaining bread crumb mixture and sprinkle with parsley. Dot with the rest of the butter. Bake at 400° for 12-15 minutes or until golden.

Curtain Call Cookbook

SUMMER DIP

1 (4¼ oz.) can chopped black olives
1 (4 oz.) can chopped green chilies
3-4 green onions, chopped
3 T. wine vinegar
1½ t. olive oil
1½ t. garlic salt
3-4 chopped tomatoes

Mix all ingredients and refrigerate. Serve with chips or crackers.

YIELD: 2 cups

Judy Chandler Murff
(Mrs. Stan)

SALMON MOLD

2 (16 oz.) cans red sockeye salmon, drained and flaked
1 (8 oz.) pkg. cream cheese, softened
½ C. finely chopped green onions
3 T. lemon juice
2 t. dill weed
2 t. prepared horseradish
½ t. pepper, freshly ground
¼ t. seasoned salt
1 t. Worcestershire sauce
¼ t. liquid smoke
Dash Tabasco
½ C. chopped pecans
½ C. parsley

Blend first eleven ingredients. Form into fish shape, pat on pecans and garnish with parsley. Chill until ready to use. Serve with assorted crackers. Freeze and defrost in refrigerator for use at any future date.

Sylvia Billingslea Collier
(Mrs. Joe A.)

Beef Burgundy Bake

2 lbs. Beef chuck or stewing beef
1 Can cream of chicken soup
1 Can cream of mushroom soup
1 Can cream of celery soup
1 Pkg. dry onion soup mix
1/2 Cup burgundy wine

Cut meat into bite size pieces and mix with all ingredients. Bake 3 hours at 300 degrees. DO NOT STIR, DO NOT ADD SALT. Multiply by 6 to serve 50. Serve over rice or noodles.

Chocolate Turtle Cake

1 German chocolate cake mix
14 Oz. pkg Kraft carmels
1 Sm. can evaporated milk
3/4 Cup butter or margarine
1 Cup Chocolate chip
1 Cup pecans

Prepare cake mix and pour 1/2 into 9 x 13 greased pan. Bake 15 minutes at 350 degrees. Melt carmels in sauce pan with evaporated milk and butter. Cool cake. Pour carmel mixture on cake, sprinkle chips on top, add 3/4 cup nuts to cake batter and spread over top. Sprinkle remainder of nuts on top. Bake 15 to 20 mins. Cool before serving. MmmMmm Good!

18, at Birmingham Seahold HS, 7:30 PM, $4. Proceeds go the the Michigan Chapter of the National Multiple Sclerosis Society. For ticket info: 649-5138 or 967-2211.

Spaghetti Dinner

Sponsored by the Oakland Branch YWCA, Feb. 18 from 5:30-7 PM. Clayton Schlotterbeck will be the chef. Tickets are $3.50 for adults and $2.50 for children and may be purchased in advance or at the door. For info: 435-9100.

Personal Growth For Single People

Sponsored by the Oakland Univ. Continuum Center will present a workshop for singles beginning Mar. 10 at the Church of Our Savior in West Bloomfield Township, from 7:30-10:30 PM. Seven-session program focuses on building self-esteem. Structured activities are used to help singles learn more about themselves and how they relate to others. $65. Pre-registration required. For info: 377-3033.

Careers In Transition

Workshop Mondays, Feb.

SMOKED OYSTER DIP

1 onion, chopped
1 clove garlic, minced
½ C. margarine
1 (5 oz.) bottle Worcestershire sauce
2 T. lemon juice (or vinegar)
Dash pepper
Dash Tabasco
1 (14 oz.) bottle catsup
1 (6 oz.) jar mustard
4 (or more) cans smoked oysters, drained

Sauté onion and garlic in margarine. Add remaining ingredients and mix well. Add smoked oysters. (May also use shrimp). May be served hot or cold with crackers.

YIELD: 1 quart

Joy Ellis McLemore

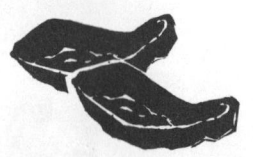

SOUR CREAM CURRY DIP

6 green onions
4 T. butter
1 T. curry powder
1½ C. sour cream
2 T. chutney

Sauté onions in butter; do not brown. Add curry powder and blend over low heat for 4 minutes. Combine sour cream and chutney. Add onion mixture and chill. Use as a dip for raw vegetables.

Normand Dufilho Wilkinson
(Mrs. Jacques)

SALMON CRÊPE HORS D'OEUVRE

6 crêpes
6 pieces smoked salmon (2"-6")
Juice of ½ lemon
6 T. grated onion
12 T. grated hard-boiled egg
¾ C. sour cream
¾ C. Hellmann's mayonnaise
6 T. caviar
Parsley

Place crêpe on salad plate and cover the middle third of crêpe with salmon. Squeeze a few drops of lemon juice on salmon. Sprinkle salmon with 1 T. grated onion and 1 T. grated egg. Fold both sides to cover middle. Garnish with 2 T. sour cream which have been mixed with 2 T. Hellmann's. Top with a teaspoon of caviar and sprinkle with 1 T. grated egg. A sprig of parsley makes this an eye-appealing hors d'oeuvre or a gourmet first course.

SERVES 6

Betty Robbins Davis
(Mrs. Charles H.)

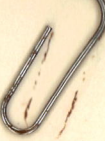

SAUSAGE PINWHEELS

2 C. flour
½ t. salt
3 t. baking powder
5 T. shortening
⅔ C. milk
1 lb. well seasoned bulk sausage

Sift flour with salt and baking powder. Cut in shortening until mixture resembles coarse crumbs. Add milk all at once and mix. Divide dough into two equal parts, roll each out ¼" thick, and spread with half the sausage. Roll up as for jelly roll. Repeat with remaining dough and sausage. Wrap in foil and freeze (this slices much better if frozen). When ready to serve, slice ⅓" or ¼" thick and bake at 400° for about 15 minutes or until golden brown. This is especially nice for morning parties and also nice for gifts.

YIELD: 2 rolls

Mrs. B. D. Bruyere

SEAFOOD DIP

1 (3 oz.) pkg. cream cheese
Juice of ½ lemon
Mayonnaise
2 (4½ oz.) cans shrimp
1 (6½ oz.) can crabmeat
Dash of Worcestershire sauce
Dash of Tabasco
Dash of salt and pepper
Dash of Accent
5 green onions and tops, finely chopped

Mash cream cheese and soften with lemon juice and mayonnaise to desired consistency. Mash the shrimp with a fork. Stir in the shrimp and crabmeat and mix well. Add the remaining ingredients and chill.

Forrest Gaumer Martin
(Mrs. J. C., Jr.)

BARBEQUED SHRIMP

2 cloves garlic, crushed
½ C. Wesson oil
1 t. salt
1 t. coarsely ground pepper
3 T. chili sauce
1 T. Worcestershire sauce
3 T. vinegar
2 T. parsley
Dash of Tabasco
3 lbs. raw shrimp, shelled and deveined

Mix in blender oil, salt, pepper, chili sauce, Worcestershire sauce, vinegar, parsley and Tabasco. Rinse shrimp and arrange on skewers. Set the skewers over a baking pan and brush with sauce several times while they refrigerate for at least 4 hours. Broil over a charcoal fire, turning frequently and brushing with marinade each time they are turned. Serve with toothpicks as an hors d'oeuvres or may be served as an entrée.

Curtain Call Cookbook

SAUSAGE SQUARES

1 lb. bulk sausage
½ C. chopped onion
¼ C. Parmesan cheese
½ C. grated Swiss cheese
1 egg, beaten plus 1 egg white
¼ t. Tabasco
2 T. chopped parsley
2 C. Bisquick
⅔ C. milk
¼ C. mayonnaise
1 egg yolk

Cook sausage and onion over low heat until brown. Drain off excess fat. Add cheeses, whole egg and egg white, Tabasco and parsley. Make Bisquick dough by mixing it with milk and mayonnaise. Spread half of dough over bottom of well greased 8" square pan. Cover with sausage mixture. Spread remaining dough over sausage. Brush with beaten egg yolk. Bake 25-30 minutes at 400°. Cut into squares and serve hot for breakfast or as an hors d'oeuvre. (I have had good luck freezing this after assembling it and taking it out to thaw overnight; then it is ready to bake for breakfast.)

Linda Berney Buie
(Mrs. James E.)

SHRIMP CHEESE BALLS

2 (3 oz.) pkgs. cream cheese
1½ t. prepared mustard
1 t. grated onion
1 t. lemon juice
Dash cayenne pepper
Dash salt
1 (4½ oz.) can shrimp, drained
⅔ C. chopped salted mixed nuts

Soften cream cheese and blend in mustard, onion, lemon juice, pepper and salt. Drain can of shrimp, break into pieces, and stir into cheese mixture. Chill. Form into ½" balls and roll in chopped nuts.

YIELD: 3½ dozen balls

Vera Mitchell Garlough

SHRIMP REMOULADE DIP

6 lbs. shrimp, deveined and cooked
2 qts. Hellmann's mayonnaise
2 (¼ oz.) can parsley flakes
2 (2 oz.) containers frozen chopped chives
1 (6 oz.) jar Kraft horseradish mustard
Juice of 2 lemons
2 T. onion salt

Cut the shrimp into small pieces. (If left whole, dip will serve less.) Add the remaining ingredients. Mix well and adjust to taste, if necessary, with additional onion salt, lemon juice or horseradish mustard. Refrigerate. Serve with saltine crackers.

SERVES 100

From Texas Tables

SHRIMP PATÉ

1 envelope gelatine
¼ C. boiling water
1 (8 oz.) pkg. cream cheese
1 lb. cooked shrimp, chopped fine
½ t. onion pureé
1/8 t. garlic powder
2 T. mayonnaise
1/3 tube anchovy paste
1 T. Worcestershire sauce
½ t. Tabasco sauce

Dissolve gelatine in boiling water. Add remaining ingredients, put into a small mold or bowl and refrigerate overnight. Unmold and serve with crackers.

Emmy Lu Huck, Dallas, Texas
Donor: Susie Moore French
(Mrs. Paul E.)

MARINATED SHRIMP AND ONIONS

3 lbs. cooked shrimp
3-4 onions, sliced

SAUCE:
1 qt. Hellmann's mayonnaise
1 bottle chili sauce
1 (6 oz.) jar horseradish (fresh is better)
2 T. Worcestershire sauce
1 T. lemon juice
Salt to taste

In a shrimp icer or a deep bowl, layer shrimp and onions. Combine sauce ingredients and pour over shrimp and onions. Marinate several hours before serving to give the onions time to wilt.

Patsy Lacy Griffith
(Mrs. J. W.)
Santa Fe, N. Mex.

GAMBAS AL AJILLO

½ C. olive oil
2 T. (or more) garlic salt OR 1—3 cloves garlic, crushed
3 bay leaves
Pinch of cayenne pepper
1 T. parsley
1 T. celery salt
1 lb. mushrooms
12 oz. fresh shrimp (or frozen)
1 lemon
Freshly ground pepper
Crusty hard rolls OR sour dough rolls

Heat olive oil and add garlic salt or garlic cloves, bay leaves, cayenne, parsley, celery salt and mushrooms. Brown mushrooms. Add shrimp. Turn once to brown both sides. (If using frozen shrimp, you might need to raise burner temperature at this time, then turn back down.) Squirt lightly with lemon juice and grind black pepper over shrimp just before serving. DO NOT OVERCOOK SHRIMP. Serve with toasted, crusty hard rolls or sour dough rolls. Tear off pieces of roll and dip into the juice. Can use cocktail forks for shrimp and mushrooms.

Marcia Burlison McDaniel
(Mrs. Stephen W.)

SPINACH FILLOS

4 pkgs. frozen chopped spinach
4 medium onions, finely chopped
1 C. olive oil
4 (8 oz.) pkgs. cream cheese
4 (8 oz.) pkgs. Ricotta cheese
2½ T. dill weed
16 green onions and tops, thinly sliced
1 C. bread crumbs (Pepperidge Farm bread)
4 T. butter
12 eggs, well beaten
1 lb. butter, melted
1 pkg. frozen Fillo Strudel pastry, thawed

Sauté spinach and onion in olive oil until moisture evaporates. Add cheeses, dill weed, green onions, bread crumbs mixed with 4 T. butter and eggs. Cut Fillo dough in quarters. (Keep other three quarters separately between damp cup towels until needed.) Paint each sheet with melted butter completely to edge. Place one teaspoon filling about 1½" from edge. Fold the sides and roll into square package. Place on a buttered cookie sheet. Brush top with butter. Bake at 425° for 20 minutes until golden brown.

Mrs. Kurt Borris

SPINACH FRITTATA

3 green onions, tops and all
2 T. olive oil
½ lb. ground beef
4 C. fresh spinach, finely chopped and steamed for a minute or two and cooled, OR 2 pkgs. frozen spinach, thawed
8 oz. sharp Cheddar cheese, grated
½ C. Parmesan cheese
4 oz. red wine
8 eggs, beaten
4 T. dry bread crumbs
½ t. thyme
½ t. Accent
½ t. garlic salt
Dash Tabasco or cayenne
1 t. salt

Sauté onions in olive oil in large skillet. Drain. Brown ground meat in the same skillet. Add onions, spinach, cheeses, wine, eggs, bread crumbs and seasonings. Stir thoroughly. Bake at 375° for 45 minutes or until golden brown. Good as an hors d'oeuvre, as a vegetable (without the meat) or as a main dish. Serve it hot, warm or cold.

YIELD: 12-3 inch squares
        50 hors d'oeuvres

Linda Ryan Butter
(Mrs. Stephen R.)

SPINACH DIP

1 (3 oz.) pkg. cream cheese
1½ C. mayonnaise
1 (10 oz.) pkg. frozen chopped spinach, thawed and drained
½ C. chopped green onions
½ C. chopped fresh parsley (if dried, use less)
1 t. salt
1 t. white pepper
Dash of Tabasco and Worcestershire sauce

Soften cream cheese and mix with mayonnaise. Add spinach and remaining ingredients. Mix and chill overnight. Serve with celery, carrots and sliced cucumbers or yellow squash.

YIELD: 1 quart

Mrs. Charles P. Dowell

STUFFED GRAPE LEAVES

30 grape leaves
2 (14 oz.) cans beef broth

FILLING:
2 C. finely chopped onions
½ C. rice
⅓ C. olive oil
2 T. finely chopped parsley
2 T. finely chopped dill
¼ C. finely chopped pistachio nuts
¼ C. finely chopped currants
1 C. finely minced lamb OR ground beef

Layer grape leaves in a pan.

FILLING:
Combine and mix all ingredients. Place filling on grape leaf and roll tucking under all ends carefully. Layer stuffed leaves in a large Dutch oven. Pour beef broth over the leaves and weight leaves down with a plate. Cook on low heat 45 minutes. Can be served hot or drain and serve chilled. May be frozen only **before** cooking.

Rose Pickens Kirkpatrick
(Mrs. Kenneth L.)

TAPENADE ORANGERIE

2 C. mayonnaise
1 (6½ oz.) can tuna, drained
1½ anchovy fillets
3 T. pitted, chopped black olives
1 scallion
¼ C. chopped onion
2 garlic cloves, minced
¼ C. minced celery
¼ C. cooked, cubed potato
½ t. Worcestershire sauce
Dash Tabasco
Salt to taste

Blend all ingredients until completely smooth. Chill. Serve as a dip for raw vegetables.

YIELD: approximately 1 quart

Cookbook Committee

SWEET AND SOUR HAM BALLS

1 lb. raw ham
1 lb. pork (ground with ham)
2 C. bread crumbs
1 C. milk
2 eggs, beaten
½ t. salt

SAUCE:
1 ½ C. brown sugar
½ C. water
½ C. white vinegar
1 t. dry mustard

Mix ingredients well and form into bite-sized balls. Put into buttered baking dish.

SAUCE:
Simmer ingredients until blended thoroughly. Pour over meatballs and bake at 350° for 1½ hours. When half-cooked, turn balls so sauce covers balls completely.

YIELD: 3½ dozen balls

Claire Smith Foster
(Mrs. Henry L.)

SWEET AND SOUR PORK

1¼ lb. lean pork, diced
2 eggs
¾ C. flour
Salt to taste

SAUCE:
¾ C. dark vinegar
1½ C. brown sugar
4 scallions
4 pineapple slices, diced
4 pieces red ginger root
1 T. cornstarch
½ C. catsup
1 t. dry mustard

Salt the pork, dip in beaten egg, roll in flour and fry in vegetable oil (peanut oil is better). Heat the oil to cooking temperature. Fry and then set aside.

SAUCE:
Simmer the vinegar and brown sugar for 10 minutes. Add scallions, pineapple and ginger root. Add cornstarch. Stir until sauce thickens. Stir in catsup and dry mustard until completely mixed. Pour over meat. This is also good on ribs. Serve in chafing dish.

Curtain Call Cookbook

TURKEY APPETIZER SPREAD

1 C. ground cooked turkey
  (baked or smoked)
3 T. Bacos
½ C. creamy type Bleu cheese
  or Roquefort dressing
Pecans or dried parsley

Grind turkey and bacos. Add dressing and mix well. Make into a flat ball, cover with nuts or parsley and chill at least overnight. Freezes well. Easily doubled to use up left over turkey.

Ivana Cella
New York, New York
Donor: Joan Nachbaur Rathbun

JALAPEÑO APPETIZER

1 (6½ oz.) can tuna, drained and mashed
1 hard boiled egg, grated
¼ C. celery, minced
2 T. onion, grated
¼ C. Miracle Whip
½ t. Worcestershire sauce
½ t. seasoned salt
Dash Tabasco
10 mild jalapeños
Paprika

VARIATION:
Add:
½ C. ground nuts
⅔ C. grated cheese

Mix thoroughly all ingredients but jalapeños and paprika; set aside. Rinse jalapeños, cut in half, and scrape out seeds. Rinse again, drain, and pat dry with paper towel. Pile tuna stuffing on jalapeño halves. Garnish with paprika. Chill before serving.

YIELD: 20 halves

Betty Robbins Davis
(Mrs Charles H.)

Richie Bell
Donor: Ethel Poday Maledon
  (Mrs. Elick)

PICKLED CURRIED EGGS

12 hard boiled eggs
Vinegar
Water
1 t. salt
½ t. pepper
1 t. curry powder
1 bay leaf
1 small onion, finely chopped

Measure with water the amount of liquid each jar will hold. Sterilize jars. Make a brine with ⅔ water to ⅓ vinegar (using measure you have made for the jar). Add seasonings. Let it come to a boil. You can substitute any spice you like. Tarragon is good. Peel eggs. Be careful not to handle jars except with tongs. Pour hot strained liquid into jars after tasting seasoning. Seal jars tightly and turn up side down to make sure of no leaks. Leave them upside down for a few hours until they cool. Eat after 3 days. Excellent cut in halves. Serve with light mayonnaise.

Patsy Lacy Griffith
(Mrs. J. W.)
Sante Fe, N. Mex.

JALAPEÑO CHEESE DIP

4 lbs. Cheddar cheese
1 large onion, cut in wedges
1 (12 oz.) can jalapeño peppers, drained and seeded
1 qt. salad dressing

Put all ingredients through blender. May be frozen.

Nancy Jordan Wright
(Mrs. Fletcher)

AVOCADO SOUP

"Garnish with cooked seafood marinated in lemon juice"

2-3 ripe avocados, mashed
4 pkgs. MBT chicken broth in 2 C. water OR 2 C. strong broth
2 C. heavy cream
1 t. grated onion
½ t. salt
White pepper to taste

In blender, combine all ingredients. Chill.

SERVES 8

Claire Smith Foster
(Mrs. Henry L., Jr.)

VARIATION I:
Add:
1 lb. potatoes, peeled and sliced
2 leeks (white part), sliced
Substitute:
1 medium onion, sliced
4 C. well-seasoned chicken broth
1 C. heavy cream

Cook potatoes, leeks, and onions in chicken broth. Blend in blender. Return to saucepan, add cream and heat through. Pour over avocados in tureen. Serve hot or cold.

SERVES 12

Carolyn Smith Russell
(Mrs. Ralph H.)

VARIATION II: Quick and Easy
1 (10 ¾ oz.) can potato soup
1 can milk

To avocados in blender, add soup and milk. Blend and chill.

SERVES 6

Betsy Kay Stites
(Mrs. William L.)

NAVY BEAN SOUP

1 lb. navy beans
10 C. water
3 lbs. ham hocks OR 2 lbs cut up cooked ham
1 C. chopped onion
1 C. chopped carrots
½ C. margarine
3 ripe tomatoes, chopped
1 T. sugar
Salt and pepper to taste

Wash beans and let soak overnight. Sauté onions and carrots in margarine. Add with all remaining ingredients to beans. Bring to a boil, reduce heat, cover, and simmer 4-5 hours.

YIELD: 1 gallon

Susie Moore French
(Mrs. Paul E.)

PINTO BEAN SOUP
"A South-of-the-Border treat —serve with Mexican Cornbread"

1 T. bacon drippings
2 green onions, cut in 1" lengths
2 cloves garlic, minced
1 medium green pepper, coarsely chopped
¼ C. tomato, peeled, seeded and chopped
1 C. cooked pinto beans, cooked in water with garlic
3 C. bean broth
1 t. dried coriander, crushed
Salt to taste
Garnishes:
¼ C. tomatoes, peeled, seeded and chopped
¼ C. chopped onions
½ C. grated Monterey Jack cheese

Sauté onions, garlic, and green pepper in drippings until slightly soft, 3—5 minutes. Add tomatoes, beans and broth, coriander, and salt to taste. Bring to a boil and boil briskly, uncovered, 10 minutes.

YIELD: 4 large servings

Linda Ryan Butter
(Mrs. Stephen R.)

BROCCOLI CHOWDER
"Great with fruit salad and toasted bread sticks"

1 lb. fresh broccoli
2 (13¾ oz.) cans Swanson's chicken broth, divided
1½ C. milk
½ C. light cream
½ C. or more cubed ham
1 t. salt
Pepper to taste
¼ t. dry mustard
3 T. butter
3 green onions, chopped
1 potato, peeled and grated
¾ C. grated Swiss cheese
1 T. chicken seasoned stock base

Cook broccoli covered in 1 can of chicken broth until tender. Remove broccoli from broth and chop coarsely. Add milk, cream, ham, salt, pepper, and dry mustard to broth. Simmer and stir occasionally. Sauté onions and potato in butter. Add the other can of chicken broth and cook until soft. Add potato mixture and the remaining ingredients to broccoli; heat just to serving temperature.

SERVES 6

Carmen Huggins Hilliard
(Mrs. George M., III)

BEEF—SAUSAGE SOUP

"Good served with egg bread—See Index"

¼ lb. lean, thick sliced bacon, diced
1 clove garlic, minced
1 lb. lean beef, cubed
Cavender's Greek Seasoning to taste
1½ C. tomato juice
1 can condensed black bean soup
1 (15 oz.) can kidney beans, undrained
1 C. carrots, diced
1 C. celery, diced
1 C. cabbage, shredded
1 C. green onions, chopped
6 beef bouillon cubes
1 t. basil
8 C. hot water
1 C. spaghetti, broken in little pieces
2 pkgs. Little Smokies (cocktail sausages), each one cut in half

Sauté bacon with garlic until brown and crisp; drain and reserve drippings. Season beef cubes generously with Cavender's Greek Seasoning and sauté until brown in reserve drippings. Add tomato juice, bean soup, vegetables, bouillon cubes, basil, and hot water. Bring to a boil and simmer for 2 hours. Add spaghetti and sausages. Simmer for another 30 minutes.

SERVES 8

Ann Killingsworth Smead
(Mrs. Hamp, Jr.)

BORSCHT

1 (20 oz.) can beets, drained, reserve juice
2 cucumbers, peeled and seeded
Salt to taste
2 C. sour cream
2 (10½ oz.) cans beef broth, undiluted
2 soup cans buttermilk
½ C. beet juice
Sour cream and caviar for garnish

Purée beets and cucumber. Drain. Put in bowl. Add salt to taste and stir. Add sour cream and stir until smooth. Add beef broth, buttermilk and beet juice. Chill. Top with sour cream and garnish with caviar.

YIELD: 3 quarts

Mrs. Kurt Borris

CANADIAN CHEESE SOUP

¼ C. butter or margarine
½ C. finely diced onions
½ C. finely diced carrots
½ C. finely diced celery
¼ C. flour
1½ T. cornstarch
1 qt. chicken stock
1 qt. milk
1/8 t. soda
1 C. processed Cheddar cheese, grated
Salt and pepper to taste
2 T. parsley, finely chopped

Melt butter in soup pot. Add onions, carrots, and celery. Sauté over low heat until tender. Add flour and cornstarch mixed together and cook until bubbly. Add stock and milk and stir, making a smooth sauce. Add soda, then cheese. (May add more cheese to taste). Season with salt and pepper. Add parsley just before serving.

YIELD: 2 quarts

Virginia Elms McRee (Mrs. J. T.)
Jill Prather Norton (Mrs. Robert W.)
Carol Morris Little (Mrs. Robert W.)

CAULIFLOWER SOUP

½ C. chopped onion
1 T. butter
½ t. curry powder
6 C. chicken broth, divided
1½ C. cooked rice
1 cauliflower
1 C. heavy cream
1 t. salt
½ t. pepper

Sauté onion in butter. Add curry powder and 2 C. broth. Simmer 15 minutes. Add rice and blend in blender. Cook cauliflower in 4 C. broth for 15 minutes. Add cauliflower and broth to rice and onion mixture. Blend. Stir in cream. Add salt and pepper to taste.

YIELD: 2 quarts

Mrs. Michael C. Macey

CHICKEN CORN CHOWDER

¾ C. celery, chopped
¾ C. onion, chopped
¼ C. margarine
2 (10 ¾ oz.) cans cream of chicken soup
1¾ C. milk
1 (1 lb.1oz.) can whole kernel corn, half-drained
½ t. basil
½ t. salt
Pepper to taste

Sauté celery and onion in margarine. Add remaining ingredients. Heat, don't boil.

SERVES 6—8

Harriett Lewis Lesikar
(Mrs. Lynwood W.)

CHICKEN GUMBO
"For those allergic to shrimp but love gumbo"

1 whole chicken
4 C. water
Celery tops
1 onion, sliced
1 t. salt
¼ t. pepper
¼ lb. bacon, cut up
1 green pepper, chopped
1 large onion, chopped
1½ C. chopped celery
2 T. chopped fresh parsley
1 (1 lb. 13 oz.) can tomatoes, mashed
Stock from chicken
2-3 C. water
1-2 t. Yogi shrimp boil concentrate
2 C. sliced okra

Boil chicken in water with celery tops, onion, salt and pepper until meat is done. When cool, remove meat from bone. Reserve stock and skim fat when cool. Sauté bacon, pepper, onion and celery until transparent. Add parsley, tomatoes, chicken stock, water, and shrimp boil concentrate and cook until vegetables are tender. Add chicken and okra and cook 10-20 minutes more. May be served over rice or as a soup.

SERVES 8-10

Marty Irons Parks
(Mrs. James R.)

CREAM OF CHICKEN SOUP

1 stewing chicken
2 qts. water
1 C. large diced onion
2 carrots, quartered
3 stalks celery, quartered
1 T. salt
Pepper to taste
1 clove garlic, minced
1 C. chopped mushrooms
½ C. chopped onion
½ C. butter
½ C. plus 1 T. flour
½ C. chopped pimientos
1 qt. light cream

Wash chicken well and remove giblets. Place in pot with water and bring to boil. Add diced onion, carrots, celery, salt, pepper and garlic. Let return to boil, then turn heat down so that liquid is barely turning over. Continue cooking until chicken is tender. Remove and strain stock. Skim fat and place stock on low heat. Sauté mushrooms and onions in butter until onions are transparent. Slowly add flour and cook until fat is absorbed and roux made. Add roux to stock. Boil 5 minutes and stir smooth. Add pimientos and chicken which has been cut into bite-size pieces. Simmer until heated and add cream.

YIELD: 3 quarts

Martha Pearce Joseph
(Mrs. George)

MRS. PAUL SCOTT'S CHICKEN CURRY SOUP
"Serve in a tureen with fried croutons"

White meat of a large chicken, steamed and chopped
½ lb. blanched almonds, chopped fine or ground coarsely
1 C. heavy cream
Salt, pepper and paprika to taste
3 C. chicken stock
Curry powder to taste

Combine almonds, chicken and cream in top of double boiler. Season highly. Add chicken stock and curry powder. Cook in double boiler for one hour.

YIELD: about 1 quart

Charity League Cookery

CHICKEN NOODLE SOUP
"A children's favorite"

1 fryer or hen, cut up
1 onion, chopped
6 stalks celery, chopped
10 carrots, chopped
2 T. chopped parsley
1 T. (or more) seasoning salt
½ jar Spice Island Chicken Seasoned Stock Base
8 oz. pkg. fine noodles

Cover chicken with water and add all remaining ingredients, except noodles. Bring to boil and simmer 1½-2 hours. Remove chicken and bone. Add meat back to soup with noodles and cook until noodles are tender. Can be made ahead and frozen.

SERVES 8-10

Susie Moore French
(Mrs. Paul E.)

BISQUE OF HAMPTON CRAB
"An easy gourmet treat"

1 C. crabmeat, picked
1 (10¾ oz.) can of cream of mushroom soup
1 (10¾ oz.) can cream of asparagus soup
1 C. light cream
1¼ C. milk
½ t. Worcestershire sauce
1/8 t. Tabasco
⅓ C. dry Sherry

Place crabmeat and soups in blender or mix and mix well. Pour into saucepan, add remaining ingredients and heat just until hot, not boiling. Can be made ahead and frozen.

SERVES 6

The Williamsburg Cookbook

CRAB GUMBO

¼ lb. bacon, diced
¼ C. butter, divided
½ C. chopped onion
1 clove garlic, pressed
2 c. sliced okra
2 C. canned tomatoes with liquid
1 (10 oz.) can Rotel tomatoes
4 thin, round slices of lemon
1 bay leaf
3 C. hot water
1 t. salt
¼ t paprika
Dash Tabasco
1 t. Worcestershire sauce
2 T. flour
1 lb. fresh crabmeat, well-picked

Cook bacon until rendered of its fat. Add 2 T. of the butter and the onion and garlic. Cool until transparent. Add okra, tomatoes, Rotel, lemon and bay leaf. Bring to a boil and add water, salt paprika, Tabasco sauce and Worcestershire sauce. Lower the heat and simmer, covered, 1 hour. Blend remaining butter with the flour and stir into simmering vegetables. When thickened and smooth, stir in crabmeat. Serve over cooked rice.

SERVES 6

Patricia Smith Houston
(Mrs. E. B.)

CUCUMBER SOUP
"For a party, substitute dry white wine to taste"

2 T. butter
¼ C. chopped onion OR 1 leek, sliced and cubed
2 C. diced, unpeeled cucumber
1 C. watercress leaves
½ C. finely diced new potatoes
2 C. chicken broth
  OR 1½ C. chicken broth and
  ½ C. white wine
2 sprigs parsley
½ t. salt
¼ t. pepper
¼ t. dry mustard
1 C. heavy cream
Chopped chives and sliced cucumbers for garnish

In saucepan, melt butter and cook onion until transparent. Add remaining ingredients except the cream and vegetables for garnish and bring to a boil. Simmer 15 minutes or until potatoes are tender. Purée in blender, correct seasonings and chill. Stir in cream and then garnish soup. If watercress is unavailable, use tender leaves of romaine lettuce. For a less rich soup, you can use light cream instead of heavy cream.

SERVES 4

Mrs. Fred Terry, Little Rock, Ark.
Donor: Rose Pickens Kirkpatrick
(Mrs. Kenneth L.)

CUCUMBER DILL SOUP

2 large cucumbers, peeled and sliced
1 medium onion, chopped
¼ C. butter
1½ C. chicken broth
1 T. lemon juice
½ t. crushed dill seed
Salt to taste
½ pt. sour cream, optional

Sauté cucumbers and onions slowly in butter until wilted. Blend in blender. Return to saucepan and add chicken broth, lemon juice, dill seed, and salt. Simmer 3-4 minutes. Chill well. May add sour cream just before serving, if desired.

SERVES 4

Ann Chreitzberg Sheppard
(Mrs. Gillett)

GARLIC SOUP
"A gourmet treat"

1 carrot, chopped
2 onions, chopped
3 T. butter
3 T. olive oil
6-8 garlic cloves
6 C. strong chicken stock
4 egg yolks
2 T. flour

Sauté carrots and onions in butter and oil. Wilt only, do not brown. Add garlic. Do not brown. Add stock and simmer covered for ½ hour. Place in blender and purée. Return to heat and bring to a boil. Beat egg yolks with flour. Combine with soup adding a little hot mixture to yolks, then adding a little at a time to hot soup. Return to very low heat to thicken. Do not boil. Serve with garlic croutons or bread sticks and parmesan cheese.

SERVES 6-8

Martha Hess Whitehead
(Mrs. R. Laughton, Jr.)

GAZPACHO ANDALUZ
"Top with sour cream seasoned with a dash of curry"

1 clove garlic, mashed
1 onion, peeled and chopped
5 very ripe tomatoes, peeled and chopped
OR 1 (16 oz.) can tomatoes
3 T. chopped parsley
2 T. vinegar
3 T. olive oil
¼ t. paprika
1 C. beef stock or beef consommé
Salt and pepper to taste

In electric blender, liquefy garlic and onion. Add other ingredients and run blender 3 minutes. Chill in refrigerator. Serve as chilled soup. Pass separately chopped cucumber, green pepper, and croutons.

SERVES 6

Joanie Marvel Abbott
(Mrs. Frank)

HAMBURGER SOUP

1 lb. ground meat
1 medium onion, sliced
1 (10½ oz.) can consommé
1 (14 ¾ oz.) can tomatoes
1 (12 oz.) can tomato juice
1 C. water
2-3 ribs celery, sliced
3-4 carrots, sliced
1 (8 oz.) can LeSueur peas, plus liquid
1 (8 oz.) can Shoepeg corn, plus liquid
1 t. thyme
1 t. salt
1 t. pepper
2 t. Worcestershire sauce
Add any one of the following:
½ C. dry rice, ½ C. dry macaroni or 1 large potato, diced.

Brown meat in large pan. Add onions and cook until wilted. Add remaining ingredients and simmer about 45 minutes or until vegetables are done. May add water if too thick.

YIELD: 3 quarts

Mrs. Bob Briggs, Venezuela
Donor: Eleanor Croxton Lawrence
(Mrs. Thomas W.)

MUSHROOM SOUP

4 T. butter
2 green onions, chopped
2 C. fresh mushrooms, sliced
1 C. chicken broth (Spice Island Stock Base)
1 T. soy sauce
1/8 t. orégano
Salt to taste
2 dashes cayenne
Few drops Worcestershire sauce
2 t. lemon juice (or to taste)
1 T. dry white wine
1 C. heavy cream

Sauté onion and mushrooms in butter until tender. Place in food processor or blender with chicken broth and purée. Return to pan, add remaining ingredients and heat through. DO NOT BOIL.

YIELD: 8 demi-tasse cups

Eleanor Croxton Lawrence
(Mrs. Thomas W.)

OATMEAL SOUP

1 C. oatmeal
½ C. butter
1 medium onion, chopped
3 cloves garlic, crushed
2 large ripe tomatoes, peeled, seeded and chopped
2 qts. chicken broth or consommé
Salt and pepper to taste

Sprinkle oatmeal into skillet and brown over low heat, stirring frequently. In a large saucepan, sauté onion and garlic in butter until onion is almost transparent and barely tender. Stir in tomatoes and chicken broth. Add browned oatmeal and boil the soup for about 6 minutes. Season with salt and pepper.

Balboa Club
Mazatlan, Mexico

ONION SOUP

5 T. butter
1 T. olive oil
4-6 red onions, thinly sliced
6 C. water
6 beef bouillon cubes
½ t. Tabasco
1 bay leaf
6 slices French bread
Grated Swiss cheese

Sauté onions in butter and olive oil just until tender. Add water, bouillon cubes, Tabasco and bay leaf. Cover and simmer 30 minutes. Toast French bread on one side. Heap Swiss cheese on untoasted side and broil until bubbly. Put slice of bread in each serving bowl. Pour soup over. Place under broiler until cheese is golden. Serve with more French bread and Parmesan cheese.

YIELD: 1½ quarts

Normad Dufilho Wilkinson
(Mrs. Jacques)

FRENCH ONION SOUP

3 lbs. onions, peeled and thinly sliced
½ C. butter or margarine
1½ t. freshly ground pepper
1 T. paprika
1 bay leaf
¾ C. flour
1 C. white wine
2 t. salt
3 qts. canned beef bouillon

Melt butter and sauté onions slowly for 1½ hours in a large pot. Add all other ingredients except bouillon and sauté over low heat 10 minutes. Add bouillon and simmer 2 hours. Season with salt to taste. Refrigerate over night. To serve: Heat soup. In a fireproof bowl, put in slices of French bread and soup. Top with grated Swiss cheese and broil until brown (about 5 minutes).

YIELD: 2 quarts

Mrs. John Ferrell

OYSTER STEW

¼ C. margarine
1 T. flour
6-8 green onions, chopped
  (separate white and
  green parts)
4 C. milk
1 stalk celery, chopped
1 t. Worcestershire sauce
Dash of white pepper
Dash of red pepper
½ t. salt
A few whole cloves
½ pt. oysters and liquor
  (or more)

Make roux of flour and margarine. Add white part of onions and cook until tender. Heat milk and add to roux. Add chopped celery, green part of onions, seasonings and cloves. Cook slowly and when thickened, add oysters and liquid. **DO NOT BOIL.** Remove cloves and serve while hot.

SERVES 3

Kathleen Ellison Loomis
(Mrs. N. E.)

CHILLED PEA SOUP

1½ C. fresh or frozen green
  peas
4 large lettuce leaves,
  shredded
⅓ C. water
⅓ C. scallions
½ t. salt
Pepper to taste
1½ C. chicken broth
½ C. sour cream
1 T. chopped mint or snipped
  chives

In a saucepan, combine peas, lettuce, water and seasoning. Simmer over low heat, covered, for 15 minutes or until soft. Add stock and simmer covered for 5 minutes. Purée the soup in a blender. Cool and chill covered. Stir in sour cream and garnish with mint or chives. Serve in chilled bowls.

YIELD: 1 quart

Cookbook Committee

CREAM OF PEA SOUP

4 C. fresh or frozen cooked
  peas
2 C. milk
1 t. green onion, chopped
¼ t. nutmeg
Salt, pepper, thyme
4 T. butter
6 T. flour
2 C. chicken broth
½ C. heavy cream
Fresh chervil
2 T. unsalted butter

Soften onions in butter. Add flour and cook until bubbly. Add milk, stirring constantly, until sauce comes to a boil. Cook, adding nutmeg, thyme and pepper to taste, 5 minutes. Add stock, stirring; add peas and cook for 5—10 minutes. Taste for seasoning. Purée soup in blender and return to pan. Just before serving, reheat, add cream, chervil and butter, without letting soup boil. May be thinned with milk to right consistency.

YIELD: 1½ quarts

Cookbook Committee

R & K VICHYSSOISE

2 large onions, chopped
1 bunch leeks OR 2 bunches green onions (½ of tops), chopped
½ C. butter or margarine
8 C. Swanson's chicken broth
3 C. potatoes, thinly sliced
1 T. (heaping) sage
1 pt. light cream
Chives

Sauté onions and leeks in butter or margarine. Cook the onions slowly; the longer they cook the better the flavor. Add chicken broth and potatoes. Cook slowly until the potatoes are done. Add sage. Let cool, then purée in blender. Add light cream. Garnish with chives.

YIELD: approximately 1 gallon

Rose Pickens Kirkpatrick (Mrs. Kenneth L.)

COLD SALMON BISQUE

½ C. minced onion
¼ C. butter
¾ C. chopped green pepper
1 C. flaked cooked salmon
4 C. milk
Sweet Hungarian paprika
Salt
White pepper
1 C. heavy cream
2 T. dry Sherry
Minced green pepper

In a large saucepan, sauté onion and butter until softened; add green pepper and sauté the mixture over moderately high heat until the pepper is tender. Stir in cooked salmon and cook the mixture for 2 minutes. Add milk, stirring constantly, and bring the liquid just to a boil. Add paprika, salt, and white pepper to taste. Let the mixture cool. In a blender in batches or in a food processor fitted with steel blade, purée the mixture. Transfer the purée to a large bowl, stir in cream, and chill the bisque covered, for at least 2 hours. Just before serving, stir in Sherry and salt and pepper to taste. Ladle the bisque into 4 chilled bowls or mugs and garnish each serving with pepper.

SERVES 4

Cookbook Committee

GUMBO
"An authentic family recipe from Louisiana"

3 lb. fryer; boiled, skinned and chopped
6 C. broth
2 T. oil or bacon drippings
3 C. okra sliced
2 C. chopped onion
2 C. chopped celery
1 clove garlic, chopped or pressed
¼ C. oil
½ C. flour
2 T. Kitchen Bouquet
1½ lbs. shrimp
1 T. Yogi shrimp boil concentrate
2 T. salt
4 C. shrimp liquor
Salt
Red pepper to taste
1 pt. oysters, optional
1 lb. fresh crabmeat OR 2 cans

Sauté okra, onion, celery and garlic in oil on low heat for about 45 minutes. Water may be added—just enough to prevent sticking. In a large iron pot make roux by slowly browning flour in oil on low heat, stirring constantly. Add Kitchen Bouquet and cook until a dark brown. Boil shrimp in enough water to cover, with shrimp boil concentrate and salt. Reserve shrimp liquor. Gradually add broth and shrimp liquor to roux. Add okra mixture, season to taste with salt and red pepper. Simmer 45 minutes to 1 hour. Add chicken and simmer 15 minutes. Add shrimp, oysters and crabmeat last. They will be tough if cooked too much. Additional Kitchen Bouquet may be added to get a rich, dark color. Additional shrimp boil concentrate may be added by teaspoons to season further. Serve over rice. Filé may be put on the table for each person to individually season his gumbo. NEVER add filé to the pot. This makes the gumbo stringy. Serve with a salad and French bread. There will be enough leftovers for the next day. Gumbo is always better the next day.

SERVES 10

Betty Cooksey Nethery
(Mrs. Tom)

SPLIT PEA SOUP

1 lb. split peas
1 large bell pepper, chopped
1 large onion, chopped
3 ribs celery, chopped
½ ham hock (or slices of ham cut in chunks.)
3 quarts water
Salt, pepper and garlic salt to taste

Mix all ingredients and bring to a boil. Let simmer 4-6 hours.

Judy Chandler Murff
(Mrs. Stan)

SEAFOOD BISQUE

1 can lobster
1 C. Sauterne
1 (10¾ oz.) can tomato soup
1 (11½ oz.) can split pea soup
1⅓ cans milk

Marinate lobster in wine for several hours. Add milk to soups and blend until smooth. Heat well. Add lobster and Sauterne just before serving.

SERVES 6

VARIATION I: To basic recipe:
Substitute:
1 (6½ oz.) can crabmeat
3 T. Sherry
1 can light cream
Add:
Dash Tabasco sauce
2 egg yolks beaten into hot soup
Salt and pepper to taste

Ann Lacy Crain
(Mrs. B. W. Jr.)

Mix all ingredients in blender. Heat and add egg yolks. Season.

SERVES 6.

Nancy Jordan Wright
(Mrs. Fletcher)

VARIATION II: To basic recipe:
Substitute:
1 C. lump crabmeat
1 C. fresh cooked shrimp
¼ C. Sherry
Add:
2 cans consommé madrilene
1 can ripe olives, julienned
Juice of 1 lemon

Mix all ingredients together and simmer 20 minutes.

SERVES 8

Mrs. Kurt Borris

CHILLED SENEGALESE SOUP

3 (10¾ oz.) cans cream of chicken soup
1 T. curry powder
2 C. sour cream
1 C. heavy cream
1½ C. (or more) light cream

Blend soup, curry powder, and sour cream well. Add heavy cream and thin with light cream. Chill. Garnish with ground chicken, parsley, sour cream or almonds.

SERVES 8

Mrs. Kurt Borris

SHRIMP BISQUE
"Serve with garlic rye toasties"

1 T. butter or margarine
3 T. chopped onion
1 T. chopped pimiento
½ C. chopped celery
½ (10¾ oz.) can cream of chicken soup
1 C. milk
1 C. cooked shrimp
1 T. chopped parsley

Sauté onion, pimiento and celery in butter about 5 minutes. Add soup and mix well. Gradually add milk and stir until smooth. Add shrimp and heat. Sprinkle parsley over top of each serving.

SERVES 4

GARLIC RYE TOASTIES

1 clove garlic
½ C. soft butter
2 dozen slices salty rye bread

Cream garlic into butter and let stand 30 minutes. Spread on bread. Toast at 400° for 7 minutes or until crisp.

Sara Richkie Whitehurst
(Mrs. Herman)

PORTUGUESE SOUPAS
"It's good served over thick slices of toasted French bread"

2½ lb. beef brisket, cut into 1" cubes
1 large onion, chopped
3 cloves garlic, crushed
4 (8 oz.) cans tomato sauce with tomato bits
¼ C. chopped parsley
2 t. salt
½ t. crushed coriander leaf (cilantro)
¼ t. pepper
1 bay leaf
2 large potatoes, cut into 1" thick cubes
1 C. dry red wine
1 bunch Swiss chard OR collards, spinach or kale

In kettle combine first 9 ingredients. Simmer covered 3 hours. Can be frozen at this point.* Stir in potatoes and wine, and simmer covered 30 minutes or until potatoes are done. Add 1 bunch of the greens and simmer 10 minutes.

SERVES 6—8

*Chopped potatoes will not freeze satisfactorily.

Rose Pickens Kirkpatrick
(Mrs. Kenneth L.)

SPRING GARDEN SOUP
"Chilled fresh vegetable soup for a summer day"

4 tomatoes, peeled and cubed
4 green onions, sliced
1 small cucumber, sliced
½ C. chopped green pepper
½ C. chopped celery
1 (13¾ oz.) can Swanson's chicken broth
1 C. tomato juice
Juice of 1 lemon
1 T. seasoned salt
¼ t. seasoned pepper
2 t. sugar

Simmer tomatoes, green onions, cucumber, green pepper and celery in chicken broth 5 minutes. Add remaining ingredients. Simmer 10 minutes. Chill.

YIELD: 5-6 cups

Rose Pickens Kirkpatrick
(Mrs. Kenneth L.)

SQUASH SOUP

½ C. butter
2 onions, chopped fine
1 dozen small yellow squash, sliced
2 C. chicken broth (Sexton)
1 t. sugar
2 C. heavy cream
Salt and pepper to taste
1 t. dill weed
Chopped parsley or chives to garnish

Sauté onions in butter. Cook squash in chicken broth. Purée in blender. Add heavy cream and seasonings. Chill. Serve hot or cold.

YIELD: 1½ quarts

Patricia Smith Houston
(Mrs. E. B.)

ZUCCHINI SOUP

1 lb. zucchini
1 small onion, quartered
1 C. chicken broth
1 t. salt
¼ t. pepper
½ t. sweet basil
1½ C. milk
½ C. light cream

Slice zucchini thickly. Combine first 6 ingredients bring to a boil and simmer for 20 minutes. Blend this mixture in blender. Combine with ½ C. milk. Blend until smooth. Return blended purée to pan and stir in remaining milk and cream. Heat to serve. Stir occasionally. Can be made ahead and frozen.

SERVES 6

Mrs. John M. Ferrell

SPINACH AND OYSTER SOUP

1 bag fresh spinach
  OR 1 box frozen, puréed
4 T. butter
¼ C. finely chopped green onions
1 C. finely chopped celery
¼ C. chopped fresh parsley
1 clove garlic, minced
1 pt. oysters, chopped
4 T. flour
3 C. light cream or milk
1 C. chicken broth
3 T Worcestershire sauce
Tabasco to taste
Salt and pepper to taste
½ t. anise seed (optional)
1 oz. annisette (optional)

Melt the butter, add onions, celery, garlic and parsley. Sauté at low heat until soft. Add oysters and cook until they curl. Stir in flour and cook until foamy. Add cream or milk and cook over low heat until thickened. Mix in broth and spinach. Bring to a boil.

SERVES 8

Linda Ryan Butter
(Mrs. Stephen R.)

ITALIAN TUNA SOUP

1 onion, chopped
½ T. olive oil
1 (1 lb.) can tomatoes
4 (10¾ oz.) cans chicken broth
1 (15 oz.) can white navy beans
½ C. water
1 t. salt
¼ t. garlic powder
1 t. Italian seasoning
6 very small zucchini, sliced
2 (6½ oz.) cans chunk light tuna, drained
Parmesan cheese

Sauté onion in olive oil. Stir in tomatoes, chicken broth, beans, water, and seasonings. Simmer uncovered 15 minutes. Stir in zucchini and simmer 10 minutes longer. Add tuna and heat through. Sprinkle liberally with Parmesan cheese.

SERVES 6—8

Mrs. Moody Lawrence
Newport Beach, Calif.

VEGETABLE SOUP

1 soup bone
½ gallon water
4-6 cans beef bouillon
4 lbs. boneless roast, cut in chunks
2 cloves garlic, pressed
2 onions, grated
1 (16 oz.) can tomatoes
3 stalks celery, chopped
3 carrots, sliced
3 potatoes, chopped
1 pkg. each frozen green peas, lima beans, corn and okra
Cabbage (optional)
1 T. sugar
4-5 chili petines (optional)
Salt and pepper to taste
Macaroni (optional)

Boil soup bone in water 1—2 hours. Add bouillon, meat, onion and garlic and simmer until meat is tender. Add vegetables, sugar, seasonings and petines. Simmer until vegetables are tender. If desired, add macaroni and simmer until macaroni is cooked. (The quantities and choice of vegetables can be varied to the taste of the individual.)

Betty Robbins Davis
(Mrs. Charles H.)

VENISON SOUP

2 lbs. venison hamburger
2 cans beef bouillon
4 cans water
2 cloves garlic, pressed
½ onion
3 stalks celery (tops only)
2-3 chili petines
Salt and pepper to taste
1 T. beef stock base
Worcestershire sauce to taste
Soy Sauce to taste
¼ C. barley
1 carrot, sliced
2-3 potatoes, chopped
1 onion, chopped
1 stalk celery, chopped
½ bell pepper, chopped
⅓ head cabbage, shredded (optional)
1 (12 oz.) can V-8 juice

Brown meat. Add bouillon, water, garlic, ½ onion, celery tops, chili petines, and seasonings. Simmer 1 hour. Add barley and simmer 30 minutes. Remove onion, celery tops and petines. Cook chopped vegetables separately until tender. Drain. Add vegetables to broth. Add V-8 juice. Simmer 30 minutes. Let cool. This soup is better if made the day before it is served and reheated.

YIELD: 4 quarts

Joyce Bander Davis
(Mrs. Bob)

Salads / Fruit 63

ANGEL SALAD
"May also be used as a light dessert"

2 eggs
2 T. water
2 T. white vinegar
1 T. butter
1 T. sugar
Dash of salt
2 C. diced pineapple, drained
2 C. marshmallows, chopped fine OR miniature marshmallows
1 C. heavy cream, whipped

In the top of a double boiler, beat eggs. Add water, vinegar, butter, sugar and salt. Cook until smooth and thick. Cool. Add pineapple and marshmallows. Fold in whipped cream. Chill 12 hours in refrigerator. Cut into squares and serve on lettuce. May be frozen.

SERVES 8—10

Mary Lynn Hartman Dawes
(Mrs. John L.)

APRICOT SALAD

2 (3 oz.) pkgs. apricot gelatine
2 C. boiling water
1 C. miniature marshmallows
2 C. apricot nectar, chilled
3 bananas
2 T. lemon juice
1 (20 oz.) can crushed pineapple, reserve juice

TOPPING:

1 whole egg, beaten
½ C. sugar
3 T. flour
½ C. pineapple juice, reserved
1 (3 oz.) pkg. cream cheese, softened
1 C. heavy cream, whipped
½ C. sugar

Dissolve gelatine in boiling water. After mixture has cooled, add marshmallows. Add cold apricot nectar. Stir. Slice bananas thinly and stir into lemon juice. Add to gelatine mixture. Chill until it begins to set. Stir in pineapple and pour into a 3 quart pyrex dish. Chill until firm.

TOPPING:

Mix beaten egg, sugar, flour, and pineapple juice together. Cook over low heat until thickened. Add cream cheese and mix well. Chill and fold in whipped cream which has been sweetened with sugar. Spread over firm gelatine mixture and chill thoroughly before serving.

SERVES 15

Alma Ruth Marks Willeford
(Mrs. Morgan L.)

Salads / Fruit

BLUEBERRY SALAD

1 (6 oz.) pkg. blackberry Jello
2 C. boiling water
1 (15 oz.) can blueberries, reserve juice
1 (8¼ oz.) can crushed pineapple, reserve juice

TOPPING:
1 (8 oz.) pkg. cream cheese softened
1 C. sour cream
½ C. sugar
½ C. chopped pecans

Dissolve Jello in boiling water. Drain blueberries and pineapple; measure liquid. Add enough water to make 1 cup; add to Jello. Stir in blueberries and pineapple. Pour into a 3 quart pyrex dish, and refrigerate until set.

TOPPING:
Combine cream cheese, sour cream and sugar. Spread over Jello layer and sprinkle pecans on top. Very sweet and rich, may also be used as a dessert.

SERVES 12—15

Mrs. Don Barnes,
Tulsa, Okla.

Donor: Ann Killingsworth Smead
(Mrs. Hamp Jr.)

SHERI'S CHERRY SALAD

2 (3 oz.) pkgs. cherry Jello
1 C. boiling water
1 (16 oz.) can sour red cherries
1 C. sugar
1½ C. chopped pecans
1 (8¼ oz.) can crushed pineapple

Dissolve Jello in boiling water. Set aside. Boil sour cherries and sugar for 10 minutes, and add to Jello. Cool. Add pecans and pineapple. Chill until firm.

SERVES 6

Dorothy Hallman Dingler
(Mrs. Clark M., Jr.)

HOLIDAY CRANBERRY MOLD

3 (3 oz.) pkgs. cherry Jello
3 C. boiling water
1 (1 lb.) can whole cranberry sauce, mashed
1 (20 oz.) can crushed pineapple, drained
1 C. chopped pecans

Dissolve Jello in boiling water. Cool until syrupy. Stir in fruit and nuts. Refrigerate in mold overnight.

SERVES 16

Doris Reeves Collier
(Mrs. John Michael)

CRANBERRY SALAD

1 (3 oz.) pkg. lemon Jello
1 ¾ C. boiling water
2 C. raw cranberries
1 large seedless orange
½ C. sugar
½ C. chopped nuts

Dissolve Jello in boiling water. Grind cranberries and orange; add sugar. When gelatine is almost set, add cranberries, orange and nuts. Chill until firm. Serve on lettuce with mayonnaise.

SERVES 6—8

Ella Tribble Love Myers
(Mrs. W. R.)

FROSTED SALAD

2 (3 oz.) pkgs. lemon Jello
2 C. boiling water
2 C. ginger ale
1 (20 oz.) can crushed pineapple, reserve juice
1½ C. tiny marshmallows
2 large bananas

TOPPING:

1 C. pineapple juice, drained from pineapple
½ C. sugar
2 T. flour
1 egg, beaten
2 T. butter
½ pt. heavy cream, whipped
Mild grated cheese

Dissolve Jello in boiling water. Stir in ginger ale. Chill until thick. Add drained pineapple, marshmallows, and bananas. Chill until set.

TOPPING:
Cook together until thick pineapple juice, sugar, flour, beaten egg, and butter. Cool. Fold in whipped cream. Spread over salad and top with grated cheese. Cut in squares and serve on lettuce leaf.

SERVES 12

Sara Skaggs Lucas
(Mrs. J. Richard)

MANGO SALAD

1 (27 oz.) can mangoes
1 (6 oz.) pkg. lemon Jello
2 C. boiling water
1 C. mango juice
1 (8 oz.) pkg. cream cheese
Sour cream
Brown sugar

Drain mangoes, reserving 1 cup juice. Dissolve Jello in boiling water and add mango juice. Blend cheese and mangoes into cooled Jello. Pour into indivdual or ring mold. Serve topped with sour cream and sprinkle with brown sugar.

SERVES 8

Ann Chreitzberg Sheppard
(Mrs. Gillett)

FROZEN FRUIT SALAD

1 (3 oz.) pkg. cream cheese
2 T. heavy cream
⅓ C. salad dressing
2 T. lemon juice
Salt to taste
½ C. maraschino cherries, chopped
½ C. Royal Anne cherries, chopped
1 C. orange sections, sliced
1 C. crushed pineapple
½ C. pecans or black walnuts, chopped
1 C. heavy cream, whipped
2 T. sugar

Mix cream cheese thoroughly with cream. Add salad dressing, lemon juice and salt to taste. Combine cherries, oranges, pineapple, and nuts. Fold in whipped cream and sugar; pour into mold and freeze. Serve on any salad leaf.

SERVES 6

Sara Richkie Whitehurst
(Mrs. Herman)

GRAPEFRUIT SALAD

2 large grapefruit OR 1 (16 oz.) can
1 (15¼ oz.) can pineapple chunks and juice
¼ lb. blanched almonds
2 t. lemon juice
2 T. gelatine
½ C. cold water
1 C. boiling water
1/8 t. salt

TOPPING:

1 (8 oz.) pkg. cream cheese
1 T. sugar
1 T. onion juice
2 T. lemon juice
2 T. Hellmann's mayonnaise
Salt and pepper to taste
Paprika to garnish

Remove white skin from grapefruit sections, cut in small pieces, and mix with pineapple, almonds and lemon juice. Soak gelatine in cold water for 5 minutes. Pour over this 1 cup boiling water. Add salt, then fruit mixture. Pour into individual molds and refrigerate. Serve on lettuce with topping.

SERVES 8

Gay Cole Howard Wheeler
(Mrs. Ridley N.)

Combine ingredients.

Aliece McHenry Mucher
(Mrs. Joseph)

ORANGE PINEAPPLE SALAD

1 pt. light cream
1 small pkg. tiny marshmallows (3¾ C.)
1 (6 oz.) pkg. orange Jello
1 (20 oz.) can crushed pineapple, drained
1 (8 oz.) pkg. cream cheese, softened

Soak marshmallows in light cream for 2 to 3 hours. Prepare Jello according to package directions and chill one hour (not firm). Blend drained pineapple and softened cream cheese. Combine all ingredients, pour into a 9" x 13" pyrex dish and chill until firm.

SERVES 12—14

Marilyn Rouse Payne
(Mrs. Hermes E.)

SPICED PURPLE PLUM SALAD

2 (17 oz.) cans purple plums
1¾ C. plum juice
1 (3 oz.) pkg. cherry Jello
1 T. gelatine, dissolved in
¼ C. cold water
¼ t. cinnamon
1/8 t. ground cloves
1/8 t. nutmeg

Drain plums and reserve juice. Add water to make 1¾ cup. Dissolve gelatine in water. Add hot liquid to Jello and gelatine. Pit plums and purée in food processor or blender. Pour plums into gelatine mixture and add spices. Pour into 6 cup mold (oiled) and chill until firm. Other fruit may be added such as drained bing cherries, mandarin oranges, pineapple tidbits, or any fruit desired.

SERVES 8

Claire Smith Foster
(Mrs. Henry L.)

SUMMER CONGEALED SALAD

1 (3 oz.) pkg. lime flavored gelatine
¾ C. boiling water
¼ C. pineapple juice (drained from crushed pineapple)
1 C. light cream
1 (20 oz.) can crushed pineapple
2 bananas, mashed
24 miniature marshmallows
¼ C. mayonnaise
1 (3 oz.) pkg. cream cheese
1 C. chopped nuts, optional
4 t. lemon juice, optional

Dissolve gelatine in boiling water. Add pineapple juice and allow to cool; then add cream. Chill in refrigerator until it reaches the mushy stage. Add remaining ingredients and mix well. Put into individual molds or one large mold and keep in refrigerator until set.

SERVES 9

Mary Lynn Hartman Dawes
(Mrs. John L.)

MIXED FRUIT SALAD

1 (10 oz.) pkg. frozen peaches, defrosted
1 (10 oz.) pkg. frozen raspberries, defrosted
¼ C. frozen lemonade, defrosted
2 T. unflavored gelatine
½ C. cold water
1 C. boiling water
¼ t. salt
1 T. sugar
1 (4 oz.) can frozen orange juice, defrosted
½ C. seeded green grapes
¼ C. walnut halves
½ C. pitted dates, sliced (optional)

Reserve juice from thawed peaches and raspberries. Pour lemonade over peaches. Soften gelatine in cold water then dissolve in hot water. Add salt, sugar, orange juice, peach juice and raspberry juice to gelatine. Chill until mixture begins to thicken. Fold in grapes, nuts and dates. Pour into a 6 cup mold and chill until firm.

Claire Smith Foster
(Mrs. Henry L.)

JELLIED WALDORF SALAD

1½ C. boiling water
1 C. cold water or cranberry juice
2 (3 oz.) pkgs. lemon Jello
¼ t. salt
½ C. white raisins (plumped in hot water)
½ C. grated carrots
½ C. chopped celery
½ C. chopped apples, skins on
½ C. pecans or walnuts
Kraft's horseradish sauce

Prepare Jello according to package directions. Add salt. Let partially set, fold in vegetables and salt. Chill in 6 quart mold. Serve with horseradish sauce.

SERVES 8

Dee Perry

Donor: Cookbook Committee

CHICKEN ASPIC

1 hen, cooked and diced
1 C. chicken stock (hot)
2 envelopes gelatine
1 C. cold water
½ C. pimiento, chopped
6 hard cooked eggs, chopped
3 T. pickle relish
2 C. diced celery
½ t. Worcestershire sauce
½ t. grated onion
1 C. mayonnaise

Dissolve gelatine in cold water. Add hot chicken stock. Combine all ingredients, adding mayonnaise last. Salt to taste. Press into a shallow greased pan. Refrigerate over-night. Cut into squares and serve on lettuce.

SERVES 8

Marilyn Rouse Payne
(Mrs. Hermes E.)

Evelyn Pegues Hight
(Mrs. Tom A., Jr.)

COLD CURRIED CHICKEN SALAD

2 C. uncooked rice
1 C. uncooked cauliflower, cut into ¼" slices
1 (8 oz.) bottle creamy French dressing
1 C. mayonnaise
1 T. curry powder
1 T. salt
1½ t. pepper
½ C. milk
6—7 C. cooked chicken or turkey, cut in large pieces
1 C. thin strips of green pepper
2 C. diagonally sliced celery
1 C. thinly sliced red onions

Cook rice until just tender and chill. Toss chilled rice with cauliflower and dressing. Refrigerate at least 2 hours. In another large bowl, combine mayonnaise, curry powder, salt and pepper. Slowly stir in milk. Add chicken and toss. Refrigerate at least 2 hours. When ready to serve, combine both mixtures; add green pepper, celery and onions. Serve with the following condiments: flaked coconut, slivered almonds, pineapple cubes, currant jelly, chutney, crumbled bacon, chopped hard-cooked eggs.

SERVES 12—15

Junior League of Houston

CARDINAL CHICKEN SALAD

1 T. lemon juice
2 C. finely chopped apples
4 C. finely chopped chicken
1½ C. finely chopped celery
1 C. green grapes, cut in half
¾ C. mayonnaise
½ t. salt
1/8 t. pepper

TOPPING:
1 (8 oz.) pkg. cream cheese
¼ C. mayonnaise

Sprinkle lemon juice over apples. Add chicken, celery, grapes, mayonnaise and seasonings. Mix lightly. Press mixture into 1½ quart bowl; chill several hours. Unmold on serving platter.

TOPPING:
Combine softened cream cheese and mayonnaise, mixing until well blended. Frost chicken salad. Garnish as desired.

SERVES 8

Marcia Burlison McDaniel
(Mrs. Stephen W.)

CHICKEN SALAD

4 lb. hen
1 stalk celery
½ t. MSG
1 large carrot
Salt and pepper to taste
1 (8 oz.) can water chestnuts, chopped in large pieces
1 (3 oz.) bottles capers, drained
2 hard boiled eggs, chopped in large pieces

CHICKEN SALAD DRESSING
½ C. chicken broth
¼ C. vinegar
¼ C. water
¼ C. chicken fat OR butter
5 egg yolks
1—2 T. prepared mustard
1 t. salt
¼ t. pepper
Dash cayenne

Boil hen with celery, MSG, carrot, salt and pepper. Cool in broth. Chop in 1 inch cubes. Moisten generously with Chicken Salad Dressing or mayonnaise and add remaining ingredients. Correct seasonings.

Florra Wheeler Anderson
(Mrs. Jack)

Heat first 4 ingredients in double boiler. Beat egg yolks; stir in mustard, salt, pepper, and cayenne. Add to hot liquid and cook, stirring until thickened. Cool. If dressing becomes too thick in storing, thin with evaporated milk, or 1—2 T. mayonnaise.

YIELD: 1½ cups

Lynne Smith Norton
(Mrs. O. L.)

CHICKEN CRANBERRY SALAD

1 pkg. gelatine
¼ C. cold water
½ C. milk
1 C. chopped celery
½ C. parsley
1 C. mayonnaise
2 C. chicken, cut up
Salt, pepper, Seasonall

TOPPING:
1 C. jellied cranberry sauce
1 pkg. gelatine
¼ C. cold water
1 (8¼ oz.) can crushed pineapple
½ C. pecans
Red food coloring, optional

Dissolve gelatine in cold water. Heat milk, and add to gelatine. Cool. Add celery, parsley, mayonnaise and chicken. Toss with seasonings. Pour into a greased 2 quart casserole dish. Chill until firm.

TOPPING:

Melt cranberry sauce and add gelatine that has been softened in cold water. Add pineapple (do not drain) and nuts. May add red food coloring for bright red color. Pour over first mixture. Refrigerate overnight. Serve on red lettuce leaf and top with mayonnaise.

SERVES 8

Joanie Marvel Abbot
(Mrs. Frank G.)

BEEF AND POTATO SALAD IN BREAD ROUNDS

2 medium Idaho potatoes
1 C. mayonnaise
3 T. Dijon mustard
1 t. dried tarragon
2 lbs. rare tenderloin of beef
¾ lb. fresh mushrooms, marinated in Vinaigrette sauce
Parsley flakes
Salt and pepper to taste
18 Pepperidge Farm round sour French rolls

VINAIGRETTE SAUCE:
2 T. red wine vinegar
6 T. salad oil
1 t. salt
1 t. dry mustard
Seasoned pepper
Minced onion
Parsley flakes
2 shallots, chopped

Peel potatoes, cook in boiling salted water until tender. Slice potatoes and while still hot, toss with mayonnaise which has been mixed with mustard and tarragon. Cut roast beef into small pieces. Toss potatoes, beef and marinated mushrooms together gently. Sprinkle with parsley flakes and season with salt and pepper to taste. Slice off top of rolls and scoop out center. Butter generously and fill with salad. Put top on and refrigerate until ready to serve.

SERVES 18

Patricia Smith Houston
(Mrs. E. B.)

SMOKED CHICKEN SALAD

2 smoked chickens
1 (8 oz.) can water chestnuts, chopped
Whitfield salad picklettes
Helmann's mayonnaise
Salt and pepper

Smoke the chickens with plenty of black pepper and hickory chips. Debone and chop chicken. Add water chestnuts and remaining ingredients to taste.

SERVES 12

Jo Ruth Edwards Maness
(Mrs. Bob)

WHEAT PILAF SALAD
"Serve with deviled eggs, sliced tomatoes and hot bread for a light dinner"

1 pkg. wheat pilaf
1 lb. fresh mushrooms, sliced or quartered
1—2 pkgs. thin sliced ham, chicken or beef
1 pkg. shredded Mozzarella cheese
1 large onion, sliced
3 yellow squash, sliced
3 zucchini squash, sliced
1 head cauliflower, flowerlets
1 cucumber, sliced
3 carrots, sliced
1 green pepper, sliced
1 C. celery, sliced

DRESSING:
1 C. olive oil
½ C. wine vinegar
½ C. lemon juice
1 clove garlic
1 t. Fine Herbes

Layer pilaf and vegetables and add dressing to each layer. At the end, mix it well and stir every few hours or so. This should be made 24 hours in advance so that the pilaf has a chance to expand. Cooked, canned vegetables may also be used (good for leftovers) and other vegetables not listed.

SERVES 18—20

Mrs. Thorton D. Saffer,
Middleburg, Va.

HAM AND CHEESE SALAD

2 C. ham, cubed
2 C. Swiss or Monterey Jack cheese, cubed
4 eggs, hard cooked

DRESSING:

1 C. sour cream
4 T. mayonnaise
3 T. prepared mustard
2 T. prepared horseradish
Salt and pepper to taste

Toss meat, cheese and eggs gently. Combine dressing ingredients and mix with salad. May add torn up pieces of lettuce greens. Serve with a fresh fruit salad.

SERVES 4

Carmen Huggins Hilliard
(Mrs. George M., III)

COLD STEAK SALAD

2 lbs. boneless sirloin, cut in ½ inch cubes
½ C. butter
¾ lb. mushrooms, sliced
1 (9 oz.) pkg. frozen artichoke hearts, cooked and cooled (may use fresh or canned)
1 C. diced celery
1 pt. small cherry tomatoes
2 T. chopped chives
2 T. chopped parsley
2 C. dressing (below)
2 t. Dijon mustard

DRESSING:

2½ C. oil
¾ C. wine vinegar
6 shallots, finely chopped
⅓ C. chopped parsley
⅓ C. dill weed
Salt and pepper to taste
1/8 t. Tabasco

In a large skillet over high heat, sauté the meat cubes in butter until browned on all sides. Transfer to a large bowl and cool. Quickly sauté the mushrooms in butter remaining in the skillet and add to bowl with artichoke hearts, celery, tomatoes, chives and parsley. Mix lightly.

DRESSING:

Combine dressing ingredients in a jar and shake.

TO SERVE:

Mix 2 cups of dressing with the mustard and pour over the salad. Toss, cover and marinate over night.

SERVES 6

Nancy Green McWhorter
(Mrs. Eugene W.)

74 Salads/Meat

ROAST BEEF SALAD
"Great way to use left-over roast beef!"

Cubed roast beef
Romaine lettuce
Red top lettuce
Iceburg lettuce
Quartered cherry tomatoes
Cubed cheddar cheese
Dill pickles, thick slices, quartered

DRESSING:
¼ C. vinegar
1/8 C. lemon juice
⅔ C. oil
½ t. red pepper
½ t. minced garlic
1 t. salt
Black pepper
¼ t. dry mustard

Combine all ingredients and toss with dressing.

Betty Hull Roberts
(Mrs. Earl , Jr.)

MOLDED BLEU CHEESE SALAD

2 pkgs. unflavored gelatine
1 quart milk, divided
2 (8 oz.) pkgs. cream cheese, softened
1 (6 oz.) pkg. Bleu cheese, crumbled

Soften gelatine in ½ C. cold milk for 5 minutes. Heat remaining milk; add gelatine and stir until dissolved. Cool until slightly thickened. Blend cream cheese and Bleu cheese, gradually add gelatine mixture, beating until smooth. Pour into mold and chill until firm. Serve with strawberries and pineapple slices.

SERVES 8

Carmen Huggins Hilliard
(Mrs. George M., III)

BAYLEY'S WEST INDIES SALAD

1 medium onion, chopped fine
1 lb. fresh lump crabmeat
Salt and pepper to taste
4 oz. Wesson Oil
3 oz. cider vinegar
4 oz. ice water

Spread half of onion over bottom of large bowl. Cover with separated crab lumps and then remaining onion. Salt and pepper. Pour oil, vinegar, and ice water over all. Cover and marinate for two to twelve hours. Toss lightly before serving.

SERVES 4

Beverly Becker Wood
(Mrs. Harold)

RICE AND CRABMEAT SALAD

2 C. cooked rice
2 small bell peppers, diced
1 (2 oz.) jar pimiento, chopped
1 lb. lump crabmeat, picked
1 C. Hellmann's mayonnaise
½ — 1 t. curry powder
½ t. chopped chives (Spice Island)
1 t. lemon juice

Mix all ingredients together. Salt to taste. Chill.

SERVES 6

Claire Smith Foster
(Mrs. Henry L.)

SEAFOOD MOLD

2½ envelopes gelatine
4 T. cold water
2 C. shrimp
2 C. crab OR 1 C. crab and 1 C. lobster
2 C. celery, chopped fine
1 clove garlic, pressed
⅓ C. ketchup
3 T. lemon juice
1½ t. salt
Pepper to taste
1 C. mayonnaise
2 t. onion juice
1 t. Worcestershire sauce
4—5 dashes Tabasco

Dissolve gelatine in cold water; then heat over hot water in a double boiler. Combine the rest of the ingredients. Add gelatine mixture. Pour into greased 2 quart mold. Chill.

SERVES 12

Alma Buchanan Brown
(Mrs. Thomas Rush)

MOLDED SALMON LOAF

1 (16 oz.) can salmon
1 hard-cooked egg, chopped
½ C. cottage cheese
½ C. chopped celery
2 T. chopped pickle
¼ C. mayonnaise
½ t. mustard
½ t. minced onion
Salt and cayenne to taste
1 T. gelatine, softened in ¼ C. cold water

SAUCE TARTARE:
1 C. mayonnaise
1 T. grated onion
1 T. minced parsley
1 T. minced sour pickle
1 T. vinegar
Tabasco to taste

Remove skin and bone from salmon and flake. Toss ingredients together and add mayonnaise. Dissolve gelatine mixture over hot water. Add to salmon mixture. Turn into a slightly greased mold or loaf pan and chill. Garnish with lemon slices and serve with Sauce Tartare. NOTE: In hot weather I use another T. of gelatine.

SERVES 6—8

Rub bowl with cut button of garlic. Fold ingredients into mayonnaise and add Tabasco to make it snappy. This sauce is also good with fried seafoods.

Mrs. Lawrence Rogers

MARINATED SHRIMP

"Can be served on lettuce as a salad or on crackers as an appetizer"

2 lbs. shrimp, cooked, cleaned and chilled
2 avocados, cut in chunks
2 small onions, sliced

MARINADE
1 C. wine vinegar
½ C. water
½ C. lemon juice
1 C. oil
3 t. salt
¼ t. pepper
2 t. sugar
1 t. thyme
1 t. dry mustard
2 t. orégano
½ t. garlic powder

Pour marinade over shrimp, avocados and onions, and refrigerate overnight. Drain and serve.

Patty Yates Shappell
(Mrs. H. D., Jr.)

Salads/Seafood 77

MOR'S SALAD

2 (4½ oz.) cans shrimp
2 (6½ oz.) cans white
  crabmeat
2 (4½ oz.) cans whole
  mushrooms
1 (8½ oz.) can LeSueur peas
1 (15 oz.) can fancy asparagus
  spears
6 hard boiled eggs
1 grapefruit, sectioned (reserve juice)
Parsley for garnish

DRESSING:
1 C. Hellmann's mayonnaise
6 T. sugar
Reserved juice from grapefruit
Juice of 1 lemon
Pepper to taste
Pinch of salt
Pinch of dry mustard

Drain shrimp and crabmeat and place on a paper towel. Drain all vegetables and reserve juices. Combine dressing ingredients and use reserved vegetable juices to thin, if necessary, but be careful that the dressing is not runny. Layer salad ingredients, pour dressing over, and garnish with parsley and additional shrimp.

SERVES 8—10

Kirsten Sonne Felker
(Mrs. Marshall L., Jr.)

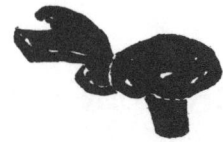

SHRIMP SALAD SUPREME

1 (6 oz.) pkg. curried rice mix
2 C. cleaned, cooked shrimp
  halved lengthwise
1 C. diced celery
½ C. diced bell pepper
½ lb. crisp, cooked bacon,
  drained and chopped
½ C. heavy cream, whipped
½ C. Hellmann's mayonnaise
1 t. curry powder

Cook rice according to directions. Put in colander and run water over. Drain well. Reserve 6 shrimp and ½ cup bacon for garnish. Combine the remaining shrimp, cooled rice, celery, green pepper and bacon. Combine cream with mayonnaise and curry powder. Stir into rice mixture. Cover and chill. Serve very cold, garnished with shrimp and bacon. Serve with chopped cashew nuts, shredded coconut and chutney as condiments.

SERVES 6

Claire Smith Foster
(Mrs. Henry L.)

SALMON RICE SALAD

3 C. steamed rice
¾ C. Basic French Dressing (see Index. Substitute lemon juice for vinegar)
3 T. mayonnaise
3 C. flaked cooked salmon
¾ C. chopped green pepper
¾ C. chopped cucumber, peeled and seeded
3 T. chopped scallion
3 T. snipped dill
Salt
Pepper

Cool steamed rice to lukewarm. In a large bowl toss rice with dressing and mayonnaise. Add remaining ingredients and mix well.

SERVES: 8

Cookbook Committee

TUNA OR CHICKEN SALAD BOMBAY
"Good and Easy"

2 (7 oz.) cans tuna packed in water, drained
1½ C. pineapple chunks
1 C. chopped celery
¾ C. walnuts meats
1 t. parsley flakes
1 t. curry powder
Hellmann's mayonnaise to taste

Combine ingredients.

SERVES 6

Barbara Hubbard Tomberlain
(Mrs. Charles)

VARIATION:

2 C. cooked diced chicken
½ C. green onions, chopped
½ t. grated lime rind
2 T. lime juice
¼ t. salt
2—3 T. chutney
¼ C. salted peanuts (add just before serving)

SERVES 8—10

Marilyn Rouse Payne
(Mrs. Hermes E.)

ORIENTAL SHRIMP SALAD

1 (10 oz.) pkg. frozen green peas, cooked and cooled
½ lb. shrimp, cooked, cleaned, and sliced
1 C. tiny whole spiced onions, drained
1 C. celery, sliced diagonally
½ C. toasted sliced almonds
½ C. mayonnaise
½ t. soy sauce
1/8 t. curry powder
1½ t. lemon juice
Dash salt

Toss all ingredients together.

SERVES 6

Claire Smith Foster
(Mrs. Henry L.)

CAULIFLOWER AND SHRIMP SALAD

1 C. cooked instant rice
3 C. cooked shrimp
1½ t. salt
Pepper
3 T. lemon juice
3 T. chopped green onions
1 C. mayonnaise
1 T. chopped stuffed green olives
2½ C. cauliflower, finely cut

Mix all ingredients together and chill for 24 hours.

SERVES 6—8

Mrs. Dan Jamison

TUNA PARTY LOAF

2 (3 oz.) pkgs. cream cheese
1 (10¾ oz.) can tomato soup
2 envelopes gelatine
¼ C. cold water
¾ C. boiling water
½ T. salt
1 t. Worcestershire sauce
3 drops Tabasco
1 T. prepared horseradish
1/8 t. dry mustard
Pinch curry powder
1 (6½ oz.) can tuna, flaked
1 C. mayonnaise
1½ T. chopped onion
20 stuffed olives, sliced

Melt cheese in soup in a double boiler stirring until smooth. Soften gelatine in cold water; dissolve in hot water. Stir gelatine into soup mixture; add seasonings and let partially set. Add tuna, mayonnaise, onion and olives. Stir until well blended. Chill in 2 quart mold.

Mrs. A. C. DeMoss

SHRIMP ASPIC

2 T. gelatine
¾ C. cold consommé
1 C. hot consommé
½ C. chili sauce
1 C. chopped celery
2 chopped dill pickles
1 lb. boiled shrimp
    OR crabmeat, diced
Juice of 1 lemon

Soak gelatine in ¾ cup cold consommé. Dissolve in 1 cup hot consommé. Cool and add remaining ingredients. Chill. Serve on lettuce with mayonnaise.

SERVES 4

Mrs. Frank Campbell
Kilgore, Texas

TUNA SALAD

1 (6½ oz.) can tuna, drained
1½—2 carrots, shredded
1 t. celery seed
1 (8 oz.) can English peas
½ C. mayonnaise (or more)
1 small onion, chopped
Canned shoestring potatoes

Mix all ingredients and just before serving add ⅔ can of shoestring potatoes and toss. May also add diced avocado.

SERVES 6

Gay Cole Howard Wheeler
(Mrs. Ridley N.)

TOSSED TUNA SALAD

½ head lettuce
2 tomatoes, cut in wedges
½ C. sliced black olives
¼ C. chopped green onions
1 (7 oz.) can Albacore tuna, drained
1 C. corn chips
½ C. grated Cheddar cheese

DRESSING:

½ t. sugar
½ C. mashed avocado
1 T. lemon juice
½ C. sour cream
⅓ C. oil
½ t. chili powder
½ t. garlic powder
¼ t. salt
¼ t. Tabasco sauce

Mix lettuce, tomatoes, olives, onions and tuna together. Pour dressing over salad. Add corn chips and toss. Sprinkle cheese on top.

SERVES 6

Su-Su Hoffman Meyer
(Mrs. Jerry)

INDIA TUNA SALAD

2 (6½ oz.) cans tuna in vegetable oil, drained
½ C. raisins
½ C. chopped green pepper
½ C. dry-roasted peanuts
¼ C. flaked coconut
2 T. chopped chutney

CURRY DRESSING:
¼ C. plain yogurt
¼ C. mayonnaise
1 t. lemon juice
1 t. curry powder
2 T. chopped green onions
¼ t. salt

Mix tuna, raisins, green pepper, peanuts, coconut and chutney together in a large bowl. Mix together dressing ingredients. Serve over salad.

SERVES 4

Eleanor Croxton Lawrence
(Mrs. Thomas W.)

CHINESE TUNA SALAD

2 (6½ oz.) cans tuna, drained
1 C. chopped celery
½ C. chopped green onions and tops
½ C. chopped bell pepper
½ C. pimiento
1 (8 oz.) can water chestnuts, sliced
½ C. ripe olives, sliced
Chinese noodles

DRESSING:
½ C. mayonnaise
1 T. vinegar
1 clove garlic
Celery salt
Seasoned salt
Pepper

Combine salad ingredients. Toss with dressing. Top before serving with noodles. Serve on cantaloupe rings.

SERVES 8—10

Betty Hull Roberts
(Mrs. Earl, Jr.)

MARINATED ASPARAGUS

4 (15 oz.) cans Green Giant asparagus
2 C. Wishbone Italian dressing
1 C. white wine
½ t. sweet basil
¼ t. orégano
1 pod garlic, crushed
¼ t. salt
¼ t. pepper
2 T. tarragon vinegar

Mix all ingredients except asparagus in a jar and shake. Let stand for some time. Place the asparagus in a serving dish and pour the marinade over all. Let this stand, covered, over night.

SERVES 12

Dorothy Robbins Kennedy
(Mrs. George E., Jr.)

ASPARAGUS CHEESE MOLD

1 envelope gelatine
½ C. cold water
Asparagus juice
1 (15 oz.) can asparagus cut fine
1 C. grated American cheese
1 (8 oz.) pkg. cream cheese
1 small bottle olives, chopped
3 hard boiled eggs, diced
½ t. salt
1 t. Worcestershire sauce
1 C. mayonnaise
Dash Tabasco sauce

VARIATION I:
Omit hard-boiled eggs
Add:
1 C. celery, chopped
1 t. onion, finely chopped

VARIATION II:
Add:
1 C. blanched slivered almonds
2 T. lemon juice

Soak gelatine in cold water; heat asparagus liquid with water added to make 1 cup and dissolve gelatine in it. Cool. Mix the remaining ingredients and add to cooled gelatine mixture. Pour into a 9" square pan and when congealed cut in squares. Serve on lettuce with favorite dressing. Sprinkle with paprika. Nice to serve with sandwiches for a luncheon salad plate.

SERVES 8

Ethel Poday Maledon
(Mrs. E. N.)

Karen Williams Frith
(Mrs. Charles E.)

Betty Lyn Bruner Collier
(Mrs. Joe)

STUFFED ARTICHOKE HEARTS

Reese's canned artichoke hearts (5-6 per can)
Italian Wishbone dressing
Cream cheese
Hellmann's mayonnaise
Anchovy paste
Stuffed olives, minced
Onion salt
Accent
Dried parsley

Marinate artichoke hearts over night in Italian dressing. When ready to serve, drain and cut bottoms of artichokes so that they will sit up straight, pull leaves apart to make petals and stuff with a mixture of the remaining ingredients to taste. Top with sliced stuffed olives.

Peggy Conner Smead
(Mrs. Hamp, Sr.)

MUSHROOM—AVOCADO SALAD

½ C. Wesson oil
3 T. tarragon vinegar
2 T. lemon juice
2 T. water
1 T. snipped fresh parsley
1 clove garlic, pressed
¾ t. salt
Dash pepper
2 avocados, sliced
8 oz. fresh mushrooms, sliced
Parsley sprigs

Combine seasonings with oil, vinegar and lemon juice. Pour over avocados and mushrooms. Chill several hours. Garnish with parsley.

SERVES 4—6

Mrs. Michael C. Macey

JELLIED GUACAMOLE PHILLIPS

3 avocados, peeled and mashed
1 tomato, peeled, seeded and chopped
1 onion, finely chopped
2 T. mayonnaise
2 T. lemon juice
1 t. salt
Dash of Tabasco
2 C. cold chicken broth
3 envelopes gelatine
½ C. cold chicken broth

Combine avocado, tomato and onion. Add seasonings. Stir in 2 cups cold chicken broth. Sprinkle gelatine over ½ cup cold broth to soften. Set the pan over simmering water and stir until it is completely dissolved. Stir the gelatine into the guacamole mixture thoroughly and pour it into a 2 quart ring mold.

SERVES 12

Ann Chreitzberg Sheppard
(Mrs. Gillett)

AVOCADO OLIVA

2 large avocados
1 (14 oz.) can artichoke hearts, quartered
½ C. oil
1 T. vinegar
1 T. lemon juice
2 T. vermouth
2 T. Dijon mustard
Salt and white pepper
2 T. chopped parsley

Cut avocados in half. Fill cavity with quartered artichoke hearts. Combine remaining ingredients, leaving the parsley for decoration. Pour the sauce over the artichoke hearts. Sprinkle with parsley and serve. Rub lemon juice on avocados if prepared ahead.

SERVES 4

Jenny Lewis Rappeport
(Mrs. Joseph H.)

AVOCADO, ONION AND CUCUMBER SALAD

2 purple onions, sliced thin
1 cucumber, sliced very thin
3 avocados, sliced

VINAIGRETTE:

¼ C. red wine vinegar
¾ C. salad oil
2 t. dry mustard
2 t. salt
Seasoned pepper

Marinate onions and cucumbers in vinaigrette for several hours in refrigerator. Add sliced avocados just before serving.

SERVES 6

Patricia Smith Houston
(Mrs. E. B.)

BEET SALAD
"Delicious with roast beef"

1 (3 oz.) pkg. lemon Jello
1 C. beet juice
1 (16 oz.) can beets, cubed
¼ C. pickle relish
2—3 T. vinegar
3—4 T. horseradish
1 t. grated onion, (optional)

Dissolve Jello in boiling beet juice. Add remaining ingredients and chill in ring mold.

Eugenia Tunstall Francis
(Mrs. Tom B.)

BROCCOLI SALAD

1 C. finely chopped onion
1 C. finely chopped celery
2—3 small yellow summer squash, unpeeled, thinly sliced
1 C. fresh mushrooms, sliced
1 (14 oz.) can artichoke hearts, drained and quartered
1 (8 oz.) can water chestnuts, drained and thinly sliced
¾ C. olive oil
⅔ C. red wine vinegar
¼ t. sugar
2 t. salt
2 (10 oz.) pkgs. frozen chopped broccoli
6 slices bacon, fried and crumbled

Combine onion, celery, squash, mushrooms, artichoke hearts and water chestnuts in large bowl. Mix oil, vinegar, sugar and salt together. Toss with vegetables. Cook broccoli in 3 quarts water for 2 minutes. Remove immediately and blanch with cold water to stop cooking process. Drain thoroughly. Toss broccoli and bacon into salad. Add more salt if needed. Chill.

SERVES 10—12

Floreid Francis Stevens
(Mrs. A. C.)

CALIFORNIA SALAD

2 C. ½ inch breads cubes
¼ C. salad oil
2 cloves garlic
2 heads Romaine lettuce
¼ t. dry mustard
¼ t. salt
¼ t. black pepper
1 C. crumbled Bleu cheese
⅓ C. lemon juice
⅓ C. additional salad oil
2 eggs

Sauté bread cubes in salad oil with garlic; stir until golden brown. Remove garlic. Break cold, crisp and well-drained Romaine lettuce into small pieces in salad bowl. Sprinkle with mustard, salt, pepper and cheese. Combine lemon juice with ⅓ cup salad oil, pour over greens. Break eggs, which have been simmered for only one minute, over greens. Toss gently. Add sautéed cubes; toss again.

SERVES 6

Etta Remer Sosland
(Mrs. Morris)

CAESAR SALAD

Juice of 2 lemons
½ C. olive oil
¼ C. wine vinegar
1 T. Worcestershire sauce
2 whole garlic cloves, peeled
2 C. bread cubes
½ C. butter
2 cloves garlic, peeled and crushed
3 heads Romaine lettuce
2 raw eggs
¼ C. Parmesan cheese
Salt and pepper

Combine first 5 ingredients and let sit several hours. Remove garlic. Toast bread cubes at 350° stirring occassionally. Melt butter with crushed garlic in frying pan. Stir in cubes until butter is absorbed. Break Romaine into pieces. Break eggs over lettuce. Add dressing and toss until all traces of egg disappear. Add cheese, bread cubes, salt and pepper and toss again.

SERVES 8

Martha Hess Whitehead
(Mrs. R. Laughton, Jr.)

COPPER CARROT PENNIES

2 lbs. carrots, peeled and sliced
1 green pepper, sliced in rings
1 onion, sliced thin

MARINADE:

1 (10¾ oz.) can tomato soup
½ C. salad oil
1 C. sugar
¾ C. vinegar
1 t. prepared mustard
1 t. Worcestershire sauce
Salt and pepper

VARIATION:

Substitute 1 lb. squash, cooked in salted water just until tender with 1 lb. carrots.

Cook sliced carrots in salted water just until tender. Drain and let cool. In bowl alternate layers of carrots, pepper and onion rings. Combine marinade ingredients and pour over vegetables. Cover and refrigerate. Keeps well. Drain before serving.

SERVES 10—12

Mrs. John M. Darby

Helen May Little
(Mrs. Earle E., Jr.)

COOL CUCUMBER MOUSSE

2 envelopes unflavored gelatine
1 C. cold water
¼ C. vinegar
⅔ C. mayonnaise
¾ t. salt
1/8 t. pepper
2 C. shredded cucumber, drained
1 C. heavy cream, whipped
1 T. grated onion

Soften gelatine in combined water and vinegar; stir over low heat until dissolved. Cool. Gradually add gelatine to mayonnaise, salt and pepper; mix well. Chill until partially set. Fold in cucumber, whipped cream and onion. Pour into a lightly oiled 5 cup mold. Chill until firm. Unmold and garnish with cucumber. Serve with chilled seafood, if desired.

SERVES 6—8

Nancy Ogletree Starr
(Mrs. Larry W.)

LIME CUCUMBER SALAD

1 (3 oz.) pkg. lime Jello
1 C. boiling water
¼ C. vinegar
1 t. salt
1 t. grated onion
1 C. sour cream
1 medium cucumber, coarsley grated
Lettuce

Dissolve Jello in water. Add vinegar, salt and onion. Chill until mixture begins to thicken. Stir in sour cream and cucumber. Pour into six molds. Chill until firm. Unmold on lettuce.

SERVES 6

Jeanie Mikeska Folzenlogen
(Mrs. Paul)

SOUR CREAM CUCUMBERS

½ t. salt
½ t. sugar
½ t. cayenne pepper
¼ C. garlic wine vinegar OR tarragon vinegar
1 C. sour cream OR yogurt
2 t. chopped chives
1 t. celery seed
1 t. dill, optional
2—3 cucumbers of medium size

Dissolve salt, sugar and pepper in wine vinegar. Whip cream until smooth; add to vinegar mixture. Add chives, celery seed and dill. Slice cucumbers after scoring with fork tines. Combine with salad dressing and allow to stand in refrigerator at least 2 hours before serving.

Marilyn Rouse Payne
(Mrs. Hermes E.)

DANISH CUCUMBER SALAD

4 cucumbers
½ C. sugar
½ C. water
½ C. vinegar
White pepper to taste
Juice of 1 lemon

Peel and slice cucumbers finely. Mix sugar, water, vinegar, pepper and lemon juice. Pour over cucumbers and chill. Gets better as the week goes on!

Kirsten Sonne Felker
(Mrs. Marshall L., Jr.)

ENGLISH PEA SALAD

6 T. mayonnaise
Juice of 1 lemon
1 small onion, finely minced OR 2 T. minced chives
2 C. frozen peas (do not thaw)
1 C. Swiss or Cheddar cheese strips
Salt and pepper to taste
2 C. lettuce, torn into bite size pieces
8 slices crisp crumbled bacon

Twenty-four hours before serving, combine the mayonnaise, lemon juice, onion, frozen peas, and cheese strips in a bowl. Stir well, add salt and pepper to taste. Cover and refrigerate. Before serving, add lettuce and bacon, toss well and taste again. **Note:** This salad must be prepared 24 hours before serving. It is unusual and delightful. Follow directions carefully.

SERVES 6

Faye Jeter Lewis
(Mrs. Harry, Jr.)

CHINESE VEGETABLE SALAD

1 C. English peas
1 C. French-style green beans
1 C. water chestnuts, sliced
1 C. Chinese mixed vegetables
1 C. sliced celery
1 onion, sliced very thin

MARINADE:

1 C. sugar
¾ C. vinegar
1 t. salt

Drain the vegetables and mix in a large bowl. Pour the marinade over them and refrigerate for 24 hours.

SERVES 10

Martha Brindley Beckworth
(Mrs. Gary)

HORSERADISH RING

"Good with any kind of meat or filled with shrimp or pea salad"

1 (3 oz.) pkg. lemon Jello
1 C. boiling water
½ C. cold water
2 T. vinegar
¼ t. salt
¾ C. prepared horseradish
1 C. heavy cream, whipped

Dissolve gelatine in boiling water. Add cold water, vinegar and salt; chill. When slightly thickened, add horseradish and fold in cream. Pour into greased mold and refrigerate.

SERVES 8—10

Carmen Huggins Hilliard
(Mrs. George M., III)

MACARONI SALAD

1 (12 oz.) pkg. macaroni, cooked
1 bell pepper, chopped
5 green onions, chopped
1 (2 oz.) jar chopped pimientoes
1 cucumber, chopped
Dash Spice Island Beau Monde seasoning
½ t. dry mustard
3 hard cooked eggs, diced
Salt and pepper to taste
1 (8 oz.) carton sour cream
2 T. mayonnaise

Mix all ingredients and let stand awhile to blend flavors.

SERVES 12

Pamela Rice Smith
(Mrs. Ned)

CAROLYN'S LAYERED VEGETABLE SALAD

1 (16 oz.) can LeSueur peas, drained
1 (16 oz.) can cut-up asparagus, drained
1 (14 oz.) can artichoke hearts, halved
2 hard-boiled eggs, sliced
Salt to taste
2 C. Hellmann's mayonnaise
2 T. lemon juice
Sliced toasted almonds

Layer vegetables and eggs in a 9" x 13" casserole. Season with salt. Mix lemon juice with Hellmann's mayonnaise and ice the salad. Just before serving, top with almonds.

SERVES 15

Mrs. Charles Dowell

ANITA'S 9-LAYER SALAD

1 head lettuce, shredded
½ C. chopped green pepper
½ C. chopped celery
½ C. chopped Spanish onion
1 (10 oz.) pkg. frozen English peas, cooked and cooled
2 C. Hellmann's mayonnaise
2 T. sugar
6 oz. grated Cheddar cheese
8 strips bacon, fried and crumbled

In a large salad bowl, layer the ingredients in the order in which they are listed. Cover tightly with plastic wrap and refrigerate 24 hours.

SERVES 10

Carol Morris Little
(Mrs. Robert W.)

VARIATION: Add:
1 head cauliflower, chopped
1 C. fresh mushrooms, chopped
½ C. Parmesan cheese

Layer cauliflower between the celery and onion; mushrooms on top of the peas; and add Parmesan cheese with grated cheese.

Joanie Marvel Abbott
(Mrs. Frank)

PATSY'S LAYERED SALAD

2 C. cabbage, shredded paper thin
1 C. carrots, sliced paper thin
2 C. lettuce, shredded paper thin
1 C. radishes, sliced paper thin
1 C. celery, sliced paper thin
1 small onion, sliced paper thin
1 bell pepper, sliced paper thin
1 C. cucumbers, sliced paper thin
1 T. sugar
3 tomatoes, peeled and thinly sliced
1 pt. Hellmann's mayonnaise
1 lb. bacon, crisply fried and chopped

In a clear glass bowl 12" in diameter with vertical sides, layer vegetables in the order listed, and press down very gently with palm of hand. Layers should show distinctly. Sprinkle sugar over top, cover and refrigerate at least 2—3 hours. When ready to serve, arrange thinly sliced tomatoes over top of cucumbers. Make a well in the center of the salad, fill with mayonnaise and cover top with bacon.

SERVES 12

Patsy Lacy Griffith
(Mrs. J. W.)
Sante Fe, N. Mex.

MARINATED VEGETABLE SALAD

3 cans small (Blue Lake type) whole string beans, well drained
3 cans asparagus spears (green) well drained
1½ cans tiny whole beets, well drained
2 large cans artichoke hearts, well drained
1 large cauliflower, boiled only until firm

SAUCE:
8 T. mayonnaise
3 T. mustard
¾ C. oil
¼ C. vinegar
Salt and pepper to taste
4—5 cloves garlic, pressed
1½ white onions, chopped fine
1 C. chopped parsley

Pile beans in the center of a large round platter. Bank the asparagus with tips up around the beans in a circle. Place an artichoke heart with a beet on top of it in the center top of beans. Secure the beet to the artichoke heart with a toothpick. Circle the asparagus with beets and artichokes. Break cauliflower into flowers and place in a circle around the edge of the platter.

SAUCE:

Combine mayonnaise and mustard; beat in oil and vinegar. Add garlic, onions and parsley. Season, using lots of pepper. The sauce can be poured over the salad and let it marinate for several hours or all day refrigerated; OR sauce can be made the day before and kept in the refrigerator. **Note:** If salad is marinated for several hours, tilt tray just enough to pour off vegetable juices but not enough to disturb salad.

SERVES 18—20

Bon Vivant Cookbook

GREEK SALAD

1 head lettuce
3 tomatoes, peeled and chopped
2 Spanish onions, sliced
1 green pepper, thinly sliced
1 C. Greek olives
¼ lb. Feta cheese, crumbled
¼ C. wine vinegar
½ t. salt
¼ t. freshly ground pepper
¾ C. olive oil
1 T. chopped basil

Tear lettuce into bitesized pieces. In a large bowl combine the lettuce with tomatoes, onions, green pepper, olives and cheese. In a jar combine vinegar with salt, pepper and oil. Shake thoroughly, pour over salad and toss well. Sprinkle with basil, if desired.

Don Brown

MARINATED GARDEN VEGETABLES

2 lbs. fresh carrots, sliced into ¼" diagonal slices
2 lbs. fresh green beans OR 2 pkgs. frozen whole green beans
1 lb. fresh asparagus OR 2 pkgs. frozen asparagus
2 T. scallions, finely minced
2 T. green pepper, finely chopped
2 T. pimiento, finely chopped
1½ C. corn oil
⅔ C. cider vinegar
2 t. sugar
2 t. salt
¼ t. pepper

Cook carrots, beans, and asparagus separately until each is tender crisp. Drain vegetables, reserving ⅓ cup liquid. Arrange carrots, beans and asparagus in a large shallow dish. Mix together the reserved liquid and remaining ingredients. Pour over the vegetables, cover, and marinate in refrigerator at least 3 hours or, preferably, overnight. To serve, drain vegetables and arrange on a large platter. Garnish with pimiento strips.

SERVES 16—20

Curtain Call Cookbook

MOLDED VEGETABLE SALAD

1½ T. gelatine
¼ C. cold water
1 C. asparagus liquid, heated
Juice of ½ lemon
1 (15 oz.) can artichoke hearts, washed, drained and chopped
1 (14 oz.) can hearts of palm, drained and cut into bite-size pieces
1 (15 oz.) can green asparagus drained
1 C. chopped celery, optional
2 green onions and tops, finely chopped
1 C. mayonnaise
1 C. heavy cream, whipped
1 t. Worcestershire sauce
Salt and cayenne to taste

Soak gelatine in cold water; dissolve in hot liquid and chill. Squeeze lemon juice over artichoke hearts and let stand. Save enough asparagus tips to radiate around the bottom of the ring mold and sieve the remainder. When gelatine is thick, add to mayonnaise with whipped cream folded in. Then add sieved asparagus, celery (if desired), green onions and seasonings. Be sure to season highly, using more lemon juice if desired. Pour a thin layer of the gelatine mixture in an oiled 3 quart ring mold and let set. Arrange the asparagus tips and then layer the artichoke hearts and hearts of palm. Pour gelatine mixture over and congeal. Ed. Note: This is a basic salad with infinite possibilities. The vegetables may be varied to include LeSueur peas, water chestnuts, avocados, toasted almonds or pecans.

SERVES 20

Cookbook Committee

MEXICAN SALAD

1 head lettuce, torn into pieces
1 tomato, chopped
1 bell pepper, chopped
1 C. chopped red onion
½ lb. longhorn cheese, grated
1 (16 oz.) can Ranch Style beans, drained
1 (6 oz.) bag small Fritos, chrushed
1 (8 oz.) bottle Catalina dressing

VARIATION: To basic recipe:
Substitute:
½ C. sliced green onions
¼ C. chopped onion
½ C. Basic French dressing
Add:
1 lb. ground beef
1 T. chili powder
½ C. water
1 avocado, sliced (optional)
1 C. chopped Spanish olives (optional)

Combine all ingredients except Fritos. Toss with dressing and add Fritos just before serving.

SERVES 6

Joyce Andres Stidham
(Mrs. Mack)

Brown meat with onion. Add beans, dressing and water. Simmer 15 minutes. Add to vegetables and toss with cheese and Fritos.

SERVES 8

Susanne Sandberg Northcutt
(Mrs. W. D., III)

PEG CORN SALAD

2 (12 oz.) cans LeSueur shoe peg corn, drained
1 medium onion, grated
1½ C. finely chopped celery
3 pimientos, chopped fine
1 small bell pepper, cut fine

DRESSING:

½ C. salad oil
½ t. dry mustard
½ t. black pepper
4 T. vinegar
1 t. salt
4 T. sugar

Combine corn, grated onion, celery, pimiento and bell pepper. Pour dressing over corn mixture and refrigerate several hours. Will keep as long as 3 weeks covered in refrigerator.

Ethel Poday Maledon
(Mrs. Elick)

RICE SALAD

2 C. cooked rice
¼ C. chopped celery
¼ C. chopped bell pepper
2 T. chopped parsley
½ carrot, diced very fine
½ C. or more mayonnaise
1 t. grated onion
1 T. mustard
1 t. India relish
1 T. diced pimiento
Salt and pepper to taste
¼ t. garlic powder

Mix all ingredients, stir well. Chill for two hours or more.

SERVES 6

Ann Lacy Crain
(Mrs. B. W.)

CURRIED RICE SALAD

1⅓ C. cooked rice
3 T. finely chopped onion
1 T. vinegar
2 T. corn oil
½ t. curry powder
1 t. salt
1 C. chopped celery
1 (10 oz.) pkg. frozen peas, cooked and chilled
¾ C. mayonnaise

Cook rice and drain while still warm. Stir in onion, vinegar, oil, curry powder, and salt. Chill at least 3 hours. Just before serving add celery, peas and mayonnaise. Even better if made 24 hours in advance and add celery, peas and mayonnaise 3 hours before serving.

Carolyn Smith Russell
(Mrs. Ralph H.)

MIXED VEGETABLE SALAD

1 C. cooked green beans, cut in 1 inch pieces
1 C. cooked diced carrots
½ C. cooked diced turnips
½ C. cooked green peas
1½ C. cooked diced potatoes
1 (6 oz.) jar marinated artichoke hearts
½ C. mayonnaise (homemade or Hellmann's)
Salt and pepper to taste
2 hard cooked eggs, for garnish
1 (16 oz.) can beet slices, drained for garnish

Combine and place in a bowl. Garnish with 2 hard cooked eggs and beet slices.

SERVES 8—10

Rose Pickens Kirkpatrick
(Mrs. Kenneth L.)

MOLÉ SALAD

"For a really special salad, add fresh crabmeat"

1 head iceberg lettuce
1 head bibb lettuce
1 head romaine lettuce
2 T. sesame seeds, toasted
Grated Romano cheese to taste

Break up lettuce, pour on dressing as needed. Sprinkle on seeds and cheese. Salt and pepper to taste.

Lottie Lipscomb Guttry
(Mrs. John S.)

DRESSING:

1 C. lemon juice
1 t. honey
1 clove garlic, crushed
Pinch of salt
1 C. salad oil

POTATO SALAD

4 large potatoes, unpeeled and cut in thirds
½ C. chopped bell pepper
4 hard boiled eggs, chopped
6 green onions, minced
¼ C. minced celery
¼ C. drained pickle relish
¼ C. chopped parsley
1—2 T. Spice Island chives
1 (2 oz.) jar pimiento, drained
1 C. Hellmann's mayonnaise
1—2 T. mustard
1—2 T. sugar
Salt and black pepper to taste
½ lb. chopped crisp bacon

Cook potatoes until done but not squshy. Let cool and peel. Dice in large pieces (they will break up), then mix all together. Sprinkle bacon over top.

SERVES 12

Claire Smith Foster
(Mrs. Henry L.)

BETTIE'S RICE SALAD

½ C. Wishbone Italian dressing
½ C. water
1 C. Minute rice
1 (10 oz.) pkg. frozen green peas, uncooked
1 small cucumber, chopped fine
1 (8 oz.) can water chestnuts, sliced
1 medium purple onion, chopped fine

Bring Wishbone dressing and water to a boil. Add Minute rice and remove from heat. Mix together peas, cucumber, water chestnuts and onion. Add to rice mixture and marinate 24 hours before serving. Store in refrigerator.

Mrs. Frank Slade

Donor: Barbara Glover Baucum
(Mrs. Joseph B.)

CURRIED RICE WINSTON SALAD

3 C. raw rice
6½ C. boiling water
3 t. salt
Juice of 2 lemons
Dash yellow food coloring
1 lb. zucchini, peeled
1 heaping T. curry powder
1 t. Accent
1½ C. mayonnaise
1 (16 oz.) can bean sprouts, drained
1 (8 oz.) can water chestnuts, chopped

Stir rice into boiling water. Add salt, lemon juice and yellow food coloring. Bring to a rolling boil, reduce heat as low as possible, cover and cook 25 minutes. Remove from heat and allow rice to reach room temperature. In the meantime, dice raw zucchini in ¼ inch squares and add curry and Accent to mayonnaise. Fold all ingredients into cooled rice.

SERVES 35

Mrs Jerry Matthews

SLAW

1 head cabbage, shredded
1 medium onion, chopped
1 bell pepper, chopped
8 or more stuffed olives, chopped
½ C. salad oil
½ C. sugar
½ C. cider vinegar
1 t. celery seed
1 t. dry mustard
¼ t. pepper
1 t. salt

Combine vegetables and olives. Mix and bring to a boil the remaining ingredients. Pour over vegetables, cover and chill at least 24 hours.

SERVES 8

Sylvia Billingslea Collier
(Mrs. Joe A.)

SPINACH MOLD WITH CUCUMBER SAUCE

7 pkgs. frozen chopped spinach, cooked and drained, reserve liquid
1 (16 oz.) pkg. Philadelphia cream cheese
1 T. grated onion
2 T. cucumber, chopped
Juice of ½ lemon
Salt, pepper and paprika to taste
3 pkgs. gelatine
1 (10½ oz.) can chicken broth
½ C. liquid from drained spinach
¾ C. toasted almonds

It is important that spinach is drained thoroughly. Grate cheese into hot spinach. Add onion, cucumber, lemon juice, salt, pepper and paprika. Dissolve gelatine in cold spinach liquid. Add to chicken broth and heat until gelatine is dissolved completely. Add to spinach mixture. Pour into well greased 10" mold and refrigerate. Serve with Cucumber Sauce. Garnish with toasted almonds.

SERVES 24

Maud Norton Bivins
(Mrs. J. K., III)

CUCUMBER SAUCE:

1 C. Hellmann's mayonnaise
3 T. grated cucumber
1 T. grated onion

BUFFET SPINACH MOLD

3 pkgs. gelatine
¾ C. cold water
6 (10 oz.) pkgs. frozen chopped spinach
12 hard boiled eggs, chopped
3 T. grated onion
½ C. Brockles dressing
1½ C. Hellmann's mayonnaise
½ C. lemon juice
Garlic salt
Onion salt
Tabasco sauce
Red pepper
Paprika
Salt

Soften gelatine in cold water. Melt over hot water. Cook spinach only until thawed. Drain well. Mix all ingredients together. Taste for seasonings. Pack into a greased 12 cup mold. May add cut up avocado and/or water chestnuts, if desired.

SERVES 20—24

Claire Smith Foster
(Mrs. Henry L.)

SPINACH SALAD

2 (10 oz.) pkgs. fresh spinach
1 cucumber
2 bunches green onions
½ lb. fresh mushrooms
4 avocados
1 lb. crisp cooked bacon, chopped

SALLY'S SPECIAL DRESSING
½ C. sugar
⅓ C. salad oil
⅓ C. white vinegar
⅓ C. water
1 egg, beaten
1 t. salt

Wash spinach and pick off stems. Dry. Slice green onions and tops very thin. Slice unpeeled cucumber very thin. Slice mushrooms and avocados and add vegetables and bacon to spinach. Toss with Sally's Special Dressing.

DRESSING:
Mix all ingredients. Bring to a boil and then refrigerate.

SERVES 8

Claire Smith Foster
(Mrs. Henry L.)

SPINACH POTATO SALAD

6 medium potatoes, boiled, peeled and cubed
8 green onions, chopped
½ pkg. (10 oz.) spinach, torn into small pieces
1 C. cottage cheese, small curd
1 C. mayonnaise
1 t. Dijon mustard
1 t. lemon juice
Salt and pepper to taste
Cayenne pepper to taste

Toss first three ingredients together. Add cottage cheese, mayonnaise and seasonings and mix well. Serve cold. May garnish with fried crumbled bacon.

SERVES 6

Carmen Huggins Hilliard
(Mrs. George M., III)

WILTED SPINACH SALAD

1 lb. fresh spinach
4 green onions, sliced tops and all
¼ t. cracked pepper
5 slices bacon
2 T. wine vinegar
1 T. lemon juice
1 t. sugar
½ t. salt
2 hard cooked eggs, sliced

Wash spinach and discard stems. Dry and tear into bite size pieces. Add onion and pepper. Fry bacon until crisp and crumble. Add vinegar, lemon juice, sugar, and salt to bacon drippings. Heat to boiling, pour over spinach and toss. Should wilt slightly. Garnish with egg slices.

SERVES 4

Rose Pickens Kirkpatrick
(Mrs. Kenneth L.)

Salads/Vegetable 99

SPINACH AND MANDARIN ORANGE SALAD

"This is delicious with fried shrimp"

1 pkg. spinach, washed and broken
1 red onion, sliced
1 (11 oz.) can mandarin oranges, drained

DRESSING:

¾ C. sugar
2 beaten eggs
1 C. vinegar (½ cider and ½ wine)
1 t. prepared mustard
1 t. salt

Bring the dressing ingredients just to the boiling point. This will be a thin dressing. Combine spinach, onion and oranges and pour dressing over salad.

Kathleen Ellison Loomis
(Mrs. N. E.)

SPINACH AND AVOCADO SALAD

½ lb. fresh spinach, washed and deveined
2 C. boiling water
2 T. salad oil
2 onions, sliced into rings
½ t. salt
1 avocado, peeled and sliced
1 hard cooked egg
Lettuce leaves
½ C. mayonnaise

Wash spinach, pour boiling water over it, and drain. Heat salad oil in skillet, add onion and salt. Sauté slightly. Place in a chopping bowl. Add spinach, avocado, and egg. Chop and blend until smooth. Chill for 1 hour. Put lettuce on salad plates, put spinach mixture on lettuce leaves. Garnish with slices of avocado and mayonnaise.

SERVES 4

Patsy Lacy Griffith
(Mrs. J. W.)

WINTER SALAD

1 lb. green beans, snapped in half
5 carrots, peeled and sliced
3 stalks celery, sliced thin
1 green pepper, cut in strips
1 small red onion sliced in thin rings
⅓ C. finely chopped parsley
4 C. Basic French dressing
1 C. thinly sliced radishes
½ C. chopped parsley

Cook green beans in boiling salted water for 10 minutes. Drain and rinse in cold water. Cook carrots until tender but crisp. Toss all ingredients with 4 cups Basic French Dressing. Sprinkle with radishes and ½ cup parsley. Chill.

SERVES 8

Susanne Sandberg Northcutt
(Mrs. W. D., III)

ASPIC RING

4 C. V-8 juice
4 envelopes gelatine
1 t. onion juice
1 (8 oz.) pkg. cream cheese
Mayonnaise
1 pt. cottage cheese, drained
1 small bunch green onions, minced
1 cucumber, seeded and chopped

Dissolve gelatine in one pint of juice. Heat remainder of juice to boiling, but do not boil. Add onion juice and gelatine and stir until dissolved. Check and correct seasonings to suit (lemon juice, salt and pepper, etc.). Pour half of mixture into a large mold and refrigerate until set. Keep other half over very low heat. Cream the cream cheese with a small amount of mayonnaise until smooth. Drain cottage cheese until dry as possible and combine with the cream cheese. Add onions and cucumber and enough mayonnaise to hold together. Do not let it get runny. Spread on top of set aspic and cover with remaining warm mixture. Refrigerate and serve filled with artichoke hearts, asparagus and avocado topped with home-made mayonnaise.

SERVES 24

Eleanor Croxton Lawrence
(Mrs. Thomas W.)

KOREAN SALAD

1 lb. spinach, torn in bite size pieces
1 (8 oz.) can water chestnuts, drained and sliced
1 (16 oz.) can bean sprouts, drained
½ C. sugar
⅓ C. catsup
⅓ C. vinegar
1 C. salad oil
5 T. Worcestershire sauce
1 small onion, grated
6 slices bacon, cooked and crumbled

Combine spinach, water chestnuts, and bean sprouts. Mix sugar, catsup, vinegar, oil, Worcestershire sauce and onion in blender. Pour over salad just before serving and toss. Sprinkle bacon on top.

SERVES 4—6

Nancy Butler Ballard
(Mrs. Jay)

TOMATO ASPIC
"Fill center with seafood or chicken salad"

2 C. tomato juice
2 bay leaves
2 cloves
Juice of 1 lemon
3 stalks celery
1 pkg. gelatine
½ C. water
1 T. sugar
Salt and pepper to taste
Juice of 1 lemon
Dash Worcestershire sauce
Dash Tabasco

Bring first 5 ingredients to a boil and boil 20 minutes. Strain and add gelatine which has been dissolved in ½ cup water. Add remaining ingredients. Cool and add chopped celery, avocado, ripe olives, etc., if desired. Chill in ring mold.

SERVES 4

Reva Harrison Ryan
(Mrs. A. B.)

Rose Pickens Kirkpatrick
(Mrs. Kenneth L.)

VARIATION I:

Use Swanson's beef broth for part of the liquid

VARIATION II:

Substitute V-8 juice for tomato juice
Add:
1 t. steak sauce
1 t. relish (chow chow)

SQUASH SALAD
"Serve with tomato wedges on lettuce"

4—5 yellow squash

MARINADE:

1 clove garlic, pressed
1 t. salt
2 t. sugar
½ t. dry mustard
Dash or two Tabasco
2 T. water
⅓ C. vinegar
¾ C. oil
1 large onion, finely chopped
   (may use Spanish for color)

Boil squash in salted water for 10 minutes or until tender but firm. Drain, cool and slice. Combine marinade ingredeints and pour over squash. Chill overnight.

SERVES 6

Mrs. Michael C. Macey

FROZEN TOMATO SALAD

1 (29 oz.) can tomatoes, well drained
1⅓ C. mayonnaise
Juice of 1 very juicy lemon
3 t. finely chopped green onions
1 t. Worcestershire sauce
2 drops Tabasco
1 t. salt
Pepper to taste
1 envelope gelatine dissolved in ⅓ C. water

Combine all ingredients in blender and whip on high speed until well blended. Place liquid in container in freezer and beat a couple of times as it freezes. When frozen, scoop out with ice cream scoop and refreeze individual servings. Serve on lettuce leaf or avocado half and top with mayonnaise seasoned with horseradish.

SERVES 6—8

Floreid Francis Stevens
(Mrs. A. C.)

TOMATO ASPIC WITH SHRIMP SAUCE

2 envelopes gelatine
½ C. cold water
1 (10¾ oz.) can tomato soup
½ C. finely chopped celery
½ C. finely chopped green pepper
1 (8 oz.) can water chestnuts, chopped
2 T. onion juice
3 (3 oz.) pkgs. cream cheese
1 C. mayonnaise

DRESSING:

1 C. mayonnaise
1 C. sour cream
1 T. paprika
2 t. Worcestershire sauce
1 garlic clove, pressed
½ lb. cleaned, cooked shrimp: chopped coarsley

Soak gelatine in water. Dissolve over hot water. Cool a little. Add soup, vegetables and onion juice. Soften cheese, mix with mayonnaise and then mix with vegetables. Put in a 1½ quart greased ring mold. Refrigerate several hours. Turn out on tray. Decorate around sides with avocado slices and tiny beets, well drained. Fill center with dressing.

SERVES 6

Patricia Smith Houston
(Mrs. E. B.)

TOMATO—AVOCADO MOLD

PART 1
2 C. tomato juice
Celery leaves
½ bay leaf
1 pkg. gelatine
¼ C. cold water
1 t. sugar
1 t. grated onion
1 T. vinegar
½ t. chili powder
Salt to taste

Heat tomato juice with celery leaves and bay leaf. Simmer for a few minutes. Do not boil. Strain. Soften gelatine in cold water. Add to hot tomato juice. Stir. Add the sugar, grated onion, vinegar, chili powder and salt. Chill until thick but not set. Pour into a 6 cup mold that has been slightly oiled.

PART II
2 pkgs. gelatine
½ C. cold water
3 large avocados
5 T. lemon juice
1 T. grated onion
1¼ t. salt
4 drops Tabasco
¼ t. Worcestershire sauce
½ C. boiling water
½ C. mayonnaise

Soften gelatine in cold water. Skin and remove pits from avocados. Purée through strainer. Add lemon juice quickly so pulp won't turn dark. Season with grated onion, salt, Tabasco and Worcestershire sauce. Add boiling water to the softened gelatine. Stir until dissolved. Add to avocado mixture. Fold in the mayonnaise. Beat until smooth. Pour into mold on top of aspic. Chill.

SERVES 10—12

DRESSING: (Ingredients to taste)

Heavy cream, whipped
Horseradish
Tabasco
Worcestershire sauce
Onion juice

Claire Smith Foster
(Mrs. Henry L., Jr.)

APRICOT DRESSING

"Serve over cantaloupe or pineapple halves filled with fruit salad"

½ C. apricots, canned and drained
2 T. mayonnaise
1 C. heavy cream, whipped
Juice of 1 fresh lime

Purée the apricots in blender. Mix with lime juice. Add mayonnaise. Fold into thickly whipped cream. Use for topping on fresh fruit salad; over this sprinkle chopped pistachio nuts.

Mrs. James R. Hansen
Burlingame, Ca.

Donor: Sara Ritchkie Whitehurst
(Mrs. Herman H.)

AVOCADO DRESSING

1 egg
½ t. dry mustard
½ C. oil
¼ C. lemon juice
1 t. Worcestershire sauce
½ t. salt
½ t. white pepper
¼ t. Tabasco
2 ripe avocados
1 T. chopped chives
4 anchovy filets
Garlic to taste
½ C. mayonnaise
½ t. powdered saffron

Blend in a blender, egg and mustard; add oil gradually. Add other seasonings. Mash avocados with anchovies, chives and garlic, beating until it forms a smooth paste. Combine with egg mixture. Combine saffron with mayonnaise and add to avocado mixture. Chill for 2 hours. Serve as a salad dressing or a dip.

Sir-Loin House
Houston, Texas

AVOCADO SALAD DRESSING

1 (3 oz.) pkg. cream cheese, softened
1 avocado, peeled and mashed
1 T. lemon juice
½ C. mayonnaise
¼ t. garlic powder
Milk

Combine and beat all ingredients except milk. Beat until smooth. Add milk to make dressing consistency. Pour over chilled Bibb and Romaine lettuce. Toss lightly.

YIELD: 2 cups

Nancy Ogletree Starr
(Mrs. Larry W.)

BASIC FRENCH DRESSING

⅔ C. salad oil
⅓ C. vinegar
1½ t. dry mustard
1½ t. salt
1—1½ T. sugar
1 t. paprika
Dash of pepper
1 clove garlic, pressed

Combine all ingredients in jar. Cover and chill. Shake well before serving. Store in refrigerator.

Thelma Holmes Williams
(Mrs. Jack T.)

BLENDER MAYONNAISE

1 whole egg
¼ t. dry mustard
½ t. salt
1 T. lemon juice
1 C. salad oil

Break egg into electric blender and add mustard and salt. Cover and blend at top speed for 30 seconds or until mixture is thick and foamy. Pour in lemon juice and blend for 10 seconds. Blending at high speed, pour oil **slowly** into center. Sauce will begin to thicken after ½ cup has gone in. If it becomes too thick, add a few drops of lemon juice.

YIELD: 1¼ cups

Peggy Moss Buckstaff
(Mrs. George)

COLE SLAW DRESSING

5 heaping T. Miracle Whip
4 heaping T. sugar
3 T. light cream
2 T. white vinegar
1 t. salt
½ t. pepper

Combine Miracle Whip, sugar and cream; mix well. Add remaining ingredients and mix well.

Mrs. Edith Hosey

CREAM CHEESE POTATO SALAD DRESSING

2 eggs
½ t. dry mustard
2 t. salt
1½ t. sugar
8 T. vinegar
2 (3 oz.) pkgs. cream cheese

Beat eggs and seasonings, scald vinegar and pour over. Cook until thick. Remove from heat and add cheese. Beat until smooth. This is enough dressing for 6 potatoes.

Rose Pickens Kirkpatrick
(Mrs. Kenneth L.)

PAULINE LANGHORNE'S SALAD DRESSING FOR SHRIMP

"A versatile sauce—dip for vegetables, dressing for shrimp or green salad"

1 C. mayonnaise
½ C. chili sauce
¼ C. wine vinegar
Onion juice OR grated onion
Garlic (on toothpick so can be removed before serving)
Bay leaf
1 C. sour cream
Parsley
1 T. Worcestershire sauce
1 t. Beau Monde seasoning
¼ t. each of: orégano, salt, powdered marjoram, rosemary
4 hard boiled eggs, grated

Mix all ingredients except eggs. Shake well and let stand overnight. Strain. Pour over eggs before serving.

Charity League Cookery

GOOD SAUCE FOR SHRIMP

1 pt. mayonnaise
2 cloves garlic, minced
2 T. curry powder
2 dashes Tabasco sauce
1 T. prepared mustard
½ C. catsup
1 small onion, minced
1 T. Worcestershire sauce
2 T. horseradish

Combine all ingredients and beat in mixer.

Aliece McHenry Mucher
(Mrs. Joseph)

CREAMY DRESSING FOR SPINACH SALAD

¼ C. olive oil
¾ C. plus 3 T. vegetable oil
5 T. vinegar
2 t. salt
1½ t. pepper
½ t. dry mustard
1 t. Dijon mustard
1 t. lemon juice
1/8 t. garlic powder
3 eggs

Combine ingredients in blender and blend thoroughly.

YIELD: 2 cups

Floreid Francis Stevens
(Mrs. A. C.)

GREEN GODDESS DRESSING
"Great for green salads, broccoli or asparagus"

1 T. lemon juice
½ C. heavy cream
2 T. tarragon vinegar
2 T. eschalot red wine vinegar
1 C. homemade mayonnaise
⅓ C. chopped parsley
¼ T. anchovy paste
¼ C. finely minced onion

Add lemon juice to cream and mix with other ingredients.

Mrs. Angus Wynne
Dallas, Texas

LIME DRESSING
"Good over melon balls"

Grated rind and juice of 1 orange
Grated rind and juice of 1 lime
Grated rind and juice of 1 lemon
1 egg, well beaten
1 C. sugar

Mix well and cook over medium heat, stirring constantly until it comes to a boil. Boil **only** 1 minute. Chill.

Mrs. Bob Patterson

POPPY SEED DRESSING
"Serve over fruit salad or shredded cabbage as slaw"

2 C. Mazola oil
¾ C. vinegar
¼ C. lemon juice
1¼ C. sugar
2 T. dry mustard
1 t. prepared mustard
1/8 C. poppy seed
2 t. salt
1 small onion, grated OR 1 T. minced onion
1 button garlic, grated OR ¼ t. garlic vinegar OR ½ t. minced garlic

Put dry ingredients in mixing bowl. Add oil slowly and beat with other ingredients. Whip 8 minutes. Store in refrigerator. Will keep for months in a covered jar.

Elizabeth Amick Cobb
(Mrs. Charles)

Betty Ruth Curtis Gray
(Mrs. Charles S.)

ROQUEFORT FRENCH DRESSING

2 T. vinegar
2 T. lemon juice
1¼ C. salad oil
½ t. salt
¼ t. pepper
¼ t. paprika
½ t. celery salt
1 t. Tabasco sauce
¾ C. Roquefort cheese, crumbled

Mix all ingredients except cheese and beat until smooth. Make a paste by adding a small amount of the mixture to the cheese. Then beat well with the remaining cheese.

YIELD: 2 cups

Katy Hall Painter
(Mrs. Paul)

ROQUEFORT SALAD DRESSING

1 (3 oz.) pkg. cream cheese
1 small wedge Roquefort cheese
½ C. light cream
¼ t. salt
1/8 t. garlic powder
¼ t. prepared mustard
½ C. mayonnaise
½ t. Beau Monde (Spice Island)
½ C. sour cream

Cream cheeses. Add the rest of the ingredients.

YIELD: 1 pint

Patricia Smith Houston
(Mrs. E. B.)

REMOULADE SAUCE

4 hard-boiled egg yolks
4 garlic pods, pressed
3 T. Creole mustard
3 C. mayonnaise
2 T. paprika
Salt and pepper to taste
2 T. Worcestershire sauce
Dash Tabasco
4 T. vinegar
4 T. parsley, chopped
3 T. horseradish

Mash hard-boiled egg yolks in blender. Add other ingredients and blend until smooth. Refrigerate 24 hours before serving.

Curtain Call Cookbook

Meats

TOURNEDOS WITH ARTICHOKE BOTTOMS AND SAUCE BÉARNAISE

6 (6 oz.) tournedos, 1½" thick
Salt and pepper
Clarified butter
6 artichoke bottoms, fresh or canned

SAUCE BÉARNAISE:
⅔ C. red wine vinegar
3 T. finely chopped shallots
1½ t. dried tarragon
12 white peppercorns, crushed
8 parsley sprigs
4 large egg yolks
1¼ C. clarified butter
1 t. salt
Cayenne pepper
1 T. fresh tarragon leaves, finely cut
1 T. fresh parsley, finely chopped

Brush tournedos with butter, salt and pepper and cook on charcoal grill. Sauté artichoke bottoms in butter. Place meat on a heated platter and set an artichoke bottom on top of each one. Fill with as much Béarnaise Sauce as they will hold and serve.

Combine the vinegar, shallots, tarragon, peppercorns, and parsley in a heavy saucepan and bring to a boil. Cook briskly until liquid is reduced to about 2 T. Remove from heat and let cool. With a whisk, beat the yolks into the saucepan until thick. Return to heat, whisking constantly. Cook until yolks have doubled in volume, lifting the pan from heat from time to time to prevent curdling. Remove from heat again and add butter in a slow thin stream. After about ¼ cup, mixture should thicken, and remaining butter may be added faster. Sauce should have consistency of mayonnaise. Strain sauce through a fine sieve. Taste and add salt, cayenne, tarragon and parsley. Sauce should be served lukewarm. Set aside to use. Do not reheat.

Carmen Huggins Hilliard
(Mrs. George M., III)

RIBEYE ROAST

5—6 lb. ribeye roast
Juice of two lemons
Liberal amount of soy sauce
¼ C. Italian Wishbone dressing
Cracked black pepper

Marinate roast several hours or overnight in other ingredients. Preheat oven at 175°. Cook roast until it registers rare on a meat thermometer. Turn off oven. Leave meat inside with door closed. About ten minutes before serving time, run roast under broiler to warm.

SERVES 10—12

Claire Smith Foster
(Mrs. Henry L.)

FILLET OF BEEF WITH GREEN PEPPERCORNS

2 T. oil
4 lb. fillet of beef
Salt and pepper
3 T. cognac, heated
1½ C. Quick Brown Sauce
1 C. heavy cream
3 T. green peppercorns
Lemon juice to taste
Salt and pepper to taste

QUICK BROWN SAUCE:
1½ t. butter
1½ t. flour
2 C. beef consommé
Salt and pepper to taste

Brown the fillet in oil on all sides over moderately high heat. Season with salt and pepper and transfer to a shallow pan. Roast in a preheated 450° oven for about 30 minutes, depending on the thickness of fillet, for rare meat. Transfer to a heated platter and let stand 10 minutes. Pour off fat from skillet, add cognac and ignite it, shaking the pan until the flames go out and stirring in the brown bits clinging to the bottom and sides of the pan. Add brown sauce, and cream and reduce over moderately high heat to 2 cups. Add remaining ingredients. Cut fillet into serving pieces, spoon some of the sauce over the slices and serve remaining sauce in sauce boat.

QUICK BROWN SAUCE:
Melt butter in a saucepan, stir in flour and cook, stirring constantly, until the color of brown wrapping paper. Gradually add consommé, bring to a boil and cook for 5 minutes, stirring constantly. Lower heat and simmer gently for 30 minutes, stirring occasionally. Skim off fat and season to taste.

Cookbook Committee

MARINATED STEAK

1 t. garlic salt
1 t. Accent
½ C. concentrated lime juice
¾ C. soy sauce
1 t. salt
5 lbs. top round steak,
    1½" thick
Cracked pepper

Mix all ingredients except steak and pepper in pan. Pepper steak well and marinate in sauce overnight. Cook on outdoor grill over gray coals about 12 minutes on each side for medium done. Slice in ½" strips before serving.

SERVES 10—12

**Mary Loomis,
Denver, Colorado**

ROAST PEPPERED RIB EYE OF BEEF

5—6 lb. boneless rib eye of beef
½ C. black pepper, coarsley cracked
½ t. ground cardamon
1 T. tomato paste
½ t. garlic powder
1 t. paprika
1 C. soy sauce
¾ C. vinegar
1 C. water
1½ T. cornstarch
¼ C. water

Trim fat from beef. Combine pepper and cardamon; rub all over beef and press into meat with heel of hand. Place roast in shallow baking dish. Mix together tomato paste, garlic powder, and paprika. Gradually add soy sauce, then vinegar. Pour soy mixture over meat, and refrigerate overnight. Spoon marinade over meat. Remove meat from marinade, reserve marinade, and let meat stand at room temperature for 1 hour. Wrap meat in foil and place in shallow pan. Roast in 300° oven for 1½ hours for a medium rare roast. Open foil, and reserve drippings. Brown roast, uncovered, at 350° while making gravy. Strain drippings, skim off excess fat. Take one cup of skimmed meat juice plus one cup water and bring to a boil. Add a little marinade (about ½ cup), if desired. Serve au jus or thicken gravy by combining cornstarch and ¼ cup water. Remove gravy from heat, beat in cornstarch mixture with a whisk. Bring to a boil, lower heat and simmer 5 minutes until thickened.

**Charlie's Cafe Exceptionale
Minneapolis, Minn.**

MUCHACHO ROAST CON COMINO

1 eye of round roast
Salt
Pepper
Ginger
Garlic powder
Flour
Oil
3 C. water
1 (15 oz.) can tomato purée
2 onions, chopped
3 T. comino (more or less according to taste)

Season roast liberally with seasonings and rub well with flour. Brown lightly in oil on all sides. Place on top of onions in a roasting pan, add remaining ingredients, cover, and cook at 350° about 3 hours.

Mrs. Robert A. Bruyere

LONDON BROIL

Flank steak
Salt
Pepper
Orégano
Garlic
Ginger
Red wine, enough to cover meat

Season steak liberally with spices. Marinate steak approximately 24 hours in wine turning once or twice. Flank steak is best rare. Cook three minutes on each side over a very hot charcoal fire. Can be served on toasted French bread as an open face sandwich. To slice: With a very sharp knife, held at an angle, almost flat to the top of the meat, slice diagonally very thin through to the bottom.

Mrs. Robert A. Bruyere

Butter
Worcestershire sauce
Garlic powder
Salt and cracked pepper

Pan broil flank steak in butter until medium rare. Remove to a hot platter. Rub liberally with butter and Worcestershire sauce. Season to taste with garlic powder, salt and pepper.

Eleanor Croxton Lawrence
(Mrs. Thomas W.)

STEAK ROLL-UPS WITH NOODLES

2 flank steaks
Basil
Marjoram
Thyme
Seasoned salt and pepper
Soy sauce
Worcestershire sauce
Parmesan cheese
½ C. margarine

Sprinkle inside of steak with all of the seasonings listed to taste. Roll steaks and tie with kitchen string. Brown evenly in margarine in an electric skillet at 340°.

SAUCE:

Combine ingredients and bring to a boil. Add rolls to sauce and simmer over low heat for about 4 hours.

SAUCE:
1 (32 oz.) can tomato sauce
2 C. water
4 pkgs. Lawry's Spaghetti Seasoning
1 (16 oz.) can whole button mushrooms
1 pkg. medium noodles, cooked and rinsed
½ C. butter
Parsley

TO SERVE:
Toss noodles with butter.
Put noodles in a deep serving dish. Cover with sauce. Cut string and slice rollups. Place on top of noodles and sauce. Garnish with parsley.

SERVES 4—6

Patricia Smith Houston
(Mrs. E. B.)

CARBONNADE A LA FLAMANDE

2½ lb. beef rump or chuck
3 T. oil
2 or 3 onions, thinly sliced
Brown sugar, a few spoonfuls
Vinegar, a few spoonfuls
1 clove garlic, finely chopped
Pinch of thyme
1 bay leaf
Beer to cover meat
1 large slice crusty bread (French)
Dijon style mustard
Salt to taste

Brown meat in oil and place in a heavy casserole. In oil remaining in pan, lightly brown onions, sprinkle with brown sugar and shake the pan over medium heat until they are caramelized. Sprinkle with vinegar and add to the meat. Add garlic, thyme, bay leaf, salt and beer to meat. Top with bread which has been spread with the mustard. Bring to a boil, cover the casserole and cook over lowest possible heat for 2 hours or until the beer is reduced by half. If it is not reducing fast enough, remove cover for last 15 minutes. The bread will dissolve, binding the sauce. Serve with steamed new potatoes in their jackets, scallions and cold beer.

SERVES 6

Eleanor Croxton Lawrence
(Mrs. Thomas W.)

POT ROAST SUPREME

¼ C. salad oil
1 (4 lb.) boned chuck pot roast
1 C. soy sauce
½ C. sugar
1 (1 inch) cinnamon stick
  OR ¼ t. ground cinnamon
2 C. water
1 C. Sherry
3 T. cornstarch
½ C. cold water

Heat oil slowly in large heavy pan or dutch oven. Brown meat well. Combine soy sauce, sugar, cinnamon stick and 2 cups water. Pour over meat. Cover and simmer 3 hours or until tender. Add sherry after first 2 hours of cooking. When meat is tender, remove to serving platter. Reserve 2½ cups of pan liquid and bring to a boil. Combine cornstarch and ½ cup cold water; mix until smooth. Add to pan liquid. Simmer, stirring constantly, until thickened. Serve over roast.

SERVES 8

Sharon Wildstein Bindler
(Mrs. Donn)

POT ROAST WITH HERBS

5 lbs. boneless pot roast
3 T. flour
½ t. pepper
1 t. salt
1 T. shortening
2 stalks celery, finely chopped
2 large carrots, finely chopped
½ green pepper, finely chopped
1 (20 oz.) can tomatoes
1 medium onion, finely chopped
1 t. basil
¼ t. garlic powder
½ t. basil

Rub meat with flour, salt and pepper. Brown in fat, then drain off fat. Place finely chopped celery, carrots and green pepper on bottom of baking dish. Set roast on vegetables. Mix tomatoes, chopped onion and 1 t. basil and pour around roast. Cover and bake 2½ hours at 350° until tender. Turn several times. Remove meat, stir in garlic powder, ½ t. basil and flour mixture. Stir and serve.

SERVES 10

Rose Pickens Kirkpatrick
(Mrs. Kenneth L.)

POT ROAST WITH RED WINE

2—3 T. bacon drippings
5 lb. chuck roast
Flour for dredging
Salt
Pepper
Orégano
Sweet basil
Marjoram
Garlic salt
1 pkg. Lipton Onion Soup Mix
2 C. water
¾ C. red wine
8 medium potatoes, quartered
12 carrots, quartered

Season roast heavily with spices, rubbing in. Dredge in flour and brown on both sides in hot bacon drippings. Remove from heat and add soup, water and wine. Cover tightly and simmer for 4 to 5 hours until meat is tender. Add carrots and potatoes the last hour.

SERVES 10—12

Eleanor Croxton Lawrence
(Mrs. Thomas W.)

JEANNE'S SLOPPY JOES

1 lb. ground beef
½ C. chopped celery
½ C. chopped onion
½ C. chili sauce
1 T. Worcestershire sauce
½ t. liquid smoke
2 (8 oz.) cans tomato sauce
1 t. chili pepper
¼ t. salt or garlic salt

Brown beef in one skillet; celery and onion in another. Pour off grease. Combine and add remaining ingredients. Simmer 30 minutes until liquid is reduced. Can be frozen.

SERVES 6

Pat McCarty Marshall
(Mrs. B. Neil)

BRISKET AND RIGATONI

3—5 lb. brisket
Salt
Pepper
Garlic salt
1 onion, chopped
1 (14 oz.) bottle catsup
2 (14 oz.) bottles water
3 T. Worcestershire sauce
Paprika
1 (12 oz.) pkg. rigatoni

Season meat well with salt, pepper and garlic salt. Place on bed of onions in a roasting pan. Mix catsup, water and Worcestershire sauce together and pour over meat. Sprinkle liberally with paprika to make roast a golden brown. Cook, covered, at 350° for 3 hours. Add rigatoni the last 30—45 minutes and cook in the gravy.

Reva G. Meyer

Donor: Su-Su Hoffman Meyer
(Mrs. Jerry)

BEEF BOURGUIGNON

6 slices bacon, chopped
4 lbs. lean sirloin, cut in ½" x 4" strips
2 cloves garlic, pressed
2 lbs. mushrooms, sliced
2 bay leaves, crushed
2 T. chopped parsley
1 t. salt
1 t. thyme
1/8 t. pepper
½ C. butter
½ C. flour
1½ (10½ oz.) cans consommé
1 C. Burgundy wine

Sauté bacon in a Dutch oven; remove and sauté meat. Add garlic and mushrooms. Add seasonings. Add bacon; cover and simmer. In a heavy saucepan, make a roux with butter and flour. Cook, stirring constantly, until mixture turns light tan. Add consommé and wine. Stir and cook until slightly thickened. Add to meat and vegetable mixture. Cover and simmer until tender, approximately 1½ hours. Serve on rice.

SERVES 10—12

Cookbook Committee

EASY OVEN STEW
"Cooks can be really creative on this simple recipe"

1½ lb. stew meat
1 (10¾ oz.) can cream of mushroom soup
1 pkg. Lipton's Onion Soup Mix
½ C. wine
Salt and pepper to taste
Fresh mushrooms
Baby carrots, optional

Mix soups, wine, salt and pepper together in a large casserole. Mix in meat which has been trimmed of all excess fat. Cover and bake at 300° for 3 hours. Add mushrooms the last 45 minutes. Serve over noodles with a salad and hot bread for an easy meal.

SERVES 6

Mrs. George M. Hilliard, Jr.
Jacksonville, Texas

BEEF STEW

2 lbs. beef, cubed
1 (10 oz.) can tomatoes
1 (8½ oz.) can English peas
2 carrots, cut in rounds
2 onions, quartered
2 potatoes, cut in cubes
1 green pepper, chopped
¼ C. raw Minute Tapioca
¼ C. soft bread crumbs
Salt and pepper to taste
Garlic salt
1 bay leaf
1 T. Worcestershire sauce
¼ t. each: thyme, orégano, basil
1½ C. dry wine, red or white

Place all ingredients in a large covered casserole. Barely cover with water. Meat will brown while cooking. If necessary add more water while cooking. The tapioca thickens the gravy. Bake at 250° for 4—5 hours. Serve with salad and cornbread.

SERVES 8

Eleanor Croxton Lawrence
(Mrs. Thomas W.)

BEEF STEW A LA FRANÇAISE

2 T. butter
2 lbs. lean stew meat
2 T. flour
1½ C. dry red wine
6 small onions, diced
4 T. butter
1 C. mushrooms, cut in half
3 carrots, sliced
1 clove garlic, crushed
Thyme
Bay leaf
Parsley
Salt and pepper
1 C. Madeira
Consommé
1 oz. brandy

Melt butter in iron casserole and brown meat. Remove meat, and add flour to make brown roux. Season paste and add red wine. Brown onions in butter. Return meat to roux and add vegetables and seasonings, plus Madeira and enough consommé to cover. Simmer, covered, 2½—3 hours, adding consommé if needed. Add brandy 30 minutes before serving. Serve over noodles.

SERVES 6—8

Susie Moore French
(Mrs. Paul E.)

KLOPS

MEATBALLS:
4 slices white bread
1 egg
1 C. heavy cream
Seasoned salt to taste
¼ t. nutmeg
¼ t. white pepper
2 t. Maggi beef extract
2 lbs. lean ground round
Flour
Seasoned salt
1 C. unsalted butter

SAUCE:
4 C. heavy cream
1 T. dill weed
1 t. seasoned salt
1 t. Maggi beef extract

Mix first 7 ingredients in blender, then pour over ground beef and mix well with hands or a fork. Taste for seasonings. Make small balls the size of large end of melon scoop and roll in flour seasoned with seasoned salt. Sauté in unsalted butter but DO NOT BROWN.

SAUCE:
Bring sauce ingredients to simmer and drop sautéed meatballs into liquid. Simmer 45 minutes to 1 hour. May be frozen. When thawed, place on low flame and add extra cream.

Mrs. Kurt Borris

DELIA'S BARBECUED MEAT LOAVES

1½ lbs. ground meat
½ lb. ground pork
1 C. milk
1 C. soft bread crumbs
1 onion, chopped
1 t. salt
Pepper to taste
Dash MSG

SAUCE:
1 C. catsup
⅓ C. vinegar
1—2 T. Worcestershire sauce
1 T. chili powder
1 clove garlic, crushed
½ C. finely chopped onion
½ C. water
½ C. chopped bell pepper, optional
2—3 T. sugar, optional

Soak bread crumbs in milk and mix with meat, onions and seasonings. Shape into loaves or patties and brown quickly in a hot skillet. Place in baking dish.

SAUCE:
Mix sauce ingredients together and bring to a boil. Pour over meat. Bake at 300° for 60 minutes or until done. Serve as meat loaves, on hamburger buns or on a bed of buttered noodles.

SERVES 8—10

Dorothy Lorimer McNally
(Mrs. Frank)

CALIFORNIA CASSEROLE

1 green pepper, chopped
1 large onion, chopped
¼ C. oil
1 lb. ground meat
Salt and pepper to taste
Chili powder to taste
Dry mustard to taste
1 (8 oz.) can tomato sauce
1 (8 oz.) can ripe olives, chopped
1 (10 ¾ oz.) can tomato soup
1 (17 oz.) can cream style corn
1 (4 oz.) jar pimiento
8—10 oz. noodles, uncooked
1 lb. cheese, grated

Sauté green pepper and onion in oil. Add meat and brown. Season with salt and pepper, chili powder and dry mustard. Add remaining ingredients except cheese. Pour into a casserole dish, sprinkle with cheese and bake at 350° for 45 minutes.

Sally Hilliard Shank
Tulsa, Oklahoma

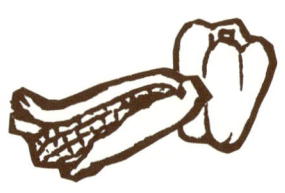

HAMBURGER PIE

CRUST:
⅓ C. shortening
1 C. flour
½ t. salt
2 t. minced onion soaked in
    ¼ C. cold water

FILLING:
1 lb. ground round or chuck
1 t. salt
¼ t. seasoned salt
½ t. sweet basil
¼ t. marjoram
1/8 t. pepper
2 t. minced onion
¼ C. catsup
1 T. Worcestershire sauce
½ C. bread crumbs
1 C. grated cheese, divided
3 tomatoes, fresh or canned

CRUST:
Cut shortening into flour and salt; add water and onions. Stir. Roll out crust and put in a 9" pie plate. Bake at 375° for 10 minutes until light brown.

FILLING:
Brown meat. Add seasonings, onion, catsup, Worcestershire sauce, bread crumbs, and ½ cup cheese. Pour into cooked crust and top with tomatoes and ½ cup cheese. Bake at 350° for 20—25 minutes.

SERVES 6

Marilyn Rouse Payne
(Mrs. Hermes E.)

STUFFED CABBAGE

1 head cabbage

FILLING:
2 lbs. ground meat
2 eggs, beaten
½ C. rice
2 slices hard, dry bread crumbled
1 small onion, chopped
2 T. brown sugar
Juice of 1 lemon
1 t. Accent

SAUCE:
1 (16 oz.) can tomatoes, mashed
1 (10¾ oz.) can tomato soup
1 (18 oz.) can tomato juice
Juice of 2 lemons
¾ — 1 C. brown sugar
Accent

Loosen cabbage leaves and steam in boiling water just long enough so they will handle easily. Shred small leaves that are too small to roll and put in the bottom of a large Dutch oven.

FILLING:
Mix all ingredients together. Put filling on cabbage leaves and roll carefully stuffing the ends in. Layer rolls on top of shredded cabbage.

SAUCE:
Combine ingredients and bring to a boil stirring constantly. Pour sauce mixture over rolls. Cover and simmer over low heat 1½ — 2 hours.

SERVES 10—12

Cookbook Committee

STUFFED PEPPERS

8—10 small bell peppers
1 lb. ground round
2 t. butter
½ C. grated onion
1 clove garlic, minced
1 C. cooked rice
½ C. Parmesan cheese
1 t. whole celery seed
Salt and pepper to taste
2 t. parsley flakes
1 (10¾ oz.) can tomato soup
½ soup can water

Parboil peppers 5 minutes, drain and let cool. Brown meat and drain. Add butter to skillet and sauté onion and garlic until clear. Add to meat along with rice, cheese and seasonings. Mix tomato soup with water and pour over peppers stuffed with meat mixture. Bake at 325° for 25—30 minutes.

SERVES 4—5

Patricia Smith Houston
(Mrs. E. B.)

SUKIYAKI

2 T. sugar
¾ C. soy sauce
2 beef bouillon cubes
1½ C. water
2—3 lbs. beef sirloin tip
2 yellow onions
1 lb. fresh mushrooms
½ lb. fresh spinach
2 green peppers
4 ribs celery
1 (8 oz.) can bamboo shoots
1 (8 oz.) can water chestnuts
Butter and oil

Mix first 4 ingredients together in a saucepan and heat until smooth. Slice meat paper thin. (Meat slices easier if slightly frozen.) Slice all vegetables very thin and bite size. Layer vegetables on a platter with meat. Put sauce in a pitcher. Heat a wok or electric skillet to melt butter and heat oil. Begin adding vegetables in order of those taking longest to cook (onions, celery, peppers). Add remaining vegetables and lastly the meat. Then some sauce. Cook until vegetables are barely cooked. (It only takes a minute.) Serve immediately. Replenish pan as needed to serve. **Note:** All vegetables and sauce can be prepared ahead of time and stored in refrigerator. Serve with rice.

SERVES 6—8

Laney Talmage Mobley
(Mrs. Ebb)

EASY-TO-DO SUKIYAKI

2 lbs. boneless beef sirloin, sliced as thinly as possible
4 stalks celery, sliced diagonally in ½" pieces
2 medium onions, thinly sliced
1 bunch green onions and tops, cut into 2" lengths
1 C. fresh mushrooms, sliced
1 (8½ oz.) can bamboo shoots, sliced
1 (8½ oz.) can shirataki, optional
1 (11 oz.) can tofu, cut in 1" cubes, optional
1½ C. Kikkoman sukiyaki sauce
2 pieces beef suet OR 1 T. salad oil

Arrange beef and vegetables attractively on a large platter. Turn electric skillet setting to 300°. Melt suet in skillet stirring until pan is well coated. Remove browned suet. (OR heat salad oil in skillet.) Add about ⅓ of the meat and cover with ½ of the Sukiyaki sauce. Add ⅔ of each vegetable, keeping meat and vegetables separate. Turn ingredients over gently while cooking, 5—6 minutes. Add another ⅓ of the meat and cook an additional 1—2 minutes. Serve Sukiyaki immediately in individual bowls or plates. Replenish skillet with remaining ingredients as needed.

SERVES 4—6

Marcia Burlison McDaniel
(Mrs. Stephen W.)

ORIENTAL STEAK

1½ lbs. round steak or top sirloin, cut in thin strips
¼ C. salad oil
2 cloves garlic, pressed
2 t. soy sauce
1 t. salt
½ C. water
1 C. green pepper, cut in strips
½ C. celery, sliced
1 C. thinly sliced onion
1 C. consommé
1½ T. cornstarch
½ t. sugar
2 fresh tomatoes, peeled and cut into eighths

Brown beef in oil. Add garlic and cook until yellow. Add soy sauce, salt and water. Cook, covered, about 30 minutes. Add vegetables and consommé, cover, and cook until barely tender. Stir in cornstarch and sugar blended with a little water. Let thicken a little, add tomato slices and let them heat. Serve over rice.

SERVES 6

Patricia Smith Houston
(Mrs. E. B.)

ORIENTAL BEEF STEW

6 breakfast steaks (2½—3½ oz. each)
Adolph's meat tenderizer
3 T. oil, divided
2 small onions, thinly sliced
1 green pepper, cut in thin strips
1 red pepper, cut in thin strips
2 ribs celery, cut in thin strips
6 fresh mushrooms, sliced
1 (8 oz.) can water chestnuts, drained and sliced
2 T. cornstarch
1½ C. water
1 beef bouillon cube
¼ t. powdered ginger
1 T. sugar
3 T. soy sauce (or more)

Prepare all surfaces of the meat as follows: Moisten the meat with water, using fingers or pastry brush. Sprinkle meat tenderizer over entire surface of meat. Use no salt. Pierce meat with a fork. Cut into ½" strips. In skillet, brown strips in 1 T. hot oil about 1½ to 3 minutes. Remove meat to dish. Add remaining 2 T. oil; heat. Add onions, peppers, celery, mushrooms, and water chestnuts. Sauté about 3 minutes. DO NOT OVERCOOK. Return meat to skillet. In small saucepan, blend cornstarch with a little of the water until smooth. Add the remaining water, bouillon cube, ginger, sugar and soy sauce. Cook over low heat until thick, about 4—5 minutes. Pour over vegetables and meat. Toss lightly and heat through.

SERVES 6

Susie Moore French
(Mrs. Paul E.)

IVANA'S BASIC MEAT SAUCE

¼ C. olive oil
1 C. celery, finely minced
Leaves from celery, finely minced
2 onions, finely minced
4 cloves garlic, finely minced
2 lbs. lean ground beef
1 lb. lean pork chops, boned and cubed
1½ T. dried parsley
4 t. salt
½ t. pepper (more if desired)
2 t. sweet basil
2 t. orégano
1 lb. fresh mushrooms, sliced
2 (10½ oz.) cans beef broth
2 (6 oz.) cans tomato paste

Sauté celery, leaves, onion and garlic in olive oil until vegetables are tender. Add meats; brown and add spices and cook over medium low heat until liquid has evaporated. Add mushrooms and cook until liquid is absorbed. Stir in broth and tomato paste and cook until thick and liquid is almost gone. Remove any excess oil. Serve on freshly cooked pasta.

IVANA'S ITALIAN CRÊPES

8 or 9 inch crêpes
Swiss cheese, thinly sliced
Mozzarella cheese, thinly sliced
Parmesan cheese, grated
Ivana's Basic Meat Sauce
Olive oil

Lightly oil an eight or nine inch round pan, place crêpe of same size on bottom, cover with meat sauce and top with cheese. Layer in the same order until top of pan is reached, ending with cheese. Bake at 350° for about 30 minutes or until thoroughly hot and cheese is melted. Turn out onto round platter and serve in wedges.

Mrs. Richard Cella,
New York, N. Y.

Donor: Joan Nachbaur Rathbun

LU-LU'S LASAGNA

SAUCE:
4 cloves garlic, minced
2 small onions, chopped
½ C. salad oil
1 lb. ground beef
2 (16 oz.) cans tomatoes
2 (6 oz.) cans tomato paste
3 tomato paste cans water
½ C. Parmesan or Romano cheese
2 T. sugar
2 t. salt
1 t. pepper
2 T. dried sweet pepper flakes
2 t. Italian seasoning
½ t. garlic powder
½ t. onion powder

CHEESE FILLING:
3—4 C. cottage cheese
2 beaten eggs
1 t. salt
½ t. pepper
½ C. Parmesan or Romano cheese
Parsley

1 lb. lasagna noodles
1 lb. sliced Mozzarella cheese

Sauté garlic and onion in oil until tender. Add meat and cook until all pink is gone. Drain off grease. Add the remaining ingredients and simmer for 1 hour. Combine filling ingredients. Cook lasagna noodles in boiling water that has been salted and oiled. Cook until tender. Do not overcook. When done, remove gently and spread on clean dishtowel wrung out in cold water. Noodles will be easier to handle.

TO ASSEMBLE:
In a greased, 3 quart casserole, place sauce, half of the noodles (or enough to make a layer), half the cheese filling, half the Mozzarella cheese, sauce and then repeat another layer. Bake at 375° for 40—45 minutes. Let stand 10 minutes to set layers before cutting. This will make at least a small casserole in addition to the larger one. The sauce can be doubled or tripled and used over spaghetti, too.

SERVES 12

Vera Mitchell Garlough
(Mrs. Harry Thomas)

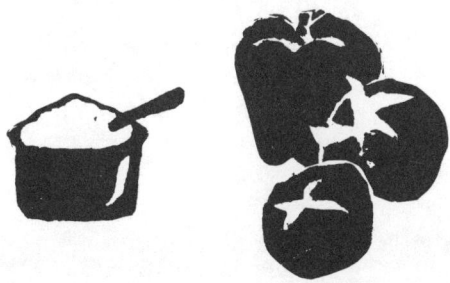

LAZY LASAGNA

2 lbs. ground round steak
1 t. salt
1 envelope Lawry's Spaghetti Sauce Mix
2 (16 oz.) cans tomatoes
1 (15 oz.) can tomato sauce
1 t. basil
Grated Parmesan cheese
1 (8 oz.) pkg. lasagna noodles
2 (6 oz.) pkgs. Mozzarella cheese

In Dutch oven or large saucepan, brown meat in salt. Add spaghetti sauce mix, tomatoes, tomato sauce, basil and a generous sprinkling of Parmesan cheese. Simmer 30 minutes. Cook lasagna noodles just until tender. In a 9" x 11" casserole, layer meat sauce, noodles and Mozzarella cheese. Sprinkle with Parmesan cheese. Repeat layers, saving enough meat sauce to pour over the top layer. Bake in 300 to 325 degree oven for 20 minutes. This is a simplified version of lasagna, yet has an authentic taste; better by far if made the day before or at least early in the morning, and then baked just before serving.

SERVES 6—8

Mrs. Ben Barnes,
Brownwood, Texas

MANICOTTI

1 lb. ground round
2 C. water
2 (6 oz.) cans tomato paste
⅓ C. chopped onion
1 (3 oz.) can sliced mushrooms
2 T. parsley
2 t. orégano, crushed
1½ t. salt
1 t. sugar
1 clove garlic
24 oz. Ricotta cheese
½ C. grated Parmesan cheese
2 eggs, beaten
¼ C. parsley
½ t. salt
8 manicotti shells

Brown meat. Add water, tomato paste, onion, mushrooms and seasonings. Simmer 30 minutes. Combine cheese, eggs, parsley and salt. Cook manicotti shells until tender, about 20 minutes. Rinse in cold water. Stuff the shells with cheese mixture (⅓ to ½ cup each). Pour half of the tomato meat sauce into a 9" x 13" baking dish. Pour remaining sauce over. Bake at 350° for 30—35 minutes. Let stand 10 minutes before serving.

SERVES 4—6

Patricia Smith Houston
(Mrs. E. B.)

LASAGNA CASSEROLE

MEAT SAUCE:
½ lb. hot pork sausage
½ lb. ground chuck or round
1 clove garlic, minced
1 T. whole basil
1½ t. salt
2 (15 oz.) cans tomato sauce
1 (10 oz.) pkg. lasagna noodles
1 pkg. sliced pepperoni, optional (layer with meat)

CHEESE FILLING:
3 C. Ricotta or creamy cottage cheese
½ C. Parmesan or Romano cheese
2 T. parsley flakes
2 eggs, beaten
2 t. salt
½ t. pepper
1 lb. Mozzarella cheese, sliced thin

MEAT SAUCE:
Brown meat slowly; skim off fat. Add all seasonings and tomato sauce. Simmer, uncovered, for 30 minutes. Stir now and then. Cook lasagna noodles until tender in a large amount of boiling, salted water. This may take 15—20 minutes. Drain and rinse in cold water.

CHEESE FILLING:
Mix the first 6 ingredients. Place ½ noodles in a 13" x 9" x 2" baking dish. Spread ½ filling, ½ meat sauce and cover with ½ Mozzarella cheese. Repeat layers. Bake at 375° for 30 minutes. Let stand 10 minutes before cutting into squares. Filling should set slightly.

SERVES 12

Susanne Sandberg Northcutt
(Mrs. W. D., III)

TUFOLI CASSEROLE

¾ pkg. tufoli
½ lb. ground beef
½ lb. ground pork
½ C. chopped celery
1 clove garlic, chopped
1 (10 oz.) pkg. frozen chopped spinach cooked and drained
1 t. orégano
Salt and pepper to taste
2 (8 oz.) cans tomato sauce
1 (10½ oz.) can tomato purée
½ lb. sharp cheese, grated
Parmesan cheese

Cook tufoli; drain and let stand in cold water. Sauté meats with garlic and celery. Add spinach and seasonings. Stuff tufoli. Combine tomato sauce and purée. In a greased 9" x 13" casserole, put stuffed tufoli and cover with sauce. Sprinkle cheeses over the top and bake at 400° for 20—25 minutes. Cover casserole with foil the first half of baking time.

SERVES 12

Clara Hurst Payne
(Mrs. William B.)

ITALIAN CASSEROLE

1½ lbs. ground beef
1½ C. chopped onion
1 (32 oz.) jar extra thick spaghetti sauce
⅓ C. water
1½ t. salt
1 t. basil
1 t. orégano leaves
1 t. sugar
¼ t. pepper
5 medium potatoes, thinly sliced
1 (8 oz.) pkg. shredded Mozzarella cheese

In a 12" skillet over medium high heat, brown meat and onions stirring occasionally. Add spaghetti sauce, water, salt, basil, orégano, sugar and pepper. Cook 2 minutes or more to blend flavors. In a 9" x 13" baking dish, evenly spoon ⅓ of meat mixture; arrange half of potatoes on top. Repeat layering, ending with meat. Cover dish tightly with foil and bake at 375° for 1 hour or until potatoes are fork tender. Remove foil, sprinkle evenly with cheese and bake 10 minutes more or until cheese melts. Let stand 10 minutes for easier cutting.

SERVES 8

Pam Rice Smith
(Mrs. Ned)

ITALIAN SPAGHETTI
"American Style"

Bacon drippings
1½ lbs. ground round
2 medium onions, chopped
1 large green pepper, chopped
1 (20 oz.) can tomatoes
1 (10½ oz.) can tomato purée
2 (3 oz.) cans mushrooms
2 garlic cloves, crushed
Chili powder to taste
Red pepper to taste
Salt and pepper to taste
Italian herbs to taste
12 oz. pkg. long spaghetti, cooked
¾ lb. Wisconsin cheese, grated

Sauté meat in a small amount of bacon drippings with onion and green pepper until brown. Add seasonings, tomatoes and purée. Simmer for at least 1 hour, stirring occasionally. Add mushrooms and heat through. Mix meat mixture and spaghetti together. Just before serving add half of the cheese and let melt. After spaghetti is placed in serving dish, top with remaining cheese.

SERVES 8

Katy Hall Painter
(Mrs. Paul)

MEXICAN SPAGHETTI SAUCE

¼ C. olive oil
1 green pepper, chopped
2 onions, chopped
1—2 cloves garlic, chopped
1 lb. ground chuck
1 C. canned tomatoes
1 (6 oz.) can tomato paste
½ C. red wine
½ C. water
1 T. chili powder
1 t. oregano
1 t. comino seeds
Salt to taste

Sauté green pepper, onion and garlic in olive oil. Stir in meat, break it into small pieces with a fork and cook until well browned. Add remaining ingredients and cook covered over low heat for one or two hours. More water and wine may be added during cooking if sauce is too thick. Serve hot over freshly cooked spaghetti.

SERVES 4—6

Eleanor Croxton Lawrence
(Mrs. Thomas W.)

SOPA

2 lbs. ground chuck or round
Garlic salt
Black pepper
Seasoning salt
1 T. vinegar
1 T. tequila or vodka
Chili powder
2 (10 oz.) cans Rotel tomatoes and green chilies, drained
1 pkg. tortillas
2 (8 oz.) pkgs. sliced Old English cheese
1 pt. sour cream

Sauté meat; add seasonings, vinegar and tequila, as the meat is cooking. The meat should be highly seasoned and well cooked. When meat is done, drain off any excess grease. Stir in Rotel tomatoes. Mix well, chopping the tomatoes into the meat. Cut tortillas in half and fry in shortening until crisp. Line pan with half the tortillas. Add half the meat mixture. Top with 1 pkg. cheese. Repeat. Top with sour cream. Cover with foil and bake at 350° for 30 minutes or until cheese is melted.

SERVES 6—8

**Cooking Under Six Flags,
Ft. Worth, Texas
Mexico Magnifico**

TACO FILLING

1 lb. ground meat
2 pkgs. Lawry's Taco Seasoning
1 (8 oz.) can tomato sauce
½ C. water
2-3 T. instant mashed potatoes
Salt to taste

Brown meat. Add other ingredients and simmer for 45 minutes. Better if prepared in advance. Fills 12 taco shells.

Patricia Smith Houston
(Mrs. E. B.)

FLAUTAS

SAUCE:
3—4 lb. lean pork roast
4 (10 oz.) cans Rotel tomatoes
2 (10½ oz.) cans beef broth
2 chopped medium onions
1 t. cumin
3 cloves garlic, minced
1 T. orégano
3 T. chili seasoning
Salt and pepper to taste

FILLING:
1 lb. ground beef
1 onion, chopped
1 t. garlic salt
Salt and pepper to taste
½ t. cumin
½ C. water
24 tortillas
½ lb. Monterey Jack cheese, grated

GARNISH:
Sour cream
Lettuce, chopped
Guacamole

Trim fat from roast and place in a large pan. Cover with tomatoes, beef broth, onions and seasonings. Simmer, covered, about 6 hours. Break meat up with a fork in sauce and mix well. This sauce freezes well.

FILLING:
Brown meat and add onion and seasonings. Add water and cook until absorbed. Dip tortillas in hot oil. Drain. Spread ground meat mixture on tortilla and some grated cheese and roll up and place in 9" x 12" casserole dish. Spoon pork sauce over entire dish and top with remaining cheese. Bake at 350° about 30 minutes until cheese is melted and bubbly.

YIELD: Two 9" x 12" casseroles

Carmen Huggins Hilliard
(Mrs. George M., III)

GLORIOUS MESS

4 lbs. ground round
3 or 4 stalks celery, chopped fine
3 onions, chopped
1 (16 oz.) can tomatoes
Ground cumin
Basil
Orégano
Worcestershire sauce
Garlic
Salt and pepper
1 (10 ¾ oz.) can mushroom soup
3 (15 oz.) cans beans (chili, pinto or brown)
Fritos or tostados

Brown meat in large heavy pot; add celery, onion, tomatoes, and seasonings to taste. Cook slowly for 1 hour. Add soup and beans and cook until heated. Serve over fritos or tostados, and garnish with any or all of the following: grated cheese, shredded lettuce, chopped tomatoes, chopped onions, chopped hot peppers, chopped olives, chili con queso and guacamole. Meat may be frozen.

SERVES 10—12

Mrs. David E. Lashley,
Fayettville, Ark.

Donor: Carolyn Smith Russell
(Mrs. Ralph H.)

BEEF ENCHILADAS

Oil
1 onion, chopped
2 cloves garlic, chopped
1 lb. lean ground chuck
3 T. chili powder
Seasoning salt to taste
Pepper to taste
2 (8 oz.) cans tomato sauce
Water, if necessary
12 tortillas
Cheddar cheese, grated
2 (10 ¾ oz.) cans cream of mushroom soup
2 C. Velveeta cheese
1 C. milk

Sauté onion and garlic in a small amount of oil; add meat and brown. Add chili powder, salt and pepper and tomato sauce. Simmer for 30 minutes, adding water if necessary to thin meat sauce. Soften tortillas in hot meat sauce and then fill each one with about 1 T. of meat and cheddar cheese. Roll up and place seam side down in a 3 quart casserole. Heat remaining ingredients together just until cheese melts, add any remaining meat sauce and pour over enchiladas. Bake at 375° for 30 minutes or until hot and bubbly.

SERVES 6

Rosemary Clark Bagwell
(Mrs. J. J., Jr.)

ENCHILADAS

1 lb. ground beef
2 onions, diced
1 (4½ oz.) can sliced ripe olives
1 lb. grated cheese
1 (8 oz.) can tomato sauce
1 (10 oz.) can mild red enchilada sauce
1½ doz. tortillas

Brown meat and onions together. Add sliced olives and cheese. Dip tortillas in hot oil to make pliable. Fill tortillas with meat mixture and roll. Put enchiladas in a 9" x 13" baking dish. Combine tomato sauce with enchilada sauce and pour over enchiladas. Sprinkle cheese over top. Bake at 350° until hot and cheese is melted.

SERVES 6

Malinda Efrid Lenhart
(Mrs. John)

GREEN ENCHILADAS

1 lb. Velveeta cheese
1 (13 oz.) can evaporated milk
2 (10¾ oz.) cans cream of chicken soup
1 (4 oz.) can green chilies, chopped
1 (7 oz.) jar pimientos, chopped
24 frozen tortillas
2 lbs. ground meat, browned
1 large onion, chopped
1 lb. sharp cheese, grated

In top of double boiler combine cheese, milk, soup, chilies, and pimiento. Heat until melted. Dip tortillas in hot grease until soft. Fill with browned meat, chopped onion and grated cheese. Roll up and place in 2 foil lined and greased 3 quart casserole dishes. Pour sauce over enchiladas and bake at 350° about 20 minutes or until hot and bubbly.

SERVES 12

Carmen Huggins Hilliard
(Mrs. George M., III)

GREEN CHILI ENCHILADAS

1 small onion, chopped
1 T. oil
1 (4 oz.) can green chilies, seeded and chopped
1 (10¾ oz.) can cream of chicken soup
1 soup can water
1 pkg. tortillas
1 lb. hamburger meat
Salt and pepper to taste
Grated cheese

Cook onion in oil until soft. Add green chilies and cook a little. Add soup and water. Put sauce aside. Fry tortillas on both sides, just until soft. Blot tortillas to get rid of excess grease. Season and brown meat. Dip tortillas in sauce and make layers of meat, cheese and tortillas. When layers are finished, pour sauce over casserole and top with cheese. Bake at 350° for 15 minutes for shallow dish, 25 minutes for deep dish.

Mrs. George McCrea,
San Angelo, Texas

CHILI PIE
"Great to have these on hand in your freezer"

1 recipe Knottie's Chili (see Index)
2 pkgs. Morrison's Corn-Kits
2 (23 oz.) cans Trappey's Jalapeño Pinto beans, drained
4 C. chopped onions
4 C. grated sharp Cheddar cheese

Cook chili down until thick. Mix Corn-Kits according to package directions. In four 4½" x 8" aluminum foil pound cake pans, layer in this order: chili (about 1½ inches), ½ can beans, 1 cup onions, 1 cup cheese and ¼ cornbread mixture. Bake in 300° oven for about 1 hour or just before brown. Remove from oven and cool, then cover with foil and place in freezer. From freezer, place directly in 300° oven until bubbly and brown on top.

YIELD: 4 pies, each will serve 4

Maud Norton Bivins
(Mrs. James K., III)

HOT TAMALES

2 lbs. ground chuck
2 T. corn oil
1 large bottle Mexine chili powder
10 garlic buttons, divided
2 t. cumin seed, divided
2 C. tomato juice, divided
3 (10½ oz.) cans consommé
2 cans water
3 C. corn meal
3 T. oil
1 small bottle Mexine chili powder
Salt to taste

Sauté meat in corn oil. Add large bottle chili powder, 5 pods crushed garlic, 1 t. cumin seed and 1 cup tomato juice. Mix consommé with water and bring to a boil. Scald corn meal with the consommé, add 3 T. oil, the small bottle of chili powder, 1 t. cumin seed, 5 pods garlic and 1 cup tomato juice. Salt to taste. This should be the consistency to spread. If not, add more boiling water. Using narrow aluminum foil, make squares approximately 8 inches. Take 1 T. meal mixture and spread it on foil. Top with 1 T. meat mixture, leaving 1½ inches at each end. Roll and seal both ends tightly. Cover with water and boil 30 minutes. Cool in water, reheat to serve, or may be frozen and reheated later.

Mrs. J. Marcus Wood

OLD FASHIONED TAMALE PIE

3 C. boiling water
1 C. yellow corn meal
2½ t. seasoned salt
3 T. margarine
1 lb. ground meat
1 C. diced green pepper
½ C. chopped onion
2 T. chili powder
1½ t. pepper
1 t. Accent
4 tomatoes, sliced
 OR 1 C. canned tomatoes
¾ C. grated cheese

Bring water to a boil, add meal and salt. Cook over low heat until thickened, and stir in margarine. Sauté meat, green pepper and onions with seasonings. In a large casserole make layers of meal, thin layer of meat mixture, tomatoes, meal mixture and top with grated cheese. Heat thoroughly at 325° for 20-25 minutes.

SERVES 10—12

Dorothy Copeland Barnett
(Mrs. W. B.)

CALDILLO

1 onion, chopped
¼ C. salad oil
Leftover roast beef, cubed
Salt, pepper and garlic powder
2 tomatoes, cubed
2 T. chopped chilies
1 C. leftover gravy OR 1 pkg. brown gravy mix

Sauté onion in oil and then add roast beef. Season well and sauté. Add tomatoes, chilies and gravy. Simmer for 20 minutes covered and 10 minutes uncovered. Excellent over rice or noodles; or in large tortilla topped with shredded lettuce, grated cheese, avocado, hot sauce, . . . as good as your imagination!

Mrs. Louis Robbins,
El Paso, Texas

Donor: Sharon Wildstein Bindler
 (Mrs. Donn)

BARBECUED HAM

2 T. salad oil
½ C. wine vinegar
½ C. chili sauce
1 t. paprika
2 t. chili powder
1/8 t. dry mustard
¼ t. salt
2 egg yolks
4 T. melted butter
1 center slice ham, ¾" thick

Combine all ingredients and pour over ham. Let marinate overnight in refrigerator. Broil ham slowly and baste with sauce while broiling.

Mrs. Holloway Mitchell

GLAZED HAM LOAF RING

1½ lbs. ground ham
1¼ lbs. ground fresh pork
1½ C. soft bread crumbs
½ C. chopped onion
2 beaten eggs
½ C. milk

SWEET SOUR GLAZE:
½ C. brown sugar
1 T. prepared mustard
2 T. vinegar
1 T. water

MUSTARD HOT SAUCE:
½ C. dry mustard
½ C. vinegar
1 egg
⅓ C. sugar
Dash salt

Thoroughly combine meats, crumbs, onions, eggs and milk. Mold by pressing mixture into lightly oiled 6½ cup ring mold. Invert on shallow baking pan and remove ring mold. Bake at 350° for 1½ hours. At the end of 45 minutes baking time, brush loaf with Sweet Sour Glaze. Continue baking loaf until done, basting loaf 3 or 4 times. Serve with Mustard Hot Sauce.

SWEET SOUR GLAZE:
Blend brown sugar and prepared mustard, stir in vinegar and water.

MUSTARD HOT SAUCE:
Mix dry mustard and vinegar in jar. Cover. Let stand overnight. In top of double boiler, beat egg, stir in sugar, dash salt and mustard mixture. Cook over hot (not boiling) water stirring constantly until mixture thickens slightly and coats spoon. Cool before serving and add mayonnaise about half and half.

Cherokee Club Kitchen

HAM IN PATTY SHELLS

8 T. butter
½ C. finely chopped onion
½ C. finely chopped green pepper
1 lb. fresh mushrooms, sliced
1 T. lemon juice
½ C. flour
4 C. milk
3 T. dry Sherry
1 t. salt
½ t. dry mustard
1/8 t. white pepper
8 C. cooked ham
18 frozen patty shells

VARIATION:
Substitute fresh boiled shrimp for half of the ham

Heat butter in large saucepan over medium heat. Sauté onion and green pepper for 1 minute. Add mushrooms and lemon juice. Continue cooking until vegetables are tender. Stir in flour, and cook 1 minute, stirring constantly. Remove from heat. Stir in milk and sherry gradually. Add salt, mustard and pepper. Return pan to heat. Cook, stirring constantly, until mixture thickens and comes to a boil. Add ham. Bring back to boiling and cook 1 minute. Serve in chafing dish on buffet. Spoon into patty shell.

SERVES 18

Carol Morris Little
(Mrs. Robert W.)

Peggy Moss Buckstaff
(Mrs. George A.)

SAVORY RUSSIAN HAM

Juice of 3 lemons
2 t. Worcestershire sauce
3 t. sugar
1½ t. dry mustard
¼ t. curry powder
1/8 t. paprika
3 t. chopped parsley
1 small green pepper, minced
6 ham steaks, ½" thick

Blend first 8 ingredients. Place a slice of ham on a deep casserole; spread with a little of the savory mixture and top with a second slice of ham. Alternate in this way until all are used. Set in a cool place for 2 hours. Then broil ham until nicely browned. Heat the remaining savory mixture from the casserole, and pour over ham.

YIELD: 6 portions

Kathryn Melton Read
(Mrs. Earl)

JAMBALAYA

1 lb. cured ham, cubed
3 slices bacon, cut in small pieces
½ C. chopped green onions and tops
Flour
1 (16 oz.) can tomatoes, chopped
1 (10½ oz.) can tomato purée
½ C. chopped celery
2 or more cloves garlic, minced
2—3 bay leaves
½ C. chopped green pepper
1 t. sugar
Accent
Savory salt
Red pepper
Salt
¼ C. chopped parsley
1 (8 oz.) can mushrooms
3 lbs. shrimp, peeled and cleaned
2 (17 oz.) cans whole kernel corn, drained
Flour
A few oysters, optional
Butter, optional

Brown ham, bacon and onion together; stir in enough flour to absorb fat. Brown lightly; add tomatoes, purée, celery, garlic, bay leaves, green pepper and season to taste with seasonings. Cover and let cook until vegetables are tender. Add parsley, mushrooms, shrimp and corn, and cook until shrimp are done. Thicken with flour and add oysters which have been browned in butter, if desired.

SERVES 6—8

Bess Vallery Topp
(Mrs. J. S.)

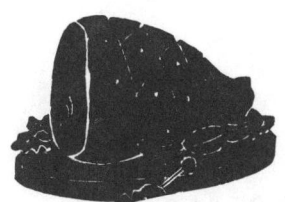

HAM BAKED IN MILK

Center slice of ham, 1½ inch thick
3 cloves
3 T. brown sugar
2 t. prepared mustard
1 C. light cream

Stud fat around ham slice with cloves. Combine brown sugar and mustard and rub into both sides of ham. Sear on both sides over quick heat in a little fat. Pour cream around it and bake, covered, at 350° about 45 minutes. Bake uncovered the last 10 minutes.

Mary Will John Sharp
(Mrs. Earl)

SPICED BAKED HAM

1 (10—12 lb.) ham
Mustard
1 C. brown sugar
1 C. mustard
1 C. Sherry
¼ t. ground cloves

Buy a good ham that does not require par-boiling. Scrub; then rub surface well with mustard. Place fat side up in a roasting pan and bake at 300° at 20 minutes per pound plus 20 minutes more. One hour before ham is done remove from oven and remove rind except around shank bone. Remove excess fat, rub with mustard and score top with a diamond formation. Insert whole cloves if desired. Combine sugar, mustard and sherry, and baste ham until golden brown. Turn oven up to 450° the last ten minutes of cooking time to form a crust. Let cool in its own juices.

Peggy Moss Buckstaff
(Mrs. George)

CHINESE SPARERIBS

4 lbs. pork ribs, cut into serving pieces (small for hors d'oeuvres)

MARINADE:
2 T. corn starch
⅔ C. dark corn syrup
⅓ C. soy sauce
1½ t. ground ginger
¼ t. salt
¼ C. vinegar
2 cloves garlic
¼ t. salt
Dash pepper
⅓ to ½ jar plum jam

Combine marinade ingredients and bring to a boil, stirring. Pour over ribs and marinate overnight or at least 4 hours. Cook ribs in 350° oven for one hour; then place ribs in broiler pan without rack and broil 10 inches from heat, basting with marinade for ½ hour. Turn occasionally.

Rose Pickens Kirkpatrick
(Mrs. Kenneth L.)

PORK ROAST WITH SOUR CREAM SAUCE
"An elegant entree"

4 T. lard
3 lb. boneless pork loin
¾ C. finely chopped onions
¾ C. finely chopped carrots
1 t. sweet paprika
1 C. chicken broth
Salt
Ground black pepper
2 T. flour
1 C. sour cream
1 T. chopped parsley
1 t. capers, drained and chopped

Heat lard. Brown pork at high heat on all sides, 10 to 15 minutes. Preheat oven to 350°. Pour off all but a thin film of fat. Add onions and cook until lightly browned (8 minutes) over medium heat. Add carrots and cook 3 minutes longer. Take the vegetables off the fire and stir in the paprika until the vegetables are coated. Add broth and bring to a boil. Stir brown bits up in pan and add roast, fat side up, salt and pepper. Bring the liquid to a boil, cover tightly and put on the middle rack in the oven. Cook 1½ hours or until tender. Baste occasionally. Put roast on heated platter. Pour the contents of the pan into a sieve over a saucepan pressing down hard on vegetables before discarding them. Skim off surface fat from pan liquid and bring sauce to simmer. Beat flour and sour cream together in a small bowl with a wire whisk and then beat mixture into sauce. Add parsley and capers. Slice meat into serving pieces and pour sauce over the meat. Serve the rest of the gravy in a gravy boat. This sauce is enough for a 6 pound roast, also.

SERVES 6

Rose Pickens Kirkpatrick
(Mrs. Kenneth L.)

PICKLED PORK

1 fresh pork ham (not cured)
¾ C. vinegar
½ C. sugar
1—2 t. salt
Half a handful of pickling spices

Mix seasonings in a large pot of water. (Use more if ham is as large as 18—20 pounds.) Place ham in pot and make sure that water covers it. Simmer covered 30 minutes per pound. Cool in juices. Refrigerate. Serve sliced and cold.

Martha Hess Whitehead
(Mrs. R. Laughton, Jr.)

PORK CHOPS JAMAICA

3 lbs. center cut pork chops (about 12)
¾ C. light stock (chicken or beef)
1 large onion, sliced
3 green peppers, sliced
2 T. butter
1 T. olive oil
1⅓ C. tomatoes (canned or fresh, cut into eighths)
¼ clove garlic
⅓ C. catsup
1 T. Worcestershire sauce
¼ t. Accent
Salt and pepper to taste

Season chops and brown in frying pan. Remove to shallow roasting pan, add stock and braise in 350° oven for 20 minutes. Meanwhile make sauce. Sauté onion and green pepper in olive oil until soft. Add remaining ingredients. Skim off any excess fat from chops and add sauce. Continue baking for 15 minutes.

SERVES 5—6

Andee Knapp Wrather
(Mrs. John D.)

DEEP DISH PIZZA PIE

1½ C. chopped onion
1 green pepper, chopped
Bacon drippings
3 lbs. highly seasoned sausage
1 (6 oz.) can tomato paste
Garlic powder
Sage, optional
Pepper, optional
2 (16 oz.) cans tomatoes, plus juice
2 (4½ oz.) cans button mushrooms
2 (8 oz.) pkgs. Mozzarella cheese, sliced
8 oz. Parmesan cheese
1 lb. sharp cheddar cheese, cut in ¾" cubes
Orégano
2 T. olive oil
2—9" pie crusts or pizza dough

Sauté onion and green pepper in a small amount of bacon drippings until soft. Add sausage and brown slightly, breaking up into small pieces with a spatula. Pour off all excess fat. Add tomato paste, juice from tomatoes, garlic powder and sage and pepper if desired. Simmer until thickened and set aside to cool. **Add no salt.** This filling may be put into two 9" pie plates lined with regular pie crust or pizza dough and brushed with 1 T. olive oil each. To assemble the pies, fill each in the following order: Parmesan cheese, Cheddar cheese, sausage mixture, tomatoes broken into pieces, mushrooms, Mozzarella cheese. Sprinkle each one with orégano and drizzle each pie with 1 T. olive oil. Bake at 450° for 25—30 minutes. Loosen from pan immediately. May be frozen. Each pie will serve 6.

Carolyn Smith Russell
(Mrs. Ralph H.)

REAL ITALIAN PIZZA

DOUGH:
2 env. Fleishman's dry yeast
1 C. warm water
1 T. sugar
6 C. unbleached flour
3 t. salt
⅓ C. olive oil
1¼ C. warm water

SAUCE:
1 (15 oz.) can tomato sauce
⅓ C. olive oil
2 T. minced dry onion flakes
½ t. dried orégano
½ t. dried basil
1½ T. garlic salt
1 T. parsley flakes
Grated Parmesan cheese
5 C. shredded Mozzarella cheese
Mushrooms
Bell pepper
Pepperoni

Dissolve yeast in 1 cup warm water with sugar. Rest 15 minutes. Add flour, salt, olive oil and 1¼ cup water. Mix together until smooth, then turn out onto table and knead well until smooth, about 10 minutes. Dough should be very smooth and stick slightly to hands. Butter a large bowl and add dough, cover and let rest in warm place for 90 minutes. (Mix sauce together at this time to allow flavor to develop). When dough is ready, divide into 3 equal pieces. On floured cloth roll with rolling pin until it fits pizza pan. Oil pizza pan well, then roll dough up on rolling pin and transfer to pan. Cover generously with tomato sauce and a third of the Mozzarella. On top of cheese a few shakes of sauce as well as a few shakes of Parmesan. Bake on lowest shelf in oven at 400° and check at 20 minutes. (Bottom of crust should be medium brown). Crust along the rim should be well browned but be sure cheese is not burned. Each pie should be baked separately. Mushrooms, bell pepper and pepperoni are good added to the top.

Mary Loomis,
Denver, Colorado

QUICK GERMAN CASSEROLE

¼ C. milk
1 (10¾ oz.) can Cheddar cheese soup
½ t. caraway seed
½ t. prepared mustard
1½ lb. canned sauerkraut, drained and snipped
1 lb. weiners OR German sausage

Stir milk into cheese soup in saucepan. Add caraway seeds and mustard. Fold in sauerkraut and heat through, stirring often. Turn into 10" x 6" x 1½" baking dish. Slash wieners at 1 inch intervals and arrange on top of sauerkraut. Bake at 375° for 15 minutes. Serve with horseradish.

SERVES 4—6

Joanie Marvel Abbott
(Mrs. Frank)

RIGATONI FLORIDA

"Serve with green salad, garlic bread and dry red wine"

1 lb. pkg. thick sliced smoked bacon
2 glasses dry white wine
2 (16 oz.) cans peeled tomatoes, cut up
Butter
Parmesan cheese
1½ (12 oz.) pkgs. rigatoni
1 pt. heavy cream
Salt and pepper to taste

Brown bacon; cook until crisp. Drain on paper towels. Crumble into a clean skillet and add wine. Cook until wine is almost absorbed. Add tomatoes and cook very slowly until almost absorbed. Add butter and Parmesan cheese to taste. Cook rigatoni in boiling salted water, until nearly done. Drain well. Return to pan and finish cooking in cream. Add bacon-tomato to mixture and salt and pepper to taste. The bacon-tomato mixture may be frozen if desired. At serving time, cook the rigatoni and mix with the thawed mixture. Delicious!

SERVES 4

Mrs. Richard Cella
New York, N. Y.

Donor: Joan Nachbaur Rathbun

SPAGHETTI CARBONARA

1 C. heavy cream
4 egg yolks
1 C. grated Parmesan cheese
2 T. bacon drippings, olive oil OR butter
1 large onion, chopped
2 cloves garlic, chopped
½ lb. fresh mushrooms, sliced
1 ripe tomato, diced
½ lb. smoked bacon, cooked, drained and crumbled
2 C. cooked ham, diced
½ C. dry wine (red or white)
¼ C. parsley, chopped
Salt and pepper to taste
1 lb. spaghetti, cooked and drained

In a small bowl, beat egg yolks with cream until smooth; stir in cheese. In a skillet, sauté onion, garlic and mushrooms in oil until tender. Add tomato, bacon, ham, wine and parsley, and stir for only a few minutes until mixture is hot and wine is absorbed. Pour cream mixture over spaghetti and toss until each strand is coated. Add vegetable, bacon and ham mixture and toss until well mixed. Serve with hot crusty Italian bread and a green salad.

SERVES 6—8

Mrs. John Clinton Robbins

ALL AMERICAN RICE CASSEROLE

2 lbs. pork sausage
2 large onions, chopped
1 large bell pepper, chopped
4 stalks celery, chopped
1 pkg. slivered almonds
3 pkgs. Lipton Noodle Soup Mix
2 oz. pimiento
1 (8 oz.) can water chestnuts, sliced
2 C. uncooked rice
Salt, pepper and soy sauce to taste
8 C. boiling water

Fry sausage and drain. Sauté onions, pepper and celery. Place in large casserole and mix all ingredients together. Add boiling water. Cover and bake at 350° for 1 hour.

SERVES 8—10

Julia Wampler Barron
(Mrs. James F.)

VEAL ORLOFF

2 C. chopped onion
¼ C. butter
1 C. rice
1 C. chicken broth
1 C. water
1 clove garlic
1 t. salt
½ t. pepper
2 C. sliced mushrooms
2 T. butter
2 T. chopped parsley
12 thin slices cooked veal, diced
½ C. grated Swiss cheese

SAUCE:
2 T. butter
2 T. flour
1¼ C. milk
½ C. grated Swiss cheese
½ t. salt
¼ t. pepper
1/8 t. nutmeg
1/8 t. cayenne
1 egg yolk

Sauté onion in butter for 5 minutes. Add rice, broth, water, garlic, salt and pepper. Bring to a boil. Cover and cook on low heat until rice is done, about 15 minutes. Sauté mushrooms in 2 T. butter for 4 minutes. Combine rice, mushrooms and parsley. Place in baking dish. Top with veal, sauce and grated cheese. Cover loosely with foil and bake at 400° for 15 minutes. Remove foil and put under broiler 3—4 minutes to brown cheese.

SAUCE:
Melt butter until foamy. Stir in flour. Cook 2—3 minutes. Do not brown. Remove. Add milk, cheese, salt, pepper, nutmeg and cayenne. Cook on medium heat for 4 minutes until thick. In bowl, combine egg yolk and small amount of sauce. Stir well and add to sauce in pan. Heat, stirring, one minute. Pour sauce over veal.

SERVES 6

Susie Moore French
(Mrs. Paul E.)

VEAL CUTLETS OSCAR

3 lbs. veal cutlets, trimmed
Salt
White pepper
Butter
24 fresh asparagus tips, cooked
6 T. lobster, cooked and cubed
2 C. Béarnaise Sauce

BÉARNAISE SAUCE:
1 C. butter
6 sprigs tarragon, finely chopped
6 springs chervil, finely chopped
4 shallots, finely chopped
½ C. tarragon vinegar
½ C. white wine
6 egg yolks
2 T. water

Cut veal cutlets into 6 serving pieces. Rub with salt and pepper and sauté in butter in a heavy skillet for about five minutes or until they are golden on both sides. Reduce the heat, cover and cook for about 15 minutes, or until it is tender. Transfer to a heated platter and arrange asparagus tips on each one, garnish with 1 T. lobster and cover generously with Béarnaise Sauce.

SERVES 6

BÉARNAISE SAUCE:
Have butter at room temperature. In the top of a double boiler combine tarragon, chervil, shallots, vinegar and wine. Cook the mixture over direct heat until it is reduced to a thick paste. Let cool slightly. Put the pan over hot, but not boiling water, add egg yolks and water. Stir the sauce briskly with a wire whisk until it is light and fluffy. Add a third of the butter and whisk the mixture constantly until it thickens slightly. Add the remaining butter in at least 2 parts, whisking briskly and constantly.

YIELD: 2 cups

Mrs. Joseph H. Croxton

SCALLOPINI AL MARSALA

1½ lbs. veal scallops (may substitute tenderized minute steaks)
Flour, salt and pepper
2 T. butter
3 T. olive oil
½ C. dry Marsala wine
½ C. chicken broth
Mushrooms, as many as desired
2 T. soft butter

Dredge meat in flour, salt and pepper. Brown in the butter and olive oil. Remove to a warm platter. Pour wine and chicken broth into the pan and bring to a boil, scraping the pan to loosen browned fragments. Add meat and simmer for 20 minutes until tender. Again, remove the meat, add mushrooms to pan, and cook rapidly a few minutes to reduce sauce. (It should be rather syrupy.) Add butter and pour over meat.

SERVES 4

Rose Pickens Kirkpatrick
(Mrs. Kenneth L.)

VEAL BIRDS GARNISHED WITH FRESH MUSHROOMS AND ARTICHOKE BOTTOMS

6 veal cutlets (6 oz.) each, well trimmed
2 C. onions, finely diced
1 C. butter, divided
2 C. bread crumbs
½ C. seedless raisins
Salt and pepper to taste
Pinch powdered thyme
¼ C. milk
¼ C. all-purpose flour
½ C. dry Sherry
2 C. Quick Brown Sauce (see Index)
1 lb. fresh mushrooms, quartered
8 artichoke bottoms, quartered
¼ C. chopped parsley

Cut veal cutlets in half, place between layer of wax paper, one at a time, and pound thin with mallet, or the side of a heavy knife blade or cleaver. Sauté onion in ½ cup butter, stirring so it does not brown. Add bread crumbs, raisins, salt, pepper, and thyme. Remove from heat, add milk and mix well. Spoon 2 T. of mixture close to one edge of each flattened piece of veal, roll up, and fasten with a toothpick. Season meat with salt and pepper, roll lightly in flour, and sauté in ⅓ cup butter. When brown, remove veal from pan, drain fat, add Sherry, and allow to boil a second or two. Stir in Brown Sauce, return meat to pan, and simmer over low heat, covered, for 20—30 minutes or until veal is tender when pierced with a fork. Sauté mushrooms and artichokes in remaining butter. Place veal birds on heated platter, cover with sauce and garnish with mushrooms, artichokes and parsley.

The Williamsburg Cookbook

VEAL PARMESAN
"Substitute eggplant for veal"

2 T. olive oil
1 clove garlic, chopped
1 (28 oz.) can tomatoes, mashed with juice
1 bay leaf
1 t. orégano or sweet basil
1 t. sugar
Salt and pepper to taste
8 veal cutlets
2 eggs, beaten
Progresso Italian flavored bread crumbs
Salt and pepper
Olive oil
8 oz. Mozzarella cheese
Parmesan cheese

Sauté garlic in olive oil until brown, add tomatoes, bay leaf, orégano, sugar, salt and pepper. Simmer about 1½ hours. Add a little water if sauce gets too thick. Dip veal in egg, then bread crumbs and sprinkle with salt and pepper. Brown in olive oil and drain on paper towels. Glaze the bottom of a greased casserole with a little sauce, add veal, Mozzarella, Parmesan and more sauce. This will make about 2 layers. End with sauce and sprinkle with Parmesan cheese. Bake at 350° for 30—45 minutes. May be prepared in advance or frozen.

SERVES 4—6

Andee Knapp Wrather
(Mrs. John D.)

ROAST LEG OF LAMB

Leg of lamb
Garlic powder
Paprika
Salt and pepper
Juice of 1 lemon
2 stalks celery
1 large onion
A little water
Catsup
Worcestershire sauce
Currant jelly

Season lamb liberally with seasonings; place in roasting pan on bed of celery and onions. Add a little water and roast uncovered 30—35 minutes a pound. One hour before lamb is done, add catsup and Worcestershire sauce to pan drippings. Thirty minutes before lamb is done, glaze with jelly.

Etta Remer Sosland
(Mrs. Morris)

MEXICAN STYLE LEG OF LAMB

1 (5—6 lb.) leg of lamb
1 C. dry red wine
½ C. orange juice
¼ C. chili sauce
¼ C. water
1 T. chili powder
1 onion, chopped
2 cloves garlic, minced
1 T. orégano
1 t. crushed cumin seed
1 T. brown sugar
Salt and pepper to taste

Place lamb in deep glass dish. Combine remaining ingredients; pour over lamb. Let stand in refrigerator 24 hours, turning occasionally. Lift lamb from marinade; drain, reserving marinade. Place lamb on rack in baking pan. Bake at 450° for 15 minutes; reduce heat to 350°. Pour reserved marinade over lamb and bake until desired doneness (we prefer medium), basting frequently. Add water to pan if juices evaporate.

YIELD: 8—10 servings

Cookbook Committee

BUFFET CRAB

2 C. cooked rice
1 (14 oz.) can artichoke hearts, drained and cut in half
1 lb. lump crabmeat OR cooked shrimp
½ lb. fresh mushrooms
2 T. margarine
1 (10 ¾ oz.) can cream of celery soup
1 T. Worcestershire sauce
Seasoned salt to taste
¼ C. dry white wine
¾ C. grated sharp cheese

Place rice, artichoke hearts, seafood and mushrooms, sautéed in margarine, in buttered casserole dish. Mix soup, salt, Worcestershire sauce, and wine and pour over mixture. Sprinkle grated cheese on top. Bake at 350° for 20 minutes or until bubbly.

SERVES 6

Carmen Huggins Hilliard
(Mrs. George M., III)

CRABMEAT IMPERIAL

1 onion, finely grated
1 bell pepper, finely chopped
¼ C. butter
2 lbs. lump crabmeat
¼ C. chopped pimiento

CREAM SAUCE:
4 T. butter
4 T. flour
2 C. hot milk
½ t. salt
¾ t. cayenne pepper

Sauté onion and bell pepper slightly in butter. Add to crabmeat that has been carefully picked of shells. Add pimiento. Make cream sauce as follows; melt butter, blend in flour, add milk stirring constantly with wire whisk. Season with salt and cayenne pepper. Add crabmeat mixture to cream sauce. Serve over hot rice.

SERVES 12

Maud Norton Bivins
(Mrs. James K., III)

KATA'S CRAB CASSEROLE

2 T. bacon drippings
2 cloves garlic, pressed
1 ½ onions, chopped fine
1 lb. whole lump crabmeat
1 cylinder (41) saltine crackers, crushed and divided into equal parts
½ C. heavy cream
½ C. light cream
½ C. butter, melted

Sauté garlic and onions in drippings. Add crabmeat and half of the cracker crumbs. Put into a 1 ½ quart casserole. Pour creams over crabmeat and add the rest of the crumbs. Pour butter over casserole. Bake at 350° for 20 minutes or until golden brown.

Katherine Edwards Crain
(Mrs. E. B.)

CRAB WITH CURRIED RICE

"Serve with tossed salad, rolls and a light dessert"

1 lb. lump crabmeat
1 qt. thick white sauce
Salt and pepper
2 T. Worcestershire sauce
2 T. Sherry
Paprika
½ C. finely chopped green pepper
1 C. finely chopped celery
½ C. pimiento
1½ C. grated sharp cheese

CURRIED RICE:
2 C. rice
2 C. chicken stock
1 T. curry powder
Salt to taste

Season white sauce with salt, pepper, Worcestershire sauce, Sherry and paprika. Combine all ingredients or arrange in layers in casserole dish. Freeze at this point or bake at 350° for 1 hour. Serve over Curried Rice.

RICE:
Combine and steam for 1 hour.

SERVES 8

Mrs. Phillip Braumell

Donor: Carolyn Smith Russell
(Mrs. Ralph H.)

OVERNIGHT CRAB CASSEROLE

1 lb. fresh lump crabmeat
3 green onions and tops, chopped
Juice of 1 lemon
3 C. French bread, cut in 1" cubes
8 oz. Velveeta cheese, grated
3—6 T. butter, melted
1¾ C. milk
3 eggs, beaten
½ t. salt
3 drops Tabasco sauce
½ t. dry mustard

Toss crabmeat lightly with onions and lemon juice. In buttered 1½ quart, shallow casserole, arrange alternating layers of bread, drizzle with melted butter, cheese and crab and onion mixture. Combine remaining ingredients. Pour over crab mixture, cover and refrigerate overnight. Remove from refrigerator 1 hour before baking. Bake, uncovered, at 350° for 50—60 minutes or until puffed and golden.

SERVES 6—8

Eleanor Croxton Lawrence
(Mrs. Thomas W.)

CRAB CASSEROLE

2 C. milk
2 large T. butter
2 T. flour
1½ lbs. crabmeat
4 hard-boiled eggs, chopped or riced
1 C. cracker crumbs
2 T. lemon juice
1 onion, grated
Lots of Tabasco
1 C. heavy cream
Salt, red pepper and paprika
Buttered bread crumbs
Butter

Make cream sauce and add crabmeat, eggs, cracker crumbs, lemon juice, onion, Tabasco, and last, the cream, salt, red pepper and paprika. Blend well. Grease casserole and fill. Top with buttered bread crumbs and dot with butter. Bake until lightly browned and bubbly, about 30 minutes. Can be frozen.

SERVES 6—8

Mrs. Henry L. Smith

CRAB FILLING FOR CRÊPES

½ C. finely chopped green onion
8 T. butter
1 lb. fresh lump crabmeat, picked over well
½ C. dry white wine
Salt and cracked pepper to taste

SAUCE:
6 T. butter
6 T. flour
1 t. salt
2 C. chicken stock
2 C. milk
3 egg yolks
¾ C. heavy cream
¾ C. grated Swiss or Gruyere cheese

Sauté onion in butter until clear. Stir in crab gently. Add wine and simmer 2 minutes. If there is too much liquid, raise heat and boil until almost gone. Season with salt and pepper and set aside.

SAUCE:
Melt butter. Add flour and salt. Cook until bubbly. Add liquid. Cook until sauce begins to thicken. Set aside. Beat egg yolks and cream together. Add hot sauce by the spoonful to egg mixture. Correct seasoning.

TO ASSEMBLE:
Add enough sauce to crab to hold it together. Put 1 T. crab mixture on each crêpe and roll. Place in a buttered shallow pan. Cover with remaining sauce and sprinkle grated cheese over-all. Bake at 325° for 20 minutes, then run under the broiler until bubbly.

YIELD: Filling for 12 Crêpes

Patricia Smith Houston
(Mrs. E. B.)

BAKED CRAB AND SHRIMP

1 lb. fresh mushrooms, sliced
¼ C. butter
2 T. flour
½ C. dry sherry
2 C. light cream
4 C. Hellmann's mayonnaise
½ C. chopped parsley
½ C. chopped green onions
4 C. white bread cubes
1 lb. fresh lump crabmeat
1 lb. fresh shrimp, cleaned and uncooked
8 hard-boiled eggs, chopped
2 (14 oz.) cans artichoke hearts, drained (not marinated)
1 C. buttered bread crumbs
½ C. Parmesan cheese

Sauté mushrooms in butter; sprinkle with flour. Stir and cool; blend in sherry and cream. Cook, stirring, until thickened; cool. Mix mayonnaise, parsley, onions, and bread cubes. Add to mushroom sauce. Gently stir in crab, shrimp and eggs. Arrange artichokes in buttered casserole; pour in seafood mixture. Sprinkle with bread crumbs and Parmesan cheese. Bake at 350° for 30—50 minutes.

SERVES 12—15

Helen May Little
(Mrs. Earle E., Jr.)

CRAB AND SHRIMP MELBA

½ C. butter
½ C. flour
2 C. light cream
2 C. milk
1 t. salt
1 t. paprika
1 t. Accent
1 t. Mei Yen seasoning powder
1 t. MSG
Dash red pepper
2 t. catsup
2 (6 oz.) cans mushrooms
1 C. sharp cheese, grated
1 lb. fresh lump crabmeat
1½ lbs. fresh cooked and cleaned medium shrimp
1 T. lemon juice
Sherry to taste
Lightly toasted buttered cracker crumbs

Make cream sauce from first four ingredients; cook until thick. Add remaining ingredients except cracker crumbs in the order given being careful not to break up lump crabmeat. Serve from a chafing dish in patty shells as an entree OR thin a little with extra cream and serve on Melba Rounds for cocktails. May also be baked in buttered individual shells and topped with crumbs. Bake only until piping hot. Freezes well.

SERVES 12 as an entrée

Peggy Conner Smead
(Mrs. Hamp, P.)

ESCARGOTS AND POTATOES

6 large Irish potatoes
3 cloves of garlic, chopped
4 shallots, chopped
2 T. parsley
¾ C. butter
35 snails and shells
Salt to taste

Boil the potatoes in salted water. While the potatoes are cooking, place the butter in a skillet and sauté the garlic, shallots and parsley. Mash the potatoes, and add 3 T. of the butter mixture to the potatoes, with salt to taste. Stuff the snails into the shells with a bit of the butter mixture. Use a decorative oven-safe dish with sides, and make a bed of the potatoes on the bottom. Place the snails and shells on the potato bed with the open end up. Bake at 350° until snails begin to bubble.

SERVES 12

Dorothy Robbins Kennedy
(Mrs. George E., Jr.)

LOBSTER THERMIDOR

6 large frozen lobster tails
2 cloves garlic, chopped
1 onion, chopped
½ C. salt
2 t. pepper
¾ C. butter, plus 3 level T. butter
½ C. flour
1½ C. light cream
9 canned mushrooms, cut up
½ t. Dijon mustard
3 T. chopped fresh parsley
1 C. Sherry
3 dashes paprika
Parmesan cheese

Put lobster tails to boil for 30 minutes in a pot of water seasoned with the garlic, onion, salt and pepper. Let cool. Remove from the pot. Remove the meat from tails. Dice; set aside and reserve the shells. Melt ¾ cup butter in a pot; add the flour, and stir until smooth. Add the cream, stirring until the sauce is thick. Take off the heat and set aside. Sauté the lobster meat and mushrooms in 3 T. butter for 5 minutes. Add the lobster meat, mushrooms, mustard and parsley to the cream sauce. Stir for 5 minutes, then add the Sherry and blend in well. Add paprika, then place the mixture in the lobster shells. Sprinkle with Parmesan cheese; put in a 450° oven and bake for 15 minutes.

SERVES 6

Cotton Country Collection

OYSTERS BIENVILLE

4 T. butter
8 green onions and tops, chopped
2 T. flour
1 C. chicken stock or broth
1 (7 oz.) can mushrooms, drained and chopped
2 egg yolks
½ C. white wine
1 (6½ oz.) can shrimp, drained and rinsed in cold water
Salt and pepper to taste
Approximately 32 raw oysters
½ C. bread crumbs
Parmesan cheese
Paprika

Sauté onions in butter until soft. Add flour and brown. Stir in broth, and add mushrooms. Beat egg yolks in wine and add to mixture. Cook until thick. Stir in shrimp. Season with salt and pepper. Divide oysters between 8 individual shells or ramekins. Place on a cookie sheet in a 400° oven for 5-10 minutes or until oysters are plump. Remove from oven and drain juice from oysters. Cover each shell with the Bienville sauce, top with bread crumbs and Parmesan cheese; dust with paprika. Bake at 350° for 15 minutes or until lightly browned and bubbly. May prepare sauce ahead of time and freeze.

SERVES 4—6 or 8 as an appetizer

Martha Hess Whitehead
(Mrs. R. Laughton, Jr.)

SCALLOPED OYSTERS

1 pt. oysters (about 2 doz.)
6 T. cream
Oyster liquor
½ C. dry bread crumbs
1½ C. cracker crumbs
½ C. melted butter (or more)
Salt and pepper
½ C. chopped celery or green pepper
Butter or grated cheese for topping

Drain oysters and reserve liquid. Combine cream and oyster liquor. Combine bread crumbs and cracker crumbs. Grease an 8" square baking pan and cover with a layer of crumbs, then a layer of oysters. Put ½ t. melted butter directly on each oyster, then proceed to build up the other layers. (Plan to use 2 layers of oysters, no more, and 3 layers of crumbs.) Season each layer with salt and pepper and pour half of the combined oyster liquor and cream over it. The oyster layers may be sprinkled with celery or green pepper (celery is better). The top layer of crumbs should be dry. Dot with butter or grated cheese.

SERVES 4

Lynn Smith Norton
(Mrs. O. L.)

DEVILED OYSTERS ON HALF SHELL

3 green onions, chopped
1 T. butter
2 T. flour
½ C. cream
¼ C. milk or oyster juice
1 t. salt
1/8 to ¼ t. nutmeg
Large dash cayenne
½ —1 t. prepared mustard
½ —1 T. Worcestershire sauce
½ —1 t. chopped parsley
3 mushrooms, chopped OR 1 can chopped mushrooms
1 pt. oysters, washed, drained and chopped
1 egg yolk
Buttered cracker crumbs

VARIATION:
3 T. crisply fried bacon, crumbled
Sherry to taste

Sauté onions in butter until soft, add flour and stir until well blended. Add liquids and all seasonings and cook until slightly thick. Add oysters. Remove from heat and mix in egg yolk. Will fill 4 large greased shells or 8 small ones. Sprinkle with crumbs and bake at 325° for 15 minutes.

SERVES 4—8

Naomi Scott Harding
(Mrs. Paul)

Add bacon with oysters. Add sherry after removing from heat.

Peggy Conner Smead
(Mrs. Hamp P.)

FRIED DEVILED OYSTERS

½ C. salad oil
¼ C. lemon juice
½ t. salt
1 t. horseradish
½ t. paprika
1 T. Worcestershire sauce
24 oysters, drained
Flour
2 eggs, slightly beaten with 2 T. water
Sifted bread crumbs

Combine first six ingredients. Pour this dressing over oysters and let stand 1 hour. Drain and wipe oysters dry. Roll in flour, dip in egg, then crumbs. Fry in hot fat, 1" deep in heavy frying pan until brown. Drain on absorbent paper and serve immediately.

Marguerite Swearingen Harrington
(Mrs. Harry M.)

OYSTERS PAN ROAST

½ C. margarine or butter
1 bunch shallots, finely chopped
2 bunches parsley, finely chopped
1½ C. flour
4 C. oyster liquid
4 doz. oysters
2 t. salt
Pepper to taste
¼ t. cayenne
1 oz. Worcestershire sauce
1 C. bread crumbs
1 lb. lump crabmeat, optional

Sauté shallots and parsley in margarine for 5 minutes. Stir in flour. Boil the oysters in oyster liquid until the edges of the oysters curl. Pour stock into flour and stir rapidly until sauce becomes thick. Season to taste with salt, cayenne and Worcestershire sauce. Add crabmeat, if desired. Place 12 oysters in each of four small casseroles or ramkins. Cover each portion with sauce. Sprinkle bread crumbs on top and bake at 475° for 20 minutes.

SERVES 4

Jenny Lewis Rappeport
(Mrs. Joseph H.)

SCALLOPS TETRAZZINI

¾ lb. scallops, fresh or frozen
½ t. instant minced onion
¼ t. salt
Dash pepper
Water (about 1 C.)
2 T. butter or margarine
2 T. all-purpose flour
¼ t. paprika
Dash leaf orégano, crushed
Dash salt
1 drop Tabasco sauce
½ C. reserved cooking liquid
½ C. milk
1 egg, slightly beaten
1 (3 oz.) can sliced mushrooms
4 oz. spaghetti, cooked and drained
2 T. grated Parmesan cheese
Whole canned mushrooms and parsley for garnish

If using frozen scallops, thaw. Cut each scallop in half. In saucepan, combine scallops, onion, salt and pepper. Add water just to cover scallops (about 1 cup). Cover and simmer 10 minutes. Drain, reserving ½ cup cooking liquid. Melt the butter; blend in flour, paprika, orégano, a dash salt and the Tabasco sauce. Add the reserved cooking liquid and milk. Cook and stir until thickened. Stir a little of the hot sauce into egg; return to sauce and mix well. Add undrained mushrooms and scallops to sauce; mix well. Spoon hot spaghetti into a 10" x 6" x 1½" baking dish; top with the hot scallop mixture. Sprinkle with grated Parmesan cheese. Brown under broiler about 5 minutes. Garnish with whole canned mushrooms and parsley, if desired.

SERVES 4

Helen May Little
(Mrs. Earle E., Jr.)

BILLIE BUTTER'S SHRIMP AND SCALLOPS GRUYERE

"Serve with rice tossed with walnuts and diced green peppers"

1 C. butter or margarine
1 C. flour
4 C. milk
1 lb. Swiss Gruyère cheese
¼ t. garlic salt
4¼ t. salt, divided
¼ t. white pepper
¼ t. Accent
¼ t. dry mustard
1 T. tomato paste
4½ t. lemon juice, divided
1½ lbs. raw scallops
¾ lb. mushrooms, sliced
3 T. butter or margarine
1½ lbs. cooked shrimp

Make a cream sauce in top of a double boiler with butter, flour and milk. Cut the cheese into small pieces and add to sauce. Cook and stir until cheese melts. Add garlic powder, 4 t. salt, pepper, Accent, mustard, tomato paste and 3 t. lemon juice. Poach scallops for about 10 minutes in water to which you have added the remaining ½ t. lemon juice and ¼ t. salt. Add 1 cup of the broth to the cream sauce. Sauté mushrooms in 3 T. butter and add to the sauce. Drain scallops and add with shrimp to the sauce. Heat for 10—15 minutes. This may be made the day before and reheated in a double boiler before serving. Thin with a little milk if necessary.

SERVES 6—8

Linda Ryan Butter
(Mrs. Stephen R.)

COQUILLE ST. JACQUES

1 lb. fresh scallops, cut in small pieces
1 lb. fresh medium shrimp OR fresh lump crabmeat
1½ C. dry white wine
½ t. salt
½ t. white pepper
3 T. butter
2 T. flour
1 C. milk
1½ C. coarsley chopped and sautéed mushrooms
½ C. grated Swiss cheese
¼ C. chopped fresh parsley
4 T. bread crumbs

Place scallops, shrimp or crabmeat, wine, salt and pepper in a large heavy saucepan; bring to a boil. Reduce heat and simmer 5 minutes. Drain and reserve liquid. Heat butter in heavy saucepan; add flour and when smooth, add reserved liquid and milk. Cook 3 minutes, stirring constantly. Add scallops and shrimp or crab and mushrooms. Cook 5 minutes, stirring constantly. Remove from heat; stir in cheese and parsley. Adjust seasonings. Fill buttered shells or individual casseroles with mixture. Sprinkle with bread crumbs, dot with butter and add a dash of paprika to each. Broil until brown.

SERVES 6

Helen May Little
(Mrs. Earle E., Jr.)

SALMON LOAF

1 small loaf unsliced bread
6 T. margarine, divided
½ C. minced onions
½ C. minced green pepper
1 C. minced celery
1 (16 oz.) can salmon
¼ C. milk
2 eggs
1 t. dill
¼ t. salt
½ t. pepper

Cut slice from top of loaf of bread and remove bread leaving ¼" all around. Crumb bread (about 3 cups). Melt 4 T. margarine in pan; add onion, green pepper and celery and cook 10 minutes or until tender. Drain salmon liquid into cup and add milk until you have ½ cup liquid. Beat liquid into eggs. Combine flaked salmon and bread crumbs; add seasonings and vegetables. Stir in egg mixture. Pack mixture into bread shell. Press top firmly down. Brush top and sides with melted margarine. Bake in pre-heated 350° oven for 50—60 minutes. Slice.

SERVES 6

Rose Pickens Kirkpatrick
(Mrs. Kenneth L.)

SHRIMP GRAND CHENIER

5 lbs. headless jumbo shrimp, in shells
1 lb. melted butter or margarine
6 T. black pepper
1 (16 oz.) bottle Wishbone Dressing
Juice of 2 lemons

VARIATION: A milder version
1½ C. melted butter
1 (16 oz.) bottle Wishbone Dressing
1 bay leaf
1 T. pepper
2 T. lemon pepper
1 T. seasoning salt
2 cloves garlic, crushed
¼ t. garlic salt

Place shrimp in a large roasting pan. Mix remaining ingredients together and pour over shrimp. Bake uncovered at 400° for 40 minutes, turning gently every 10 minutes. Serve sauce in individual bowls for dipping.

SERVES 6

Forrest Gaumer Martin
(Mrs. J. C., Jr.)

Mix together all ingredients and pour over shrimp. Bake, covered, at 400° for 35 minutes.

Claire Roberts Harris
(Mrs. Jerry S.)

FRENCH FRIED SHRIMP

2 lbs. raw shrimp, cleaned and deveined
1 C. flour
1 t. baking powder
½ t. sugar
½ t. salt
1 egg
1 C. ice water
3 T. oil

Beat together all ingredients except shrimp to make a batter and refrigerate for 1 hour or until cold. Cut shrimp down the back until almost cut in half. Dip in batter and fry in hot oil. Drain and serve at once with sauce.

Bess Vallery Topp
(Mrs. J. S.)

SAUCE:
1 C. mayonnaise
½ (14 oz.) bottle catsup
1 T. chopped ripe olives
¼ C. chopped dill pickle
1 T. minced onion
Chopped parsley

ÉTOUFEE

1 C. butter OR ½ C. butter, ½ C. fat
½ C. flour
6 C. chopped onions
3 C. chopped celery
6 green onions with tops, chopped
1 green pepper, chopped
4 cloves garlic, minced
1¼ C. tomato sauce
½ C. chopped parsley
2½ C. water
4 T. Worcestershire sauce
3 bay leaves
1 T. Tabasco sauce
1 T. sugar
1 t. sweet basil
Salt to taste
3 lbs. peeled crawfish tails or shrimp

Make a dark roux with the flour and butter. Add onion, celery, green onions, green pepper and garlic; saute until tender. Add remaining ingredients except crawfish (or shrimp), and simmer for 2—3 hours, adding more water when necessary. Twenty minutes before serving, add crawfish (or shrimp).

SERVES 6—8

Normand Dufilho Wilkinson
(Mrs. Jacques)

SHRIMP DIVINE

½ C. butter
1 C. chopped onions
1 C. chopped bell pepper
1 clove garlic, chopped
1 (10¾ oz.) can tomato soup
1 (10¾ oz.) can cream of
  shrimp soup
1 C. heavy cream
3—4 T. cream sherry
Salt and pepper to taste
1—1½ lbs. cooked shrimp

Sauté onions, bell pepper, and garlic in butter until soft. Add remaining ingredients and heat through. Serve over noodles or rice.

SERVES 4

Mrs. Kurt Borris

SHRIMP ORLEANS

1 T. butter
1 medium onion, sliced
1 clove garlic, crushed
1 (10¾ oz.) can cream of
  mushroom soup
¼ C. tomato catsup
1 (3 oz.) can mushrooms,
  drained
2 C. cooked shrimp
1 C. sour cream

Sauté onion and garlic in butter until tender. Add the soup and catsup; mix well. Add mushrooms and shrimp; heat thoroughly. Just before serving, fold in sour cream and serve on chow mein noodles or rice.

SERVES 8

Linda Ann Black Holliday
(Mrs. Robert E.)

SYLVIA'S SHRIMP AND RICE

1 small pkg. frozen shrimp
  pieces
½ C. chopped onion
½ C. chopped celery
¼ C. butter or margarine
1 (10¾ oz.) can cream of
  shrimp soup
1 C. sour cream
1 C. grated Cheddar cheese
1 t. garlic salt
1 t. pepper

Place shrimp in boiling water according to package directions. Sauté onion and celery in butter. Add soup and sour cream. Add grated cheese to mixture. Stir until all is blended well. Add garlic salt and pepper. (Do not add salt to this recipe.) Drain shrimp and add to mixture. Serve over rice.

SERVES 6

Doris Reeves Collier
(Mrs. John Michael)

SHRIMP CASSEROLE

1 C. chopped onion
1 C. chopped green pepper
1 C. chopped celery
3 cloves garlic, chopped
½ C. margarine
⅓ C. parsley
1 C. green onion tops
1 (4 oz.) can pimiento and juice
3 C. cooked shrimp
1 (10¾ oz.) can cream of mushroom soup
1 (10¾ oz.) can Cheddar cheese soup
½ t. pepper
1 t. salt
2 T. Tabasco (will be HOT, adjust to taste)
2 slices bread, toasted and crumbled
2 C. cooked rice

Cook onion, green pepper, celery, and garlic in margarine. Add parsley, onion tops, pimientos and juice, shrimp and both soups. Mix gently. Add seasonings, stir in toast and rice. Pour into a 3 quart casserole dish, sprinkle with bread crumbs and grated cheese. Bake at 350° for 30 minutes. Can be made ahead of time and frozen or make only a day ahead and refrigerate.

SERVES 12-15

Sally Hoffmann Stevenson
(Mrs. Charles A.)

SUPER SHRIMP CREOLE

½ C. green pepper, chopped fine
1 onion, chopped fine
¼ C. chopped celery
4 buttons garlic, chopped fine
½ C. butter
2 T. flour
2½ C. water
1¼ C. tomato sauce
1 bay leaf
4 drops Tabasco sauce
1 t. salt
1 T. Worcestershire sauce
½ t. pepper
½ t. thyme
2 T. parsley flakes
1 lb. cleaned raw shrimp
1 C. red wine

Sauté green pepper, onions, celery and garlic in butter. Add flour to mixture and brown. Add water and tomato sauce and simmer. Add seasonings and simmer 15 minutes, covered. Add shrimp and wine. Cook until shrimp is done. Serve over buttered rice.

SERVES 6

Jeanie Mikeska Folzenlogen
(Mrs. Paul D.)

BASIC CURRY FOR SEAFOOD OR CHICKEN

½ C. butter
½ C. flour
1 t. salt
1—2 T. curry powder
Cayenne to taste
Dash paprika
3 C. milk
1 C. light cream
2 T. catsup
1 C. cooked, sliced fresh mushrooms
3 C. cooked turkey, chicken or shrimp
1—2 T. Sherry
Rice

Melt butter and blend in flour, salt, curry, cayenne and paprika. Cook until bubbly. Add milk and cream, and cook, stirring occasionally, until thick; stir in catsup, mushrooms, chicken or shrimp and Sherry. Serve over white or wild rice with accompaniments. (See Index)

SERVES 8

Peggy Conner Smead
(Mrs. Hamp P.)

VARIATION I: To basic recipe Add:
½ C. chopped onion
½ C. chopped celery

Sauté onion and celery in butter until tender, then proceed as above.

Muriel Dilworth Deam
(Mrs. J. P.)

SUBSTITUTE:
2½ C. chicken stock (fat removed) for milk
1½ C. tomato juice for light cream
May use lamb or veal
Omit: paprika, catsup, mushrooms and Sherry

VARIATION II: To basic recipe Add:
1 tart apple, cored, peeled and chopped
½ t. ground ginger

Sauté apple with onion and celery until tender and proceed as in Basic Curry.

Claire Smith Foster
(Mrs. Henry L., Jr.)

SUBSTITUTE:
2 C. chicken broth for milk
2 C. heavy cream for light cream
Omit: paprika, catsup and mushrooms

INDIAN EMBASSY CURRY

SAUCE:
4 slices bacon, chopped
¼ C. thinly sliced celery
¼ C. thinly sliced onion
½ garlic clove, chopped
2 T. vegetable oil
¼ C. flour
½ C. applesauce
¼ C. curry powder
3 T. tomato paste
1 T. sugar
1 T. lemon juice
2 chicken bouillon cubes
1¼ C. water
Salt to taste

1 C. heavy cream
Whole cooked shrimp (or cubed meat or poultry)
Steamed rice

Condiments (see index)

In a saucepan, sauté the bacon, celery, onion and garlic in vegetable oil for 10 minutes. Sprinkle with flour and cook the mixture over low heat, stirring frequently for 5 minutes. Add next 8 ingredients and cook covered, over low heat for 45 minutes. If the sauce is not to be used at once, it can be cooled and either refrigerated or frozen. To serve the curry combine 1 cup of sauce with 1 cup cream. Add shrimp, poultry or meat and heat through.

SERVES 4

Eleanor Croxton Lawrence
(Mrs. Thomas W.)

COLD SHRIMP CURRY

2 lbs. shrimp, cooked, cleaned and peeled

SAUCE:
3 C. Hellmann's mayonnaise
2 T. curry powder
1 T. onion juice
¼ t. garlic powder
2 t. Worcestershire sauce
5—6 dashes Tabasco

VARIATION: To above recipe:
Substitute 1 C. sour cream with 2 C. mayonnaise

Add:
1 T. lemon juice
2 t. soy sauce

Combine sauce ingredients and mix with shrimp. Serve with condiments.

Patricia Smith Houston
(Mrs. E. B.)

BROILED SHRIMP STUFFED WITH CRABMEAT

1 lb. jumbo shrimp
¾ C. dried bread crumbs
¼ C. diced onion
¼ C. mushrooms
¼ C. Sauterne wine
Salt and pepper to taste
1 C. fresh crabmeat
1 clove garlic, minced

Peel, devein and split uncooked shrimp. Put bread, onion, and mushrooms through a fine sieve. Add Sauterne and season with salt and pepper. Mix into a fine paste. Shred crabmeat, add to mixture and blend in garlic last. Stuff shrimp. Top each with butter and broil 4-5 minutes to a golden brown.

SERVES 4-6

Martha Pearce Joseph
(Mrs. George)

SHRIMP SUPREME

1 lb. fresh mushrooms
½ C. butter
9 hard boiled eggs
Mayonnaise
Chutney
2 lbs. cooked shrimp
2 C. rich white sauce (made with butter and light cream)
2 C. grated Cheddar cheese, divided

Sauté mushrooms in butter. Spread on bottom of a 3 quart casserole. Devil the eggs with mayonnaise and chutney. Place stuffed halves on top of mushrooms. Place shrimp on top of eggs. Add 1 cup grated cheese to white sauce. Simmer, then pour over shrimp. Spread another cup of cheese over top. Bake at 350° until bubbly, about 30 minutes.

SERVES 6—8

Mrs. Kurt Borris

FLOUNDER STUFFED WITH CRABMEAT

6 T. butter
2 T. chopped green pepper
¼ C. finely chopped green onion
1 C. fresh crabmeat, well picked
1 t. chopped parsley
Salt and freshly ground pepper to taste
1 T. lemon juice
Dash Tabasco
4 (1 lb.) flounders
Seasoned salt

Melt butter in skillet, add green pepper and onion and cook until onion is transparent. Add crabmeat, parsley, salt, pepper, lemon juice, and Tabasco sauce and mix well. Stuff flounders loosely with crab mixture and close with skewers and string. Arrange the fish on a buttered baking pan and sprinkle with seasoned salt. Broil slowly on both sides basting frequently with additional lemon juice and butter until flounder is golden.

SERVES 4

Patricia Smith Houston
(Mrs. E. B.)

SEAFOOD CRÊPE PIE

"Prepare 8 to 10 inch crêpes. See Basic Crêpe Recipe"

FILLING:
4 C. prepared seafood; crab lobster, shrimp or a combination
¼ C. butter
1 clove garlic, pressed
½ C. green onions, minced
½ C. water chestnuts, minced
¼ C. Madeira
1 t. salt
1/8 t. cayenne
½ t. dry mustard
¼ t. nutmeg
½ C. parsley, minced

SAUCE:
4 T. butter
4 T. flour
2 C. fish stock OR clam juice
½ C. milk
1 C. grated Gruyere or mild Swiss, (4 oz.)
1 C. heavy cream
½ t. salt
½ t. seasoned salt
Pinch of garlic powder
Cayenne to taste
¼ t. saffron
1 T. vermouth
1 T. Madeira wine
1 C. remaining seafood
1 T. minced chives

FILLING:
Melt butter, sauté garlic and onions until soft, but not browned. Add water chestnuts and 3 cups seafood. Cook for 2 minutes. Add wine and seasonings; toss over moderate heat until liquid almost evaporates. Stir in parsley and set aside.

SAUCE:
Melt butter for sauce, stir in flour until smooth and gradually add stock. Stir over low heat until thick and smooth. Add milk, cheese, cream, salts, cayenne and garlic powder. Dissolve saffron in vermouth and add with lemon juice and Madeira. Carefully stir in 1 cup remaining seafood and chives. Check for seasonings.

PIE:
Stir ½ cup of sauce into the filling. In a buttered 9" pie plate, layer crêpes and filling, beginning and ending with crêpes. Wrap and store overnight or freeze. Store remaining sauce. If frozen, let thaw 1 hour before baking. Pour 1 cup of sauce over pie and bake 30 minutes in a 350° oven or 1 hour if pie has been frozen. Cut in pie shaped wedges "a table" and pass remaining sauce.

Cotton Country Collection

SEAFOOD NEWBURG

2 T. butter
2 T. flour
¾ t. salt
Dash cayenne pepper
2 C. light cream
4 egg yolks, well beaten
¼ C. Sherry
2 lbs. seafood

Melt butter, stir in flour, salt, and cayenne. Blend well and cook until bubbly. Slowly add cream and cook over low heat until smooth and sauce boils. Stir a little sauce into the eggs, then add to the rest of the sauce. Add Sherry and seafood. Serve with saffron rice.

SERVES 6—8

SAFFRON RICE:
Add ¼ — ½ t. saffron to rice while cooking

Claire Smith Foster
(Mrs. Henry L., Jr.)

DEVILED SEA FOOD
"Prepare the day before"

2 lbs. fresh or frozen fillet of haddock
1 lb. scallops, fresh or frozen
1 lb. shrimp, cooked, shelled and deveined
½ C. butter
9 T. flour
1 C. cream
1½ C. consommé
2 T. cornstarch
A little milk
1 T. lemon juice
1 T. Worcestershire sauce
¼ C. catsup
1 T. horseradish
1 large clove garlic, crushed
1 t. dry mustard
½ t. salt
1 t. soy sauce
2 t. MSG
¼ t. cayenne
¼ C. chopped parsley
¼ C. Sherry
Buttered crumbs

If frozen fish is used, thaw. Place in the top of a greased double boiler and steam for 20 minutes or until done. Cool and cut into bite size pieces. Make a cream sauce using butter, flour, cream, milk and consommé. Cook until thick and add cornstarch blended with a little milk. Cook until no starchy taste remains. Add remaining ingredients except crumbs and correct seasonings. Mix with fish and pour into a greased 3 quart casserole or individual shells. Sprinkle top with crumbs and refrigerate. Before baking, let come to room temperature. Bake at 350° for 30 minutes or until hot throughout.

SERVES 12

Ella Tribble Love Myers
(Mrs. W. R.)

BASS WITH MUSHROOMS AND ALMONDS

1 large or 2 small bass fillets
Juice of 2 lemons
½ C. butter
1 large or 2 small pods garlic, minced
3 C. sliced fresh mushrooms
½ C. toasted almonds

Place fish in pyrex pan, and cover with lemon juice on both sides. Let stand for at least one hour in the refrigerator. Melt butter over heat in a large pan, and add garlic and mushrooms. Sauté just until limp. (Add more butter if the mushrooms absorb too much.) Strain and reserve the butter and add this to the fish in the pyrex pan. Turn and coat fish on both sides. Let stand in the refrigerator until ready to cook. Turn broiler on and let heat with door closed for 5 minutes. Place fish 15" from heat, and leave door propped open. Cook for 15—25 minutes, depending on the thickness of the fish. Baste ocasionally. When done, remove from heat and add mushrooms and almonds, and serve promptly.

Dorothy Robbins Kennedy
(Mrs. George E., Jr.)

BAKED FISH WITH TOMATO SAUCE

4 slices bacon
2 C. chopped onions
1 C. celery, sliced
2 (16 oz.) cans tomatoes
1 T. chopped parsley
1/8 t. thyme
2 bay leaves
Salt and pepper
5 lbs. red fish or red snapper
Seasoned salt and seasoned pepper
Melted butter
Lemon juice
Tabasco

Fry bacon, remove bacon and wilt onions in bacon fat. Add tomatoes, chopping them up with a spoon. Add parsley, thyme, bay leaves, chopped bacon, salt and pepper. Cook until most of the water has cooked out and the sauce is thick. Season fish inside and out with salt and pepper. Pour melted butter, lemon juice, and Tabasco over generously. Cook at 400° for 15 minutes in a preheated oven. Spread with sauce and finish baking at 350° for 15 minutes.

SERVES 6

Linda Ryan Butter
(Mrs. Stephen R.)

STUFFED SALT-WATER FISH

2 fresh fish (flounder, red snapper, red fish, etc.) 2½ lbs. each, deboned
8 T. melted butter, divided
1 medium onion, minced
2 ribs celery, finely chopped
¼ bell pepper, chopped
1 (3 oz.) can mushrooms, chopped
1 doz. fresh shrimp, chopped
½ lb. crabmeat
1 T. Worcestershire sauce
1 small bay leaf
Pinch thyme leaves
¼ lb. browned and chopped almonds
½ C. cream
Bread crumbs
Salt and pepper
Juice of ½ lemon
2 T. cooking oil
3½ oz. Sherry or white wine, divided

Sauté onion, celery and bell pepper in 4 T. butter until soft. Add shrimp and mushrooms with their liquor, sautéeing until shrimp are pink. Add crabmeat, thyme, bay leaf, Worcestershire sauce, almonds, salt and pepper, cream and enough bread crumbs to hold all together; add 3 oz. wine. Stuff fish. Melt 2 T. oil plus 2 T. butter in broiler pan and place fish on top. Broil slowly under a low flame, spooning remaining 2 T. butter and ½ oz. wine over fish to keep it moist. When fish is golden brown it will be cooked through. When served, spoon sauce from pan over fish and sprinkle juice of ½ lemon over it.

Patty Yates Shappell
(Mrs. H. D., Jr.)

CHARCOALED RED SNAPPER FILLETS

2 lbs. red snapper fillets
½ C. oil
¼ C. lemon juice
2 t. salt
½ t. Worcestershire sauce
¼ t. white pepper
Dash liquid hot pepper sauce
Paprika

Cut fillets into serving size portions and place in well-greased, hinged wire grills. Combine remaining ingredients, except paprika. Baste fish with sauce and sprinkle with paprika. Cook about 4 inches from moderately hot coals for 8 minutes. Baste with sauce and sprinkle with paprika. Turn and cook for 7—10 minutes longer or until fish flakes easily when tested with a fork.

SERVES 6

Nancy Ogletree Starr
(Mrs. Larry W.)

BAKED RED SNAPPER IN CREOLE SAUCE

3 lbs. red snapper (or other large fish)
6 T. butter, melted
½ C. chopped onion
2 C. chopped celery
¼ C. chopped bell pepper
3 C. canned tomatoes
1 T. Worcestershire sauce
1 T. catsup
1 t. chili powder
½ finely sliced lemon
2 bay leaves
1 clove garlic, minced
1 t. salt
½ t. red pepper

Dredge fish inside and out with seasoned flour. Sauté onion, celery and bell pepper in butter. Add remaining ingredients and simmer for 15 minutes more. Pour sauce around fish. Bake fish for about 45 minutes, basting frequently with sauce.

Patty Yates Shappell
(Mrs. H. D., Jr.)

FILET OF RED SNAPPER ROQUEFORT

2 lbs. filet of red snapper, cut into 6 portions
Salt and pepper
Juice of 1 lemon
Chopped green onions

SAUCE:
½ C. butter
½ C. Parmesan cheese
¼ C. bread crumbs
2 T. lemon juice
Parsley
1 C. Roquefort salad dressing (See Index)

Sprinkle red snapper filets with salt, pepper and lemon juice. In a shallow pan, place snapper on top of bed of green onions. Pour more lemon juice over filets and broil. When partially cooked, cover each piece with the sauce, return to the broiler and finish cooking.

SAUCE:

Melt on top of stove, butter, Parmesan cheese, bread crumbs, lemon juice and parsley. Combine with Roquefort salad dressing.

Carolyn Smith Russell
(Mrs. Ralph H.)

CORAL GABLES FISH

6 fish fillets
1 C. frozen grapefruit juice, mixed as directed
¼ C. butter or corn oil
Seasoned salt
2 C. mayonnaise
Paprika
Parsley

Marinate fish in grapefruit juice 3 hours. Remove and place in baking pan. Coat with the butter and seasoned salt. Bake at 350° for 30 minutes. Remove and cover fish with mayonnaise and paprika. Broil until golden. Garnish with parsley. Note: A boat captain in Coral Gables gave me this recipe for dolphins. I have also used it for red fish and bass. It is equally good with fresh water fish.

SERVES 6

Ann Chreitzberg Sheppard
(Mrs. Gillett)

TUNA CHEESE CASSEROLE

6 T. butter or margarine
6 T. flour
1 t. salt
3 C. milk
2 C. Velveeta cheese, grated
2 (7 oz.) cans white tuna
3 C. cooked noodles
30 crushed saltine crackers
25 black olives, sliced

Melt butter or margarine in top of double boiler or heavy sauce pan. Add flour and salt and cook until bubbly. Slowly add milk, stirring constantly, and cook until thick and smooth. Add grated cheese and stir over low heat until melted. Remove from heat, add tuna, noodles, olives and most of the cracker crumbs, (reserve some for topping). Pour into a buttered 2 quart casserole, top with remaining cracker crumbs, and dot with butter. Bake at 325° until brown and bubbly.

SERVES 8—10

Katy Hall Painter
(Mrs. Paul)

Poultry & Game

BREAST OF CHICKEN WITH ARTICHOKE HEARTS

6—8 large chicken breasts
1 T. salt
1 t. poultry seasoning
Paprika
½ C. melted butter
1 (10½ oz.) can beef consommé
½ C. Sherry
½ lb. fresh mushrooms
2 (14 oz.) cans artichoke hearts, drained

Place chicken breasts skin side up in roasting pan. Season with salt, poultry seasoning and paprika. Bake at 325° for 1 hour, basting every 20 minutes with melted butter and consommé. Add Sherry to drippings in pan and bake 30 minutes longer. Remove chicken, add mushrooms and artichoke hearts to drippings in pan and heat. Pour over chicken.

SERVES 6—8

Claire Smith Foster
(Mrs. Henry L., Jr.)

CHICKEN BREASTS DELIGHT

4 whole chicken breasts split, skinned and boned
Salt and pepper to taste
Flour
¼ C. oil
¾ C. Sauterne wine
1 (10¾ oz.) can cream of chicken soup
1 (8 oz.) can water chestnuts, drained and sliced
1 (3 oz.) can sliced mushrooms, drained
2 T. chopped green pepper
¼ t. thyme

Roll chicken in seasoned flour and brown lightly in oil. Place chicken in 3 qt. baking dish. Add Sauterne to drippings. Add remaining ingredients and simmer for 2 minutes. Pour over chicken. Bake covered at 350° for 45 minutes. Uncover. Bake until tender.

SERVES 8

Barbara Hubbard Tomberlain
(Mrs. Charles)

GARLIC BAKED CHICKEN

6—8 chicken breasts
½ C. softened margarine
4 T. flour
1 pkg. Good Season's Garlic Salad Dressing Mix
2 T. lemon juice
½ t. salt

Remove skin from chicken. Wash and dry. Arrange in a baking dish bones down. Mix margarine, flour, salad mix, lemon juice and salt to a spreadable paste. Add more lemon juice if necessary. "Ice" the chicken with paste. Bake at 350° until brown and done. DO NOT COVER.

SERVES 6

Marilyn Rouse Payne
(Mrs. Hermes E.)

TWO SAUCE CHICKEN

6 chicken breasts
Garlic salt
Seasoning salt
Fresh ground black pepper
½ C. butter
3 green onions, chopped
⅔ C. red wine
½ C. Hollandaise sauce (See Index)

Highly season chicken with all seasonings on both sides. Brown in butter over medium heat until golden brown. Add onions, tops and all, and wine. Cover and simmer about 45 minutes. Remove chicken to serving platter. Remove pan from heat. Add Hollandaise to pan and combine with pan juices on low heat; let boil up very gently one time. Stir constantly so as to combine well and pour over chicken. May be prepared ahead except for Hollandaise—chicken may be reheated and Hollandaise added then. No additional salt is needed. This is very rich.

SERVES 6

Eleanor Croxton Lawrence
(Mrs. Thomas W.)

EAST—WEST CHICKEN

3 T. flour
Salt and pepper
3 lbs. fryer parts (or 8 chicken breasts)
2 T. butter
6 slices bacon, cooked and crumbled
½ C. chopped onion
1 clove garlic, chopped
2 t. curry powder
1½ T. flour
1 (10¾ oz.) can chicken broth
2 T. lemon juice
1 t. sugar
1 (2¼ oz.) can sliced ripe olives, drained

Mix 3 T. flour, salt and pepper. Lightly coat chicken pieces and place skin side up in a 9" x 13" pyrex dish. Dot with pats of butter. Bake for 20 minutes at 450° until browned. Cook bacon and drain. Brown onion, garlic, and curry powder in 1½ T. bacon drippings (from cooked bacon) until soft. Stir in 1½ T. flour. Add chicken broth and cook, stirring until thickened. Stir in remaining ingredients. Cook gently for 5 minutes. Spoon over the browned chicken. Reduce oven temperature to 350° and bake 30 minutes longer or until the chicken is tender. Serve with tiny buttered noodles or with rice.

SERVES 6 (or 8 for bridge with chicken breasts).

Martha Hess Whitehead
(Mrs. R. Laughton, Jr.)

CHICKEN IN WINE

8 chicken breasts, skinned
Seasoned salt, seasoned pepper and garlic salt
½ C. margarine
2 C. Sauterne Wine, divided
2 (10¾ oz.) cans cream of mushroom soup
1 pkg. Italian salad dressing mix
2 (3 oz.) pkgs. cream cheese softened

RICE:
4¼ C. water
3 T. chives
1 pkg. Italian salad dressing mix
2 C. rice

Season chicken breasts with seasoned salt, pepper and garlic salt. Brown in margarine in heavy skillet. Pour 1 cup of the wine over chicken. Set aside. Mix soup, 1 pkg. salad dressing mix, cream cheese and remaining wine. Stir well and let stand until room temperature. Heat oven to 350°. Place chicken breasts and wine in shallow baking dish. Pour soup mixture over chicken. Bake uncovered for 1 hour.

RICE:
Bring salted water to a boil. Add chives, 1 pkg. salad dressing mix and rice. Stir. Reduce heat to low and cover tightly. Cook approximately 20 minutes or until rice is done. Serve chicken with rice.

SERVES 8

Mrs. Henry Cooksey,
Olla, La.

Donor: Betty Cooksey Nethery
(Mrs. Tom)

FRENCH STYLE CHICKEN

1 fryer, cut up
4 T. butter
½ C. flour
2 t. salt
¼ t. pepper
¼ t. thyme
1 (3 oz.) can mushrooms, drained
4 green onions, chopped
2 T. lemon juice
⅓ C. apple juice
1½ t. sugar
1 t. salt
2 canned or fresh tomatoes, diced

Melt butter in large skillet. Mix flour, salt, pepper and thyme in bag. Add chicken and shake until each piece is coated. Brown in butter. Add mushrooms and onions and cover. Simmer 3 minutes. Mix fruit juices, sugar and salt. Add to chicken and simmer 5 minutes, covered. Add tomatoes and cover. Simmer 1 hour.

SERVES 4

Nancy Jordan Wright
(Mrs. Fletcher)

FRUITED CHICKEN

6—8 pieces chicken (breast, leg, thighs)
⅓ C. flour
1½ t. salt
½ t. paprika
1 t. curry powder
4 T. oil
1 C. dry white wine
6—8 orange segments
1 C. pitted bing cherries
6—8 pineapple spears
1 avocado, cut in crescents
Sprigs of mint

Shake chicken pieces in paper bag with flour, salt paprika and curry powder. Brown gently on all sides in oil. Remove to a large baking dish. Add wine, cover and bake at 375° for 20 minutes. Remove from oven and arrange orange segments, cherries and pineapple spears over chicken. Return to oven and bake uncovered 20—25 minutes. Garnish with avocado and mint.

SERVES 6—8

Linda Ann Black Holliday
(Mrs. Robert E.)

CHICKEN WITH SHRIMP

2 frying chickens, cut in serving pieces
Flour
¼ C. butter
3 large onions, chopped
2 cloves garlic, crushed
2 (8 oz.) cans tomato sauce
1 C. Burgundy wine
1 T. chopped parsley
1 T. orégano
1 T. basil
1 T. salt
¼ t. pepper
1 lb. raw shrimp, cleaned and deveined

Dust chicken pieces with flour, and sauté in a large skillet until golden. Remove from pan. In the same skillet, cook onion and garlic stirring frequently until onions are tender but not brown. Stir in tomato paste and all other ingredients except shrimp. Return the chicken to the pan, cover, and cook over low heat for about 45 minutes or until tender. Transfer the chicken to a warm platter. Bring the sauce to a boil and add the shrimp. Cook over moderate heat until they turn pink. Pour sauce over chicken and serve over hot steamed rice. May be prepared ahead, adding shrimp when it is reheated.

SERVES 6—8

Ann Chreitzberg Sheppard
(Mrs. Gillett)

LOUISIANA CHICKEN

8 chicken halves
1 T. red pepper
Salt to taste
¾ lb. margarine
6 oz. (or less) Evangeline sauce, to taste
3 cloves garlic, pressed
2 T. sugar
4 T. Worcestershire sauce
¼ C. vinegar
1 T. black pepper
2 C. water

Sprinkle chicken with red pepper and salt; let stand for a while. Combine remaining ingredients to make sauce and simmer for 10 minutes. Cook chicken slowly over a charcoal fire and baste with sauce.

Forrest Gaumer Martin
(Mrs. J. C., Jr.)

LEMON BAR—B—Q CHICKEN

1 fryer, cut up
¼ C. butter
Flour
Salt and pepper
Paprika

LEMON SAUCE:
1 clove garlic, crushed
½ C. lemon juice
2 t. chopped onion
½ t. pepper
½ t. thyme

Dip chicken in flour and season with salt, pepper and paprika. Preheat oven to 400°. Melt butter in baking dish and turn each piece in melted butter. Place skin side down and bake 30 minutes. Turn chicken and pour LEMON SAUCE over. Cook 30 minutes longer.

SERVES 4

Susie Moore French
(Mrs. Paul E.)

CHICKEN CACCIATORE

Olive oil
1 fryer, cut into serving pieces
1 C. chopped onion
½ C. chopped green pepper
2 cloves garlic, minced
1 (16 oz.) can stewed tomatoes
1 (8 oz.) can tomato sauce
3 t. salt
½ t. pepper
½ t. allspice
2 bay leaves
½ t. thyme
½ C. red wine

Brown chicken pieces in olive oil. Remove and fry onions, green pepper, garlic. Add remaining ingredients. Simmer chicken in sauce 45 minutes. Serve over buttered spaghetti sprinkled with parmesan cheese.

SERVES 4—6

Betty Cooksey Nethery
(Mrs. Tom)

COQ AU VIN FLAMBÉ

2 broiler fryers, cut in pieces
Flour for dredging
½ C. butter
1 slice raw ham, chopped
10 small white onions, peeled and left whole
1 clove garlic, finely chopped
¼ t. thyme
1 sprig parsley
1 bay leaf
8 whole mushrooms
Salt and freshly ground pepper
2 oz. cognac, warmed
1 C. dry red wine

Preheat oven to 300°. Dredge chicken with flour. In a skillet, heat the butter, add the chicken and brown. Transfer the chicken to an earthenware casserole, and add the ham, onions, garlic, thyme, parsley, bay leaf, mushrooms, salt and pepper. Pour the heated cognac over and ignite. When flame dies, add the wine. Cover and bake until the chicken is tender, about 2½ hours.

SERVES 10

Claire Smith Foster
(Mrs. Henry L., Jr.)

COQ AU VIN

1—3 lb. chicken, cut into 8 pieces, washed and well dried
3—4 T. cooking oil
Salt and pepper
1 medium onion, diced
¼ C. sifted flour
3 C. red wine
1½—2 C. beef stock or bouillon, divided
2—3 shallots, chopped
3—4 cloves garlic, chopped
1 t. (heaping) tomato paste
1 bouquet garnish (parsley, thyme, bay leaf and celery)
24 baby onions
½ lb. mushrooms, quartered and sautéed in butter
⅓—½ lb. smoked bacon, cut into ½" pieces
Parsley

Season chicken on both sides and brown in oil (skin side down first) in large casserole. Add diced onion and brown. Sprinkle flour over chicken and onion. Shake pan and turn chicken so that flour will mix with the fat and brown. Add wine and half of the bouillon; stir well with wooden spatula. If the sauce is too thick, add the other half of the stock to thin. Add shallots, garlic, tomato paste, and bouquet garni. Adjust seasonings. Cover and simmer in 350° oven or on the stove for 30 minutes. Blanch bacon. (To blanch, bring bacon to a boil in cold water, drain; pour cold water over and drain again.) Boil baby onions until tender. Drain and glaze with a little sugar. Sauté bacon in the pan the onions were glazed in. Take chicken out and keep warm. Strain sauce and degrease. Return chicken to the pan and add onions, mushrooms and bacon and heat with chicken in strained sauce. To serve, place chicken on platter; spoon sauce and garniture over it and sprinkle with parsley.

SERVES 4—6

Mrs. Sam Mack

CHINESE CHICKEN

½ C. butter or margarine
1 fryer, cut into pieces OR 4 chicken breast, halves

SAUCE:
1 rounded T. cornstarch
½ C. sugar
½ t. ginger
½ t. Accent
1 t. salt
1 T. water
¼ C. vinegar
¼ C. soy sauce
1 can pineapple tidbits and juice

Melt butter in baking pan large enough to hold amount of chicken used. Roll chicken pieces in melted butter and lay pieces flat in pan. Place in 450° oven and bake until golden brown.

SAUCE

Mix first 5 ingredients in saucepan, add liquids including juice from pineapple and cook until clear and thickened. Pour over browned chicken. Turn oven to 350° and bake 25-30 minutes until chicken is tender. Add pineapple last 5 minutes.

SERVES 4

Marcia Burlison McDaniel
(Mrs. Stephen W.)

CHICKEN MOONGATE

4—6 whole chicken breasts, cut into 2" strips
Flour
Butter
1" piece fresh ginger, thinly sliced
½ C. water
¼ C. brown sugar
3 T. cornstarch
¼ C. vinegar
2—3 T. soy sauce
½ t. salt
2½ C. pineapple chunks
1 green pepper, cut in strips
1 onion, thinly sliced
¾ C. blanched almonds
1 C. fresh mushrooms, sliced
½ pkg. snow peas

Dredge chicken in flour and brown in small amount of butter. Add ginger and stir in water. Cover and simmer until tender, about 30 minutes. Remove ginger. Drain pineapple and reserve syrup. Combine sugar, cornstarch, syrup, vinegar, soy sauce and salt. Add to chicken; cook and stir until gravy thickens. Add pineapple, green pepper, onion, mushrooms, nuts and snow peas. Cook 3-5 minutes. Serve over hot rice. Pass extra soy sauce.

SERVES 6—8

Helen May Little
(Mrs. Earle E., Jr.)

SWEET AND SOUR CHICKEN

2½ lb. fryer, cut up
1 t. garlic salt
1/8 t. pepper
1 ¾ C. boiling water
2 T. cornstarch
¼ C. sugar
1 C. pineapple chunks
⅓ C. raisins
¼ C. vinegar
3 T. soy sauce
1 green pepper, cut in strips

Cook first four ingredients covered about 40 minutes or until chicken is tender. Save broth, remove meat from bones and cut in bite size pieces, put into 1 ¼ C. broth (retain remainder of broth for cooking rice). Mix cornstarch and sugar thoroughly and stir into chicken. Add remaining ingredients and cook uncovered until broth is clear and thickened, stirring as needed to prevent sticking. Serve over rice or chinese noodles.

SERVES 4—6

Carolyn Council Seale
(Mrs. Fred)

CHICKEN BREASTS WITH BACON

8 chicken breasts halves, boned and skinned
8 slices bacon
1 (2½ oz.) jar dried beef, cut up
1 C. sour cream
1 (10 ¾ oz.) can cream of mushroom soup
¼ C. vermouth

Wrap each chicken breast in bacon. Place in a greased casserole. Combine remaining ingredients and pour over chicken. Bake at 300° for 2 hours. May be prepared ahead of time.

SERVES 8

Susie Moore French
(Mrs. Paul E.)

CHICKEN SPAGHETTI SAUCE

1 (3 lb.) hen, cooked in seasoned water
4 C. chicken stock
2 C. onion, chopped
1 (8 oz.) can mushrooms, drained
¼ C. garlic, chopped fine
2 (6 oz.) cans tomato paste
cayenne
Paprika
Tabasco sauce
Salt to taste
Flour and water to thicken

Bone chicken and cut into bite-sized pieces. Simmer onion, garlic, tomato paste, cayenne, paprika, Tabasco and salt in stock until tender. Add chicken and mushrooms. Thicken with flour and water. Serve over spaghetti.

SERVES 6

Gladys Olvey Sample
(Mrs. Clark)

CREAMY CHICKEN SPAGHETTI

2 large fryers OR 1 fryer and 2 whole breasts
1 each bay leaf, carrot and onion
3 medium onions, chopped
2 garlic cloves, minced
Olive oil
1 (7 oz.) jar pimientos
2 (8 oz.) cans sliced mushrooms
1 small can evaporated milk
2 (8 oz.) cans tomato sauce
8 strips bacon, fried and crumbled
1 lb. extra sharp cheese, grated
2½ (10 oz.) pkgs. vermicelli, cooked in chicken broth and drained

Cook chicken until tender in water with bay leaf, celery, carrot and onion added. Reserve broth. Cool chicken and cut into bite size pieces. Brown onions and garlic in olive oil. Stir all ingredients together and put in large casserole. Bake at 350° until bubbly.

SERVES 12

Mrs. Shipton Pickens
Little Rock, Ark.

Donor: Rose Pickens Kirkpatrick
(Mrs. Kenneth L.)

CHICKEN SPAGHETTI

"Serve with tossed green salad and toasted English mufffins"

1 large hen OR 2 fryers
3 qts. broth
2 C. finely chopped celery
2 C. finely chopped onions
2 C. finely chopped green pepper
2 (12 oz.) pkgs. spaghetti
8 t. chili powder
1 (3 oz.) can mushrooms
1 (20 oz.) can tomatoes
3 cloves garlic, chopped fine
Salt and pepper to taste
Tomato juice to thin (if necessary)
½ lb. American cheese, grated
½ lb. cheddar cheese, grated

Cook hen in enough water to make about 3 quarts of broth. Take chicken off bone and set aside. Add celery, onions green pepper and spaghetti to boiling broth. When tender, add chili powder, mushrooms, tomatoes, garlic, salt and pepper. (May add tomato juice if mixture seems too dry.) Add chicken. Put in 3 quart baking dish and cover with grated cheese. Bake, covered, at 350° for 20 minutes. Freezes well.

SERVES 10—12

Barbara Glover Baucum
(Mrs. Joseph B.)

OLD-FASHIONED CHICKEN PIE

PASTRY:
- 1¼ C. flour
- 4 T. shortening
- 2 T. butter, chilled and cut in ¼ inch pieces
- 1/8 t. salt
- 3 T. ice water

FILLING:
- 1—5 lb. roasting chicken
- 4 qts. chicken stock
- ½ t. salt
- ½ t. pepper
- 12—16 small white onions, chopped
- 4 large carrots, scraped and sliced in ½" thick rounds
- 1 C. small English peas
- 1 C. celery, scraped and diced in 1" pieces
- ¼ t. onion salt
- ¼ t. celery salt
- ¼ t. seasoning salt
- 1 t. sage
- 1 t. poultry seasoning
- 1 C. butter
- 1 C. flour
- ½ C. heavy cream
- 1 T. melted butter

PASTRY:
In a large mixing bowl, combine and work pastry ingredients into a compact ball. Dust lightly with flour, wrap in wax paper and chill for at least ½ hour. Roll the dough on a lightly floured surface into a rectangle about 10" x 14".

FILLING:
Place the chicken in an 8 quart soup pot and cover it with the chicken stock. Add salt and pepper and bring to a boil over high heat. Skim off the broth. Simmer the chicken until tender but not falling apart (about 1½ hours). Remove the chicken and set aside to cool. Add vegetables to the stock, and simmer, covered, about 20 minutes or until vegetables can be easily pierced with a fork. Stir in seasonings. Remove vegetables with a slotted spoon to a small bowl. Remove the skin from chicken, cut the meat away from the bones, and cut into 1½" chunks. In a small saucepan, melt the butter over moderate heat. Take off the heat, stir in flour and mix until smooth. Skim the fat from the stock and pour 5 cups of stock into the saucepan in a slow stream stirring with a wire wisk. Return the pan to moderate heat and cook, whisking, until the sauce is smooth and thick. Stir in cream and taste for seasoning. Preheat the oven to 375°. Pour the sauce into a 3 quart casserole. Add the chicken and vegetables and spread them out evenly. Drape the pastry over the top of the pan. Crimp the pastry around the sides to seal and secure it. Brush with melted butter. Make two small slits in the pastry to allow the steam to escape. Bake the pie in the middle of the oven for about 45 minutes, or until the crust is golden brown.

SERVES 8—10

Ongie W. Thompson

Donor: Rose Pickens Kirkpatrick
   (Mrs. Kenneth L.)

BILLIE BUTTER'S CHICKEN TETRAZZINI

2½ lb. chicken, cut up
2¼ C. boiling water
1 bay leaf
1 T. celery leaves
1 onion
2 whole cloves
½ t. salt
½ t. pepper

SAUCE:
1½ T. chicken fat or butter
2 T. flour
½ t. paprika
½ t. salt
Few grains pepper
⅔ C. broth
1 C. evaporated milk
1¼ C. grated American cheese
2 T. Sherry
3 C. cooked spaghetti
¾ C. canned mushrooms

Put chicken in kettle and add all seasonings. Cover and boil gently 1¼ hours or until tender. Leave chicken in the broth until cool. Dice.

SAUCE:
Melt fat in sauce pan, stir in flour. Add seasonings and stir in broth and cook until it thickens, stirring constantly. Blend in milk and ¾ cup cheese and cook slowly until cheese melts. Add Sherry. Divide sauce in two portions and add spaghetti and mushrooms. Place in greased baking dish. Make a hollow in center to form nest. Add remaining sauce to chicken and pour in to center of nest. Sprinkle top with ½ cup cheese and bake at 350° for 20 minutes.

SERVES 4

Linda Ryan Butter
(Mrs. Stephen R.)

SWISS ENCHILADAS

1 onion, chopped
2 T. oil
1 clove garlic, crushed
1 (8 oz.) can tomato sauce
1 (4 oz.) can green chilies, drained and chopped
2 C. cooked, chopped chicken
Salt, pepper and Cavender's seasoning
1 C. sour cream
1 C. chicken broth
1 C. cream
1 doz. flour tortillas
½ lb. grated Monterey Jack or Swiss cheese

Sauté onion in oil. Add garlic, tomato sauce, green chilies, chicken, salt, pepper and Cavender's seasoning to taste. Mix sour cream, chicken broth and cream. Dip tortillas in cream sauce. Spoon chicken mixture on tortilla, roll and place in baking dish. Pour cream sauce over enchiladas. Top with grated cheese. Bake at 350° for 30 minutes covered with foil. Remove foil to brown. Garnish with avocado slices or ripe olives.

SERVES 6—8

Marilyn Rouse Payne
(Mrs. Hermes E.)

CHICKEN ENCHILADAS

4½—5 lb. hen
5 onions
2 bay leaves
Salt and pepper
¼ C. butter
1 large onion, sautéed in butter
2—3 cans green chilies, drained
2 pints sour cream
1 pkg. frozen chopped spinach, cooked and drained
24 soft tortillas
½ lb. Monterey Jack cheese, grated

Cook chicken with onions, bay leaves, salt and pepper. Reserve broth. Remove meat from bones and cut into large chunks. Sauté onions in butter. Put green chilies through blender. Mix these with the sour cream, onions, and chopped spinach. Dip each tortilla in broth until limp. Fill each tortilla with a spoonful of chicken and a large T. of sauce. Roll and put in 9" x 13" baking dishes seamside down. Pour remaining sauce over tortillas and top with grated cheese. Bake at 350° for 20—30 minutes. These may be prepared ahead and may be frozen.

SERVES 12

Susie Moore French
(Mrs. Paul E.)

CHICKEN TOMATO CRÊPES

3 C. cooked chicken, chopped coarsely
1 C. peeled fresh tomato, cut in strips
¾ C. heavy cream
1 C. grated Gruyere cheese
Salt and pepper to taste

SAUCE:
6 T. butter
6 T. flour
1 t. salt
2 C. chicken stock
2 C. milk
3 egg yolks
¾ C. heavy cream
¾ C. grated Swiss or Gruyere cheese

SAUCE:
Melt butter. Add flour and salt. Cook until bubbly. Add liquid. Cook until sauce begins to thicken. Set aside. Beat egg yolks and cream together. Add hot sauce by the spoonfull to egg mixture. Correct seasoning.

TO ASSEMBLE:
Put 1 T. of chicken on each crêpe and roll. Place in a buttered shallow pan. Cover with sauce and sprinkle grated cheese overall. Bake at 325° for 20 minutes, then run under the broiler until bubbly.

YIELD: Filling for 12 crêpes

Patricia Smith Houston
(Mrs. E. B.)

TOMATO CHICKEN

1 small onion, chopped
½ green pepper, chopped
1 clove garlic, chopped
½ C. margarine
1 T. flour
1 (15 oz.) can Hunt's tomato sauce with tomato bits and peppers
1 C. chicken broth
3 C. chicken, chopped
1 C. toasted almonds
1 (8 oz.) can sliced mushrooms
Salt and pepper to taste

Sauté onion, green pepper and garlic in margarine until tender. Add flour and cook slightly. Add tomato sauce and chicken broth and cook until thickened. Add chicken, almonds, mushrooms, salt and pepper; heat thoroughly. Serve over fluffy rice.

SERVES 4—6

Reva Harrison Ryan
(Mrs. A. B.)

CAJUN CHICKEN CASSEROLE

2 fryers
1 C. water
1 C. Sherry
1½ t. salt
½ t. curry powder
½ C. diced celery
1 onion, chopped
½ lb. mushrooms (canned or fresh)
¼ C. margarine
2 (6 oz.) pkgs. wild rice
1 C. sour cream
1 (10¾ oz.) can cream of mushroom soup
1 pint oysters, optional

Boil fryers in water, sherry, salt, curry powder, celery and onion. Debone chicken. Reserve broth. Sauté mushrooms in margarine. Prepare rice according to package directions using reserved broth as liquid. Combine chicken, rice, mushrooms, sour cream and soup. Refrigerate overnight. Bake at 350° in a large casserole dish for 1 hour. This may be prepared ahead or frozen.

SERVES 6—8 (or more)

Note: Simmer oysters in juices until edges curl. Drain and chop. Add to above.

Mrs Henry Cooksey,
  Olla, La.

Donor: Betty Cooksey Nethery
(Mrs. Tom)

CHICKEN AND WILD RICE CASSEROLE

1 pkg. Uncle Ben's Wild Rice Mix, cooked
3 C. cooked chopped chicken
¼ C. pimiento, chopped
2 T. parsley
1½ t. salt
¼ t. pepper
½ C. chopped onions
1 (6 oz.) can mushrooms, drain and reserve liquid
½ C. butter
¼ C. flour
1½ C. light cream
½ C. slivered almonds

Prepare rice according to package directions. Combine chicken, pimiento, parsley and seasonings and set aside. Sauté onions and mushrooms in butter until tender. Add mushroom liquid and enough chicken broth to make 1½ cups and slowly stir into flour mixture. Add cream and cook until thickened. Add rice, vegetables and chicken mixture. Pour into a greased 2 quart casserole, sprinkle with almonds. Bake at 350° for 25—30 minutes.

SERVES 6—8

Judy Fite Shiver
(Mrs. John D.)

VARIATION: Add:
1 C. celery or water chestnuts, sauteed
½ C. white wine
1 C. sliced fresh mushrooms, sauteed (instead of canned)

CHICKEN HASH
"Serve over Mexican cornbread for brunch"

1 large hen, cooked, boned and chopped
6 C. chicken broth, well seasoned
2 green peppers, chopped
4 garlic cloves, chopped
2 C. celery, chopped
2 large onions, chopped
4 pimientos, chopped
4 (8 oz.) cans water chestnuts, chopped
4 t. chopped parsley
4 (10¾ oz.) cans cream of mushroom soup
1½ t. Worcestershire sauce
¼ C. white wine
½ t. cracked black pepper

Add peppers, garlic, celery, onions and pimientos to chicken broth and cook until tender. Add chicken and the rest of the ingredients and simmer for 30 minutes. If the mixture is too thin, add more soup; if too thick, add more broth. Serve over chinese noodles.

SERVES 25

Ann Lacy Crain
(Mrs. B. W., Jr.)

CHICKEN D'WANGO

1 chicken
½ C. margarine
1 onion, chopped
1 C. chopped celery
1 C. chopped bell pepper
1 C. mushrooms, chopped
1 C. pimiento, chopped
2 C. chicken broth
1 (10¾ oz.) can cream of
   mushroom soup
½ lb. American cheese (or
   more)
Juice of 1 lemon
1 large pkg. spinach noodles

Cook chicken. Remove and cut in bite size pieces. Reserve stock. Melt margarine and saute onion, celery, bell pepper, mushrooms and pimiento. Add 2 C. chicken broth, soup, cheese and lemon juice. Simmer sauce until it thickens. Add cut up chicken. Cook noodles in broth or water. Layer noodles and chicken mixture. Bake at 350° for 35 minutes. Freezes well.

SERVES 6

Mrs. O. B. Canon

COLD CHICKEN SOUFFLÉ

2 envelopes unflavored
   gelatine
½ C. cold water
2 (10¾ oz.) cans cream of
   chicken soup
2 T. curry powder
6 C. cooked chicken chunks
   (8 large chicken breasts)
Seasoned salt and pepper to
   taste
2 C. heavy cream, whipped
Toasted sesame seeds
½ C. cooked chicken slivers
Chutney

DAY BEFORE:
In a large bowl, sprinkle gelatine over cold water; set aside to soften. In saucepan, prepare soup as label directs. Add curry powder. Pour hot soup over gelatine. Stir until gelatine dissolves. Sprinkle chicken chunks with salt and pepper. Add to soup. Chill until mixture thickens, (slightly). Make a collar by folding a 30" piece of foil in half lengthwise. Grease lightly. Wrap collar around outside of greased 1½ quart soufflé dish and secure with tape. Fold whipped cream into cooled chicken mixture, pour into soufflé dish and refrigerate.

AT SERVING TIME:
With metal spatula, loosen foil collar from soufflé; remove. Sprinkle with Sesame seeds. Garnish with chicken slivers. Serve with chutney.

SERVES 8—10

Mrs. Marjorie Marberry Loper

Donor: Susanne Sandberg Northcutt
   (Mrs W. D., III)

CASSEROLE OF CHICKEN

2 (3½ —4 lb.) chickens
1½ t. salt
1 t. MSG
3 stalks celery with leaves
1 carrot
1 large clove garlic
Parsley, several sprigs
Water to cover
1½ lbs. fresh mushrooms
Butter for sautéeing
4 T. butter
5 T. flour
4 C. chicken broth
½ C. heavy cream
1 t. dried sweet basil
¼ t. cayenne pepper
½ t. black pepper
4 egg yolks, well beaten
½ C. Maderia or Sherry wine (optional)

Combine first eight ingredients and cook slowly until chicken is tender. Remove chicken. Strain broth and set aside in a cool place to allow fat to rise to top. Bone chicken and cut in bite-size pieces. Sauté mushrooms in butter until tender; remove from pan. Make cream sauce from the 4 T. butter, flour, broth and cream. When sauce is quite thick, remove from fire and add seasonings and egg yolks. If desired, add wine. Mix sauce with chicken and mushrooms and pour into a 3 quart casserole. Bake at 350° for 30 minutes. This may be prepared ahead and refrigerated. Allow to reach room temperature before baking. Arrange grilled toast points around casserole and serve with white or wild rice.

SERVES 12

Ella Tribble Love Myers
(Mrs. W. R.)

CURRIED CHICKEN CASSEROLE

1 large fryer, cooked, boned, cut up
2 T. butter
1 medium onion, sliced
1 (4 oz.) can mushrooms, drained
1 (8 oz.) can water chestnuts, sliced
¼ C. chopped parsley
1½ t. seasoned salt
Pepper
Pinch of basil
1½ t. curry powder
1 C. sour cream
1 (10¾ oz.) can cream of chicken soup
Canned biscuits
Paprika

Boil chicken in seasoned water until tender. Cut in bite size pieces. Sauté onion in butter. Combine all ingredients except biscuits and paprika. Place in a casserole, and top with canned bisquits. Sprinkle with paprika. Bake at 350° for 30 minutes.

SERVES 4-6.

Susie Moore French
(Mrs. Paul E.)

SAUCE PIQUANTE

2 T. flour
2 T. cooking oil
2 onions, chopped
¼ C. chopped ham
Chicken breasts and thighs (4 lbs.)
1 (6 oz.) can tomato paste
½ can water
3 pods garlic, crushed
3 ribs celery, chopped
¼ C. parsley, chopped
3—4 green onions, chopped
15 green olives, sliced
1 sour pickle, chopped fine
Rind of 1 lemon, grated
1 pt. mushrooms (canned) and juice
Salt and pepper to taste
1½ C. Sauterne wine
2 doz. oysters

In heavy iron dutch oven, make roux by browning flour in shortening until dark brown. Add onions and cook until tender. Add ham and chicken. Cook slowly with lid on for 30—45 minutes. Remove chicken, and debone, and remove skin. Return chicken to pot. Add tomato paste and water. Cook 45 minutes. Add garlic, celery, parsley, and green onions. Cook 45 minutes longer. Add olives, sour pickle, and lemon rind. Cook 45 minutes longer. Add mushrooms and juice. Cook 45 minutes longer. Salt, black and red pepper may be added at any time. The entire cooking period cover 4—5 hours. Use a deep iron pot or dutch oven with the lid on during the entire cooking time. At no time should the mixture boil, but rather simmer slowly. Stir only enough to prevent sticking. About 30 minutes before serving add Sauterne. Add oysters and juice 20 minutes before serving. If desired, may be thickened with paste of flour and water. Serve over rice. Serves 6—8 generously. **Note:** In my opinion, this is Creole cuisine at its best. Serve with individual salads of asparagus, artichoke hearts, boiled eggs, and mayonnaise (home-made is best), and hot French bread. When one make this the first time, one feels one has to wear the recipe pinned to one's breast or glued to one's nose for fear of missing one ingredient or step, but the results are well worth the effort! Better if allowed to set and season in refrigerator for a day.

Betty Cooksey Nethery
(Mrs. Tom)

CHICKEN 'N PEPPERS

1 t. oil (or so)
1 clove garlic, minced
1 pinch orégano
4 large boneless chicken breast
Flour
2 (15½ oz.) jars Ragu Marinara Sauce
2 (3 oz.) cans mushrooms
1 (16 oz.) jar sweet peppers
Salt and pepper to taste

Heat oil in a skillet. Add garlic, orégano and chicken which has been dusted with flour. Sauté until done and tender, but **not brown**. Add remaining ingredients and simmer for 1 hour. Serve over rice.

SERVES 6

Patricia Dooley Flatt
(Mrs. Doyle Edwin)

PHEASANT MADEIRA

2 pheasants, cut into fourths
Salt to taste
Pepper to taste
½ C. butter
15 small onions, glazed in butter with 1 t. sugar
1 (8 oz.) can undrained mushrooms
1 C. Madeira wine
1 egg yolk, beaten

Salt and pepper pheasant and brown in butter. Add glazed onions and mushrooms. Add wine to pan onions were cooked in and stir for a minute or two, then add to pheasant. Cover and continue to cook slowly until tender. Add egg yolk to pan juices to thicken.

SERVES 6—8

Reva Harrison Ryan
(Mrs. A. B.)

TURKEY AND OYSTERS IN CREAM SAUCE

3 C. cooked turkey, cut into chunks
1 pt. oysters, drained; reserve liquid
6 T. butter
6 T. flour
3 C. rich milk
1 (2¼ oz.) can deviled ham
Chicken Broth Seasoning

Make a cream sauce by melting butter, stir in flour and cook a few minutes. Pour in milk and cook and stir until thick and smooth. Blend ham into sauce. Add turkey and oysters and liquid. Season with Chicken Broth Seasoning. Heat thoroughly. Serve in patty shells or over cornbread, biscuits or muffins.

SERVES 8

Linda Ryan Butter
(Mrs. Stephen R.)

BAKED DUCK IN ORANGE SAUCE

1 duck
Celery leaves
1 onion
Water to cover
Salt
1 small jar tart jelly
10 oz. orange juice

Parboil duck with celery leaves and onion for 20 minutes. Remove from water, salt and place in a covered roasting pan. Mix jelly and juice together and pour over duck. Baste often for 1 hour. When done, slice and let soak in pan juices in warm oven until ready to serve.

Virginia Elms McRee
(Mrs. J. T.) Dallas, Texas

CROCK POT QUAIL WITH WHITE WINE

12 quail
½ C. butter or margarine
2 C. sliced fresh mushrooms
½ C. chopped green onions
1 C. dry white wine
1 (10¾ oz.) can cream of chicken soup
2 T. lemon juice
Salt and pepper to taste
Cooked wild rice

Brown quail in butter; remove and set aside. Sauté mushrooms and onions in butter. Place quail, mushrooms, and onion in Crock Pot and add wine mixed with chicken soup, lemon juice, salt and pepper. Cook on high 5—6 hours. (OR place in baking dish and bake at 350° for 1½ hours.) Serve with wild rice.

Kathryn Anderson Reagan
(Mrs. Bill)

TURKEY CREME

1 small onion, chopped
4 T. butter
3 T. flour
½ C. turkey stock
½ C. white wine
½ t. salt
¼ t. white pepper
Sliced turkey or chicken
2 C. cooked and drained spinach, chopped
Salt and pepper
1 can mushroom caps, drained
Parmesan cheese

Sauté onion in butter until tender but not brown. Add flour, mixing into a smooth paste and cook, stirring constantly, for 2 minutes. Stir in stock and wine gradually making a smooth thick cream sauce. Add salt and pepper. Season spinach with salt and pepper and place in a greased casserole. Arrange turkey slices on spinach, cover with cream sauce, top with mushrooms, and sprinkle liberally with Parmesan cheese. Heat in a 350° oven for 25 minutes.

SERVES 4

Gayle Whitehurst Hansen
(Mrs. James R.) Burlingame, Calif.

CORNISH GAME HENS
"Festive entrée for a dinner party"

4 cornish game hens, split
8 sheets foil
½ C. olive oil
Salt, pepper and paprika to taste
8 t. Worcestershire sauce
8 T. red wine
1 t. thyme
1 t. poultry seasoning
4 T. chopped parsley

Place hen halves on sheets of foil. Brush with olive oil. Season. Combine remaining ingredients and pour over hens. Fold hen into foil packet. Place on cookie sheet, and bake at 300° for 45 minutes. Open packets and brown under broiler. Save juice and serve with hens.

SERVES 6

Claire Smith Foster
(Mrs. Henry L., Jr.)

VENISON STEAK

1½ C. water
2 slices lemon
1 t. whole pepper
½ T. poultry seasoning
¼ t. mace
2 T. salt
1 C. vinegar
½ medium onion
6 whole cloves
3 or 4 sprigs parsley
2—2½ lbs. venison steak
Flour
Oil
2 cloves garlic, divided
1 T. butter
3 T. oil
1 small onion
1 C. consommé
1 scant C. thick tomato juice
1 scant C. dry wine (Claret)
½ t. rosemary
1 T. chopped parsley

Simmer first 10 ingredients 30 minutes and cool. Pour over steak and marinate 5—6 hours, then dry with cloth. Roll lightly in flour and brown in oil with 1 garlic clove. Drain and place meat in roasting pan, combine remaining ingredients and pour over venison. Cook at 350° for 1 hour.

SERVES 4

Mrs. Frank Dana
Kilgore, Texas

Eggs & Chese

BAKED EGGS

6 t. butter
12 eggs
1 (6 oz.) jar marinated artichokes
2 C. sour cream
¼ C. grated Swiss cheese
2 T. dry white wine
1 T. Dijon mustard
Salt and pepper to taste
Dash of cayenne
Parmesan cheese

Melt butter in six ramekins. Break two eggs into each dish. Mix artichokes, sour cream, Swiss cheese, wine, mustard and seasonings and pour over eggs. Sprinkle Parmesan cheese over top. Set ramekins in a shallow pan of water. Bake in a 350° oven until eggs are set, about 10 minutes.

Carmen Huggins Hilliard
(Mrs. George M.,III)

CHEESE BLINTZES

1 C. flour
½ t. salt
4 eggs
1 C. water

FILLING:
1 lb. dry cottage cheese
1 whole egg
1 T. butter, melted
3 T. sugar
1 t. cinnamon

Combine ingredients to make smooth batter. Grease a 6" skillet with butter; put small amount of batter in pan; pour off excess and fry until sides pull away. Put filling in center of crepe, roll over and tuck in ends. (May be frozen at this point.) When ready to serve, fry on both sides until brown OR bake at 350° for 20 minutes.

YIELD: 18 blintzes

Joyce Andres Stidham
(Mrs. Thomas Mack)

SPANISH EGGS

½ C. butter
½ C. chopped bell pepper
½ C. chopped ripe olives
½ C. chopped onions
½ C. sliced mushrooms
½ C. tomato purée
12 eggs, beaten slightly
Salt and cayenne to taste

Sauté peppers, olives, onions, and mushrooms in butter for 5 minutes. Add purée and cook 5 minutes. Season eggs and scramble in sauce until done. Serve in chafing dish to keep hot. For a large crowd, each recipe of sauce may be made the day before and put in jars in the refrigerator. When ready to serve, heat sauce in skillet and heat. Add beaten eggs and scramble.

Bess Vallery Topp
(Mrs. J. S.)

EGGS COUNTRY PLACE

8 slices bacon, fried crisp drained and crumbled
2 large onions, chopped
2 large green pepper, chopped
1 (16 oz.) can tomatoes, drained and reserve juice
Salt and pepper to taste
2 T. butter
8 slices American cheese
1 doz. hard boiled eggs, sliced

Fry bacon and remove most of bacon drippings. Sauté onions and peppers in remainder of grease. Add tomatoes with about half of the juice; add seasonings and simmer about 30 minutes. Melt 2 T. butter in a 9" x 13" baking dish. Place sliced eggs in dish. Place cheese slices over eggs. Sprinkle on crumbled bacon. Top with sauce. Bake at 325° for 30-40 minutes.

SERVES 12

Barbara York Richardson
(Mrs. Kenneth C.)

WILLIAMSBURG INN FANTASIO OMELET

1 medium apple, peeled and diced
1 slice stale bread
¼ C. butter, divided
2 oz. sausage meat
1 t. chopped walnuts OR pecans
3 eggs
1 T. light cream
¼ C. Cheddar cheese, shredded

Trim slice of bread and cut into croutons. Fry until brown and crisp in 1 T. butter turning to brown on all sides. Reserve. Crumble sausage meat and cook; drain and reserve. Crumble sausage meat and cook; drain and reserve. Sauté apple in drippings and when almost done, add chopped walnuts or pecans. Combine croutons, sausage, apple, and nuts. Beat eggs and cream until light and foamy. Salt and pepper to taste. Heat remaining butter in an omelet pan over high heat. Remove pan from heat, and eggs and return to heat. When eggs begin to set, lift edges with fork or spatula so that uncooked eggs will run to bottom of pan. Shake the pan to prevent sticking. When eggs are completely set, mound apple mixture and cheese on half the omelet; fold and roll onto warm plate and serve at once.

SERVES 2-3

Camen Huggins Hilliard
(Mrs. George M., III)

CHEESE SOUFFLÉ

3 T. butter
2 T. flour
1 C. scalded milk
½ C. grated dairy cheese
½ t. salt
4 eggs, separated

Melt butter in upper part of double boiler. Stir in flour; when well blended, gradually add the milk, cheese and salt, stirring constantly, until sauce is thick and smooth. Remove from heat. Beat egg yolks until thick and pale, and stir in the milk mixture. Cool. Fold in the stiffly beaten egg whites. Pour into a buttered baking dish and set in a pan of hot water. Bake at 325° for 35-45 minutes for a firm soufflé; if it is preferred soft, bake at 375° for 20-25 minutes. Serve at once. You may add more cheese to this recipe and not alter the texture.

SERVES 3-4

Gloria Haggard Hawthorn
(Mrs. Neal A.)

BRUNCH CASSEROLE SUPREME

2 lbs. sausage
1 (6 oz.) jar marinated artichoke hearts coarsely chopped, reserve marinade
½ lb. mushrooms, sliced
1 bunch green onions, chopped (use half of tops)
9 slices bread, buttered
2 C. grated Cheddar cheese
6 eggs
3 C. milk
1 t. salt
Dash Tabasco
1 t. paprika
1 t. dry mustard
1 t. Dijon mustard
Dash nutmeg
2 t. Worcestershire sauce
1 C. crushed potato chips
½ C. butter
Paprika

Cook sausage; drain and crumble. Sauté mushrooms and green onions in marinade from artichoke hearts. Line bottom of a 3 quart baking dish with 6 slices of bread (cut in half into triangles). Sprinkle with layers of ½ cheese, sausage, mushrooms and green onion mixture, and artichoke hearts. Cut the remaining three slices of bread into sixths and place on top of filling layer. Add another layer of remaining sausage, etc.. Beat well, eggs and milk. Add seasonings. Pour over casserole mixture. Can be refrigerated overnight or several hours now. Before serving, top with potato chips and pour melted butter over top. Sprinkle with paprika. Bake at 350° for 30-45 minutes or until potato chips brown and eggs are set. Slice in squares.

YIELD: 12-15 squares

Linda Ryan Butter
(Mrs. Stephen R.)

EGG CASSEROLE

6 eggs
1 C. milk
1 t. dry mustard
½ t. salt
1 C. cubed bread
1 C. cubed mild cheddar cheese
1 C. cubed cooked ham

Beat eggs, milk, mustard and salt in blender. Grease an 8 x 8 inch pan and place cubed ingredients within. Pour liquid over. Bake at 350° for 45 minutes or until golden. Cut into squares.

SERVES 6

Malinda Efrid Lenhart
(Mrs. John.]

VARIATION: To above recipe Add:
Pepper to taste
¼ C. minced onion
2 t. Worcestershire sauce
Dash Cayenne
1 (16 oz.) can asparagus pieces (optional)
1 C. crushed potato chips
½ C. melted butter

Add seasonings to milk mixture. Combine asparagus with bread, cheese and ham. Top with chips and pour butter over the top.

CHILI RELLENOS

2 (4 oz.) cans green chilies
¾ C. grated mild Cheddar cheese
4 beaten eggs
½ t. salt
½ t. dry mustard
½ C. milk

Remove seed from chilies. Put flat in the bottom of the casserole. Make layer of chilies and then cheese. Cover with the mixture of eggs, salt, dry mustard and milk. Bake at 350° for 30 minutes.

SERVES 4

Helen Martin Johnston
(Mrs. E. C., Jr.)

CHILI CON QUESO

"Use on rolled tortillas for a main course"

1 large onion, chopped
1 bell pepper, chopped
2 T. bacon drippings
2 T. flour
1 T. Mexene chili powder
1 t. jalapeño peppers, chopped (optional)
1 (10 oz.) can Rotel tomatoes
2 lb. Velveeta cheese

Sauté onion and pepper in bacon drippings. Add all other ingredients, except cheese, and cook until thickened. Melt cheese in double boiler and add to first mixture. May be served in chafing dish with tortilla chips. May be frozen.

Nancy Rogers Smith
(Mrs. Robert H.)

ENCHILADAS

SAUCE:
½ C. bacon grease
1 small onion, chopped
6 buttons garlic, chopped
4 heaping T. chili powder
4 T. flour
2 (8 oz.) cans tomato sauce
Water

2 doz. tortillas
2 lbs. cheese, grated
3 onions, finely chopped

Sauté onions and garlic in bacon grease. Add chili powder and flour. Mix well, add tomato sauce and enough water to make a thick sauce.
TO ASSEMBLE:
Soften 3 tortillas at a time in sauce. Spread about ¼ t. onion over tortilla, then cover generously with cheese. Roll up and place on rimmed cookie sheet, seam side down. Grate cheese over all and bake at 350° until cheese is melted, about 10 minutes. If sauce gets too thick, thin with water.

Virginia Elms McRee
(Mrs. J. T.), Dallas, Texas

FETTUCCINE RENÉ

½ lb. fettuccine OR noodles
2 shallots, chopped
1 T. butter
1 C. chicken stock
½ C. heavy cream
1 C. sour cream
¼ C. grated Parmesan cheese
2 T. chopped chives

Cook fettuccine in boiling salted water until tender. Drain thoroughly. In a saucepan, sauté chopped shallots in butter for a few minutes. Stir in chicken stock and boil the mixture for 3 minutes. Remove the pan from heat and gradually stir in cream. Add the pasta, sour cream, grated Parmesan cheese and chopped chives. Toss mixture well.

SERVES 4

Cookbook Committee

NOODLES AU TIM

1 (8 oz.) pkg. medium noodles
2 C. cottage cheese
2 C. sour cream
¼ C. butter, melted
¼ C. onion, chopped
1 clove garlic, minced
1 t. Worcestershire sauce
Dash Tabasco
Salt & pepper to taste
Grated Parmesan cheese

Cook noodles in boiling salted water for 10 minutes. Drain the noodles and rinse in cold water. Combine cottage cheese, sour cream, butter, onion, garlic, Worcestershire sauce, Tabasco and salt and pepper in mixing bowl. Stir in noodles and pour a buttered 2 quart casserole. Bake at 350° F. for 45 minutes. Serve them hot with a side dish of grated Parmesan cheese. Can be prepared ahead.

SERVES 8

**The Windjammer,
Seattle, Wash.**

HANAHO FONDUE

8 slices bread (1" thick), remove crusts and cut in cubes
¾ lb. sharp Cheddar and/or Old English cheese, grated
5 eggs, beaten
2 C. milk
1 t. salt
¼ C. melted butter

Put layer of bread cubes in buttered 2 quart baking dish, then a layer of grated cheese. Repeat until dish is full, with the bread layer on top. Beat together eggs, milk and salt. Pour over bread and cheese. Let set in refrigerator overnight. Before baking, cover with melted butter. Set casserole in pan of hot water, and bake at 325° for 45-60 minutes.

SERVES 4-5

Claire Smith Foster
(Mrs. Henry L.)

SWISS FONDUE

½ lb. Swiss cheese, grated
1 C. light DRY wine
2 T. Kirsch
2½ t. cornstarch
1/8 t. salt
Dash of MSG
Dash of white pepper

Combine cheese and wine in chafing dish on top of stove and heat, stirring constantly, until melted. Continue stirring adding the cornstarch which has been blended with Kirsch. Continue cooking 2 or 3 minutes or until fondue begins to bubble. Serve with French bread cubes.

SERVES 3

Kathleen Ellison Loomis
(Mrs. N. E.)

CHEESE GRITS

3 C. boiling water
¾ C. grits (not instant)
½ lb. sharp cheese, grated
2 eggs, beaten
6 T. butter or margarine
1½ t. seasoned salt
¼ t. salt
Dash Tabasco (more if you like)

Boil grits 2 to 3 minutes. Stir constantly. Add the rest of the ingredients. Bake at 350° in a greased 2 quart casserole for 1 hour.

SERVES 8

Kathleen Ellison Loomis
(Mrs. Norman E.)

ITALIAN BRUNCH

½ lb. Italian sweet sausage
2 T. olive oil
1 C. potatoes, peeled and diced
½ C. thinly sliced onion
¼ chopped green pepper
1 C. tomatoes, peeled, seeded and diced
8 eggs
¼ C. light cream
Salt and pepper to taste
Thick slices of Italian bread, toasted
Orégano
Grated Romano cheese

In skillet, sauté sausage in oil until sausage is no longer pink. Add potatoes, onions and green pepper and cook, stirring occasionally, until potatoes are brown and onion and pepper are limp. Lightly beat eggs, cream and seasoning together. Pour into skillet and cook stirring until eggs are set but still moist.
TO SERVE:
Serve these dressed-up eggs on thick slices of Italian bread toasted. Sprinkle with orégano and grated Romano cheese.

Mary Ann Hollandsworth Nelson
(Mrs. Tom)

PATÉ BRISÉE

1½ C. flour
¾ stick butter, cut into small pieces
2 T. Crisco
¼ t. salt
3 T. ice water

In a large bowl, combine flour, butter, Crisco and salt. Blend until well combined and add ice water. Toss the mixture until water is incorporated and form the dough into a ball. Knead the dough lightly for a few seconds with the palm of the hand to distribute fat evenly and reform it into a ball. Dust the pastry with flour, wrap it in wax paper, and chill it for 1 hour. Roll out 1/8" thick and bake in a pie plate at 450° for 10-12 minutes.

YIELD: 1-9" crust

QUICHE LORRAINE

1 recipe Paté Brisée
½ lb. bacon
½ C. Swiss cheese
1 C. Cheddar cheese
½ C. grated onion
3 eggs
1 C. milk
1 t. salt
Tabasco to taste
1 (4 oz.) can mushrooms
½ (4 oz.) jar pimiento

Bake quiche pastry in quiche dish or 9" pie plate at 450° for 10-15 minutes. Fry bacon and crumble. grate cheeses and onion. Beat eggs and add milk and seasonings. Layer ingredients in the following order in pastry: bacon, Swiss cheese, onion, mushrooms, pimiento, and Cheddar cheese. Pour egg mixture over the layers. Bake at 325° for 45 minutes.

Marilyn Rouse Payne
(Mrs. Hermes)

ONION PIE

1—10" partially baked pie shell (made with paté brisée dough)
1 lb. yellow onions, sliced plus 1 for fried rings
2 T. bacon fat
2 eggs
2 eggs yolks
2 t. Dijon mustard
½ C. grated Parmesan cheese
1¼ C. light cream, scalded

BEER BATTER:
1 (12 oz.) can beer
1—1¼ C. flour
1 T. salt
1 t. paprika
½ t. baking powder

Cook onions in bacon fat until limp (about 5 minutes). Drain. Beat together lightly eggs, egg yolks, mustard and cheese. Stir in onions. Add cream slowly so as not to curdle eggs. Pour into pie shell and bake in preheated 350° oven for 25 minutes.

BEER BATTER
This should be made at least 1-2 hours before serving. Add flour to beer, let thicken. Add salt, paprika and baking powder. Let stand at room temperature. Slice and separate onion into rings. Dust with flour, dip in batter and deep fry in 2" of hot fat. Garnish pie with fried onion rings.

Julia Dannenbaum
Gritti Palace Cooking School, Venice, Italy

Doner: Gay Cole Howard Wheeler
(Mrs. Ridley)

SPINACH RICOTTA PIE

1 recipe Paté Brisée, partially baked

FILLING:
1 pkg. frozen chopped spinach, thawed
1 lb. Ricotta cheese
¼ lb. fresh mushrooms, chopped
1 egg
½ C. Swiss cheese, grated
½ C. freshly grated Parmesan OR Romano cheese
¼—½ t. thyme
Salt and pepper to taste

SAUCE:
1 (8 oz.) can tomato sauce
1 clove garlic
Salt to taste
1 t. Italian seasoning

Combine filling ingredients and put in pie shell. Bake at 350° for 30 minutes. Combine sauce ingredients, heat well, and serve along with pie.

Jan Crawford

TOMATO QUICHE

FRESH TOMATO PUREÉ
¾ C. minced onion
2 T. butter
4 large tomatoes; peeled, seeded, squeezed and chopped
½ t. salt
¼ t. pepper
1/8 t. sugar
Bouquet garni (4 sprigs each parsley and thyme & 1 bay leaf)

CUSTARD:
1 C. heavy cream
½ C. light cream
2 eggs, beaten
2 egg yolks, beaten
Fresh tomato purée
¼ C. grated Swiss cheese
¼ C. grated Parmesan cheese
½ t. salt
¼ t. white pepper

1½ recipes Paté Brisée
Tomato slices ½" thick
Salt, pepper, thyme to taste
3 T. grated Swiss cheese
3 T. grated Parmesan cheese
Butter
Parsley

PUREÉ
Sauté onion in butter until golden. Add tomatoes and seasonings. Cook mixture, covered, over low heat for 10 minutes. Remove the cover, increase heat and cook until mixture is thick. Remove bouquet garni and cool.

CUSTARD:
Mix first nine ingredients thoroughly and reserve.

CRUST:
Roll Paté Brisée out on a floured board into a circle 15" in diameter. Lift the dough over a rolling pin into a 11" French shallow falsebottomed flan pan with a removable flute ring and press dough firmly into pan. Cut off excess dough. Prick the bottom of the shell with a fork and chill for 1 hour. Line the shell with wax paper, cover the paper with foil and fill the foil with raw rice. Bake the shell in the bottom third of a 400° oven for 10-15 minutes or until it begins to set. Carefully remove the foil, rice and wax paper. Bake the shell until lightly colored. Remove shell from oven and cool.

TO ASSEMBLE:
Fill shell with reserved custard mixture, cover the top with tomato slices and sprinkle with salt, pepper and thyme. Sprinkle with cheeses and dot with butter. Bake quiche on top rack of 375° oven for 25-30 minutes or until the custard is set and crust is golden. Remove quiche from pan and cool slightly. Sprinkle with parsley.

SERVES 8

**Patricia Smith Houston
(Mrs. E. B.)**

MACARONI LOAF AND SAUCE

2 C. cooked macaroni
1 C. bread crumbs
3 eggs, well beaten
¾ C. grated cheese
½ C. pimiento
1 T. grated onion
1 T. chopped fine green pepper
½ t. salt
¾ C. milk

SAUCE:
4 T. butter
4 T. flour
1 C. chicken broth
1 C. milk cooked
1 lb. chicken, cooked until tender and removed from bones
1 C. mushrooms
½ C. Spanish olives, chopped
Salt and pepper to taste

Combine ingredients and pour into a greased loaf pan. Bake at 350° about 45 minutes.
SAUCE
Melt butter, add flour and cook until bubbly. Stir in liquids and cook until sauce thickens. Add chicken, mushrooms and olives. Serve with loaf.

SERVES 6-8

Laura Bass Skipper
(Mrs. L. N. Jr.)

WELSH RAREBIT

2 T. butter
2 T. flour
2 eggs, beaten
1 C. milk
2 C. cheese (cubed)
½ t. dry mustard
1 T. Worcestershire sauce
1/8 t. cayenne
1 C. beer, (optional)

Melt butter, add flour and blend well. Add milk and cheese to beaten eggs. Add to butter mixture. Continue to cook, stirring until cheese melts and mixture thickens (8-10 minutes). Add seasoning and mix thoroughly. Serve on crisp toast or crackers.

Marguerite Swearingen Harrington
(Mrs. Harry M. Jr.)

BARLEY CASSEROLE

½ C. butter
1 C. barley
1 onion, chopped
1 C. sliced mushrooms
1 envelope Lipton's Onion Soup Mix
2 C. chicken broth (made with 2 bouillon cubes)
1 C. slivered almonds

Melt butter. Add barley and onion and brown. Put into a 2 quart casserole dish. Add remaining ingredients. Bake uncovered at 350° for 1 to 1½ hours. Stir occasionally and add more broth or water if additional liquid is needed.

SERVES 6

Linda Berney Buie
(Mrs. James E.)

VARIATION:
Omit Lipton's Onion Soup Mix
Add:
1 C. chopped celery
½ C. chopped pimiento
Salt and pepper to taste

BROCCOLI SOUFFLÉ
"Fill center with creamed chicken, ham or seafood"

2 C. chopped broccoli, cooked and drained
1 C. mayonnaise
1 T. butter, melted
1 T. flour
3 eggs, well-beaten
½ t. salt
½ t. sugar
Cayenne to taste
1 C. light cream

VARIATION:
Add:
Juice of ½ lemon
1 T. grated onion

Add mayonnaise and butter to broccoli. Sprinkle flour over mixture. Add eggs, salt, sugar, cayenne and cream. Mix well and pour into a 6 C. buttered ring mold or 1½ qt. casserole. Place in a pan of warm water and bake at 350° for 45 minutes. Serve at once. Can be served hot or cold as a salad or a vegetable.

SERVES 6

Leita Young Kelly
(Mrs. George A.)

Mrs. Frank Campbell
Kilgore, Texas

ELIZABETH'S BROCCOLI

1 pkg. frozen chopped broccoli, steamed and drained
½ C. butter
1 onion, chopped
2 T. flour
1 C. milk
1 beaten egg yolk
¾ C. Parmesan cheese
Finely crushed buttered cracker crumbs

Sauté onion in butter until soft. Add flour and let cook about 2 minutes, stirring constantly. Add combined milk and egg yolk. Cook until thickened and add cheese and broccoli. Sprinkle with cracker crumbs. Bake at 350° in a greased 1 quart casserole for 30 minutes.

SERVES 4

Eleanor Croxton Lawrence
(Mrs. Thomas W.)

QUICK BAKED BEANS

"Add cooked ground meat for a supper dish"

6 slices bacon, chopped
1 t. (or more) Worcestershire sauce
2 buttons garlic, chopped
1 medium onion, chopped
2 (16 oz.) cans pork and beans
2 T. bacon grease
1 C. catsup
1 T. sugar
Salt and pepper to taste

Fry bacon until crisp. Drain. Sauté garlic and onion in bacon grease until tender (not brown). Drain. To beans in a greased 2 quart casserole, add remaining ingredients. Mix thoroughly. Bake at 350° for 1 hour until brown and slightly thickened.

SERVES 8

Reva Harrison Ryan
(Mrs. A. B.)

BUTTER BEAN CASSEROLE

"Add cooked, chopped ham for a main dish"

1 (16 oz.) can peeled tomatoes, chopped
3 T. flour
2 T. chopped green pepper
2 T. chopped onion
1 T. oil
3 C. cooked butter beans
1 C. grated sharp cheese

Heat tomatoes and thicken with flour. Sauté pepper and onion in oil. Season to taste. Add to tomatoes and drained butter beans. Pour into a 1½ quart buttered casserole; sprinkle with cheese. Bake at 350° for 30-40 minutes.

SERVES 6-8

Mrs. Ira Rathbun

BRUSSELS SPROUTS AND ARTICHOKE HEARTS
"Good with prime rib"

1 pkg. frozen brussels sprouts
1 (14 oz.) can artichoke hearts, drained
⅔ C. mayonnaise
½ t. celery salt
¼ C. grated Parmesan cheese
½ C. melted butter
2 t. lemon juice
¼ C. sliced almonds

Cook frozen brussel sprouts according to package directions until barely tender. DO NOT OVERCOOK. Arrange with artichoke hearts in a greased 1½ qt. oblong casserole dish. Mix remaining ingredients and spoon over the vegetables. Bake uncovered at 425° for 10 minutes.

SERVES 6

Martha Hess Whitehead
(Mrs. R. Laughton, Jr.)

BRUSSELS SPROUTS

2 pkgs, frozen brussels sprouts, cooked and drained
½ C. slivered almonds
1 C. seedless white grapes (fresh or canned)
¾ C. sour cream
½ C. drained mushrooms
¼ C. chopped pimiento
1 t. sugar
2 t. salt
½ t. pepper
¾ C. grated cheese
Paprika

Combine almonds, grapes, sour cream, mushrooms, pimiento, sugar, salt, and pepper. Add brussels sprouts. Heat in double boiler for 7 minutes. Remove, place in serving dish, sprinkle with cheese and paprika.

SERVES 8

Mrs. Douglas Humble
Kilgore, Texas

CARROTS WITH ALMONDS

5 large or 8 small carrots, peeled and sliced
½ t. salt
1 T. honey
¼ t. sweet basil
2 T. butter
1 pkg. almonds, toasted
¼ t. dill

Place carrots in water to barely cover. Add all ingredients except almonds and dill, and cook covered until just tender, but not mushy. Place on a serving dish and sprinkle almonds over top. Sprinkle dill over all. Serve hot.

SERVES 6

Dorothy Robbins Kennedy
(Mrs. George E., Jr.)

CARROT CASSEROLE

2 lbs. carrots, peeled
2 T. finely chopped onion
1 C. heavy cream
1 t. sugar
Salt to taste
4 T. butter
½ C. Ritz cracker crumbs

Cook carrots until tender. Mash carrots. Add onion, cream, sugar, salt and butter. Put into a greased 2 quart casserole and sprinkle crumbs on top. Bake uncovered at 350° for 20—25 minutes or until done.

SERVES 8

Marcia Burlison McDaniel
(Mrs. Stephen W.)

CREOLE CABBAGE

2 lbs.(8 C.) green cabbage, shredded
1 t. salt
2 T. oil
¾ C. thinly sliced onion
1 ¾ C. canned tomatoes
2 T. chopped green pepper
1 t. salt
2 whole cloves
1 bay leaf
1 t. sugar

Cook cabbage, covered, with salt in a small amount of water until tender. Drain well. Brown onions in hot oil, add tomatoes, green pepper and seasonings. Simmer uncovered for 20 minutes. Remove cloves and bay leaf from sauce and pour over cabbage while tossing lightly with fork.

SERVES 8

Bess Vallery Topp
(Mrs. J. S.)

VARIATION: To above recipe:
Substitute:
4 T. bacon drippings
Add:
1 C. celery

Steam cabbage in sauce until tender.

Cherokee Club

CELERY HEARTS

2 (16 oz.) cans celery hearts
½ C. butter
½ C. flour
1½ C. milk
½ lb. American cheese, grated

Heat celery hearts and drain. Make cheese sauce of butter, flour, milk and cheese. Cover celery hearts with cheese sauce, sprinkle with Parmesan cheese and paprika. Run under broiler until bubbly.

SERVES 6

Patricia Smith Houston
(Mrs. E. B.)

BRAISED RED CABBAGE

1 medium head red cabbage
4 T. butter cut into small pieces
1 T. sugar (to taste)
1 t. salt
⅓ C. water
⅓ C. white vinegar
¼ C. red currant jelly (or grape)
1 grated apple

Preheat oven to 325°. Shred enough cabbage to equal nine cups. Combine butter, sugar, salt, water, vinegar in heavy casserole or stainless on top of stove. When water is boiling and butter is melted, add cabbage. After it comes to a second boil, remove from stove and cover. Put casserole in the center of the oven and braise for two hours. Add a little water if necessary during cooking time. After about 1 hour and 50 minutes, stir in the jelly and grated apples. Complete cooking process.

Kirsten Sonne Felker
(Mrs. Marshall L., Jr.)

CORN PUDDING

½ C. corn meal
1 t. salt
½ C. cold milk
1½ C. scalded milk
2 T. butter
1 C. cream style corn
Pepper
Paprika
1 green chile
2 eggs, beaten

Combine corn meal, salt and cold milk in double boiler. Add scalded milk and cook 10 minutes, stirring until smooth. Remove from heat. Combine corn, pepper, paprika and green chile. Add to corn meal mixture. Slowly stir in eggs. Bake at 350° in a greased 2 quart casserole for 45 minutes.

SERVES 6—8

Agnes Scruggs

CORN AND CHEESE FONDUE

⅓ C. bread cubes
1½ C. cream style corn
¼ C. minced onion
¼ C. green chilies, chopped
¾ C. grated cheese
½ t. salt
2 eggs, well-beaten
½ C. hot milk

Mix ingredients together and pour into a greased loaf pan. Set in a pan of hot water and bake at 350° until set, about 1 hour.

SERVES 4

Eleanor Croxton Lawrence
(Mrs. Thomas W.)

DRESSING FOR TURKEY

1 9" X 13" pyrex dish of cornbread
1 small can biscuits, cooked
6 slices white bread
1 box long grain & wild rice
½ C. butter
2 onions, chopped
1 stalk celery, chopped
1 bell pepper, chopped
1 bunch green onions, chopped
1 T. sage
1 T. poultry seasoning
1 T. black pepper
3½ quarts of rich chicken stock
Salt to taste
1 can water chestnuts, drained, and chopped
5 eggs, beaten
2 T. butter
1 package slivered almonds

Crumble dried cornbread, dried biscuits and dried bread in a large, deep pot. Add rice which has been cooked in chicken stock; set aside. Sauté onions, celery, bell pepper and green onions in butter. Add to bread and rice mixture along with sage, poultry seasoning and black pepper. Add 3 quarts of boiling chicken stock and cover immediately to allow dressing to steam for 15 minutes. Add salt to taste, correct seasoning and mix well. Add additional chicken stock if dressing seems too dry. At this point dressing may be refrigerated for a day or two, or frozen. Before cooking, add water chestnuts and eggs; mix well. Place dressing in pyrex dishes and sprinkle with slivered almonds which have been sautéed in butter. Bake at 350° until golden brown (1¼ to 1½ hrs.). Makes one 9" X 13" dish and one small casserole.

SERVES 20

Betty Robbins Davis
(Mrs. Charles H.)

MASHED POTATO DRESSING

1 onion, chopped
2 stalks celery, chopped
1½ C. margarine, divided
15 slices day-old bread
Salt and pepper to taste
2 medium potatoes, mashed
2 eggs, beaten
1 pkg. Pepperidge Farm Herb Seasoned Stuffing
Chicken broth

Sauté onions and celery in ½ cup of margarine for 20 minutes. Trim crust from bread and cube. Brown cubes in a large roasting pan with 1 cup margarine, stirring often. Add potatoes, eggs, stuffing and sautéed vegetables. Moisten with broth. Season to taste. Bake at 350° for 45 minutes—1 hour until brown.

SERVES 6—8

Mrs. S. W. Hawkins,
   Ft. Smith, Ark.

Donor: Elaine Carpenter Carter
   (Mrs. E. H., Jr.)

EGGPLANT CASSEROLE

2 large or 3 small eggplant
1 large onion, grated
1 bell pepper, chopped
1 clove garlic, pressed
3 eggs, beaten
1 t. Worcestershire sauce
1 can Rotel tomatoes and chilies
1 (10¾ oz.) can mushroom soup
2 C. grated cheese
2 C. cracker crumbs
¼ C. margarine
Salt and pepper to taste

Cook eggplant until tender. Drain and mash. Add all ingredients except cheese and crackers. Mix well. Layer eggplant mixture with cheese and crumbs in a large casserole. Repeat, ending with crumbs. Pour margarine over crumbs. Bake at 350° for 50 minutes.

SERVES 12—14

Mrs. G. A. McCreight

NEW ORLEANS EGGPLANT

1 large eggplant; peeled, sliced, boiled until tender, and drained
1 large onion, chopped
1 large green pepper, chopped
Butter
Salt and pepper to taste
2 eggs
1 C. aged Cheddar cheese
1 T. flour
1 (8 oz.) can oysters, drained
1 C. cooked shrimp
¼ t. celery seed
¼ C. butter or chicken fat
Light cream
Buttered cracker crumbs

Sauté onion and pepper in butter until tender. Add all ingredients, except crumbs, to mashed eggplant. Add small amount of light cream if mixture seems dry. Top with cracker crumbs. Bake at 250° for 1 hour or longer in a 2 quart casserole.

Florra Wheeler Anderson (Mrs. Jack)

FIDEO

1 (8 oz.) pkg. vermicelli
¼ C. salad oil
1 medium onion, chopped finely
1 clove garlic, minced
1 (16 oz.) can tomatoes
1 (10½ oz.) can chicken broth
Salt and pepper to taste
1 T. cumin powder

Sauté vermicelli in salad oil until light brown. Drain on paper towels. Place in a casserole. Brown onion and garlic. Add tomatoes and chicken broth. Add remaining ingredients. Cover the vermicelli with sauce. Cover casserole and cook for 1 hour, adding more chicken broth as liquid is absorbed.

Seasoned With Sun Cookbook

SCALLOPED EGGPLANT

1 large eggplant (2-2½ C.), diced
2 T. butter
½ C. onion
⅓ C. milk
1 (10¾ oz.) can cream of mushroom soup
1 egg, slightly beaten
¾ C. herb-seasoned stuffing
2 t. butter, melted
½ C. crushed herb-seasoned stuffing
1 C. shredded Cheddar cheese

Cook eggplant in boiling salted water until tender. Drain. Sauté onion in butter. Add milk to soup in mixing bowl. Blend in egg. Add eggplant, onion and ¾ C. stuffing. Pour into a greased 1½ quart casserole. Toss crumbs with butter. Sprinkle over casserole. Top with cheese. Bake at 350° for 30 minutes. Can be prepared in advance and frozen.

SERVES 8

Patricia Dooley Flatt
(Mrs. Ed)

TONI'S SUPER GREEN BEANS

2 (1 lb.) cans seasoned French style green beans, drained
1 onion, chopped
1 (8 oz.) carton sour cream
1 (8 oz.) water chestnuts, sliced and drained
2 C. grated Cheddar cheese divided

Mix all ingredients together, reserving 1 C. cheese. Place in a buttered 2 quart casserole dish and top with remaining cheese. Bake at 350° covered for 15 minutes and uncover for 15 minutes.

Helen May Little
(Mrs. Earle E., Jr.)

RIVER ROAD GREEN BEANS HORSERADISH

2 (16 oz.) cans whole green beans
1 large onion, sliced
Several bits of ham, bacon or salt meat
1 C. mayonnaise
2 hard cooked eggs, chopped
1 heaping T. horseradish
1 t. Worcestershire sauce
Salt and pepper to taste
Garlic salt to taste
Celery salt to taste
Onion salt to taste
1½ t. parsley flakes
1 lemon, juiced

Cook beans with sliced onion and meat for 1 hour or more. Blend mayonnaise with remaining ingredients and set aside at room temperature. When beans are ready to serve, drain. Spoon mayonnaise mixture over beans. These are excellent left over or cold.

SERVES 8

Susanne Sandberg Northcutt
(Mrs. W. D., III)

PIQUANT GREEN BEANS

2 lbs. string beans
4 strips bacon, cut into
   ½" strips
2 T. diced pimiento
2 T. red wine vinegar
¼ t. sugar
1 T. Worcestershire sauce
¼ t. dry mustard
Tabasco sauce
1 (8 oz.) can water chestnuts,
   drained and sliced

Steam beans until tender. Sauté bacon until crisp. Remove bacon from fat and add to beans. To bacon fat in skillet add pimiento, vinegar, sugar, Worcestershire, mustard and 2 or 3 drops Tabasco. Bring to a boil stirring constantly. Pour over beans. Add water chestnuts. Mix well.

SERVES 6

Barbara Glover Baucum
(Mrs. Joseph B., Jr.)

WILLIAMSBURG GREEN BEANS

1 (16 oz.) can Blue Lake green
   beans, drained
8 bacon slices; fried, drained
   and crumbled
½ C. butter
1 large onion, minced
4 medium zucchini, sliced ¼"
   thick
Salt and pepper to taste

Sauté onions in butter. Increase heat to medium high and add zucchini. Stir cook until tender crisp. Add bacon, green beans and seasonings. Cook about 1 minute.

SERVES 6-8

Barbara Hubbard Tomberlain
(Mrs. Charles)

GOURMET HOMINY BAKE

2 (29 oz.) cans white hominy
2 (4 oz.) cans green chilies,
   minced
Salt and pepper to taste
½ C. butter
1 C. sour cream
½ C. heavy cream
1 C. shredded Monterey Jack
   cheese

Drain and rinse hominy. In a greased 2½ qt. casserole, layer hominy and chilies; salt and pepper. Dot with sour cream and butter. Repeat layers. Pour cream over all. Sprinkle with cheese. Bake at 350° for 25—30 minutes.

SERVES 12

Cookbook Committee

MUSHROOM, CARROT, TOMATO CASSEROLE

1½ lbs. fresh mushrooms, sliced
4 carrots, sliced
1 onion, sliced
2—3 tomatoes, peeled and sliced
1 T. butter
1 T. flour
1 C. sour cream
1 T. lemon juice
½ t. salt
1/8 t. pepper
1½ oz. cognac
1 T. chopped parsley
4 oz. butter

Layer vegetables in a 2 quart casserole. Melt butter over low heat. Stir in flour and cook until bubbly. Add the rest of the ingredients except parsley and butter. **DO NOT BOIL.** Pour sauce over vegetables. Dot with butter. Sprinkle with parsley. Bake at 350° degrees 45 minutes to 1 hour. Test carrots for doneness. Can be prepared ahead.

SERVES 8—10

Mrs. Michael C. Macey

MUSHROOM PIE

2 lbs. mushrooms, cleaned and trimmed
4 T. butter
Juice of ½ lemon
Salt and pepper to taste
1 recipe paté brissé (See Index)

SAUCE:
2 T. butter
3 T. flour
1½ C. chicken stock
½ C. Madeira wine
½ C. heavy cream
Salt and pepper to taste

Sauté mushrooms in butter with lemon juice and seasonings. Place mushrooms in a greased 3 quart baking dish. To the pan juices add butter, stir in flour. Gradually add stock and cook until thickened. Stir in wine, cream and adjust seasoning. Pour over mushrooms and cover with paté brissé. Bake at 400° for 15 minutes. Reduce heat to 350° and bake 10—15 minutes longer.

SERVES 12

Emily Wood McWhirter
(Mrs. A. M.)

MUSHROOMS AND TOMATOES

2 T. butter
4 slices bacon, diced
½ C. finely chopped onions
16 medium mushrooms, stems removed
3—4 peeled tomatoes, cut into eighths
Salt and cracked pepper to taste

Brown bacon in butter until golden. Add onions and cook until clear. Stir in mushrooms. Add tomatoes, season, and stir until hot. DO NOT OVERCOOK.

Patricia Smith Houston
(Mrs. E. B.)

SCALLOPED MUSHROOMS

1½ lbs. fresh mushrooms
¼ C. butter
½ C. heavy cream
Salt
Red and black pepper
1½ C. Monterey Jack cheese, grated

Sauté mushrooms in butter for about 5 minutes. Add cream and cook until liquid is almost gone, stirring when needed. Add seasonings and pour mixture into a greased casserole. Cover with cheese and bake at 400° ONLY UNTIL CHEESE MELTS and mushrooms are hot.

Rita McEacharn Curtis
(Mrs. William)

MUSHROOMS IN SOUR CREAM

8 T. butter
2 onions, thinly sliced
1 lb. large fresh mushrooms
1 C. sour cream
1 t. lemon juice
1 t. salt
Black pepper, freshly ground
2 t. chopped fresh parsley

Melt butter in a heavy 10" skillet over medium heat. Sauté onion until clear. Stir in mushrooms and cook for 3—4 minutes. Add sour cream, lemon juice, salt and pepper. Heat through only. Serve immediately.

SERVES 6—8

Patricia Smith Houston
(Mrs. E. B.)

BAKED CRABMEAT POTATOES

4 potatoes
1 C. grated sharp cheddar cheese
½ C. light cream
½ C. butter
4 t. grated onion
Salt and pepper
1 (6½ oz.) can crabmeat
  OR ¾ C. lump crabmeat

Bake potatoes until done. Halve the potatoes and scoop out pulp. Mash the potatoes, add other ingredients and mix well. Refill potato skins and heat in a 400° oven for 10 minutes. These may be made in advance. In preparing a larger amount, freeze any extra filling. When ready to use, put into sea shells and bake.

SERVES 4

Carolyn Smith Russell
(Mrs. Ralph H.)

CHEESE POTATOES

2 (10 oz.) boxes frozen hash brown potatoes, thawed OR 6 potatoes, peeled and chopped
1 t. salt
½ t. pepper
2 T. minced onion (or more)
1 (10 ¾ oz.) can cream of chicken soup
1 C. sour cream
½ C. grated Cheddar cheese
4 T. butter

Mix potatoes with salt, pepper, onion, soup and sour cream. Pour into a 2 qt. casserole. Sprinkle cheese on top and dot with butter. Bake at 350° 1 hour, or until brown and bubbly.

SERVES 10

Floreid Francis Stevens
(Mrs. A. C.)

STUFFED BABY NEW POTATOES

"A great substitute for potato salad"

Small new potatoes
Sour cream
Green onions, chopped
Salt and pepper to taste

Scrub and cook desired amount of very small new potatoes in salted water until done. Cool. With melon ball scoop, cut out top of potato. Fill cavities with sour cream seasoned with chopped green onions, salt and pepper. Chill. Taste improves if made several hours in advance. It takes about 1 t. sour cream for each potato. If potatoes are small enough can be used as pick up food.

Mrs. Joseph H. Croxton

CLAY'S FAVORITE SWEET POTATOES

3 (1 lb. 7 oz.) cans sweet potatoes, drained
¾ C. brown sugar
3 T. butter
½ t. ground cloves
¾ t. cinnamon
¾ t. nutmeg
¼ t. salt (or to taste)
1 C. heavy cream

Mix first seven ingredients well with electric mixer, then blend in cream. Pour mixture into a 3 quart buttered casserole and bake in a pre-heated 400° oven for 30 minutes. Can be made in advance and frozen.

SERVES 8—10

Eleanor Croxton Lawrence
(Mrs. Thomas W.)

PAPRIKA RICE

½ lb. bacon
1 medium onion, chopped
1 medium bell pepper, chopped
1 T. paprika
1 (2 oz.) can pimiento, chopped
1 (1 lb. 4 oz.) can tomatoes, chopped
1 C. water
2 t. salt
1 C. uncooked rice
1 C. grated Cheddar cheese

Cook bacon until crisp. Drain. Sauté onion, bell pepper and paprika in bacon drippings until tender. Drain. Add pimiento, tomatoes, water and salt. Mix well, heat to boiling point and add rice. Cover and cook about 20 minutes or longer. Crumble bacon into mixture and top with cheese.

SERVES 6

Vera Mitchell Garlough
(Mrs. Harry Thomas)

RICE PILAF

½ C. margarine
2 C. long grain rice
4 C. chicken stock (Spice Island stock base)
¾ C. chopped carrots
¾ C. chopped celery
¾ C. chopped parsley
½ C. chopped green onions
1 C. thinly sliced water chestnuts OR almonds

Brown rice in margarine, stirring often. Add chicken stock. Bake at 375° in a greased 2 quart casserole for 30 minutes. Stir once or twice. Add chopped, uncooked vegetables. Stir well, fluff and serve.

SERVES 10—12

Carmen Huggins Hilliard
(Mrs. George M., III)

WILD RICE CASSEROLE

1 c. wild rice
1 C. grated Cheddar cheese
1 C. ripe olives, chopped
1 C. canned tomatoes, WELL drained
1 C. sliced mushrooms
½ C. chopped onion
½ C. salad oil
1 C. hot water
Salt and pepper to taste (a lot!)

Soak rice in water 2 days and drain. Add remaining ingredients and bake at 350° for 1 hour. Stir 2 times during cooking.

SERVES 8

Patty Yates Shappell
(Mrs. H. D., Jr.)

BAKED RICE

¼ C. margarine
1 C. raw rice
½ t. salt
1/8 t. black pepper
1/8 t. red pepper
½ t. garlic salt
½ C. chopped celery
¼ C. chopped green onion
1 T. parsley
1—2 T. Worcestershire sauce
1 (10½ oz.) can beef broth
½ soup can water

Melt margarine in pyrex dish. Add rice and seasonings. Add chopped celery, onions, parsley and Worcestershire sauce. Add beef broth and water. Bake uncovered at 350° for 45 minutes or until water is absorbed. Cover and steam for 15 minutes at 350°

Marilyn Rouse Payne
(Mrs. Hermes E.)

RICE JULIA
"Good with roasted meats"

1 T. bacon drippings
1 large onion, chopped
1 C. rice
1 (10½ oz.) can beef consomme
½ C. water
½ t. ground orégano
½ t. ground comino
1 T. Worcestershire sauce
Salt & pepper to taste

Lightly brown onion in hot drippings. Add rice and brown lightly. Remove to top of double boiler and add remaining ingredients. Cover partially and steam about 30—45 minutes or until done. Can be prepared ahead and reheated.

SERVES 4

Anne Price Mackenzie
(Mrs. Douglas)

SPINACH SOUFFLÉ

1 box frozen spinach
1 onion
1 clove garlic, pressed (optional)
3 T. butter
3 T. flour
1 C. light cream or milk
¼ t. salt
¼ t. pepper
3 eggs, separated
½ C. grated cheese
Buttered bread crumbs

Cook spinach with onion. Remove onion and drain spinach. Purée spinach. Make a sauce of butter, flour, milk and seasonings. Add gradually the beaten egg yolks. Add spinach. Fold in cheese and stiffly beaten egg whites. Put in a buttered baking dish. Sprinkle top with bread crumbs. Set in pan of hot water and bake at 350° about 25 minutes or until firm. Serve with Hollandaise sauce or mushroom sauce.

Verne Monday Smith
(Mrs. Bruner)

JALAPEÑO SPINACH

2 pkgs. frozen chopped spinach
2 T. chopped onion
2 T. butter
2 T. flour
½ C. evaporated milk
½ C. vegetable liquid
½ T. pepper
¾ T. celery salt
½ T. garlic powder
1 (6 oz.) roll Kraft Jalapeño cheese, chopped
Buttered bread crumbs

Cook spinach, drain and reserve liquid. Sauté onion in butter. Stir in flour and cook for 2 minutes. Add evaporated milk, vegetable liquid, pepper, celery salt, garlic powder and chopped cheese. Cook until melted. Add drained spinach and mix in a 2 quart casserole. Top with buttered bread crumbs. Bake at 350° for 30 minutes.

SERVES 8

Carolyn Smith Russell
(Mrs. Ralph H.)

SPINACH CUPS

1 pkg. frozen chopped spinach
¾ C. butter, melted
8 slices white bread, crusts trimmed
2 eggs, beaten
½ C. creamed style cottage cheese
⅓ C. Parmesan cheese
½ C. heavy cream
Garlic salt to taste
Dash Worcestershire sauce
Pinch sugar
Salt & pepper to taste
Paprika

Cook and drain spinach. Melt butter in skillet. Dip bread slices (both sides) in cooled butter. Press each bread slice into a muffin cup. Add the rest of the ingredients to spinach and fill bread-lined muffin cups. Sprinkle with paprika. Bake at 325° for 30 minutes. Let cool a minute for easy removal. NOTE: Add sliced mushrooms or chopped artichokes to spinach cups or omit bread and butter and bake in a greased 2 quart casserole.

SERVES 8

Jane Castleberry Cunningham

PARTY SQUASH

5 lbs. little neck yellow squash
½ C. butter
1 C. light cream
Salt and pepper to taste
2 onions, thinly sliced
1 lb. cheese, grated

Parboil squash in salted water. Drain well. Melt butter in cream. Add to mashed squash and season. In a buttered 3 quart casserole layer squash mixture, onions, and cheese. Bake at 350° for 45 minutes.

SERVES 10—12
Ann Lacy Crain
(Mrs. B. W.)

STUFFED SQUASH

12 yellow squash
1 lb. bulk sausage, browned and drained
3—4 green onions, chopped
¼ C. margarine
Salt and pepper to taste
2 T. Worcestershire sauce
1 egg, beaten
1 C. Progresso bread crumbs
Pinch orégano
½ C. grated Swiss cheese
½ C. grated Old English cheese

Parboil squash in salted water until barely tender. Drain, halve and scoop out, retaining pulp. Combine pulp and remaining ingredients and stuff shells. Bake at 325° for 20 or 30 minutes. Note: Squash may be cooked, drained, mashed, and combined with remaining ingredients, and baked in a 2 quart casserole.

SERVES 12

Susie Moore French
(Mrs. Paul E.)

SQUASH BAKE

½ C. margarine
2 onions, chopped
1 (13 ¾ oz.) can Swanson's chicken broth
1 can water
1 C. rice
1 t. salt
½ t. sugar
¾ t. pepper
1 (4 oz.) can green chilies, chopped
2 (6 oz.) rolls garlic cheese, sliced
4—5 medium squash, sliced
1 (16 oz.) can tomatoes, chopped with juice

Sauté onions in margarine. Add broth, water, rice, seasonings, chilies and cheese and cook until cheese is melted. Pour into a 3 qt. casserole, add squash and tomatoes and bake covered at 325° for 45 minutes. Freezes well. If prepared early in the day, to freshen appearance at serving time, cover with grated cheese and bake uncovered 30 minutes at 325°.

SERVES 15

Nancy Blakeley Ruff
(Mrs. Jon B.)

SQUASH—PEPPER CASSEROLE

3 yellow squash, sliced
1 small onion, sliced
2 tomatoes, sliced
1 medium size green pepper, sliced
1 stalk celery, sliced
2 t. salt
2 t. black pepper
2 T. uncooked regular rice
2 T. butter or margarine
1 T. brown sugar

Combine all ingredients except butter and brown sugar in a 1½ quart casserole. Dot with butter and sprinkle with brown sugar. Bake at 350° in covered casserole for 45—50 minutes.

SERVES 4—6

Maud Norton Bivins
(Mrs. James K., III)

REGINA'S HERBED SQUASH CASSEROLE

2 lbs. zucchini or yellow squash, sliced
1 medium onion, sliced
2 carrots, sliced
2 T. butter or bacon drippings
½—1 C. sour cream
1 (10¾ oz.) can cream of chicken soup
2 C. Pepperidge Farm Herb or Cornbread Seasoned Stuffing
½ — ¾ C. margarine, melted
Salt and pepper to taste

The following ingredients are optional:
1 (2 oz.) jar pimiento, drained and chopped
1 can water chestnuts, sliced
Dash Tabasco
Dash Worcestershire sauce

Steam sliced squash, carrots and onion in a covered skillet with butter or drippings. Combine sour cream, soup and seasonings. Mix margarine with stuffing. Line a greased 2 quart casserole with ½ of stuffing mixture. Layer vegetables in casserole, cover with sour cream mixture and top with remaining stuffing mixture. (If desired, vegetables may be mashed and added to sour cream mixture.) Bake at 350° for 30 minutes.

SERVES 8

Martha Hess Whitehead
(Mrs. R. Laughton, Jr.)

Joan Nachbaur Rathbun

Karen Williams Frith
(Mrs. Charles)

Andee Knapp Wrather
(Mrs. John D.) Ft. Lauderdale, Fla.

SCALLOPED TOMATOES, HEARTS OF PALM AND ARTICHOKE HEARTS

1 (35 oz.) can whole plum tomatoes
1 (14 oz.) can artichoke hearts, quartered
1 (14 oz.) can hearts of palm, sliced
½ C. green onion, finely chopped
2 T. shallots, finely chopped
¼ lb. butter
½ t. leaf basil
¾ t. orégano
2 T. sugar
3 T. lemon juice
½ t. lemon rind
2 t. Wondra flour
2 t. salt
Pepper to taste

Drain tomatoes, artichoke hearts and hearts of palm; rinse artichokes and hearts of palm in water. Sauté onions and shallots in butter until tender. Add tomatoes, artichokes, hearts of palm, basil and orégano. Heat 2 or 3 minutes, stirring gently. Season with sugar, lemon juice and rind, salt and pepper. Shake in Wondra flour to thicken. Bake in greased casserole at 325° for 10—15 minutes or until vegetables are heated through.

SERVES 8

Patricia Smith Houston
(Mrs. E. B.)

BAKED TOMATO VERTIS

8 tomatoes
3 T. butter
2 C. raw spinach, chopped
2 medium carrots, chopped
1 small green pepper, chopped
3 large stalks celery, chopped
1 onion, chopped
1 C. dried bread crumbs
½ C. milk
1 egg, beaten
½ t. salt
1/8 t. pepper
1 t. basil
1 T. parsley
1 C. grated cheese

Cut the tops from the stem end of tomatoes. Scoop out seeds and pulp. Sauté vegetables in butter until they are brown. Add remaining ingredients except cheese and mix thoroughly. Fill tomatoes and sprinkle with cheese. Place in a greased pan and bake at 400° for 20 minutes or until tomatoes are tender.

Mrs. Harry Stewart
Camden, Arkansas

BAKED SAVORY TOMATOES

8 tomatoes, peeled
½ C. wild rice, cooked
6 slices bacon
4 large sweet onions, chopped
1 C. mushrooms, chopped
Salt and pepper to taste

Cut a slice off the tops of the tomatoes. Scoop out the centers carefully, leaving a good sustaining wall. Fry bacon until crisp and drain. Cook the onions and mushrooms in a small amount of bacon drippings until tender, but not brown. Add bacon and rice. Season. Mix well with a fork and stuff the tomatoes with this mixture. Bake at 350° for about 20 minutes or until tomatoes are soft. Ed. Note: You might use Uncle Ben's Wild Rice and White Rice Mix.

Bess Valery Topp
(Mrs. J. S.)

PEARLINE'S BAKED TOMATOES

1 (28 oz.) can tomatoes, drained
½ small onion, chopped
5—6 slices bread, crumbled
¼ C. sugar
¼ t. red pepper
½ C. butter, melted
¼ t. salt
¼ C. butter

Combine tomatoes, onion, bread crumbs, sugar, red pepper, melted butter and salt. Pour into a greased 1 qt. casserole. Dot on top with the remaining butter and bake at 350° for 30—40 minutes or until set. Can be prepared in advance and frozen.

SERVES 4

Ann Chreitzberg Sheppard
(Mrs. Gillett)

MEXICAN VEGETABLES

1½ lbs. yellow squash, sliced
½ C. chopped onion
¼ C. green chilies
1 (16 oz.) can whole kernel corn
½ lb. cheese, grated
1 tomato, chopped
½ t. crushed coriander leaf (cilantro)
½ t. salt

Boil squash and onion in a small amount of water until barely tender. Pour off excess liquid and mash. Mix all ingredients; place in a 2 quart casserole. Bake at 350° for 30 minutes.

SERVES 8

Eleanor Croxton Lawrence
(Mrs. Thomas W.)

BAKED VEGETABLES WITH SOUR CREAM

2 C. chopped green pepper
⅔ C. chopped scallions
3 T. butter
1⅓ C. grated carrots
½ C. minced parsley
4 yellow squash, cut into thin strips 2 inches long and ½ inch wide
1½ t. salt
½ t. basil
½ t. orégano
Pepper to taste
1 C. sour cream
⅔ C. freshly grated Parmesan cheese
⅓ C. freshly grated Parmesan cheese

In a large skillet, sauté green pepper and scallions in butter for 3 minutes. Add carrots and parsley and sauté the mixture for 3 minutes. Add the squash strips to the skillet and sauté them for 3 minutes. Add seasonings. Remove the skillet from the heat and add sour cream and ⅔ C. Parmesan cheese. Combine the mixture well, pour it into a buttered 1½ quart souffle dish, and sprinkle the top with ⅓ C. Parmesan cheese. Bake the vegetables in a preheated 350° oven for 35 minutes, or until the squash is tender.

SERVES 6

Carolyn Smith Russell
(Mrs. Ralph H.)

SUMMER VEGETABLE CASSEROLE

4 slices bacon, chopped fine
1 C. chopped onion
1 lb. zucchini squash, diced OR ½ lb. yellow, ½ lb. zucchini
1 lb. eggplant, peeled and diced
4 T. margarine
1 t. seasoned salt
¼ t. lemon pepper marinade
2 T. parsley, chopped
2 large tomatoes, sliced OR 1 (1 lb.) can sliced tomatoes
½ C. Cheddar cheese or 1 C. Mozarella cheese

Cook bacon partially. Pour off all but 2 T. drippings and add vegetables and seasoning. Cook 5—10 minutes over medium heat. Stir occasionally. Stir in parsley. Layer vegetables, tomatoes and cheese in a 2 quart casserole. Cover with bacon. Bake at 350° uncovered for 1 hour.

SERVES 4—6

Linda Ryan Butter
(Mrs. Stephen R.)

VEGETABLE BAKE

"This is good with any meat and kids love it"

8 carrots, sliced 2 large onions, sliced 2 large potatoes, quartered ¼ lb. butter 1 t. thyme 1 T. chopped parsley Salt and pepper to taste	Layer vegetables in a casserole dish with a cover. Dot with butter and sprinkle with thyme and parsley. Bake covered in 350° oven until they are tender (about 1 hour). SERVES 4 Rose Pickens Kirkpatrick (Mrs. Kenneth L.)

INDIAN SUMMER VEGETABLES

2 ears fresh corn 3 T. butter or margarine 2 medium green peppers, cut into strips 2 medium onions, sliced ¼ C. water 4 medium tomatoes, quartered Salt 1½ t. coarsely ground black pepper ¼ t. sweet basil ½ C. grated Parmesan cheese	Cut corn off cob. Preheat fry-pan to 360°. Add butter and melt. Add green peppers and onions. Cover and cook 5 minutes, stirring once or twice. Add ¼ cup water and remaining ingredients except cheese. Cover and cook 10 minutes or until vegetables are crisply tender, not mushy. Shake occasionally during cooking time. Serve with grated cheese. Note: Zucchini may also be included in this recipe. SERVES 10—12 Mary Ann Hollandsworth Nelson (Mrs. Tom)

FRIED ZUCCHINI

"Serve sprinkled with Parmesan cheese or with a dip for an appetizer"

3-4 lbs. zucchini, cut into long strips, ¼" wide 2 eggs 2 C. light cream 2 C. flour ¾ C. whole-wheat flour ¾ C. corn meal 1 T. celery salt 2 t. garlic powder 1 T. white pepper 1 t. thyme 2 t. salt 1 t. paprika	Whip eggs and light cream together; strain. Mix all dry ingredients together. Immerse zucchini in egg mixture and drain. Coat slices in breading mixture. Deep fry. Drain well on paper towels. SERVES 10-12 Cookbook Committee

ZUCCHINI CASSEROLE

1 lb. zucchini, trimmed and scrubbed
Dried dill weed
1 clove garlic
½ lb. fresh mushrooms, sliced
3 T. butter
2 T. flour
1 C. sour cream
Buttered bread crumbs
Salt and pepper to taste

Slice zucchini into ½ inch slices. Bring zucchini to boil in salted water and add dill and garlic. Simmer until barely tender. DO NOT OVERCOOK. Drain zucchini but reserve 2 T. cooking liquid. Discard garlic. Sauté mushrooms in butter for 5 minutes. Stir in flour and cook 2 minutes longer. Add sour cream, zucchini and reserved cooking liquid stirring constantly. Correct seasonings and heat thoroughly but DO NOT BOIL. Transfer to casserole and top with butter bread crumbs. Brown quickly under broiler.

SERVES 6

Patricia Smith Houston
(Mrs. E. B.)

RATATOUILLE

"Use this versatile dish as an appetizer, salad, vegetable or filling for crêpes"

½ lb. eggplant, peeled
½ lb. zucchini
Salt
4 T. olive oil
1½ C. sliced onion
1 C. sliced green pepper
2 cloves garlic, pressed
Pepper
1 C. drained, canned pear-shaped tomatoes OR 1 lb. peeled, seeded and juiced tomatoes (1½ C. pulp)
3 T. minced parsley

VARIATION:
Add:
1 t. thyme
1 t. bay leaf, crushed

AS A FILLING FOR CRÊPES:
Sprinkle crêpes with grated Parmesan and/or Swiss cheese.

Slice eggplant and zucchini lengthwise 3/8" thick. Salt in bowl and let stand 30 minutes. Heat olive oil in a non-stick pan. Sauté eggplant and zucchini until lightly brown on both sides. Remove to a side dish. Add more oil (if necessary) and sauté onion and green pepper slowly until soft. Stir in garlic and season with salt and pepper. Slice tomatoes in strips and place over onions and peppers. Cover; cook 5 minutes. Uncover; raise heat and boil several minutes until tomato juice almost evaporates. Season with salt and pepper and fold in parsley. Layer into 2½ quart casserole 2" deep alternating ⅓ of the tomato mixture with ½ of the eggplant and zucchini. Cover. Simmer over low heat 10 minutes; uncover, tip casserole and baste with juices rendered and correct seasonings if necessary. Raise heat slightly and boil until juice almost evaporates. Serve hot or cold.

Mrs. William C. Morris
New Orleans, La.

Donor: Nancy Weaver Morgan
(Mrs. Stephen)

ZUCCHINI SOUFFLÉ

1 lb. small, firm zucchini
Salt
2 T. butter

BECHAMEL SAUCE:
2 T. butter
3 T. flour
¾ C. milk
Salt and pepper to taste
3 eggs, separated
Butter

SAUCE:
⅔ C. tomato purée
Salt, sugar, garlic, Fine Herbes
1 C. heavy cream
½ C. grated Parmesan cheese

Coarsely grate zucchini; arrange in layers in bowl and salt. Let stand ½ hour. Squeeze moisture out. Sauté in butter for 7-8 minutes until well dried and lightly colored. Prepare Bechamel Sauce by melting butter, stir in flour and cook a few minutes. Add milk and seasoning stirring over medium heat until mixture thickens. Let cool before adding beaten egg yolks. Stir egg mixture into zucchini. Beat egg whites until peaked. Fold ⅓ of whites into mixture; then fold in remaining whites. Put into buttered quart mold. Set mold in a pan of hot water and bake at 350° for 20-25 minutes. Remove mold and let cool for 10 minutes before unmolding onto a shallow baking dish.

SAUCE:
Whisk together purée and cream. Season liberally. Pour over unmolded soufflé. Sprinkle cheese over surface. Bake at 450° for 20 minutes.

Richard Onley-Gritti Palace Cooking School
Donor: Gay Cole Wheeler
(Mrs. Ridley)

ROYAL ZUCCHINI PARMESAN

2 medium onions, chopped
1 green pepper, chopped
2 garlic cloves, chopped
2 T. salad oil
1 (16 oz.) can tomatoes
1 (8 oz.) can tomato sauce
1 (6 oz.) can tomato paste
2 C. water
1 t. salt
¼ t. cracked pepper
¾ t. orégano
6 8 zucchini, cut in ¼" slices
1½ C. grated Cheddar cheese
1 C. grated Parmesan cheese

Sauté onion, green pepper and garlic in oil until limp. Add tomatoes, sauce and paste. Add water and seasonings; cook slowly until sauce is thick (about 35 minutes). Add sliced zucchini and cook 10 minutes. Remove from heat, stir in cheese and blend well. Put into buttered 3 qt. casserole. Sprinkle with Parmesan cheese. Bake at 350° for 45 minutes. Can be frozen.

SERVES 8—10

Helen May Little
(Mrs. Earle E.)

EARLENE'S CHOP-CHOP

¼ C. Hellmann's mayonnaise
¼ C. sour cream
1 T. melted butter
1 onion, chopped very fine
3 T. capers, chopped fine
Dash black pepper
1 T. Season All salt
1 T. lemon juice

Mix all ingredients together and heat. DO NOT BOIL. Pour over hot, cooked vegetables.

YIELD: 1 cup

Aliece McHenry Mucher
(Mrs. Joseph)

MUSTARD SAUCE FOR GREEN BEANS

2 T. butter
1 T. flour
1 t. salt
Dash pepper
1 T. prepared mustard
1 egg yolk, slightly beaten
¾ C. milk
1½—3 t. lemon juice

Melt butter in double boiler on medium heat. Stir in flour, salt, pepper and mustard. Combine egg yolk and milk and add to above mixture. Cook, stirring constantly, until smooth and thickened (about 5 minutes). Remove from fire and add lemon juice just before serving. Serve over hot, seasoned and well drained vegetables.

SERVES 5—6

Martha Apple Johnson
(Mrs. W. B.)

MUSTARD MAYONNAISE

2 C. mayonnaise
½ (6 oz.) jar horseradish mustard

Heat (do not boil or will curdle). Pour over green vegetables.

Susie Moore French
(Mrs. Paul E.)

ORANGE SAUCE

1½ C. fresh orange juice
1 T. lemon juice
1 C. sugar
2 T. cornstarch
1 T. butter
Grated orange and lemon peel

Combine all ingredients and cook until clear. Good to serve with cooked carrots or beets.

Peggy Moss Buckstaff
(Mrs. George)

Verne Monday Smith
(Mrs. Bruner)

BASIC CRÊPE BATTER

2 eggs, beaten
1 C. all purpose, pre-sifted flour
½ t. salt
1½ C. milk
1 T. butter, melted

Mix eggs with flour and salt, using a wire whisk. Gradually add milk, stirring constantly until mixture is smooth. Add butter and blend. Allow this to stand at least 30 minutes before using. To use the traditional method, spray a 6" crêpes pan with Pam or similar coating, brush lightly with butter, and pour in about 1 tablespoon of batter. Tilt pan to cover bottom. When edge browns in 25 seconds, turn and cook quickly for 10 seconds. Add more milk for thinner batter. Add 1 tablespoon of sugar for dessert crêpe. For new crêpes pan, use only 1 cup of milk. Stack cooled crêpes between double layers of wax paper. They freeze perfectly. Thaw and warm before using.

YIELD: 20-24 crêpes.

Betty Robbins Davis
(Mrs. Charles H.)

SWEDISH PANCAKE BATTER

2 eggs separated
3 C. milk
1 C. sifted flour
2 T. sugar
½ t. salt

ORANGE SAUCE:
1 (6 oz. can) frozen orange juice, concentrate
1 C. water
1 C. sugar
2 rounded T. cornstarch
¼ C. butter

Beat egg yolks until frothy and gradually add the remaining ingredients. Beat until smooth as silk. Let stand for 2-3 hours in refrigerator. When ready to bake, fold in 2 stiffly beaten egg whites. Use heavy frying pan as griddle. Be sure the pan is sizzling hot. Add butter and when butter is slightly brown, pour batter a tablespoonful at a time. Roll each pancake with cottage cheese and serve with sour cream and orange sauce. This makes a good brunch dish.

Dilute orange juice with water and add sugar. Bring to a boil. Thicken with cornstarch. Add butter and serve hot.

Aliece McHenry Mucher
(Mrs. Joseph)

PENNY'S BUTTERMILK BISCUITS

2 C. sifted flour
1½ t. baking powder
½ t. soda
1 t. salt
½ C. Crisco
⅔ C. buttermilk

Heat oven to 450°. Sift together flour, baking powder, soda, and salt. Cut in shortening. Stir in buttermilk. Round up on lightly floured board. Knead lightly 10-15 times. Roll out 1/8" thick. Spread with melted butter. Fold over and cut double biscuits. Place on ungreased baking sheet. Bake 10-12 minutes.

YIELD: 30 small biscuits

Mrs. Michael C. Macey

CARAWAY CHEESE GEMS

1 large egg
½ C. sour cream
1 C. flour
1½ t. baking powder
¼ t. soda
1½ t. caraway seed
¾ C. grated (medium-fine) extra-sharp Cheddar cheese

In a medium mixing bowl, beat egg slightly; add sour cream and beat to blend. Combine dry ingredients and cheese. Add to egg mixture and stir only until moistened and still lumpy. Spoon into paper muffin cups almost full or into small muffin tins. Bake in a preheated 375° oven until done, about 25 minutes.

YIELD: 6 large or 12 small muffins

Cookbook Committee

QUICK CHEESE BREAD

½ C. milk
1 egg, beaten
1½ C. biscuit mix
2 T. chopped parsley
1 T. minced onion
1 C. shredded Cheddar cheese, divided
¼ C. melted butter or margarine

Combine milk and egg. Add biscuit mix, parsley, onion and ½ C. cheese. Pour into a greased 8" or 9" round pan. Sprinkle remaining ½ C. cheese on batter; pour melted butter over top. Bake at 350° for 25 minutes or until golden brown.

SERVES 6-8

Eugenia Tunstall Francis
(Mrs. Tom B.)

CHEESY FRENCH BREAD

1 C. butter, softened
½ lb. cheese, grated
1 clove garlic, crushed
Parsley or paprika

Blend butter, cheese and garlic. Spread on slices of French bread or a loaf split into two sections. Broil until bubbly. Sprinkle with parsley or paprika.

Linda Ryan Butter
(Mrs. Stephen R.)

OVEN BUTTERED CORNSTICKS

4 T. butter or margarine
2 C. packaged biscuit mix
1 (8¾ oz.) can cream style corn

Melt butter or margarine in 15½"x10½"X½" baking dish. Combine biscuit mix and corn and knead until dough is formed. Roll to 6" x 10" rectangle. Cut rectangle in half lengthwise. Then cut in 3" fingers. Dip fingers in melted butter and place in pan and bake at 450° for 10-12 minutes.

YIELD: 2 dozen

Maud Norton Bivins
(Mrs. James K., III)

MEXICAN CORN BREAD

1 C. corn meal
1 C. sweet milk
3 eggs
3 jalapeño peppers, seeded and chopped
½ C. chopped onion
1 t. garlic powder
1½ C. shredded cheese
½ t. soda
½ t. salt
½ t. sugar
1 C. (1 small can) whole kernel corn
1 (2 oz.) can chopped pimiento
⅓ C. bacon drippings or corn oil

Mix all together well and cook in a greased skillet at 350° for 45 minutes.

Karen Williams Frith
(Mrs. Charles E.)

DALLAS CADDO CLUB HUSH PUPPIES

2 C. corn meal
1 C. flour
¼ C. sugar
¼ t. soda
3 t. baking powder
2 t. salt
1 t. black pepper
1 t. poultry seasoning
1 t. Accent
¼ C. parsley flakes
1 onion, chopped
2 eggs
1 C. buttermilk
1 T. butter, melted

Combine all ingredients. Drop in hot oil from a tablespoon making one inch balls. Cook until brown. Mixture will keep for several days in the refrigerator.

YIELD: 36

Nancy Blakeley Ruff
(Mrs. Jon B.)

NASHVILLE EGG BREAD

2 C. cornmeal
2 eggs
½ t. salt
Pinch of soda
2 t. baking powder
1¼ C. milk

Combine ingredients. Pour batter into hot greased 10" skillet or 9x9x2" greased cake pan. Bake at 400° for 25 minutes.

Ann Killingsworth Smead
(Mrs. Hamp, Jr.)

MELBA ROUNDS

½ C. butter
1 t. dill weed
2 t. parsley flakes
¼ t. garlic powder
1 t. tarragon
Pepperidge Farm thin sliced bread

Melt butter and add seasoning. Cut bread into rounds with biscuit cutter. Brush both sides of each round liberally with butter mixture. Place on cookie sheet and bake in 200° oven until golden brown and very crisp.

Patricia Smith Houston
(Mrs. E. B.)

SOUR CREAM CORNBREAD

⅓ C. vegetable oil
1 t. salt
2 eggs
1½ C. Cinch cornbread mix
1 (8 oz.) can cream style corn
1 (8 oz.) carton sour cream

Mix all ingredients together, and bake at 350° for 30 minutes.

Mrs. Virgil Howie, Gulfport, Miss.
Donor: Gay Cole Howard Wheeler
 (Mrs. Ridley N.)

ORANGE NUT BREAD

1 C. ground orange rind
½ C. water
2 T. sugar
2¼ C. unsifted all-purpose flour
1 C. sugar
2½ t. baking powder
1 t. salt
⅔ C. milk
3 T. melted Crisco
2 eggs
¾ C. walnuts (chopped)

In advance, grind orange rinds of 2 or 3 large oranges FINE. Use 1 C. in a saucepan, add water and 2 T. sugar. Cover and cook over low heat 10 to 15 minutes until most water is absorbed. Cool. Sift flour, sugar, baking powder and salt in a large bowl. Add milk, shortening and eggs. Beat at low speed until smooth. Add cooked orange rind and nuts. Put batter into two greased 9"x5"x3" loaf pans. If desired, sprinkle top with mixture of ½ t. cinnamon, 2 T. sugar before baking.

Sue Roth Fite
(Mrs. John)

ORANGE PRUNE BREAD

2 C. sifted flour
⅔ C. sugar
2 t. baking powder
½ t. salt
½ t. baking soda
⅔ C. coarsely chopped pecans
1 C. coarsely chopped cooked prunes
½ C. prune juice (from cooked prunes)
1 egg, slightly beaten
2 t. orange peel
¼ C. butter, melted
1 t. vanilla

ORANGE BUTTER:

2 t. orange peel
1 T. orange juice
¼ C. soft butter
1 (8 oz.) pkg. cream cheese (softened)

Sift flour, sugar, baking powder, salt, and soda together. Add pecans. Combine prunes, prune juice, the egg, orange peel, melted butter, and vanilla. Add this mixture to the dry mixture. Stir until just well mixed. Pour into a greased and floured loaf pan and bake at 350° for 50 minutes, or more, if necessary, until done. May be served with orange butter, if desired. May be frozen.

YIELD: 1 loaf

Laney Talmage Mobley
(Mrs. Ebb)

OLIVE BREAD

"It is delicious served with soft cream cheese"

2 C. flour
2 t. baking powder
1 t. salt
¼ t. soda
½ t. dry mustard
1 C. chopped stuffed olives
1 C. chopped pecans
¼ C. sugar
2 T. butter
2 eggs
¾ C. milk

Sift together flour, baking powder, salt, soda, and mustard. Add nuts and olives. Set aside. Cream butter and sugar; and eggs one at a time, beating well. Add milk and dry ingredients, alternately, stirring only enough to blend well. Pour into greased and floured loaf pan. Let sit 20 minutes before baking. Bake at 350° for 1 hour.

YIELD: 1 loaf

Mrs. Lala Guttry, Kilgore, Texas

ONION SHORTCAKE

2 (6 oz.) pkg. cornbread mix
⅓ C. milk
1 egg
3 jalapeño peppers, chopped finely
1 C. cream style corn
1 onion, thinly sliced into rings
¼ C. butter
1 C. sour cream
¼ t. dill weed
½ t. salt
1¾ C. grated Cheddar cheese

Mix cornbread mix, egg, milk, corn, and the jalapeño peppers, and pour this into a greased 8" by 12" casserole. Set aside. Sauté slightly the onion rings in the butter. Add dill weed, salt, and ¾ C. of the cheese to the sour cream. Spread this mixture over the cornbread mixture. Sprinkle the remaining cup of grated cheese over the top. Bake at 325° for 40 minutes. Let the cornbread set for 10 minutes before cutting.

SERVES 10

Maud Norton Bivins
(Mrs. James K., III)

PARMESAN—WINE BREAD

2 C. Bisquick
1 T. sugar
1 T. instant onion
½ t. orégano
½ C. melted butter
¼ C. white wine
1 egg, beaten
½ C. milk
½ C. Parmesan cheese, divided

Combine all ingredients (¼ C. cheese) and beat. Pour into an 8" round pan. Top with ¼ C. cheese. Bake at 400° for 25 minutes.

Patty Yates Shappell
(Mrs. H. D., Jr.)

POLLY'S PUMPKIN BREAD

3⅓ C. flour
½ t. baking powder
2 t. soda
1½ t. salt
1 t. cinnamon
½ t. cloves
2⅔ C. sugar
⅔ C. vegetable oil
4 eggs
1 (16 oz.) can pumpkin
⅔ C. water
⅔ C. raisins

Combine the flour, baking powder, soda, salt, cinnamon, and cloves in mixer, and mix at low speed. Add the sugar, and, mixing well after each addition, the oil, eggs, pumpkin, water and raisins. Bake at 350° for 35 to 40 minutes. After cooking, cool loaves and wrap in foil. Let sit for 2 or 3 days for a very moist bread. May be frozen.

YIELD: 4 medium sized loaves.

Judy Fite Shiver
(Mrs. John D.)

STRAWBERRY NUT BREAD
"A moist and pretty bread for the holidays"

3 C. sifted flour
1 t. soda
1 t. salt
1 t. cinnamon
2 C. sugar
4 eggs, beaten
1¼ C. oil
2 (10 oz.) pkgs. thawed frozen strawberries and juice
1¼ C. chopped pecans

Sift flour, soda, salt, cinnamon and sugar into a large bowl. Combine eggs, oil, strawberries and pecans. Make a well in the center of the dry ingredients. Add liquids, stirring just enough to moisten. Pour into 2 greased 9"x5"x3" pans. Bake at 350° for 1 hour. (May use 6-6"x3"x2" pans and bake 40 minutes.) Remove from oven and let stand 5 minutes before removing from pans. Freezes well.

Jill Prather Norton
(Mrs. Robert W.)

VARIATION:
Omit nuts
Add:
1 t. Red food coloring
FILLING:
½ C. strawberry juice, reserve from strawberries
1 (8 oz.) pkg. cream cheese

FILLING:
Cream juice in blender. Spread on cool bread.

Jeanette Kimble West, Enid, Oklahoma

ZUCCHINI BREAD

3 eggs
2 C. peeled and grated zucchini
1 C. oil
2 C. sugar (may use half white and half brown)
2 t. vanilla
3 C. flour
1 t. salt
1 t. soda
½ t. baking powder
1 t. cinnamon
½ C. chopped nuts

Beat eggs, add zucchini, oil, sugar and vanilla. Beat well. Sift dry ingredients. Add to creamed mixture. Mix well. Add nuts. Bake in greased 8½" x 4½" x2 5/8" bread pans. Bake at 325° for one hour or until done. Can be frozen. Ed. note: ½ C. dried currants can be added to the batter.

Diane Dulin Atkinson
(Mrs. Dennis)

BLUEBERRY COFFEE CAKE

2 C. flour
1½ C. sugar
⅔ C. margarine
2 T. baking powder
1 t. salt
2 eggs, separated
1 C. milk
1 (15 oz.) can blueberries (drained) or 1½ C. fresh berries

Sift the flour and the sugar in a large bowl. Cut in the margarine with a pastry fork until small pea-sized balls form. Reserve ¾ C. for the topping. Add the baking powder, salt, egg yolks, and the milk. Beat for 3 minutes. Beat the egg whites until stiff in a separate bowl, and fold gently into the above mixture. Arrange the blueberries over the batter which has been placed in a greased 9"x13"x2" pan, or 2 round 9" pans. Sprinkle the remaining reserved topping on the top. Bake at 350° for 40 to 45 minutes. May be frozen.

Sue Roth Fite
(Mrs. John)

RICH SWEET DOUGH

¾ C. milk
½ C. sugar
2 t. salt
½ C. margarine
½ C. warm water
2 yeast cakes
1 egg
4 C. unsifted flour

Scald the milk. Stir in the sugar, salt, and margarine. Cool to lukewarm. Measure the warm water into a large bowl. Add the yeast, and stir until dissolved. Stir in the lukewarm milk mixture, the egg, and half of the flour. Beat until smooth. Stir in the remaining flour to make a stiff batter. Cover tightly with waxed paper. Refrigerate the dough at least 2 hours.

PECAN STICKY BUNS

1 recipe Rich Sweet Dough
1 C. margarine
2½ C. brown sugar, divided
1½ C. chopped pecans, divided

Prepare the dough. Before shaping, melt the margarine. Stir in 1½ C. brown sugar, and 1 C. chopped pecans. Spoon into greased muffin pans. Combine the remaining 1 C. brown sugar, and ½ C. chopped pecans. Divide the dough in half. Roll out each half to a 12" square. Sprinkle each half with brown sugar-pecan mixture. Roll up lengthwise as for a jelly roll. Cut into 1" slices, and place in prepared pans. Cover, and let rise in a warm place until doubled in bulk, about 1 hour. Bake for 25 minutes at 350°.

YIELD: 2 dozen.

Sara Skaggs Lucas
(Mrs. J. Richard)

GLASS MOUNTAIN COFFEE CAKE

1 C. butter or margarine
2 C. sugar
2 eggs
4 T. brown sugar
1 C. sour cream
1 t. vanilla
2 C. sifted flour
1 t. baking powder
¼ t. salt
1 t. cinnamon
1 C. chopped pecans

Cream butter and sugar well. Add eggs one at a time, beating well after each addition. Add brown sugar and mix thoroughly. Fold in sour cream and vanilla. Add sifted dry ingredients. Add chopped pecans. Pour into a heavy oiled and floured tube pan and bake at 350° for 45 to 60 minutes. Cool cake at least 10 minutes before turning out of pan. Sprinkle with powdered sugar.

Mrs. L. C. Fisher, Jr.
Donor: Martha Pearce Joseph
(Mrs. George)

REFRIGERATOR GINGER BREAD MUFFINS

4 C. flour
2 t. soda
1 t. baking powder
2 t. ginger
¼ t. allspice
¼ t. cinnamon
1 C. butter
1 C. sugar
4 eggs
1 C. molasses
1 C. sour cream

Combine all dry ingredinets. Cream the butter and sugar. Beat in the eggs. Add the molasses and sour cream. Add the dry ingredients. Fill the muffin pan ½ full. Bake at 350° for 15 minutes. May be served hot with or without icing. The dough may be stored in the refrigerator for up to 3 weeks.

YIELD: 4 dozen

Carmen Huggins Hilliard
(Mrs. George M.)

APPLE COFFEE CAKE

"This is great with scrambled eggs for breakfast."

1 C. flour
1 C. sugar
¼ t. salt
1 t. cinnamon
½ t. nutmeg
1 t. soda
1 egg
2 T. melted margarine
2 C. chopped, peeled tart apples
1 C. chopped nuts

Sift together in a large bowl flour, sugar, salt, cinnamon, nutmeg, and soda. Add remaining ingredients and mix until well moistened. Pat into a greased 9" round pan. Bake at 350° for 30-35 minutes.

Sally Hilliard Shank
Tulsa, Oklahoma

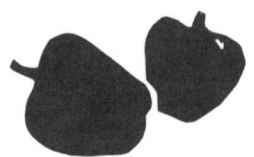

BOHEMIAN COFFEE CAKE

1 C. vegetable oil
1 C. brown sugar
1 C. white sugar
1 C. buttermilk
2 eggs
2½ C. flour
1 t. salt
1 t. soda
1 t. cinnamon
1 t. nutmeg
1 t. vanilla
1 C. coconut
1 C. pecans

Mix all cake ingredients. Pour into a greased, floured pan. Bake at 350° for 1 hour and 10 minutes. Cool before icing. Cream together the cream cheese, margarine, and the powdered sugar. Add the almond extract, and vanilla. Sprinkle with the toasted almonds.

Mrs. Bill Ratliff
Donor: True Sandlin Mann
   (Mrs. Jack C. Jr.)

ICING:

1 (8 oz.) pkg. cream cheese
¼ C. margarine
1 box powdered sugar
½ t. almond extract
1½ t. vanilla
1 C. sliced, toasted almonds

BRAIDED COFFEE CAKE

DOUGH:
1 pkg. dry yeast
½ C. lukewarm water
1 egg, slightly beaten
½ C. margarine
¾ t. salt
¼ C. sugar
½ C. boiling water
4 C. flour

FILLING:
¾ C. margarine, divided
1 C. granulated sugar
1 C. brown sugar
Cinnamon to taste
Chopped nuts

ICING:
Confectioner's sugar
Water

Stir dry yeast into lukewarm water. Let stand 5 minutes and add egg. Melt margarine, sugar and salt in boiling water. Cool, add to yeast mixture, and stir in flour. Put dough in greased bowl, cover, and refrigerate overnight. Next day let dough come to room temperature. Then knead 4-6 times. Divide the dough into two balls. Roll one ball out thin. Spread half of margarine over dough surface. Combine sugars, cinnamon, and nuts. Sprinkle ½ of mixture over dough. Slice dough into 3 strips. Roll and seal each strip. Braid 3 strips together. Let rise 1 to 1½ hours. Repeat process with second ball of dough. Brush with margarine and bake at 350° 15 to 20 minutes. Cool. Mix confectioners sugar with small amount of water until it reaches a syrup-like consistency. Dribble this over the coffee cakes. May be frozen without icing. Add later.

Mrs. John N. Darby

CRANBERRY COFFEE CAKE

1 C. margarine
1 C. sugar
2 eggs
1 t. baking powder
1 t. soda
1 t. salt
2 C. flour
1 C. sour cream
1 t. almond extract
1 (7 oz.) can cranberry whole berry sauce
½ C. chopped nuts

GLAZE:
2 T. warm water
½ t. almond extract
¾ C. powdered sugar

Cream the margarine, and add the sugar and eggs. Combine dry ingredients. Add the dry ingredients alternately with the sour cream. Add the almond extract. Pour half of the batter in a greased and floured bundt pan. Spread half of the cranberry sauce over the batter. Pour the remaining batter in the pan. Top with the remaining cranberry sauce and the nuts. Bake at 350° for 55 to 60 minutes. Cool. Make a glaze by mixing together the warm water, almond extract, and powdered sugar. Spread on top of the cake. Serve warm. May be frozen.

SERVES 16—20

Marilyn Rouse Payne
(Mrs. Hermes E.)

BOURBON BREAD

1 pkg. dry yeast
1 C. flour
¼ C. light brown sugar
½ C. lukewarm water
2¼ C. unsifted flour
2 eggs, plus 1 white, beaten
1 t. salt
⅓ C. melted butter
½ C. warm milk
¼ C. Bourbon

Combine the first 4 ingredients in a large bowl. Beat the mixture well, and set the bowl in a dishpan of warm water. Cover with a towel. Let the dough rise for approximately 1 hour. Beat the eggs and the egg white until light. Then beat the eggs, and all the remaining ingredients, into the yeast mixture. Beat this mixture hard, using your hands, for approximately 4 minutes. The dough should be light, but with a good body. Add up to ¾ C. more flour if needed. Replace the dough in the bowl, and then in the pan of warm water. Cover. Let rise for approximately 45 minutes to 1 hour. Beat hard again. Then place in a greased bread pan. Set the pan in the warm water again, and cover with a towel. Let the dough rise until it reaches the top of the pan. Place the pan in a cold oven. Set the temperature at 400°, and bake for 15 minutes. Turn the oven down to 325° for another 25 minutes. Turn the bread onto a wire rack to cool, and cover lightly with a cloth. Freezes well.

Kirsten Sonne Felker
(Mrs. Marshal L., Jr.)

ETHIOPIAN HONEY BREAD

1 pkg. yeast
½ C. warm water
1 egg, beaten
½ C. honey
1 t. salt
1 t. coriander
1 T. cinnamon (or less)
1 t. cloves
1 C. warm milk
4 T. (or more) butter, softened
4-4½ C. flour
2 T. butter, softened

Add yeast to warm water. Combine egg, honey, salt and spices. Add yeast mixture, milk, and butter. Add flour and roll into a soft ball. Knead with more flour until fairly firm. Then knead remaining butter into dough. Place in bowl, set in warm place to rise. Let double, punch down. Divide in half, making 2 loaves, adding more butter for a richer bread, as your knead. Place in 2 greased 8" x 5" bread pan. Let rise until double. Bake at 300° for about 1 hour.

YIELD: 2 loaves

Jan Crawford

PARTY ROLLS

4 cakes yeast or 6 packages dry yeast
½ C. warm water
1 C. sugar
1 C. Crisco
2 t. salt
4 eggs
1½ C. lukewarm milk
7 C. all-purpose flour, sifted
1½ sticks butter, melted

Dissolve yeast in water and set aside. Cream sugar and shortening, add salt and eggs; mix well. Combine lukewarm milk and yeast mixture; stir into first mixture. Fold in flour until mixture reaches a good dough stage, not too dry and not sticky. Scrape into a large greased bowl (I use the largest Tupperware bowl) and cover with a damp cup towel. Place the dough in a warm place for 2 hours or until double in volume. Turn out on a floured board, handling as little as possible. Roll to ½" thickness, cut with a biscuit cutter, dip in butter, and fold each roll in half as it is placed in pan. At this point, rolls may be refrigerated for several days or frozen. To bake, allow rolls to reach room temperature and to rise until double in volume (about 1 hr.). Bake in middle of oven at 350° for 20-25 minutes until golden brown. I buy foil pans and give extras to friends.

YIELD: 80-100 rolls

Betty Robbins Davis
(Mrs. Charles H.)

MONKEY BREAD

½ C. margarine
1 C. milk
½ C. sugar
½ t. salt
1 pkg. dry yeast
½ C. warm water
2 eggs, beaten
4 C. flour
½ C. margarine, melted

Scald the milk. Add the margarine, sugar, and the salt. Dissolve the yeast in the warm water. Add the yeast, eggs, and ½ of the flour to the milk mixture. Beat with a spoon. Add the rest of the flour. Beat well. Cover with a damp cloth and place in the refrigerator overnight. Take out 2½ hours before needed. Flour hands and pinch off dough. Roll into balls the size of a walnut. Drop the balls into the melted margarine, and then into a ring mold pan. Let rise. Bake at 375° for 40 minutes.

Mrs. Edwin Duncan, Tyler, Texas

SWEDISH RYE BREAD LIMPA

2 C. milk
2 C. water
1 C. brown sugar
1 C. molasses
1 T. anise seed
1 T. ground orange rind
1 T. salt
½ C. butter
⅓ C. water
1 T. sugar
2 cakes yeast
6 C. Bohemian rye flour
6 C. all-purpose flour, divided
3 T. butter

Scald milk (not necessary if canned) and cool. Combine next 5 ingredients in saucepan, bring to a boil and boil 5 minutes. Add salt and ½ C. butter and cool to lukewarm. Soften yeast in ⅓ C. water and 1 T. sugar. Combine all above ingredients in large bowl. Add rye flour and mix well. Beat until smooth. Add 4 C. white flour; knead in next 2 C. flour or as much as is necessary to make smooth and elastic. Knead about 10 minutes. Place in greased bowl and let rise until double (about 2 hours). Punch down and divide into 4 loaves. Place in pans. Melt 3 T. butter and brush tops. Let rise until double. Bake at 350° for 45-55 minutes.

YIELD: 4 loaves

Mrs. Paul Glaske

TWO HOUR ROLLS

1 C. milk
2 T. butter
1 yeast cake
½ C. lukewarm water
2 T. sugar
3 C. flour
1 t. salt
1 C. butter, melted

Scald the milk. Add the butter and cool. Dissolve the yeast in the water. Add the sugar. Sift the flour and salt together. Pour the yeast and milk mixtures into a mixing bowl. Add 1½ C. flour. Beat until smooth. Add the remaining flour. Mix well. Cover and let rise in a warm place for 30 minutes. Roll and cut into desired shape. Dip each roll in the melted butter. Place in baking pan and let rise for 30 minutes more. Bake at 350° until brown, approximately 10 to 15 minutes, and serve at once.

YIELD: 2 dozen (3")

**Gay Cole Howard Wheeler
(Mrs. Ridley N.)**

FRENCH BREAD

1¼ C. warm water (not hot)
1 pkg. dry yeast
1½ t. salt
3 T. soft shortening
4 C. sifted flour
1 egg white
2 T. water

Measure the water and yeast into a mixing bowl. Stir to dissolve. Then add the remaining ingredients. Add the flour and stir with a wooden spoon until smooth. Put out onto floured board, and knead until the dough is smooth and elastic and doesn't stick to the board. Grease a large bowl with margarine, and put rounded dough in bowl. Turn it over to bring greased side up. Cover with a damp cloth and put in a warm place to rise for 1½ hours. I always put mine in the oven to rise, and put a pan of hot water on the bottom shelf. This helps with the rising. Change the water from time to time during the period of rising. To test it, press 2 fingers into the dough. When dough is doubled, it will leave indentations. Punch the dough down and turn it over and let it rise for 30 minutes more. At the end of this time, shape into one large loaf, or two smaller loaves. Roll the dough with your hands, making it smaller at each end. Don't work with the dough any more than you have to. Place the loaf diagonally across a large baking sheet which has been lightly greased with margarine and sprinkled with cornmeal. If you are making two loaves, place on one large baking sheet, treated the same way, and place about 4" apart so that when they rise, they won't join each other. Make ¼" slashes in the dough at 2" intervals with a very sharp knife. Brush the top with cold water. Let stand uncovered for 1½ hours. Brush again with water, and bake in pre-heated oven for 20 minutes at 375°. Take out and brush with a mixture of 1 egg white and 2 T. water. Put back in the oven and bake for 25 minutes for 1 loaf, and 20 minutes for 2 loaves.

Kathleen Ellison Loomis
(Mrs. Norman E.)

WHITE BREAD

½ C. warm water
2 pkgs. dry yeast
1 ¾ C. lukewarm milk
2 T. sugar
1 T. salt
2 T. soft shortening
7 C. flour

Add part of sugar to water before adding yeast. Measure ½ C. warm water in large mixing bowl and add yeast, stirring to dissolve. Set bowl in pam of very hot water until yeast starts to work and foam. Stir in milk, sugar, salt, shortening and then start adding flour and stir. Add flour until it handles easily and doesn't stick. Put dough on floured board and knead until it is smooth and elastic and no longer sticks to board. Round up in greased (butter) bowl. Turn to bring greased side up. Cover with damp cloth and put in oven with a pan of hot water on lower shelf. Let dough rise until doubled in bulk, approximately 1½ hrs. Punch down and turn dough over; cover with damp cloth again and let rise for about 30 minutes. Divide dough into 2 equal parts. Let rest on board (covered with dry tea towel) for 10 minutes; knead again and shape into loaves and put in greased bread pans. Put in oven, cover pans with dry cloth. Put pan of hot water on bottom rack of oven, and let rise for 45 minutes to 1 hour. This will make the loaves rise until almost to top of bread pan. Turn oven on after removing towel and pan of water, to 375°. Starting in a cold oven lets the loaves rise a little more as the oven heats. Bake approximately 35 minutes. Take out of pans, put on rack and brush tops of loaves with butter. Cover with dry tea towel to prevent loaves from cracking on top.

Kathleen Ellison Loomis
(Mrs. Norman E.)

MY MOTHER'S BREAD

1 yeast cake
1 C. shortening
1 C. sugar
2 C. warm water
1 t. salt
5 C. flour

Dissolve yeast in 1 cup of warm water. Cream shortening with sugar. Add salt, and remaining water. Add the yeast. Stir in the flour, approximately 5 cups, until dough is not sticky. Cover and let rise for 2 hours. Stir down, and place in pans. Let rise again. Bake 30 to 40 minutes and 350°. Makes 2 loaves and a pan of rolls.

Mrs. Jerry Martin, Lubbock, Texas

HOT ASPARAGUS SANDWICH

1 (16 oz.) can asparagus tips, drained
4 oz. cream cheese
Juice of ½ lemon
2 hard-boiled eggs, sieved
½ t. seasoned salt
Butter
Parmesan cheese
16 slices sandwich bread, trimmed

Mix well first five ingredients and beat until smooth. Spread on 8 slices of trimmed bread. Cover with 8 additional slices of bread to make sandwiches. Spread the outside top and bottom of sandwiches with softened butter and sprinkle on side with grated Parmesan cheese. Cut sandwiches in half. Place under broiler until golden brown. Sprinkle the other side with cheese and broil as before. These may be cut into finger-sized sandwiches also.

YIELD: 16 sandwich halves

Dorothy Robbins Kennedy
(Mrs. George E., Jr.)

CRAB SANDWICHES

1 C. fresh or canned crabmeat
½ C. chopped or sliced ripe olives
½ C. diced celery
2 T. chopped green onions
½ C. shredded process mild Cheddar cheese
½ C. mayonnaise
3 English muffins, halved

Combine first 6 ingredients and spread on buttered English muffin halves. Broil until hot and brown.

SERVES 6

Mrs. Harry R. Moore, Dallas, Texas
Donor: Susie Moore French
(Mrs. Paul E.)

CHICKEN SALAD LUNCHEON SANDWICHES

English Muffins
Chicken salad
Asparagus spears
Swiss or American cheese grated

Top sliced English muffins with generous servings of chicken salad (or sliced ham, chicken or turkey). Top meat with asparagus spears and grated Swiss or American cheese. Heat in 250°—300° oven until warm and cheese melts. To be eaten with knife and fork.

Mrs. Mack Williams, Gainesville, Fla
Donor: Katy Hall Painter
(Mrs. Paul)

HAM SANDWICHES

½ lb. soft margarine
3 T. prepared mustard
1 t. Worcestershire sauce
½ grated onion
20 Sesame buns
1 lb. chopped ham (chipped)
20 slices Swiss cheese

Cream together well; margarine, mustard, Worcestershire and onion. Spread mixture on both halves of the buns thinly. Put meat and cheese on buns and wrap in foil. Bake in a 325° oven for 25 minutes. Can rewarm and freeze.

Barbara Hubbard Tomberlain
(Mrs. Charles)

ESSIE'S HOT OPEN-FACED TURKEY SANDWICHES

6 slices whole wheat bread, buttered
6 slices cold cooked turkey (smoked is best)
6 slices Swiss cheese
6 slices crisp bacon
6 hard-cooked eggs, sliced
Salt and pepper to taste
Herbed Mayonnaise

HERBED MAYONNAISE:
¾ C. mayonnaise
¾ t. poultry seasoning
1½ T. capers
¾ t. instant minced onion

Have all ingredients cold. Place on each slice of buttered bread in order given: turkey, cheese, bacon and 1 sliced hard-cooked egg. Sprinkle with salt and pepper to taste. Top each with 2 T. Herbed Mayonnaise. Place under broiler to brown. Serve piping hot.

SERVES 6

Fay Jeter Lewis
(Mrs. Harry, Jr.)

GRILLED MUSHROOMS AND CHEESE SANDWICHES

⅓ C. mayonnaise
2 t. Worcestershire sauce
1 t. prepared mustard
¼ t. salt
1/8 t. cayenne
2 C. Cheddar cheese, grated
½ C. Bleu cheese, crumbled
1 (4 oz.) can mushroom stems and pieces, drained
2 T. green onions finely chopped
16 slices white bread
3 beaten eggs
½ C. milk
2 T. grated Parmesan cheese

Combine mayonnaise, Worcestershire sauce, mustard, salt, and cayenne. Add cheeses, mushrooms, and onions. Make sandwiches. In a shallow dish, combine egg, milk, and Parmesan. Dip both sides of sandwiches into egg mixture. Cook on buttered griddle over medium heat until golden.

YIELD: 8 sandwiches

Carmen Huggins Hilliard
(Mrs. George M., III)

AMBROSIA CAKE

½ C.+ 1 T. butter
⅓ – ½ C. Crisco
3 eggs
2 C. sugar
½ t. salt
2 t. soda
1 C. sour milk
3 C. cake flour
½ t. cloves
1 t. cinnamon
½ C. boiling water
2 squares chocolate

FILLING:
3 C. sugar
1½ C. milk
1 t. baking powder
1 pinch soda
1 grated coconut
1 C. chopped dates
1 C. chopped nuts
1 orange, juice and grated peel
¼ C. butter, melted

Cream sugar and shortening. Add eggs. Dissolve soda in milk. Combine dry ingredients. Add milk alternately with dry ingredients. Bake at 325° for 30 minutes.

YIELD: 3 thin 9" layers

FILLING:
Combine sugar, milk, baking powder and soda in a saucepan and cook until soft ball stage (232°). Combine fruits and pour syrup over. Mix and spread on cake.

Cookbook Committee

APPLE RUM CAKE

½ C. butter
1 C. sugar
1 egg
2 C. peeled, grated apple
1 C. sifted flour
1 t. soda
1 t. cinnamon
¾ t. nutmeg
½ t. salt

HOT RUM SAUCE
½ C. butter
1 C. sugar
½ C. heavy cream
¼ t. nutmeg
1 t. vanilla
3 T. dark rum

Cream butter, sugar and egg until light. Add part of apple. Gradually add dry ingredients and the rest of the apple. Bake at 400° for 35 minutes in a a greased 9" square pan.

SERVES 16

SAUCE:
Combine butter, sugar and cream and cook over low heat 15-20 minutes. Add spices and rum and pour over hot cake.

Patsy Lacy Griffith, Santa Fe, N. Mexico (Mrs. J. W.)

BANANA NUT CAKE

1 C. butter
3 C. sugar
2 t. soda
8 T. buttermilk
3 C. flour
4 eggs, separated
5 ripe bananas, mashed
2 t. vanilla
1 C. pecans
½ t. salt

ORANGE ICING:
½ C. butter
2 (16 oz.) boxes powdered sugar
Fresh orange juice

Cream butter and sugar; dissolve soda in buttermilk; add alternately with flour. Add beaten egg yolks, mashed bananas, then vanilla, pecans and salt. Add last, stiffly beaten egg whites. Bake in four 9" cake pans at 350° until done. Ice with orange icing.

Cream butter with half the powdered sugar. Add orange juice and remaining sugar alternately, to make the right consistency to spread. Spread between layers of cake and on top and sides.

Peggy Conner Smead
(Mrs. Hamp, Sr.)

BANANA SPLIT CAKE

1½ pkg. fine graham cracker crumbs
¾ C. melted margarine

FILLING:
2⅓ C. powdered sugar
2 eggs
½ C. margarine, softened
2 bananas, cut lengthwise
1 (16 oz.) can crushed pineapple, drained
1 (9 oz.) tub Cool Whip
Maraschino cherries to garnish
Pecans to garnish

Combine crumbs with margarine. Mix well. Press into 8"x10" casserole.
FILLING:
Beat sugar, eggs and margarine together until smooth. Layer bananas. Add pineapple. Top with Cool Whip. Garnish with cherries and pecans. Cover with foil and refrigerate for 12 hours.

SERVES 10-12

Pam Rice Smith
(Mrs. Ned)

BLUEBERRY CHEESE CAKE

3 (8 oz.) pkgs. cream cheese
1 pt. sour cream
3 T. cornstarch
5 eggs, separated
¾ C. sugar
Juice of 1 lemon
1 t. vanilla

CRUST:
1 box Zwieback crumbs
½ C. margarine
½ C. sugar
Dash cinnamon
Dash nutmeg

Cream cheese. Add sour cream and cornstarch paste, made with a little milk. Mix egg yolks, sugar and add lemon juice and vanilla. Fold in well-beaten (soft peaks) egg whites.

CRUST:
Mix crust and coat spring-form pan over all. Bake at 250° for 1 hour and 10 minutes. Let it set in oven overnight or at least 1 hour. Top with can of blueberry pie filling.

Mrs. Maury Rolnick
Dallas, Texas

BUTTER PECAN CAKE

1 pkg. Betty Crocker Butter Pecan Cake Mix
4 eggs
½ C. oil
1 C. water
1 pkg. Betty Crocker Butter Pecan Frosting Mix
1 C. chopped pecans
1 C. grated coconut

Combine first four ingredients. Mix well. Fold in frosting, nuts and coconut. Bake at 350° in a greased and floured tube pan 1 hour. Cool 10 minutes. This cake is better two or three days old.

Verne Monday Smith
(Mrs. Bruner)

Dorothy Lorimer McNally
(Mrs. Frank)

CARAMEL FUDGE CAKE

½ C. butter or margarine
2 C. brown sugar (packed, light brown)
2 eggs beaten
2 C. sifted flour
2 t. baking powder
Pinch salt
2 C. pecans
1 t. vanilla

Melt butter; add sugar and mix well. Cool. Add eggs and beat. Add rest of ingredients and mix. Turn into a greased flat pan and bake at 350° for 20 minutes.

Cookbook Committee

CHOCOLATE APPLESAUCE CAKE
"A moist and different holiday cake"

1 C. sugar
2 C. flour
½ t. salt
2 T. cocoa
1 t. cinnamon
½ t. allspice
¼ t. ground cloves
2—4 C. pecans, broken
1 C. dates (chopped with sugar)
¾ C. candied cherries, sliced
½ — ¾ C. candied pineapple, chopped
½ C. butter
1½ C. applesauce
2 t. soda
⅓ C. milk

Sift dry ingredients together. Combine fruits and nuts and combine with sifted ingredients. Add butter and applesauce. Stir soda in milk and add to batter. Line tube pan with foil and grease. Bake at 350° for 1 hour. Cool. Pour liquor or brandy over cake and store in cake tin. Serve with whipped cream.

SERVES 20-30

Vivienne Johnson Calk
(Mrs. Earl, Jr.)

DEVIL'S FOOD CAKE

2 C. sugar
¾ C. cocoa
1 C. shortening
2 eggs
1 C. buttermilk
2½ C. flour
2 t. soda
¼ t. salt
1 C. boiling water
1 t. vanilla

ICING:
1½ C. sugar
½ C. cocoa
10 T. cream
2 T. butter
1 t. vanilla
1 C. chopped nuts, optional

Mix sugar and cocoa. Add shortening, eggs and buttermilk. Sift flour, soda, and salt. Add boiling water and vanilla. Bake at 300° for 30 minutes in a long pan.

Mix together sugar, cocoa and cream. Cook over low heat to the soft ball stage. Add butter and cool. Add vanilla and beat until consistency to spread. Add nuts, if desired.

Reva Harrison Ryan
(Mrs. A. B.)

FIESTA CAKE

3 C. flour
2 C. sugar
1 t. soda
1 t. salt
1 t. cinnamon
1 C. chopped almonds
3 eggs
1½ C. Wesson oil
1 t. almond extract
2 C. chopped (firm) ripe bananas
1 (8 oz.) can crushed pineapple and juice (heavy syrup)

Mix and sift dry ingredients. Stir in nuts. Beat eggs, combine with oil and almond extract, bananas, pineapple and juice. Mix thoroughly, but do not beat. Spoon into a well greased and floured tube pan. Bake at 325° for 1 hour and 20-25 minutes. Cool in pan 15 minutes. Remove from pan, cool thoroughly and frost.

CREAM CHEESE FROSTING

1 (8 oz.) pkg. cream cheese
½ C. butter or margarine
1 lb. powdered sugar
1 T. instant chocolate OR Suisee Mocha instant coffee

Soften cream cheese and butter to room temperature. Cream together with sugar and instant chocolate. Frost cake and refrigerate. Can be frozen.

Sylvia Billingslea Collier
(Mrs. Joe)

GREEK SPICE CAKE

2½ C. flour
1 t. salt
1 t. cinnamon
1 t. cloves
1 t. nutmeg
1 t. soda
1 t. baking powder
1 C. shortening
1 C. brown sugar
1 C. white sugar
3 eggs
1⅓ C. buttermilk
2 t. almond extract
1 C. chopped nuts

Sift flour and other dry ingredients. Cream shortening and sugars. Add eggs one at the time, and cream. Add dry ingredients alternately with buttermilk. Add extract and nuts. Pour into a 9" x 13" greased and floured pan and bake at 350° for 35 minutes.

Boil water and sugar for 2 minutes. Cut cake into squares in the pan, while hot; pour syrup over cake. Serve from the pan.

Carolyn Council Seale
(Mrs. Fred)

ICING:

2 C. white sugar
¾ C. water

HARVEY WALLBANGER CAKE

1 pkg. Duncan Hines orange cake mix
1 (3¾ oz.) pkg. vanilla instant pudding (4 servings)
4 eggs
½ C. orange juice
½ C. Wesson oil
½ C. Galliano liquer
2 T. vodka

GLAZE:
1 C. sifted powdered sugar
1 T. orange juice
1 T. Galliano liquer
1 t. vodka

Combine all ingredients in a mixing bowl. Beat at low speed ½ minute, then medium speed for 5 minutes. Pour into greased and floured bundt pan. Bake at 350° for 45 minutes. Cool 10 minutes.

GLAZE:
Combine ingredients and glaze the warm cake.

SERVES 12

Claire Smith Foster
(Mrs. Henry L., Jr.)

HERSHEY BAR CAKE

1 C. margarine
2 C. sugar
4 eggs
8 Hershey bars, melted
2 t. vanilla
2½ C. flour
¼ t. salt
1/8 t. soda
1 C. buttermilk
1 C. chopped pecans

Cream margarine and sugar together. Add eggs one at a time. Add melted Hershey bars and vanilla. Sift dry ingredients together and add alternately with buttermilk. Add pecans. Bake in a tube pan lined with greased wax paper at 300° for 1 hour 45 minutes.

Dale Coe Simons
(Mrs. James K.)

JAM CAKE

1 C. butter
2 C. sugar
4 eggs
1 C. blackberry jam
1 C. strawberry preserves
1 C. chopped nuts
1 C. buttermilk
1 t. soda
3 C. sifted flour
1 t. cinnamon
1 t. allspice
1 t. cloves

Cream butter and sugar; add eggs, beat well; add jam, preserves and nuts. Dissolve soda in buttermilk. Add alternately with flour which has been sifted with spices. Bake in long pan or in layers. Ice with caramel icing or a cream filling. (See Index)

Bess Vallery Topp
(Mrs. J. S.)

LOIS JACKSON'S LEMON CHEESE CAKE OR LANE CAKE

1 C. butter
2 C. sugar
1 t. vanilla
3½ C. sifted flour
3 t. baking powder
¾ t. salt
1 C. milk
8 eggs, separated (reserve yolks for frosting)

LEMON CHEESE FROSTING:
8 egg yolks
2 C. sugar
½ t. salt
1 C. butter
Juice of 3 lemons and grated rind

LANE FROSTING:
8 egg yolks
1 C. sugar
Pinch of salt
½ C. butter
1½ C. coarsely chopped pecans
1 C. seedless raisins, chopped
1½ C. coconut
1½ C. quartered candied cherries
1 C. wine, bourbon or brandy

Cream butter and sugar and beat until fluffy. Add vanilla. Sift dry ingredients together 4 or 5 times. Add flour mixture to butter mixture alternately with milk beginning and ending with flour. Beat egg whites until they stand in soft peaks. Fold gently into batter. Grease and line each pan with wax paper. Measure 1 C. batter for each 9" cake pan. There should be 6 layers. Bake at 375° until barely firm to touch, about 10 minutes. Do not brown. The secret to cake moisture is to cook it just enough. Ice with either frosting below.

Beat egg yolks until lightened in color. Cream butter, sugar and salt until fluffy. In the top of a double boiler, cook egg yolks and butter mixture 30-40 minutes. Add lemon juice and rind. Cook enough to stand in slight mounds when tested. Spread between layers and all over.

Beat egg yolks until light; add sugar and salt and continue until fluffy. Melt butter in top of double boiler; add egg mixture and cook until it thickens. Mixture should look almost transparent. Remove and stir in other ingredients. Cool. Spread between layers and all over. This cake freezes well. Freeze cake unwrapped to avoid the filling from sticking to the wrap, then wrap.

Ann Killingsworth Smead
(Mrs. Hamp P. Jr.)

PLUM CAKE

2 C. sugar
1 C. Wesson oil
3 eggs
2 C. flour
1 t. soda
1½ t. ground cloves
1½ t. cinnamon
1 C. chopped nuts
2 small jars strained plums (baby food)

Combine all ingredients and mix well. Grease and flour pan and bake at 350° for 1 hour.

Verne Monday Smith
(Mrs. Bruner)

ORANGE FLUFF CAKE

8 egg yolks, well beaten
1¼ C. sugar
1 C. flour, sifted several times
4 T. orange juice
8 egg whites
Pinch of salt
1 t. cream of tartar

ICING:
2 C. sifted powdered sugar
2 T. butter
Grated orange rind
Orange juice

Gradually, add sugar to egg yolks. Add flour and orange juice. Add cream of tartar to stiffly beaten egg whites, then fold into first mixture. Bake in a greased and floured pan at 325° for 1 hour.

Combine powdered sugar, butter, grated orange rind, and enough orange juice so that icing will spread evenly on cake.

Martha Pearce Joseph
(Mrs. George)

PERSIMMON CAKE

2 C. chopped nuts
2 C. seedless raisins
2 C. persimmon pulp
2 C. sugar
2 T. shortening
3 C. sifted flour
¼ t. ground cloves
2 t. cinnamon
1 t. salt
1 C. milk OR ½ C. milk and ½ C. brandy

Combine nuts, raisins, pulp, sugar and shortening. Add sifted dry ingredients. Stir in liquid and mix well. Bake at 325° for 1½ hours or until done in a greased tube pan or 2 loaf pans.

SERVES 10

Dorothy Hallman Dingler
(Mrs. Clark)

BUTTERMILK POUND CAKE

1 C. butter
3 C. sugar
5 egg yolks
1 C. buttermilk
¾ t. soda
1/8 t. salt
3 C. sifted flour
5 egg whites, beaten stiff
2 t. lemon flavoring, 2 t. rum extract, or 2 t. almond extract may be added for extra flavoring. (optional)

Cream butter, add sugar and cream again. Add yolks, one at a time, beating well after each. To ½ cup buttermilk, add soda and stir. To other ½ cup buttermilk, add salt and stir. Add flour alternately with buttermilk, beginning and ending with flour, to butter and sugar mixture. Fold in whites. Grease bottom of tube pan lightly. Pour in batter and bake at 350° one hour or until small cracks appear in top of crust. Let cool. This cake freezes well.

Mrs. Clark Sample, Jr.

CHOCOLATE POUND CAKE

½ lb. butter
½ C. Crisco
3 C. sugar
5 eggs
3 C. flour
½ t. salt
½ t. baking powder
½ C. cocoa
1½ C. milk
1 t. vanilla

ICING:
2 C. sugar
1 stick butter
2 squares baking chocolate
⅔ C. evaporated milk
1 t. vanilla

Cream butter, Crisco and sugar; add eggs one at a time, beating after each addition. Sift together dry ingredients and add alternately with milk to creamed mixture. Add vanilla. Bake at 325° for 1½ hours.

Combine all ingredients; bring to a boil, cook for 2 minutes. Let cool and beat.

Mrs Bill Wheeler

Donor: Martha Pearce Joseph
(Mrs. George)

RUM POUND CAKE

1 C. margarine
½ C. Crisco
3 C. sugar
5 eggs
3 C. flour
1 t. baking powder
½ t. salt
1 C. milk
1 t. coconut extract
1 t. rum extract

GLAZE:
1 C. sugar
½ C. water
1 t. almond extract

Cream margarine and Crisco. Add sugar very slowly. Beat well. Add whole eggs, one at a time. Mix dry ingredients, and add alternately with milk. Add extracts. Bake in a greased bundt pan or spring form pan at 300° for 1—1½ hours. THIS CAKE REQUIRES MORE BEATING THAN MOST.

GLAZE:
Mix glaze ingredients in saucepan and let come to a boil. Cool. Brush on cake while cake is hot.

SERVES 12

Mrs. Carl Price
Eldorado, Ark.

Donor: Linda Ryan Butler
(Mrs. Stephen R.)

MRS. J. H. LAIRD'S POUND CAKE

2 C. real butter
4 C. sugar
12 large eggs
2 T. lemon juice (generous)
4 C. sifted cake flour

Cream butter and sugar well until very light. Add eggs one at a time, beating well after each. Add lemon juice. Add flour slowly, mixing well. Pour into greased and floured pan. Bake at 325° until done, about 1 hour. Makes two bundt size cakes.

GLAZE:
⅓ C. lemon juice or orange juice
1½ C. sifted powdered sugar

Laney Talmadge Mobley
(Mrs. Ebb)

PRUNE CAKE

½ C. shortening or butter
1 C. sugar
2 eggs
⅔ C. stewed prunes, chopped
⅔ C. sour milk
1⅓ C. flour
½ t. each: soda, salt cinnamon, nutmeg, allspice, and baking powder, and cocoa

Blend shortening with sugar, add eggs. Add chopped prunes. Stir in milk. Add to this the sifted dry ingredients. Bake in 2 layers at 350° for about 25 minutes.

Mrs. G. A. McCreight

CREAMY ICING:
1 (8 oz.) pkg. cream cheese
½ C. margarine
1 lb. powdered sugar
Vanilla
1 C. pecans

Beat all ingredients together and spread on cake.

Freida Strauss Frost
(Mrs. Wayne)

WHISKEY CAKE
"A good holiday cake"

¾ lb. butter
2 C. sugar
6 eggs, separated
¾ C. whiskey
4 C. sifted flour, (save ½ C. to flour raisins and nuts)
1 t. baking powder
1 lb. white raisins
1 qt. ground pecans

Cream butter and sugar. Beat egg yolks and add whiskey very slowly. Add butter and sugar to egg yolks. Combine flour and baking powder and add to sugar mixture. Beat egg whites until stiff. Fold egg whites into batter. Flour raisins and pecans and add to batter. Bake at 200° in a greased and floured tube or Bundt pan for 3 hours.

Dale Coe Simons
(Mrs. James. K)

ANGEL FOOD MOCHA TORTE

1 angel food cake
1 T. gelatine
¾ C. cold water
1 C. powdered sugar
2 T. mocha essence
  OR strong coffee
6 egg yolks
1 t. vanilla
2 C. heavy cream, whipped
½ C. slivered almonds,
  toasted OR ½ lb. pecan
  brittle, crushed

Bake cake according to favorite recipe. Soften gelatine in cold water. Dissolve over hot water and add sugar and mocha essence or coffee. Beat egg yolks until light, adding gelatine mixture and vanilla. Mix. Fold in whipped cream. Chill. Spread mixture between layers and over top and sides of the angel food cake which has been cut in two a little above center. Caution: Chill the mixture until it begins to stiffen before spreading. Sprinkle with almonds or pecan brittle. Chill several hours before serving.

SERVES 12-16

Mrs. Rogers Lacy

BLACK FOREST TORTE

4 squares unsweetened
  chocolate
⅔ C. butter
1¾ C. flour
1¾ C. sugar
1¼ t. soda
1 t. salt
¼ t. baking powder
1¼ C. water
1 t. vanilla
3 eggs

CHOCOLATE FILLING:
2½ bars German chocolate
¾ C. butter
½ C. toasted almonds

CREAM FILLING:
2 C. heavy cream
2 T. sugar
1 t. vanilla

Preheat oven to 350°. Melt chocolate over water, add butter and cool. Sift dry ingredients together and add to butter mixture: add water and vanilla and beat for 2 minutes before adding eggs and beat 2 minutes more. Pour ¼ of the batter into each of four 9" buttered round pans. Bake 15 minutes and cool. Remove from pan and cover with waxed paper to prevent drying.

CHOCOLATE FILLING:

Melt the German bars with butter and toasted almonds. Cool in refrigerator.

CREAM FILLING:

Whip the cream until stiff and add the sugar and vanilla.

TO ASSEMBLE:

Layer 1. cake, 2. chocolate, 3. cake 4. cream 5. cake 6. chocolate, 7. cake 8. cream. Top with shaved chocolate.

Dorothy Robbins Kennedy
(Mrs. George E., Jr.)

CHERRY TORTE

2 C. canned red cherries, drained
1¼ C. sugar
1 C. flour
1 t. cinnamon
1 t. baking soda
Pinch of salt
½ C. chopped nuts
1 egg, well beaten
1 T. melted butter

Mix dry ingredients into cherries and nuts. Add well beaten egg and melted butter. Pour into 9" x 13" pan and bake at 350° for 30—35 minutes.

Cook until thickened. Chill and serve over torte. Top with spoonful of whipped cream or ice cream.

Jeanie Mikeska Folzenlogen
(Mrs. Paul)

CHERRY SAUCE
1 C. cherry juice
1 T. cornstarch
½ t. salt
½ C. sugar
1 T. butter

BISQUE TORTONI

"Definitely a dessert for an Italian meal!"

½ C. ground macaroons
1 C. light cream
⅓ C. sugar
¼ C. Sherry
1 C. heavy cream, whipped
½ C. blanched almonds, minced and toasted

Soak the ground macaroons in the light cream for 30 minutes. Add sugar and sherry; freeze until mushy. Fold whipped cream and pack into 8, ¼ C. paper or foil cups. Sprinkle with almonds and freeze until firm.

SERVES 8

Patricia Dooley Flatt
(Mrs. Doyle Edwin)

SWEDISH DESSERT WAFFLES

1½ C. butter
3 C. cake flour
3 eggs
1½ C. sugar
½ t. salt

Cream butter and flour. Add eggs one at a time, beating after each. Add sugar and salt, and mix well. Drop rounded tablespoon of batter onto pre-heated (lowest setting) waffle iron. Bake until done but not brown.

Lucy Reid Peacock
(Mrs. Donald R.)

MARY LEWIS'S CARAMEL ICING

2 T. butter, melted
2 T. shortening, melted
1 C. brown sugar
¼ C. milk
1½ C. powdered sugar

Combine butter, shortening, sugar and milk. Let boil slowly 4 minutes. Cool and add sugar.

Charity League Cookery

LEMON FILLING FOR ANGEL FOOD CAKE

1 C. sugar
3 T. cornstarch
1 C. boiling water
Juice and grated rind of 1 lemon
2 T. butter
2 egg yolks, well beaten
1 pt. heavy cream, whipped
Dash of yellow cake coloring

Cook sugar, cornstarch and water until thick. Add juice and rind of lemon, butter and egg yolks. Cook one minute and cool. When cold, add cream with cake coloring. This will ice one large cake. Split the cake in the middle and ice as a two layer cake. This can be prepared early. Keep refrigerated. It never soaks in the cake.

Dorothy Turner Clendenen
(Mrs. Wade H.)

SHERRIED CHOCOLATE SAUCE

"For a delicious parfait, spoon over coffee ice cream"

6 oz. unsweetened chocolate
1¼ C. boiling water
1¼ C. evaporated milk
2⅓ C. sugar
1 T. dark corn syrup
2 t. vanilla
2 T. medium dry Sherry

Mix chocolate and boiling water to a smooth paste. Heat milk and sugar together in a saucepan and add to chocolate. Return to saucepan, add syrup and cook until thick, stirring occasionally. Remove from heat, cool to lukewarm, stir in vanilla and Sherry and cool thoroughly. This is excellent whenever a chocolate sauce is required.

YIELD: 5 cups

Floreid Francis Stevens
(Mrs. A. C.)

STRAWBERRY TOPPING

3 C. strawberries
1 C. sugar
1½ C. orange juice
1½ C. lemon juice
¼ C. Grand Marnier

Stem berries and blend with sugar. Add fruit juice and liqueur. Freeze and put over ice cream.

Peggy Moss Buckstaff
(Mrs. George)

CANDIES

TIPS FOR CANDY MAKING

1. A thermometer helps take the guessing out of candymaking.
2. Stages for Cooking Candy:
Thread (230°—234°)—Syrup spins a thread from spoon 3" long
Soft Ball (234°—238°)—In cold water, syrup will form ball with pressure.
Firm Ball (244°—248°)—The ball will hold its shape without pressure.
Hard Ball (248°—254°)—The ball holds its shape, but still plastic.
Very Hard Ball (254°—260°)
Light Crack (270°—285°)—Syrup in cold water separates into hard threads.
Hard Crack (290°—300°)—Syrup in cold water separates into brittle threads.
Carmelized Sugar (310°—338°)
3. THE WEATHER IS A FACTOR. Cook candy 2° higher in moist, hot weather.
4. The cooking pot should be 4 times as much as the ingredients used, and the pot should be greased with butter 2" deep around the top of the pot. (To avoid syrup run-over.)
5. Cooking:
    a. Stir over low heat until sugar dissolves.
    b. Cover 1st 3 minutes to avoid crystals on side of pan.
    c. Candies with corn syrup must be cooked to higher temperatures.
    d. Candies with butter, cream, milk, chocolate or molasses are apt to burn if not stirred while cooking. Dissolve ingredients over quick heat. Cook slowly when boiling point is reached.
6. DO NOT BEAT CANDIES UNTIL THEY ARE COOL—ALMOST COLD.
7. Grease pans with butter.

ARLYNE FLANAGAN'S DIVINITY

PART I:
1 C. sugar
½ C. water
3 egg whites, beaten

PART I:
Boil sugar and water together until it spins a thread when dropped from spoon. Pour very slowly over beaten egg whites.

PART II:
3 C. sugar
1 C. white Karo syrup
¾ C. water
Vanilla to taste
2 C. broken pecan meats (or more)

PART II
Have cooking in another pan sugar, Karo and water. Boil together until it spins a thread when dropped from spoon. Add to first mixture. Beat all together in electric mixer until still a little warm. Add vanilla to taste. Add pecans, if desired. Pour into large oiled platter. Cut into squares when cool.

Charity League Cookery

ANNE GODDARD'S ENGLISH TOFFEE

1 C. sugar
1 C. butter, do not substitute
3 T. water
1 t. vanilla
4—5 small plain Hershey bars
¼ C. finely ground pecans

Combine sugar, butter and water. Boil to 300° (using candy thermometer), stirring constantly. Add vanilla. While you are cooking the above, put a pizza pan in a warm oven and keep it there until toffee has reached 300°. Pour onto warm, greased (with butter) pan. Lay Hershey bars on sheet of hot candy. As it softens, spread evenly. While still warm, put pecans on top. Put in refrigerator until ready to serve. It is too brittle to cut, so it has to be broken.

Kathleen Ellison Loomis
(Mrs. N. E.)

FUDGE

¼ C. butter
2 heaping T. cocoa
1 C. milk
2 C. sugar, divided
1 C. chopped pecans
1 t. vanilla

Melt butter; add cocoa, then milk. Bring to a boil and add 1 C. sugar. Stir until dissolved over medium heat, then add 2nd C. of sugar. Boil slowly, stirring frequently, until soft ball stage is reached. Set in pan of cold water. Do not beat until cold, then add pecans and vanilla and beat well. Drop by teaspoonful onto waxed paper. If candy becomes too hard to drop, soften by adding a few drops of milk.

Kathryn Adamson Booth
(Mrs. J. Willis, Jr.)

ORANGE PRALINES

1½ C. sugar
½ C. fresh orange juice
1½ C. pecans
2 t. grated orange rind

Boil sugar and orange juice until it makes a soft ball in cold water. Add nuts and orange rind and beat until cool. Drop on waxed paper. Foolproof.

Susanne Sandberg Northcutt
(Mrs. W. D., III)

ORANGE OR GRAPEFRUIT STICKS

½ C. sugar
¼ C. hot water
Peel of an orange

Wipe fruit, remove peel in quarters and cut in narrow strips with scissors. Place peels in sauce pan and cover with cold water, let boil up once and drain. Repeat five times to extract the bitter taste. Heat the sugar with the hot water and when dissolved add peel. Cook slowly until syrup is nearly evaporated, drain and roll the strips in granulated sugar. For grapefruit weigh the peel and use an equal amount of sugar.

Aliece McHenry Mucher
(Mrs. Joe)

PEPPERMINT CRUNCH CANDY

1 C. evaporated milk
1 C. sugar
2 T. corn syrup (Karo)
1 (6 oz.) pkg. chocolate chips
6 oz. unsweetened baking chocolate
1 C. coarsely chopped peppermint stick candy
2 C. nuts, chopped

In a heavy saucepan, cook milk, sugar and Karo until mixture is bubbling all over. Boil for 2 additional minutes, stirring constantly. Take off heat. Stir in chocolate until melted and smooth. Cool 10 minutes. Add nuts and candy. Drop by teaspoons on wax paper. Let cool and set.

YIELD: 60 small pieces

Joan Marvel Abbott
(Mrs. Frank)

PRALINES

2 C. sugar
1 C. light brown sugar
½ C. white Karo
½ t. baking soda
1 C. buttermilk
¼ C. oleo
¼ t. salt (add when almost done)
3 C. pecan halves
2 t. vanilla (add after taking off stove)

Cook sugars, Karo, soda, buttermilk and oleo in large pan. (This foams up.) When half done, add 3 cups pecans halves. Using candy thermometer, cook to 236° then add vanilla. Beat until smooth. The approximate time of stirring is about 10 minutes and you need to work very fast (in fact you will need another helper) to drop it on wax paper spread on baking pan. This will take approximately 45 minutes from beginning to end.

Kathleen Ellison Loomis
(Mrs. N. E.)

APRICOT BALLS

1 lb. dried apricots
½ whole orange, including skin
2 C. sugar
Powdered sugar

Grind together apricots and orange, including skin (remove seeds). Stir in 2 cups sugar and cook over low heat, stirring constantly, until mixture is thick and sugar is melted. Cool slightly and form into 1" balls. Roll each ball in powdered sugar and set on waxed paper to "firm up" Keeps very well in tight container.

YIELD: 84 balls

Vera Mitchell Garlough
(Mrs. Harry Thomas)

APRICOT BARS

2½ C. cooked and drained apricots
1¾ C. sugar, divided
¼ C. water
2 C. sifted flour
1 t. salt
½ t. baking soda
¾ C. butter or margarine
1½ C. flaked coconut
½ C. chopped pecans

Combine cooked apricots, ¾ cup sugar, and water; cook about 5 minutes, stirring occasionally, until slightly thickened. Cool. Sift flour, salt, and soda together. Cream butter, gradually adding 1 cup sugar; beat well. Blend in dry ingredients. Stir in coconut and pecans. Press 3 cups of this crumbly mixture in bottom and halfway up the sides of a greased 9" x 13" pan. Bake at 400° for 10 minutes. Spread apricot mixture over crust. Sprinkle remaining crumbs over top. Bake 20–25 minutes longer. Cool and cut into squares. Top with whipped cream if desired. Freezes well.

Martha Pearce Joseph
(Mrs. George)

BEACON HILL MINT COOKIES

1 (6 oz.) pkg. Nestle's semi-sweet mint drops
2 egg whites
Dash of salt
½ C. sugar
½ t. vanilla
½ t. vinegar
¾ C. chopped nuts

Melt semi-sweet over hot water. Beat egg whites with a dash of salt until foamy. Add sugar gradually, beating until stiff peaks form (not dry). Add vanilla and vinegar. Fold slightly cooled chocolate into above meringue, then add nuts. Drop by teaspoon onto greased cookie sheet. Bake at 350° for 9 minutes (again not too dry).

Jane Weeks Johnston
(Mrs. J. Glenn)

BAKLAVA

1 pkg. fillo dough, defrosted and covered top and bottom with damp cloths.
2 C. ground nuts
1 lb. unsalted clarified butter, heated until boiling

SYRUP:
1½ C. sugar
1 lemon, juice and peel
½ C. water

Remove sheets of dough carefully one at a time. Place 1 t. of nuts along edge of each sheet, fold over 2" and lap back. Pleat and twist ends. Place each pleated sheet on ungreased cookie sheet. Trim edges and cut in ¼'s. Sprinkle generously with chopped nuts over all. Pour butter over all. Bake at 350°, 20—25 minutes. Remove from oven and blot up extra butter around cookies with paper towel.

SYRUP:
Boil ingredients until tacky. Pour over all cookies.

YIELD: 80—100 cookies

Nell Bell Wrather
(Mrs. John)

BROWNIE BONBONS

1 package (15½ oz.) fudge brownie mix
½ C. chopped walnuts
1 egg
1 T. water
18 milk chocolate kisses

Pre-heat oven to 375°. Mix brownie mix, walnuts, eggs and water thoroughly. Wrap dough by rounded tablespoonfuls around each chocolate kiss; seal edges. Place on ungreased baking sheet. Bake until bonbons are set, 8 to 10 minutes. Note: Caramel candies, pitted dates or walnuts halves can be substituted for the chocolate kisses.

YIELD: 18

Simone Fanchier Kibbe
(Mrs. Robert)

FUDGE SQUARES

1 C. sugar
½ C. butter
2 eggs
1 C. flour
3 T. cocoa
1 t. vanilla
1 C. chopped pecans

Cream sugar and butter; add eggs. Sift flour and cocoa; add to creamed mixture. Add vanilla and pecans last. Bake in a greased 8" x 8" square pan at 350° until toothpick come out clean. Cut into squares and roll in powdered sugar.

YIELD: 16—2" squares

Mrs. Robert Wood

GOOD RICH BROWNIES

⅓ C. shortening
1 C. sugar
2 eggs
1 t. vanilla
2 (1 oz.) squares chocolate, melted
⅔ C. flour
¼ t. salt
½ t. baking powder

ICING:
2 T. water
1 T. butter
¼ t. vanilla
1 C. powdered sugar
1 oz. square chocolate

Cream shortening and sugar, add eggs and vanilla. Beat well. Add cooled melted chocolate and blend. Add sifted dry ingredients, stir in nuts. Bake at 350° in a 8" square pan **only** 35 minutes.

YIELD: 16—2" squares

ICING:
Heat icing ingredients and beat until spreading consistency. Spread on brownies.

Mrs. Curtis DeMoss

MINT-FLAVORED BROWNIES

2 (15½ oz.) boxes regular size brownie mix
2 C. chopped pecans
2 t. peppermint flavoring
36 after-dinner mints (chocolate covered ½ oz. peppermints)
2 T. water (or more)

Mix according to package directions using only one egg per box and no vanilla. Add pecans and peppermint flavoring. Cook according to directions on the package. Do not overcook. Cool before icing. Unwrap mints and melt in the top of a double boiler with 2 T. water. Spread while hot on top of the cool brownies.

Curtain Call Cookbook

BUTTER CRISP COOKIES

1¼ C. butter
1½ C. powdered sugar
1 egg, beaten
Dash of salt
3 C. flour
1 C. chopped pecans or almonds
1 t. vanilla

Cream butter and sugar. Add egg, flour, pecans and salt. Mix well. Place by teaspoonsful on buttered cookie sheet. bake at 275°.

Cherokee Club

CHOCOLATE CARAMEL BARS

1 (14 oz.) pkg. light caramels (about 50)
⅓ C. evaporated milk
1 pkg. German Chocolate cake mix
1 T. water
½ C. butter or margarine, softened
1 C. chopped nuts
1 (6 oz.) pkg. semi-sweet chocolate pieces

Preheat oven to 350°. Grease and flour a 9" x 13" pan. Combine in heavy saucepan, the first 2 ingredients. Cook over low heat, stirring constantly, until caramels are melted. Keep warm. Combine, in a large bowl, the remaining ingredients, except chocolate pieces. Stir with fork until dough is crumbly but holds together. Press half of dough into prepared pan, reserve remaining dough for topping. Bake at 350° for 6 minutes. Sprinkle chocolate pieces over baked crust. Spread caramel mixture over all. Spread reserved dough over caramel mixture. Bake 15—20 minutes. Cool completely.

YIELD: 3 dozen bars

Jeannine Wallace Faires
(Mrs. Gene R.), Beaumont, Texas

CREWS CHOCOLATE CRINKLE COOKIES

½ C. cooking oil
4 squares unsweetened chocolate, melted
2 C. sugar
4 eggs
2 t. vanilla
2 C. sifted flour
½ t. salt
2 t. baking powder
1 C. confectioner's sugar

Mix oil, chocolate and sugar; blend in 1 egg at a time until mixed well; add vanilla and stir in flour, salt and baking powder. Chill several hours or overnight. Drop teaspoonfuls of dough into confectioner's sugar and roll into balls. Bake 2" apart on greased cookie sheet at 350° about 10 min. Tastes wonderfully chewey right out of the freezer.

YIELD: 50—60 cookies

Mrs. Robert A. Bruyere

CINNAMON STICKS

1 C. margarine
1 egg yolk
3 t. cinnamon
1 C. sugar
2 C. flour
Chopped nuts, optional
1 egg white

Mix first 5 ingredients and spread thin on cookie sheet. Press in nuts on top, if desired. Beat egg white stiff; spread on. Bake at 250°—275° for 1 hour. Cut in sticks.

Mrs. Earl Breedlove

DATE NUT TORTES

MERINGUES:
3 egg whites
½ t. baking powder
1/8 t. salt
1 t. vanilla
1 t. vinegar
1 t. water
1 C. sifted sugar

FILLING:
2 eggs, well beaten
1(13 oz.) can evaporated milk
½ C. milk
1 C. sugar
1 T. flour
¼ t. salt
8 oz. pitted dates, chopped
1 C. broken pecans
1 t. vanilla
¾ C. bourbon

Beat egg whites, baking powder and salt in an electric mixer until frothy. Slowly, add vanilla, vinegar and water. When whites are stiff, add sugar 1 T. at a time. Continue beating for several minutes after all sugar has been added. On a lightly greased cookie sheet, shape by using a pastry bag or spoons into 12 individual torte shells or 48 bite sized shells (great for pickup party fare). Be sure to indent centers so they will hold filling. Bake at 275° for 1 hour.

FILLING:
Mix flour, sugar and make a custard of eggs, milk, and salt, cooking over very low heat, stirring constantly. Cook until very thick. Just before removing from heat, stir in dates. Mix well. Allow to cool, then add bourbon, nuts and vanilla. Chill for several hours. Just before serving, spoon filling into shells and top with sweetened whipped cream. Very rich, but oh so good!

YIELD: 12 individuals or 48 miniatures

Mrs Joe H. Croxton

DATE TARTS

3 eggs, beaten
¾ C. sugar
2 T. flour
1 t. vanilla
1 C. nuts
1 pkg. dates, pitted and chopped

GLAZE:
Juice and grated rind of ½ lemon
Juice and grated rind of ½ orange
Powdered sugar to stiffen

Mix all ingredients and beat well. Bake at 350° in small greased and floured muffin tins until done.

GLAZE:
Combine ingredients and glaze tarts. Freezes well.

Mrs. Robert A Rowland
Austin, Texas

JELLY RIBBON COOKIES

1½ C. butter
2 eggs, beaten
¾ C. granulated sugar
1 t. vanilla
½ t. salt
4⅔ C. sifted flour
1 (16 oz.) jar rasberry or favorite preserves

ICING:
2 C. confectioner's sugar
4 T. water

Cream first four ingredients in warm bowl. Add salt and sifted flour. Knead together until well blended and form smooth ball. Put in cookie press; use star form. Press out 3 strips lengthwise on ungreased cookie sheet. Make sure the strips are touching so they can bake together. Pour preserves in pastry tube. Squeeze jelly between rows of each ribbon. Bake at 325° for 25 minutes until light brown. While warm in pan drizzle with icing. Cut immediately into 1 inch diagonal strips, let cool and then remove from pan. Freezes well.

YIELD: 12 dozen

Shirley Rodgers Griffin
(Mrs. John)

LUSCIOUS LEMON BARS

1 C. margarine
½ C. powdered sugar
2 C. flour
¼ t. salt
4 eggs, beaten
1¾ C. granulated sugar
¼ C. flour
1 T. grated lemon rind
4 T. lemon juice
Powdered sugar to sift over the top

Soften margarine and blend well with powdered sugar, flour and salt. Press into the bottom of a 9" x 13" pan and bake at 350° for 20 minutes. Blend together the remaining ingredients and pour over the first layer. Continue baking for 25 minutes. Sift additional powdered sugar over the top immediately after removing from the oven. Cool and cut in squares.

YIELD: 3 dozen

Eleanor Hopper Heinz
(Mrs. J. B.)

PRALINE COOKIES

½ C. butter
1 egg, beaten
1 C. flour
1 C. brown sugar
1 t. vanilla
½ C. pecans

Soften butter and mix with remaining ingredients. Drop by teaspoonfuls on an ungreased cookie sheet. Bake at 350° for 20 minutes.

YIELD: 3 dozen

Susanne Sandberg Northcutt
(Mrs. W. D., III)

PECAN SLICES

1 C. flour
½ C. softened butter
¼ t. salt

FILLING:
2 eggs, beaten
1½ C. brown sugar
2 T. flour
½ C. grated coconut
1 C. pecans or black walnuts, chopped
½ t. baking powder
½ t. salt
1 t. vanilla

ICING:
1½ C. sifted powdered sugar
Lemon juice

Sift and measure flour. Combine with softened butter. Add salt. Mix to a smooth paste. Spread in a 9" x 13" pan. Bake at 350° for 12 minutes. Spread with filling and bake at 350° for 25 minutes. When slightly cool, spread with powdered sugar moistened with lemon juice to frosting consistency.

Sara Richkie Whitehurst
(Mrs. Herman)

RANGER COOKIES

1 C. butter
1 C. brown sugar
1 C. white sugar
1 t. salt
1 t. soda
1 t. baking soda
2 eggs
2 C. flour
1 C. chopped nuts
2 C. oatmeal
2 C. Rice Krispies or Special "K"
1 T. vanilla

Mix well. Drop by teaspoonsful on ungreased cookie sheet. Bake at 350° about 8—10 minutes or until done. **Do not overcook.** Cool and pack in cans. Serve hot or cold.

YIELD: 100 cookies

Ethel Poday Maledon
(Mrs. E. N.)

SAND TARTS

½ lb. butter
½ C. sifted powdered sugar
2 C. sifted cake flour
1 C. chopped pecans
1 t. vanilla

Cream butter; add sugar, stir well and add flour, nuts, and vanilla. Shape into balls or crescents and bake on ungreased cookie sheet at 325° for 20 minutes or until a light brown. Roll in powdered sugar while warm. Will keep indefinitely.

YIELD: 4 dozen

Helen Corbitt's Cookbook

SAUSAGE COOKIES

1 lb. fresh pork sausage
1½ C. flour
½ C. brown sugar
1 t. baking powder
¾ t. salt
1 egg, beaten
⅓ C. orange juice
1 t. grated orange rind
¼ C. drippings
¼ C. chopped nuts (optional)

Lightly brown sausage breaking into pieces. Remove sausage to paper toweling, and reserve ¼ cup drippings. Mix flour, brown sugar, baking powder, and salt. Combine egg, orange juice, orange rind, and reserved drippings, and stir into dry ingredients. Stir in sausage and nuts. Drop by spoonfuls onto baking sheet. Bake in hot oven, 400° for 12—15 minutes. Store in refrigerator.

YIELD: 6 dozen

Mrs. Paul Glaske

OLD FASHIONED SOFT SUGAR COOKIES

2 C. sifted all-purpose flour
½ t. baking soda
½ t. salt
½ C. shortening
1 C. granulated sugar
1 egg, separated
½ C. buttermilk or sour milk
½ t. vanilla

Preheat oven to 350°. Sift flour, soda and salt. Mix shortening, sugar and egg yolk until light and fluffy. Add flour mixture alternately with buttermilk; then mix in vanilla. Fold in stiffly beaten egg white. Drop by rounded tablespoons 3 inches apart onto a greased cookie sheet. With spatula, flatten until ½ inch thick. If desired, sprinkle with sugar mixed with chopped nuts, raisins or grated lemon rind. Bake 20 minutes or until golden brown.

YIELD 1½ dozen

Susan Bowling Randolph
(Mrs. Joe N.)

CRUMBLE APPLE DESSERT

4—6 apples, sliced
⅔ C. light brown sugar
Dash of cinnamon
3 T. butter
2 T. cold water

TOPPING:
½ C. brown sugar
½ C. butter
1 C. flour
Pinch of salt

VARIATION:
8 fresh peaches, peeled and sliced
1 C. sugar
Eliminate water

Slice apples into deep baking dish. Cover with brown sugar, cinnamon, and butter. Sprinkle cold water over all.

Combine the topping ingredients to form a crumbly mixture to put on top of apples. Bake in a 375° oven for 30-40 minutes or until apples are tender and the crust a golden brown.

SERVES 4-6

Mary Lynn Hartman Dawes
(Mrs. John L.)

Combine all dry ingredients and sprinkle over peaches. Bake at 375° for about 45 minutes. Serve warm with ice cream or whipped cream.

Barbara York Richardson
(Mrs. Kenneth L.)

BREAD PUDDING WITH BRANDY SAUCE

10 slices day-old bread, broken in pieces
4 C. milk, scalded
1 C. heavy cream
4 eggs, beaten
1 C. sugar
1 t. vanilla
1 t. cinnamon
½ t. nutmeg
¼ C. butter, melted
½ C. seedless raisins

BRANDY SAUCE:
3 egg yolks
1 C. sugar
1 t. vanilla
1½ C. milk
1 T. cornstarch
¼ C. water
1 oz. brandy

Combine bread, milk and cream. Add sugar to beaten eggs and mix well. Stir in bread mixture and add vanilla, cinnamon and nutmeg. Stir in butter and raisins. Pour into buttered 2 qt. baking dish. Place dish in a pan of warm water about 1" deep. Bake at 350° for 1 hour or until knife inserted in center comes out clean.

SERVES 8

Slightly beat egg yolks in a saucepan. Add sugar, vanilla, milk and blend well. Cook over low heat until mixture comes to a boil. Blend cornstarch in water and stir into hot mixture. Continue cooking until thickened. Remove from heat and stir in brandy. Cool. Pour over pudding before serving.

Jane Weeks Johnston
(Mrs. J. Glenn)

BANANAS FOSTER

2 T. brown sugar
1 T. butter
1 ripe banana, peeled and sliced lengthwise
Dash cinnamon
½ oz. banana liqueur
1 oz. white rum

Melt sugar and butter. Add banana and sauté until tender. Sprinkle with cinnamon. Pour in liquer and flame. Serve over vanilla ice cream.

SERVES 2

Brennan's Restaurant
New Orleans, La.

EASY DESSERTS TO SERVE WITH MEXICAN FOOD

Pour 1 oz. of tequila over a large dip of orange, lemon, lime, or pineapple sherbet in frosted, stemmed glass. OR pour 1 oz. of Kahlua over chocolate chip ice cream. Top with toasted coconut, and serve in frosted, stemmed glasses.

Note: The sherbert or ice cream can be placed in sherbets or wine glasses in freezer ahead of time to facilitate serving.

Betty Robbins Davis
(Mrs. Charles H.)

ENGLISH TOFFEE DESSERT

1½ C. vanilla wafer crumbs
1 C. chopped nuts
½ C. butter
1 C. powdered sugar
3 eggs, separated
1½ oz. unsweetened chocolate
½ t. vanilla
1 C. heavy cream, whipped

Mix wafer crumbs and chopped nuts, using half of mixture to cover bottom of a 9" x 9" pan. Cream butter and sugar until fluffy, add egg yolks, chocolate and vanilla. Mix thoroughly. Fold in stiffly beaten egg whites. Pour mixture in pan over crumb and nut mixture, then pour remaining crumbs and nut mixture over top. Store overnight in refrigerator. Cut in squares and serve with whipped cream.

Reva Harrison Ryan
(Mrs. A. B.)

CRÊPES SUZETTE

½ C. butter
8 T. sugar
Lemon rind ½" square
Orange rind ½" square
Juice of 1 orange
Juice of ½ lemon
1 pony of brandy or cognac
12 crêpes (See Index)
1 pony of Grand Marnier
Confectioner's sugar
1 orange, cut into wedges to garnish

To do this dessert justice, one should prepare it in front of the guests. In a large, flat skillet or French crêpes pan, melt butter over hot flame and add sugar to make a syrup. Slice thin slivers of orange and lemon rinds into pan. Squeeze the orange and the lemon halves into the syrup and mix thoroughly with a fork. When mixture simmers rapidly, add warmed brandy and continue heating until ready to ignite. Tip pan to allow flame to ignite sauce, allow flame to burn down, and lower heat to add crêpes. Add crêpes, one at a time, dipping each side into the sauce, then folding them twice to make a triangular shape. Raise heat and when mixture simmers rapidly, add warmed Grand Marnier and ignite. Serve each guest 2 crêpes, garnishing with powdered sugar and an orange wedge.

SERVES 6

Betty and Charley Davis

FABULOUS ORANGE & LEMON DESSERT

2 doz. lady fingers, split
¼ lb. butter
1 C. sugar
½ pt. heavy cream, whipped
3 eggs, separated
Juice of 1 large orange
Juice of 1 lemon
1 T. orange rind
1 t. lemon rind
¼ C. finely chopped nuts
Rum

Cream butter and sugar. Beat egg yolks with a whisk and add to creamed mixture. Add fruit juices, rind and nuts. (This looks awful but will smooth out with cream). Add whipped cream. Beat egg whites with a pinch of cream of tartar and add last. Line 1½ qt. mold (or bundt cake pan) with buttered wax paper. Then, line bottom and sides with split lady fingers. Sprinkle with rum and add ½ of mixture, then a layer of lady fingers, rum, 2nd half of mixture and top with lady fingers and rum. Freeze for 2 to 2½ hours.

SERVES 12-18

Peggy Moss Duckstaff
(Mrs. George)

QUICK CHOCOLATE MOUSSE GLÜCK

1 (6 oz.) pkg. chocolate bits
2 whole eggs
3 T. very strong hot coffee
3—4 T. orange flavored liqueur
¾ C. scalded milk
Heavy cream

Blend the mixture at high speed for 2 minutes. Pour mousse into six small cups and chill. Serve with unsweetened cream whipped. This will make a blender full. It is very rich.

SERVES 6

Eleanor Croxton Lawrence
(Mrs. Thomas W.)

FRESH FRUIT DESSERT

Sliced fresh fruit, pineapple, strawberries OR seedless green grapes
Sugar
Lemon juice
Sour cream
Brown sugar

Place fruit in individual bowls. Sprinkle with sugar and lemon juice. Top with a tablespoonful of sour cream. Sprinkle with brown sugar. Garnish with a piece of fruit.

Cookbook Committee

KING'S PUDDING

3 C. granulated sugar
1 C. water
16 egg yolks, lightly beaten
1 t. ground cinnamon
¼ C. light rum
1 C. heavy cream, whipped
5 egg whites
1 C. confectioner's sugar
1 Sara Lee pound cake cut into thin slices
½ C. toasted chopped almonds

Boil the sugar in a cup of water until it reaches a thin thread stage. Remove from heat; cool, and add the lightly beaten egg yolks and cinnamon. Cook mixture over a low flame, stirring constantly, until thick. Remove from stove and add the rum. Beat the heavy cream in peaks. Beat the egg whites along with the confectioner's sugar until stiff and this mixture stands in peaks. Fold whipped cream into egg white mixture. In a deep long serving dish, arrange a layer of cake slices, follow with a layer of egg yolk cream, a layer of whipped cream and repeat until all ingredients are used. Top with almonds. Refrigerate.

SERVES: 12

Maud Norton Bivins
(Mrs. J. K., III)

FROZEN DESSERT

1 (18 oz.) jar Bama apricot preserves OR orange marmalade
1 (6 oz.) can frozen lemonade, thawed
½ gallon GOOD vanilla ice cream, softened
Lemon slices OR mint leaves

Blend preserves and lemonade concentrate with ice cream in a large bowl. Return to freezer for at least 12 hours. Serve in sherbert or champagne glasses and top with slice of lemon or mint leaves.

SERVES 20

Dorothy Lorimer McNally
(Mrs. Frank)

PASHKA

4 (8 oz.) pkg. cream cheese
½ C. butter
1 (1 lb.) pkg. powdered sugar
3 egg yolks, beaten
Grated rind of 1 lemon
1 (5 oz.) can toasted, unsalted almonds
¼ C. citron
¼ C. candied orange peel
¼ C. candied lemon peel
1 t. vanilla

THIS RECIPE MUST BE PREPARED 24 HOURS AHEAD. Cream together cheese and butter. When well mixed, add sugar, then egg yolks, mixing well after each addition. Add other ingredients and mold either in a new flower pot or a colander lined with plastic wrap. Freeze. This will keep at least a month. Serve on sesame seed crackers or with fresh strawberries or pineapple spears.

SERVES 20-24

Agnes Scruggs

BRANDY PEACHES

16 canned cling peach halves
1 C. maple syrup
1 C. brown sugar
⅓ C. melted butter
Pinch of ground cinnamon
⅓ C. brandy

Place peach halves cavity side up in baking pan and pour a little syrup around peaches. Put 1 T. maple syrup, 1 t. butter, and 1 T. sugar in each peach. Sprinkle with cinnamon. Bake uncovered at 325° for 20 minutes. Pour brandy over peaches. Place peach half in sherbert glass and top with vanilla ice cream.

SERVES 16

Frances Birdwell Booth
(Mrs. Talmadge E)

RASPBERRY DELIGHT

1 oz. can Eagle Brand milk
½ C. lemon juice
½ C. pecans, chopped
½ pt. heavy cream, whipped
2 T. seedless raspberry jam
½ box vanilla wafers

Mix slowly milk, lemon juice and pecans. Fold in cream and add jam. Make a layer of wafers in pan. Pour in half of mixture, make another layer of crumbs and cover with the other half of mixture. Top with crumbs. Chill overnight.

SERVES 6

For 36 people, use 6 cans of milk, 2½ pts. cream, 2½ C. lemon juice, 2½ C. pecans, 10 T. jam and 3 boxes vanilla wafers.

Susan Sandberg Northcutt
(Mrs. W. D., III)

STRAWBERRY-BANANA TRIFLE

1 (3¾ oz.) pkg. vanilla pudding mix
1 pkg. yellow cake mix
3 (10 oz.) cartons frozen strawberries
4 medium bananas
1 C. chilled heavy cream
¼ C. sugar
¼ C. toasted, slivered almonds

Make pudding according to directions on the package. Bake cake according to directions on package. Use one layer and freeze one for future use. Cut the layer to be used crosswise in half. Place first half in bottom of bowl and cover with ½ strawberries, ½ bananas, and ½ pudding. Repeat, Cover and chill for four hours or as long as 8 hours if possible. In a chilled bowl, beat cream and sugar until stiff. Spread over trifle and sprinkle with almonds.

SERVES 12

Ann Killingsworth Smead
(Mrs. Hamp, Jr.)

STRAWBERRIES ROMANOFF

12 medium-size fresh strawberries
2 scoops vanilla ice cream
1 C. fresh heavy cream, whipped
2 t. sugar
1 oz. Grand Marnier
1 oz. brandy
1 oz. Triple Sec

Wash strawberries; remove stems and set aside. Put a scoop of vanilla ice cream in 2 serving dishes. Combine cream, sugar, Grand Marnier, brandy and Triple Sec for sauce; pour over ice cream and garnish with strawberries.

SERVES 2

Helen May Little
(Mrs. Earle E., Jr.)

LOIS JACKSON'S NO-COOK ICE CREAM

BASIC RECIPE:
6 eggs
3½ C. sugar
2 (13 oz.) cans Carnation milk
1 can Eagle Brand milk

PEACH ICE CREAM:
Basic recipe
Peaches (1 blender full)
½ C. sugar
3 t. vanilla

BUTTER PECAN ICE CREAM:
Basic recipe
2 C. chopped pecans
½ C. butter
3 T. Rum Sauce (if not available, double the vanilla)
1½ t. vanilla

Beat eggs until frothy; then add other ingredients, stirring well.

Blend peaches with sugar in blender. Add to basic recipe with vanilla. Pour into freezer. Finish filling freezer to fill line with whole milk.

Sauté pecans in butter until thoroughly heated. Add with other ingredients to the basic recipe. Pour into freezer and finish filling to fill line with whole milk.

Ann Killingsworth Smead
(Mrs. Hamp, Jr.)

LEMON ICE CREAM

2 quarts milk, (may use low fat)
3 C. sugar
1 C. lemon juice
Rind of 1 lemon, grated

Combine ingredients and freeze in ice cream freezer.

Mrs. Michael C. Macey

LEMON SHERBERT

Juice of 4 lemons
2 C. sugar
1 (13 oz.) can evaporated milk
1 quart milk
Rind of 2 lemons

VARIATION: Lemon Velvet
Substitute:
Heavy cream for evaporated milk
1 t. lemon extract for rind of 1 lemon

Dissolve sugar with lemon juice, add milk and lemon rind. Stir well and freeze in electric or hand freezer.

YIELD: ½ gallon

Cherokee Club Kitchen

Helen Corbitt

MILKY WAY ICE CREAM

1 (13 oz.) can Pet milk
6 Milky Way candy bars
1 can Eagle Brand milk
½ C. sugar
1 t. vanilla
2 boxes vanilla junket
Milk to finish filling freezer

Melt candy bars in Pet milk. Combine with remaining ingredients and freeze in an ice cream freezer.

YIELD: 1 gallon

Mrs. Arliss Mallory

STRAWBERRY ICE CREAM

2 C. heavy cream
4 egg yolks
1 t. grated lemon peel
1½ C. sugar
3 full baskets of fresh strawberries
2 t. fresh lemon juice
1 C. light cream

In the top of a double boiler, mix together the cream, egg yolks, and lemon peel. Cook on low heat, stirring until thickened. Add sugar and stir until dissolved. Strain and cool. Purée all but a few berries. Chop the rest fine and sprinkle with the lemon juice. Add the berries to the cooled custard, stir in light cream and churn freeze. Note: Be sure to add the lemon juice to the berries and not to the cooking custard.

Dorothy Robbins Kennedy
(Mrs. George E., Jr.)

FLAKY PASTRY

2 C. flour
2 t. sugar
1 t. salt
½ C. butter
½ C. Crisco
3 T. cold water

Blend flour, sugar and salt. Cut butter and Crisco with pastry fork into flour mixture being careful not to overwork. Pastry should resemble coarse meal. Sprinkle water evenly over the mixture and mix until pastry sticks together but is not sticky. Before rolling, divide the pastry into two parts, and place between two sheets of waxed paper. Refrigerate for 1 hour. This is a very flaky pastry, and cooling makes if manageable. If you are making a cobbler or a sweet pie, add extra sugar. Bake at 425° until golden brown. Pastry can be frozen.

YIELD: 2—9" pastries

Dorothy Robbins Kennedy
(Mrs. George E.)

EASY PIE CRUST

1 C. plus 2 T. flour
½ t. salt
7 T. Crisco
2 T. plus 1 t. water (cold)

Sift flour and salt into mixing bowl. Blend in Crisco with a pastry blender. Add water, stirring with a fork. Roll out on floured board.

Trudy White Canon

FLAKY PASTRY WITH SOUR CREAM

2 C. flour
1 t. salt
⅔ C. cold butter, divided
4—6 T. sour cream

Sift flour and salt into a chilled mixing bowl. With pastry fork, cut in ⅓ C. butter until mixture resembles coarse meal. Cut in another ⅓ C. butter to make lumps the size of small peas. Add sour cream 1 T. at a time and stir into dough gently with a fork until it can be gathered together and cleans the bowl. Form the dough into a ball, wrap in wax paper and chill 30 minutes. Roll out dough in a rectangle about ⅓" thick and cover with 3 T. hard butter, cut into thin shavings. Fold the upper ⅓ of the dough over the center and fold the lower ⅓ of the dough over the upper flap making 3 layers. Give the dough a quarter turn, roll it out thinly in a rectangle and fold again in thirds. Wrap the dough in wax paper and chill overnight or at least several hours. For regular pastry, substitute cold water for sour cream.

Patricia Smith Houston
(Mrs. E. B.)

EASY BLACKBERRY COBBLER

1 C. butter (room temperature)
1 C. sugar
2 C. flour

FILLING:

5 C. blackberries, drained
1 C. sugar
½ C. butter

Mix crust ingredients using a pastry cutter until crumbly. Place blackberries in a rectangular baking dish, dot with butter and cover with sugar. Pour crumbly crust over fruit and bake at 350° for 1 hour. Top with ice cream or whipped cream. Note: This same recipe can be used for other fresh fruits; apples or peaches. Additional spices may be added nutmeg, cinnamon, cloves.

SERVES 6-8

Doris Reeves Collier
(Mrs. Mike)

ARMY'S BLACKBERRY COBBLER

PASTRY:
2 C. flour
1 t. salt
1 T. sugar
12 T. Crisco
3—4 T. water

FILLING:
2 cartons fresh blackberries
2½ C. sugar
1 t. vanilla
Dash nutmeg
2 T. flour
½ C. water
¼ C. butter

Combine dry ingredients. Cut in Crisco with pastry fork. Add water a T. at a time until dough mixes into a ball. Roll out the desired shape to fit baking dish. Line baking dish and bake at 350° until golden. Make pastry strips for top of cobbler.
FILLING:
Cook blackberries in water (enough to cover the berries) with sugar for 20 minutes. Mix flour with water and add to berries. Add butter, vanilla and nutmeg. Pour into baked pastry. Top with strips and bake at 350° until brown.

SERVES 10

Sara Skaggs Lucas
(Mrs. Richard)

CARAMEL APPLE PIE

Pastry for 2 crust (9") pie

FILLING:
6 apples, pared and sliced
1 T. cornstarch
1 t. cinnamon
¼ t. salt
3 T. sugar
3 T. margarine, melted
⅓ C. dark Karo syrup

TOPPING:
2 T. flour
2 T. margarine
¼ C. brown sugar
3 T. dark Karo syrup
¼ C. chopped nuts

Put apples in crust. Mix the remaining ingredients. Pour mixture over apples. Top with crust and bake at 425° for 45 minutes.

TOPPING:
Combine ingredients in pan and cook until margarine is melted. Spread topping over cooked pie and return to oven 8—10 minutes or until bubbly.

Marilyn Rouse Payne
(Mrs. Hermes E.)

SOUR CREAM APPLE PIE

1 9" flaky pastry with sour cream, unbaked
6 tart cooking apples
1 C. sugar
2 T. flour
1/8 t. salt
1 t. ground cinnamon
1 t. grated lemon peel
1/8 t. ground cloves
½ C. flour
¼ C. sugar
1/8 t. salt
½ C. grated Cheddar cheese
Sour cream

Peel, quarter and core apples. Slice thinly. Combine first six ingredients and toss apples lightly in this mixture. Arrange apples, overlapping the slices in the pastry-lined pan. Combine flour, sugar, salt and cheese. Mix in butter and sprinkle mixture over apples. Bake at 400° for 40 minutes until topping and crust are golden brown. Let the pie cool slightly. Top each slice with a generous spoonful of sour cream.

Patricia Smith Houston
(Mrs. E. B.)

GRANDMOTHER'S KENTUCKY PIE

1 (9") unbaked pie shell
3 C. brown sugar
½ C. cream
3 eggs
½ C. butter
1 t. vanilla
Pinch of salt

Cream butter and sugar; add eggs, cream, salt, and vanilla. Cook in unbaked shell 40 minutes at 300°.

Jenny Lewis Rappeport
(Mrs. Joseph H.)

OLD FASHIONED CHESS PIE

1 (9") unbaked pie shell
1½ C. sugar
½ C. butter
4 eggs
2 T. cream
1 t. vanilla
2 T. vinegar

Boil sugar, butter and vinegar together slowly until dissolved. Cool and add eggs, cream and vanilla. Bake in unbaked pie shell in moderate oven, 350° until pie is set.

Florra Wheeler Anderson
(Mrs. Jack)

CHOCOLATE ANGEL STRATA

1 (9") baked pie shell
2 eggs, separated
½ t. vinegar
¼ t. salt
¼ t. cinnamon
½ C. sugar
¼ C. water
1 C. (6 oz.) pkg. chocolate chips, melted
¼ C. sugar
¼ t. cinnamon
1 C. heavy cream, whipped

Beat egg whites with vinegar, salt and cinnamon. Add sugar gradually, beating until meringue stands in peaks. Spread in bottom of pie shell. Bake at 325° for 15-18 minutes or until slightly browned. Cool.
FILLING:
Add water and slightly beaten egg yolks to chocolate chips. Spread 3 T. or more over cooled meringue. Chill remainder. Combine sugar, cinnamon and cream. Beat until thick. Spread ½ of mixture over chocolate in shell. Combine remaining cream with chocolate mixture and spread over whipped cream in shell. Chill at least 4 hours.

Mrs. P. H. Brammell, Lafayette, La.
Donor: Carolyn Smith Russell
      (Mrs. Ralph)

CHOCOLATE CREAM PIE

1 (9") baked pie shell

FILLING:
1½ C. sugar
½ t. salt
2½ T. cornstarch
1 T. flour
2½ C. milk
½ C. light cream
3 squares unsweetened chocolate cut-up
3 egg yolks (room temperature), slightly beaten
1 T. butter
1½ t. vanilla

MERINGUE:
3 egg whites
¼ t. cream of tartar
3 T. sugar

Combine dry ingredients in a heavy saucepan. Stir in milk and cream gradually. Add chocolate. Cook over medium heat, stirring constantly until mixture thickens and boils. Remove from heat. Slowly stir a small amount of chocolate mixture into egg yolks. Blend into hot mixture, boil 1 minute stirring constantly. Remove from heat and blend in butter and vanilla. Cool. Pour into cooled baked pie shell.

MERINGUE:
Beat egg whites with cream of tartar and sugar until peaked. Top pie with meringue and bake at 400° for 10 minutes.

Eleanor Hopper Heinz
(Mrs. James B.)

MISSISSIPPI MUD PIE
"Easy and children love it"

1 C. flour
½ C. margarine
1 C. chopped nuts

FIRST LAYER
1 C. powdered sugar
1 (8 oz.) pkg. cream cheese
1 C. Cool Whip

SECOND LAYER
1 pkg. chocolate instant pudding (4 servings)
1 pkg. vanilla instant pudding (4 servings)
3 C. cold milk

TOPPING
1 C. Cool Whip
2 Hershey bars, grated
Chopped nuts

Combine flour margarine and nuts; line a 9" x 13" baking dish. Bake at 350° for 20 minutes. Cool completely.

FIRST LAYER:
Whip all ingredients together and spread on crust.

SECOND LAYER:
Whip ingredients until thickened and spread over cheese mixture.

TOPPING:
Top with 1 cup Cool Whip. Garnish with grated chocolate and or pecans. Chill overnight. Can be frozen.

SERVES 15—20

Deen Summers, Dallas, Texas

Donor: Carolyn Smith Russell
(Mrs. Ralph)

Jean Williamson Bright
(Mrs. William Delbert)

FUDGE PIE

2 squares chocolate
½ C. butter
4 eggs, beaten
1¼ C. sugar
1 T. flour
1 t. vanilla

Melt chocolate and butter in a double boiler. Add sugar and the rest of the ingredients. Mix well and pour into greased 9" pie plate. Put pie plate in a pan of hot water and bake at 450° for 15 minutes, or until brown. Reduce heat to 300° and cook for 35 minutes.

Cherokee Club

CHOCOLATE CHESS PIE

1 (9") unbaked pie shell
1½ C. sugar
3½ T. cocoa
¼ C. margarine, melted
2 eggs, beaten
1 (5.33 oz.) can evaporated milk
1 t. vanilla

Mix all ingredients and pour into pie shell. Bake at 350° for 35 minutes or until set.

Barbara York Richardson
(Mrs. Kenneth)

COFFEE ICE CREAM PIE

18 Hydrox chocolate cookies, crushed
¼ C. butter
2 squares unsweetened chocolate
⅔ C. evaporated milk
½ C. sugar
1 qt. Coffee Ice Cream
½ C. chopped pecans or walnuts

Line a 9" pie plate with cookie crumbs mixed with butter. Refrigerate. Stir and cook chocolate, milk and sugar until thick in a double boiler. Cool. Fill crust with ice cream. Pour chocolate mixture over ice cream. Sprinkle with nuts. Freeze for at least 2 hours.

Mrs. Edwin Duncan
Tyler, Texas

Donor: Verne Monday Smith
(Mrs. W. Bruner)

GRASSHOPPER PIE

1 (9") baked pie shell
2 t. unflavored gelatine
⅓ C. heavy cream
¼ C. sugar
4 egg yolks
¼ C. Creme de Cocoa
¼ C. Creme de Menthe
1 C. heavy cream, whipped

Soften gelatine in ⅓ cup cream, dissolve over boiling water. Beat sugar into egg yolks. Stir in liqueurs and dissolved gelatine. Add a drop of green food coloring if desired. Chill until slightly thick. Fold in whipped cream and pour into prepared crust. Chill 4 hours. Top with shaved chocolate.
Note: A chocolate wafer crumb crust makes this dessert more striking and delicious.

Julia Wampler Barron
(Mrs. James Ferrell)

HARVEST PIE

1 (10") baked pastry shell
2 C. pumpkin
1 C. evaporated milk
¾ C. water
3 egg yolks, slightly beaten
1 C. brown sugar, packed
1 t. salt
1 t. cinnamon
1 t. nutmeg
½ t. ginger
1½ envelopes gelatine
½ C. cold water
3 egg whites
3 T. brown sugar
1 t. vanilla
1 C. chopped walnuts
1 C. heavy cream
1 t. vanilla
2 T. powdered sugar
¼ C. toasted walnuts

Combine pumpkin, milk, water, egg yolks, brown sugar, salt and spices in the top of a double boiler. Cook for 12 minutes. Soften gelatine in water and blend into pumpkin mixture. Chill until slightly thickened and cool. Beat egg whites until foamy and gradually beat in 3 T. of brown sugar. Add vanilla and beat until stiff. Fold into pumpkin mixture along with nuts. Pour into cooled baked pie shell. Whip cream with vanilla and powdered sugar. Top pie with cream and sprinkle with toasted walnuts.

Reva Harrison Ryan
(Mrs. A. B.)

JAMOCA ALMOND FUDGE PIE

CRUST:
18 Oreo Cookies
¼ C. margarine

FILLING:
1 qt. Baskin-Robbins Jamoca Almond Fudge Ice Cream
3 sqs. unsweetened chocolate
¼ C. oleo
⅔ C. sugar
1 small (5 oz.) can evaporated milk
1 C. heavy cream
3 T. powdered sugar
¼ C. toasted almonds or shaved chocolate

Put oreos in blender (5-6 at a time). Mix oreo and margarine. Put in 9" pie pan and freeze.
FILLING:
Pour ice cream into frozen crust and freeze. Melt chocolate and oleo in double boiler. Add alternately sugar and milk. Cook on low heat and stir until mixture reaches the softball stage. Cool to room temperature. Pour onto frozen ice cream and freeze. Whip cream with powdered sugar. Put this on top of frozen chocolate and refreeze. Sprinkle with slivered almonds and chocolate shavings. Serve immediately!

Mrs. John Price

IMPOSSIBLE PIE

4 eggs
½ C. flour
2 C. milk
½ t. salt
1 t. vanilla
1 C. sugar
1 C. coconut (3½ oz. can)

Put all ingredients in blender. Blend 10 seconds at a time for 3 or 4 times. Pour into buttered and floured 10" pie pan. Bake at 350° for 50 to 60 minutes.

Mrs. Delbert Freeman

PEACH MELBA ICE CREAM PIE

1 (3½ oz.) pkg. flaked coconut
¼ C. chopped nuts
2 T. melted butter
1 qt. Swenson's fresh peach ice cream
1 pt. Swenson's old fashion vanilla ice cream
1 pkg. frozen peaches, thawed OR 1 C. fresh peaches

MELBA SAUCE:
1 pkg. frozen red raspberries, thawed
½ C. sugar
3 T. cornstarch

VARIATION: To above recipe
Substitute:
Graham cracker crumbs for nuts
Vanilla ice cream for peach ice cream
Omit peaches

Add:
2 T. currant jelly to Melba Sauce for color

Mix coconut, butter and nuts and press into a buttered 9" pie plate. Bake at 325° for 10 minutes. Cool and then chill in freezer. Spoon softened peach ice cream over crust and freeze. Spoon softened vanilla ice cream over peach and freeze. Spoon peaches and syrup over ice cream and freeze.

SAUCE:

Drain raspberries, reserving syrup. Combine sugar and cornstarch. Add syrup. Heat in a saucepan to a boil and cool until thick. Stir constantly. Fold in raspberries. Cool. When ready to serve, pour over pie.

Joan Marvel Abbott
(Mrs. Frank)

Mrs. O. B. Canon

GRANDMOTHER'S PUMPKIN PIE
"A custard pie"

6 (9") unbaked pie shells
4 eggs, beaten
3 C. sugar
3 pts. milk
1 quart strained pumpkin
1 t. ginger
4 t. cinnamon

Combine ingredients and pour into pie shells. Bake at 450° for 10 minutes and then reduce heat to 325° and bake until set, or until inserted knife comes clean.

Cassandra Cobb Northcutt
(Mrs. LeGrande)

STRAWBERRY PIE

1 (9") baked pie shell
1 carton fresh strawberries
1 C. sugar
2 C. juice (Made from puréed strawberries combined with pineapple juice)
3 T. cornstarch
1 (3 oz.) pkg. cream cheese, softened and thinned with cream to spread
1 C. heavy cream, whipped

Sugar strawberries and let stand for 1 hour. Purée strawberries. Combine purée, juice and cornstarch and cook until it is thick and clear. Cool. Line pie shell with cream cheese. Pour cooled filling into shell. Chill. Top with whipped cream just before serving. Filling can be made ahead, but do not assemble very long before serving.

Dorothy Lorimer McNally
(Mrs. Frank)

STRAWBERRY CUSTARD PIE

CRUST:
1 C. flour
2 T. powdered sugar
6½ T. margarine, melted

FILLING:
2 C. milk
½ C. margarine, melted
5 T. flour
1 C. sugar
1 t. vanilla
Cool Whip

CRUST
Combine flour and sugar. Pour margarine into flour-sugar mixture and stir. Press into 9" pie plate with both hands. Bake at 325° for 25 minutes.

FILLING:
Combine flour and sugar in a heavy saucepan. Add milk gradually. Pour in margarine. Cook until thick. Remove from heat and add vanilla. Cool thoroughly.

TO ASSEMBLE:
Put fresh sliced strawberries over pastry. Add cooled custard. Top with Cool Whip.

Barbara York Richardson
(Mrs. Kenneth)

STRUDLE

2 C. oleo
4 C. flour
1 pint sour cream
⅓ C. apricot preserves
⅓ C. coconut
⅓ C. white raisins
⅓ C. chopped nuts

Blend with knives; oleo, flour and sour cream. Chill overnight. Divide into six parts. Roll each in thin rectangles. Spread with preserves, coconut, white raisins, and chopped nut mixture. Roll like jelly roll. Bake at 450° for 15 minutes or 375° for 25 minutes. Slice cold or frozen. This can also be frozen, baked or unbaked. Makes 6 loaves. Each may be cut into 12 pieces.

YIELD: 6 loaves

Joyce Andres Stidham
(Mrs. T. M.)

WHITE CHRISTMAS PIE

1—9" baked pie shell, chilled
1 T. plain gelatine
¼ C. cold water
1 C. sugar
4 T. flour
½ t. salt
1½ C. milk
¾ t. vanilla
¼ t. almond extract
½ C. heavy cream
1 C. coconut
3 egg whites
½ t. cream of tartar

Soften gelatine in water. Mix ½ cup sugar with flour and salt in sauce pan. Stir milk in gradually. Cook over low heat, stirring until it boils for one minute. Remove from heat. Stir in softened gelatine. Cool. When partially set, beat with rotary egg beater until smooth. Blend in vanilla and almond extract. Gently fold in meringue made with egg whites, cream of tartar and remaining sugar. Pour into chilled pie shell. Sprinkle a little coconut on top. Set in refrigerator for one hour before serving. This pie is truly snow white.

Barbara Hubbard Tomberlain
(Mrs. Charles)

Accompaniments

HOT APPLESAUCE

5 apples
4 T. butter
Juice of 2 oranges
Juice of one lemon
½ C. sugar
Pinch of salt
Cinnamon

Chop apples in big chunks. Sauté in butter and add juice of lemon and oranges, sugar and salt. Sprinkle on some cinnamon. Simmer, slowly, for a half hour or bake at 250° for an hour. Very good with pork, ham, or chicken.

SERVES 4-6

Betty Lyn Bruner Collier
(Mrs. Joe)

BAKED FRUIT CASSEROLE

3 C. canned fruit
½ C. white raisins

SAUCE:
½ C. margarine
3 rounded T. flour
½ C. sugar
¾ C. fruit juice

Soak raisins in water until plump. Drain off water. Cut canned fruit into bite-size pieces and reserve juice. Combine fruit mixture and raisins.
SAUCE:
Combine ingredients and make sauce. Cool until thick and mix with fruit and bake at 350° until hot and bubbly.

Susan Hill Perry
(Mrs. Milton A.)

SPICY BROILED GRAPEFRUIT

3 grapefruit, halved
¼ C. brown sugar
¼ C. melted butter
1 t. cinnamon
Dash of cloves
½ t. ginger
½ t. grated orange peel

Cut out centers and seeds and loosen sections of grapefruit. Combine ingredients and spread each grapefruit with mixture. Add a cherry in middle of each grapefruit before serving. Broil 5 minutes and serve.

SERVES 6

Carmen Huggins Hilliard
(Mrs. George M.)

CHERRY SAUCE FOR HAM

1 can cherry pie filling
1 C. orange juice
¼ t. cinnamon
¼ t. cloves

Combine ingredients and bring to a boil. Serve warm or cold.

YIELD: 3 C.

Mrs. John Ferrell

PEACH CONSERVE

18 large peaches
3 oranges
3 lemons
18 C. sugar
1 (8 oz.) jar maraschino cherries, diced

Peel and grind peaches. Juice the lemons. Juice the oranges and grind, and add to the peaches. Measure the mixture and add 1½ C. sugar for every cup. Boil for 1 hour, stirring. Add cherries and juice. Cook 10 minutes longer. Pour into sterilized jars and seal.

YIELD: about 11 pints

Carmen Huggins Hilliard
(Mrs. George M., III)

CRANBERRY JELLY

4 C. cranberries
2 C. boiling water
2 C. sugar

Put cranberries in stew pan with boiling water and boil 20 minutes. Run through a sieve. Add sugar and cook five minutes. Turn into a mold or jelly glasses and let cool. Pour paraffin over top to seal.

Peggy Moss Buckstaff
(Mrs. George)

H & H MAYHAW JELLY

Mayhaw
Water
Sugar

Put fresh mayhaws in a large kettle and add water until you can see it through the top layer of fruit. Bring to a boil, and simmer approximately 10 minutes. Pour juice into a jelly bag, or cheesecloth, to strain. Measure 4 C. of the strained juice. Place this and 3 C. sugar into a large enamel or stainless steel pan, and bring to a rolling boil. Cook for 23-25 minutes, until the syrup thickens. Pour immediately into hot, sterilized jars and seal.

YIELD: 3 (10 oz.) jars or 4 half pint jars

Eleanor Hopper Heinz
(Mrs. J. B.)

Patricia Smith Houston
(Mrs. E. B.)

BLENDER HOLLANDAISE SAUCE

½ lb. butter
4 egg yolks
2 T. lemon juice
¼ t. salt
Pinch cayenne

Heat butter until bubbly. Put eggs, lemon juice and salt in blender and turn on and off. Turn blender on again while slowly pouring in hot butter. Add cayenne. Serve immediately.

Lindy Ryan Butter
(Mrs. Stephen R.)

HOT MUSTARD

1 C. (2 cans) Coleman's mustard
1 C. vinegar
1 C. sugar
2 eggs, beaten

Mix mustard and vinegar. Let stand for 2 hours. Add sugar and eggs. Cook in top of a double boiler until thick, stirring frequently.

Curtain Call

SWEET AND SOUR SAUCE
"Excellent with Crab Rangoon—see Index"

1 C. pineapple juice
3 T. catsup
1 C. sugar
½ C. vinegar
4½ t. cornstarch
½ t. salt (or less)
Few drops red food coloring

Cook over low heat until thick and clear. Stir often.

Dorothy Lorimer McNally
(Mrs. Frank)

QUICK BROWN SAUCE

1½ t. butter
1½ t. flour
2 C. beef consommé
Salt and pepper to taste

Melt butter in a saucepan. Stir in flour and cook, stirring constantly, until the color of brown wrapping paper. Gradually add consommé, bring to a boil, and cook for 5 minutes, stirring constantly. Lower heat and simmer gently for 30 minutes, stirring occasionally. Skim off fat and season to taste.

Cookbook Committee

PICKLED SQUASH

8 C. thinly sliced squash (¼" thick)
2 C. thinly sliced onions (1/8" thick)
½ C. chopped bell pepper
1 T. salt
1 C. vinegar
1 ¾ C. sugar
½ t. celery seed
½ t. mustard seed

Sprinkle salt over squash, onion, and bell pepper. Let sit awhile. Mix vinegar, sugar, celery seed and mustard seed, and let it come to a boil. Add vegetables. Bring back to a boil, remove from fire and put into scalded jars and seal while hot.

YIELD: 5 pints

Fay Jeter Lewis
(Mrs. Harry, Jr.)

MOTHER'S CHOW CHOW

3 C. chopped green tomatoes
3 C. chopped cucumbers
2 large onions, chopped
1 medium head cabbage, chopped
1 (7 oz.) jar pimientos
1 bell pepper, chopped
1 hot pepper (or more if hotter chow chow is desired)
1 t. turmeric
½ t. cinnamon
½ t. allspice
1½ C. vinegar
1 C. packed brown sugar
1 C. white sugar
1 T. mustard
8—12 whole cloves (tied in small rag so they can be removed)

Mix vegetables and sprinkle generously with salt. Stir and let stand until juice is drawn out, about 3-4 hours. Squeeze out juice and put vegetables in a large pan. Add remaining ingredients and bring to a boil. Cook until vegetables are tender. Seal in sterilized jars.

Liz Amick Cobb
(Mrs. Charles)

HOT SAUCE

2 medium onions, chopped
2 cloves garlic, pressed
3 T. olive oil
2 (10 oz.) cans tomatoes and green chilies
1 t. ground cumin
1 t. salt

Sauté chopped onions and garlic in olive oil until limp. Stir in tomatoes and green chilies, add cumin and salt. Simmer 10 minutes.

GREEN TOMATO PICKLE RELISH

1 gallon green tomatoes, chopped (approx. 22)
1 gallon chopped onion (approx. 18)
½ pt. hot peppers, chopped (approx. 6)
6 C. sugar
2 qts. vinegar
1 T. allspice
1 T. cloves
½ C. salt

Mix together all ingredients. Bring to a boil and take off the stove. Pour into hot jars and seal.

Claire Smith Foster
(Mrs. Henry L.)

QUICK, EASY, NO-SOAK DILL PICKLES

MIX:
1 hot pepper
2 garlic cloves
½ t. mustard seed
½ t. celery seed
2 flowers of fresh dill (or 1 heaping t. dill seed)

BOIL:
2 C. white distilled vinegar
5 C. water
½ C. salt

Pack the following ingredients at room temperature with cucumbers in quart jars.

Bring vinegar, water and salt to a boil. Pour boiling mixture over the ingredients already in the jars and seal with hot rings and lids. Let set for 2-3 weeks before serving.

Linda Green McCaffity
(Mrs. Jerry)

CRISP, CRUNCHY SWEET PICKLES

1 gallon sliced cucumbers
2 C. pickling lime powder
2 gallons water

MIX:
8 C. sugar
5 C. vinegar
4 t. salt
1 box pickling spice
1 gallon sliced cucumbers that have been soaking

Mix in a plastic or glass container, and soak for 24 hours. Wash and soak in clear water for 3 hours to remove lime mixture.

Soak in sugar and vinegar solution for 24 hours. Cook mixture slowly for 1½ hours. Pour in jars and seal.

Linda Green McGaffity
(Mrs. Jerry)

SLANG JANG
"A delicious relish served with cream peas or black-eyed peas"

1⅔ C. chopped ripe tomatoes
1 C. chopped bell pepper
2 C. chopped onions
2 T. salad oil
⅓ C. sugar
½ C. vinegar
3 t. Accent
Salt and pepper to taste

Combine vegetables and toss with the oil. Add all other ingredients and mix well. Place in covered jar or bowl and let stand several hours.

Cherokee Club Kitchen

BARBEQUE SAUCE

1 (46 oz.) can tomato juice
3/8 C. Worcestershire sauce
½ onion, grated
2 T. vinegar
3 t. salt
⅓ C. brown sugar
1 t. cayenne
3 (14 oz.) bottles catsup
¼ C. lemon juice
¼ C. Woody's Barbecue Sauce

Combine all ingredients. Simmer over low heat until seasonings blend (about 15 minutes). The sweetness of catsup varies from brand to brand Adjust sweetness according by increasing or decreasing amount of brown sugar. This is enough sauce for 5 or 6 chickens and several slabs of ribs, with plenty left over for serving with the meal.

YIELD: 5 quarts

Tom Nethery
Kingsport, Tenn.

CURRY ACCOMPANIMENTS
"Use a combination of flavors and textures when selecting curry accompaniments—sweet, sour, salty and crunchy"

Crumbled bacon
Chutney
Toasted coconut
Toasted almonds
Chopped peanuts or cashew nuts
Pineapple cubes
Orange slices
Banana or avocado slices in lime juice
White raisins, plumped in sherry or brandy
Watermelon rind or sweet pickles, chopped
Fresh or candied ginger, grated

Chili sauce with hot chili powder
Chopped hard boiled eggs
Hearts of palm
Sliced ripe or stuffed green olives
Cucumbers, sliced in vinegar
Fresh vegetable chutney (onion, green pepper, tomato chopped in lemon juice)
Sour or dill pickles, chopped
Green pepper, chopped
Green onions, thinly sliced
Fried onion rings
Crumbled potato chips
Pearl onions
Currant jelly

MARINATED VEGETABLES
"Serve as an appetizer or salad"

VEGETABLES:
8 (4 oz.) cans button mushrooms
5 (14 oz.) cans Heart of Palm, cut in ¾" slices
4 (14 oz.) cans artichoke hearts

MARINADE:
3½ jars Durkee's dressing
Olive oil
Wine vinegar (5 dashes)
1 heaping T. mayonnaise
1 level soup spoon prepared mustard
½ bottle capers and juice
1 t. parsley flakes
1 t. dried chives

Drain vegetables and set aside. Rinse out Durkee's bottle with ½ inch of olive oil. Add wine vinegar. Mix all of the ingredients together and add vegetables. Marinate in the refrigerator for 12 hours or longer. This will keep for several weeks.

SERVES 60

Kenneth L. Kirkpatrick

DILLED COCKTAIL MEATBALLS

6 slices bacon
2 lbs. ground round
1 lb. mild sausage, ground
2 eggs, beaten
2 t. salt
1 large onion, minced
¼ t. garlic powder
4 T. flour
2 cans beer
1 C. tomato paste
1 t. powdered dill weed
1 C. pimiento stuffed olives
1 C. salad olives

Fry bacon to produce bacon fat. Reserve bacon for other use. Mix ground beef, sausage, eggs, salt and onion. Form into small cocktail-size meatballs. Brown on all sides in bacon fat. Remove meatballs and drain. Discard all but 2 T. of the fat. Add garlic powder and stir in flour. Cook, stirring, until the flour is lightly brown. Little by little add the beer, stirring constantly. Cook until the sauce is smooth and thickened. Stir in tomato paste and dill. Add meatballs. Cover and cook over low heat for 10 minutes. Add olives and cook for 2 minutes. Serve in chafing dish with small amount of sauce. Toothpicks will spear meatballs and olive portions. May be made with larger meatballs and serves with sauce over noodles as main dish.

YIELD: 80—100 small balls

E. S. Farrington, M. D.

JOE CROXTON'S 1000 ISLAND DRESSING

½ lb. finely grated cheese
½ medium onion, diced
2—3 T. Heinz sweet pickle relish plus juice
1 (4¼ oz.) can chopped ripe olives, drained
3 dashes Worcestershire sauce
4—5 dashes Tabasco
1 medium green pepper, chopped fine
1½ small pimiento, chopped
10—15 pecan halves, optional
1 qt. mayonnaise
Salt and pepper to taste
Chili sauce for color (about 5 T.)
3—6 hard boiled eggs, chopped

Mix in order given and let stand overnight. Makes wonderful open-face chicken sandwiches.

DAVE ABBOTT'S GERMAN POTATO SALAD

4 lbs. Russet potatoes (3 or 4 qts. when peeled and diced) cooked
1 C. celery, diced
1 C. chopped onions
6 slices bacon, cooked and crumbled
2 T. snipped parsley
2 t. salt
¾ C. margarine
½ C. flour
¾ t. dry mustard
4½ T. sugar
2¼ t. salt
½ t. Tabasco
1 can beer

Mix potatoes, celery, onion, bacon, parsley and salt together and set aside. Melt margarine and add flour, dry mustard, sugar, salt and Tabasco. Stir until smooth. Add beer and cook until mixture thickens and comes to a boil. Mix with potato mixture. Refiegerate overnight. Before serving, cover and heat at 375° for 25 to 30 minutes.

SERVES 12

Joanie Marvel Abbott
(Mrs. Frank G.

COLD CHEESE SOUP

4 (3 oz.) pkgs. cream cheese
2 C. beef boullion
¾ t. curry powder
1 garlic clove, pressed

Blend ingredients and correct seasonings. Chill.

YIELD: 1 qt.

Holloway Mitchell

PORTUGUESE SOUP

2 C. onions, chopped
6 cloves garlic, chopped (or garlic powder)
6 T. oil
1 lb. garlic flavored smoked pork sausage, cut into bite-size pieces
10 C. beef stock
1 (15 oz.) can kidney beans with liquid
1 head green cabbage, chopped into medium pieces
12 small new potatoes, quartered
¼ to ½ C. vinegar (or less to taste)
1 (16 oz.) bottle catsup (or more)
Salt and pepper to taste

Sauté onions and garlic in oil. When the vegetables are just transparent, add sausage slices and brown lightly. Add beef stock and all other ingredients. Bring soup to a boil, stirring to keep the bottom of the pot from burning. Reduce heat. Allow to simmer for 35-45 minutes or longer if you like, stirring occasionally. Correct seasonings to taste. This soup freezes well, except for the potatoes. Flavor of the soup is best when made ahead of time. Keeps about 1 week in the refrigerator.

YIELD: About 1 gallon

Jack Barcley
Donor: Dorothy Hallman Dingler
(Mrs. Clark M., Jr.)

FILET MIGNON WITH CHICKEN LIVERS

8 filet mignon steaks, cut 1½-2" thick (not bacon wrapped)
4 Spanish onions, chopped
32 chicken livers, chopped
1 C. butter
4 C. dry red wine
8 large fresh mushroom caps, sliced
4 t. salt
1 (4½ oz.) bag slivered almonds, toasted
8 t. chopped parsley
16 whole chicken livers, sautéed

Sauté onions and chopped chicken livers in butter until the onions are tender. Add wine, mushrooms and salt and simmer for 5 minutes. Broil the steaks to the desired degree of doneness and keep warm. On 8 sheets of aluminum foil, spread a portion of the onion-chicken liver-mushroom mixture. Lay the steaks on the sauce and spoon another portion of the sauce on top. Add toasted almonds and parsley. Seal the bags and bake at 500° for 5 minutes. Unseal the bags and transfer the contents to a serving plate. Add to each portion 2 chicken livers, which have been separately sautéed to crispness. Packages may be made in advance and run in a hot oven just before serving time.

SERVES 8

E. S. Farrington, M. D.

BEEF STROGANOFF

2 lbs. beef tenderloin
Butter
1 C. chopped white onion
4—6 large cloves garlic, finely chopped
1 (9—10 oz.) can sliced mushrooms
4 T. flour
4 t. Wilson's B-V Beef Flavor Sauce
1 T. catsup
½ t. salt
¼ t. pepper
1 (10½ oz.) can beef broth
1 t. Spice Island dill weed (not seed)
½ C. red wine
2 (8 oz.) cartons sour cream

Cut beef in finger sized bits or strips. Sear in butter; remove meat. Combine onions and garlic in butter and cook slowly for about 5 minutes. Add more butter if necessary. Add mushrooms and cook another 5 minutes. Add more butter if necessary. Add mushrooms and cook another 5 minutes or until onions change color. Remove from heat. Add flour, B-V, catsup, salt and pepper and combine. Return to low heat and slowly add bouillon while stirring constantly. When thoroughly combined, simmer about 5 minutes, stirring frequently. Sprinkle in dill weed and combine. Add wine and combine, then add sour cream and thoroughly combine mixture. Return meat to stroganoff sauce (drain off liquid from meat and discard). Stir meat and mixture well and let stay in warm oven for 2 hours, stirring occasionally. Serve over rice or noodles. This dish improves with one or two days of age in refrigerator.

SERVES 6-8

Brewster Welch

ELEGANT BEEF STROGANOFF

1 clove garlic, minced
½ C. chopped onion
2 T. shortening
1 lb. sirloin steak, cut into 2 x 2½" strips
¼ C. all-purpose flour
½ t. salt
1/8 t. pepper
1 (3 oz.) can sliced mushrooms
2 T. catsup
½—1 C. beef bouillon
½ C. sour cream
Cooked wide noodles
Poppy seed

Sauté garlic and onion in hot shortening. Remove from skillet. Dredge beef strips in combined flour, salt and pepper. Brown evenly over low heat. Return onion and garlic to skillet; add undrained mushrooms, catsup and ½ C. bouillon. Cover tightly and cook over heat for 1 hour until tender. If the sauce is too thick, add more bouillon. Uncover and quickly add sour cream and heat thoroughly. Serve immediately over noodles sprinkled with poppy seed. Garnish stroganoff with minced green onion or parsley.

SERVES 6

J. Glen Johnston

KNOTTIE'S CHILI

4 lbs. extra lean ground chuck
4 onions, finely chopped
4 cloves garlic, chopped
2 cans Rotel tomatoes
1 (28 oz.) can Hunt's tomatoes
2 (18 oz.) cans V-8 juice
3 t. M.S.G.
2 t. salt
1 t. black pepper, cracked
1 t. cracked red pepper
1½ oz. Gebhardt's chili powder
½ oz. ground cumin
1 t. orégano
3 C. water

In a large pot, brown meat in its own juice, and after browning, add onions and garlic and cook 4 minutes more, stirring frequently. Add both tomatoes, V-8 juice, and seasonings. Bring to a boil and add water. Cook on low heat for 1½ hours.

James K. Bivins, III

VEAL SCALLOPINI

1½ lbs. white veal or lean tender beef
Parmesan cheese
½—1 C. olive oil
1 C. Sweet Florio Marsala wine, divided
1 large white onion, sliced
6 cloves garlic, pressed
2 (5 oz.) jars sliced mushrooms
1 large green pepper, sliced
½ t. salt
½ t. pepper
½ t. cayenne
½ t. Italian seasoning
1 T. orégano
1 T. thick liquid beef gravy base
1 T. parsley
1 T. capers
1 (12 oz.) can tomato paste
1 (15 oz.) can tomato sauce

Cut meat into bit-size pieces. Coat meat with cheese. Sear meat in oil. Remove meat to bowl or platter. Add ½ C. of the wine to meat and let meat absorb it. Sauté in the same skillet: onions, garlic, mushrooms, pepper and seasonings. Add meat, tomato paste and sauce. Simmer 30 minutes. Add the other ½ C. of wine and simmer another 30 minutes.

SERVES 6

Brewster Welch

CHICKEN JOSEF

1½ C. chopped onions
¾ C. cooking oil
8 lbs. chicken pieces
Salt and pepper
Italian herb seasoning
Flour
1 bell pepper, chopped
1½ C. chopped celery
¼ C. chopped parsley
4 carrots, cut into 1½" pieces
White wine

Sauté onions in cooking oil until light brown. Remove from oil. Salt, pepper and flour chicken pieces and sear in remaining oil. Add onions and other ingredients. Add white wine to almost cover chicken. Cover and cook for 1 hour at a low temperature. May be prepared ahead and reheated before serving. Note: The secret of this dish is in the seasoning. Use LIBERAL amounts of salt, pepper and Italian herbs. Wine seems to absorb salt, so keep tasting.

SERVES 12

Joseph Bramlette

QUAIL CARGILL STYLE

Salt, pepper and flour quail. Brown in deep fat in iron skillet. Don't cook too done. Place in roaster and bake in oven at 300°. Baste with white wine 2—3 hours. Thirty minutes before serving add fresh mushrooms.

GRAVY:
Reserve drippings and a few mushrooms, place in iron skillet and add a little flour. Brown. Add water or milk and stir until the right consistency. Do not make gravy too thick.

Robert Cargill

Donor: Paula Cargill Kaplan
       (Mrs. Charles A.)

BARBEQUED FISH

Large fish filets
Several slices bacon, fried, crumbled, reserve grease
Butter
Seasoned salt
Pepper
Lemon juice
½ C. barbeque sauce, warmed

Place large fish filet on heavy duty foil. Make platter of foil by crimping up edges around fish. Pour bacon grease over fish, sprinkle crumbled bacon top. Dot with butter and season with seasoned salt, pepper and lemon juice to taste, depending on size of filet. Place on grill. Leave about 20 minutes. Baste fish with warm barbeque sauce. Poke holes in foil and let juices drain onto fire. Cook for a few more minutes until done.

Ira Gray Rathbun

HOLLY LAWRENCE'S WILD DUCK

"The gravy's as good as the duck—serve it on wild rice"

4 wild ducks
1 C. flour
1 C. Wesson oil
4 C. cold water
4 buds garlic, finely chopped
1 heaping t. crushed whole ground red pepper, per duck
2 level t. celery seed, per duck
2 level t. chili powder, per duck
2 level t. salt, per duck

Make a roux, in a deep kettle, by browning flour until dark brown in the oil. Stir constantly. When flour has become very dark brown, place kettle in sink of cold water immediately to prevent scorching. When mixture has cooled, return to heat and add 4 C. cold water. Stir until completely blended, then add garlic. Place inside each duck; red pepper, celery seed, chili powder and salt. Put ducks in roux and cook, covered, at 325° about 3 hours.

Thomas W. Lawrence

SAUTÉED CUCUMBERS

8 medium cucumbers, peeled
3 T. butter
1 t. granulated sugar
Salt
1 t. chopped chives

Cut the cucumbers in half lengthwise, and use a spoon to remove the seeds. Slice the cucumber halves into 1" pieces, cover with boiling salted water, and boil for about 5 minutes. Heat the butter into a large skillet. Drain the cucumbers thoroughly, and sauté in the melted butter until nicely golden on all sides. Sprinkle sugar over the pieces as they cook. When all the pieces are sautéed, transfer the vegetable to a serving dish, season with salt and sprinkle with chopped chives.

SERVES 8

E. S. Farrington, M. D.

MONTERREY BEANS

2 lbs. pinto beans, soaked overnight
½ lb. bacon, diced
2 large tomatoes, chopped
1 large onion, chopped
4 pods garlic, crushed
Green chilies to taste, chopped
½ t. dried corriander

Fry all ingredients except beans together. When cooked add beans and enough water to cover. Cook slowly until done.

SERVES 12

Thomas W. Lawrence

STUFFED MUSHROOMS

24 large fresh mushrooms
Juice of ½ lemon
¼ C. grated Swiss cheese
½ C. bread crumbs
¼ C. chopped parsley
1 clove garlic
2 T. grated or minced onion
Salt, pepper or dash cayenne
3 T. butter
¼ C. Sherry
1 (4¼ oz.) can chopped ripe olives
Bread crumbs for topping
Butter

Wash and remove stems from mushrooms carefully. Reserve stems. Squeeze a little lemon juice into each cap. Combine cheese, crumbs, parsley, garlic, onion, salt and pepper. Chop mushroom stems finely and sauté in butter. Pour over bread mixture and add other ingredients; pile lightly into caps and mound high. Sprinkle with additional bread crumbs and dot with butter. Put on baking sheet.(Cover and refrigerate if made ahead of time.) Bake at 350° for 45 minutes.

Donn Bindler

YORKSHIRE PUDDING

1 C. flour
1 egg
1 C. milk
Dash salt and pepper

Mix all of the ingredients by hand until all lumps have dissolved. Pour into greased muffin pan and bake at 400° for 15-20 minutes.

YIELD 12

John L. Dawes

CHARLEY'S PIMIENTO CHEESE

2 lbs. hoop cheese, grated
1 onion, grated
2 (4 oz.) cans pimientos, drained and chopped
6 candied dill strips, minced
1 C. mayonnaise
2 T. Worcestershire sauce
Dash of Tabasco
Seasoned salt to taste
Pepper to taste
1 t. dill weed
2 T. white Karo

Combine cheese, onion, pimientos, and dill strips; mix well. Add mayonnaise, Worcestershire, Tabasco, salt, and pepper; mix thoroughly. Add additional mayonnaise if needed for spreading consistency. Add dill weed and Karo; mix well. This can be refrigerated for two weeks. I use a food grinder instead of grating the cheese, onions, and pickles.

YIELD: 1½ quarts

Charles H. Davis

JALAPEÑO PEPPER SAUCE

5 onions, chopped
2 bell pepper, chopped
12—14 small ripe peeled tomatoes, chopped
6 garlic cloves, chopped
¾ C. jalapeño peppers, chopped
1 C. sugar
1 C. vinegar
1 C. cooking oil
1 C. water
4 T. salt
4 t. black pepper

Combine all ingredients and cook 2½-3 hours until thick. Pour while hot into sterilized fruit jars and seal.

Jim Heller

CHERRIES JUBILEE

1 C. black Bing cherry juice
1 T. cornstarch
¼ C. sugar
½ C. pitted black Bing cherries
1 T. butter
2 T. Kirsch
2 T. brandy
2 or 3 oz. good cognac, warmed

Bring juice to a boil. Mix cornstarch, sugar, and a little of the juice and add to boiling mixture. Boil 1 minute, stirring constantly. Add the cherries. Remove from heat; add butter, Kirsch, and brandy. At this point you may serve this hot over ice cream. It is much more fun to place cherry mixture in a silver chafing dish, keeping it hot. Add warmed cognac and ignite. When flames die, serve over vanilla ice cream. This is an easy, delicious gourmet dessert.

SERVES 6

Charley Davis

BOILED CUSTARD

6 eggs
1½ C. sugar
½ gal. sweet milk

Beat eggs while gradually stirring in sugar. Add milk and stir well. Place mixture in large container that is in another large container of hot water. Cook slowly until mixture thickens, stirring continuously (about 1 hour). Note: Never let the water boil hard. A cake rack may be used in bottom of pan of water on which to set pan of custard mixture.

George M. Hilliard, M. D.

FROYLAN'S MARGARITAS

1 oz. fresh lime juice
1 oz. Cointreau
2 oz. Tequila
⅔ blender full of ice

Rub rim of champagne glass with lime and dip in salt. Combine ingredients in blender with ice until mushy.

SERVES 2

Casa Tres Changos
Acapulco, Mexico

NEGRONI

½ gin
½ Campari
1 drop sweet Vermouth
Lemon twist

Mix ingredients and serve over ice.

Stephen R. Butter

BANANA DAIQUIRI

1½ oz. white rum
2 T. lime juice
½ large banana, sliced
2 T. sugar
2 maraschino cherries
Ice, shaved

Blend ingredients with blender ⅓ full of shaved ice until it has a slushy consistency. Pour into champagne glasses.

SERVES 2

A. C. Stevens, M. D.

CAFE MARRAKECH

1 oz. brandy
1 oz. Creme de Cacao
Hot freshly brewed coffee
Lightly sweetened whipped cream
Bitter chocolate shavings

In a stemmed 6-8 ounce glass, put brandy and creme de cacao and fill the glass with hot coffee. Spoon whipped cream over the top and sprinkle the cream with shavings of cocolate.

SERVES 1

Jon B. Ruff

THOUGHTS ON WINE

Ernest Hemingway's eloquent words provide us with food for thought on wine:

Wine is one of the most civilized things in the world that has been brought to the greatest perfection, and it offers a greater range for enjoyment and appreciation than, possibly, any other purely sensory thing which may be purchased. One can learn about wines and pursue the education of one's palate with great enjoyment all of a lifetime . . . (from "Death In The Afternoon")

Wine has been around since the dawn of recorded history, yet many of us are just beginning to realize how much it adds to our entertaining as well as to our day-to-day living. Keeping this in mind, let us share with you some thoughts on wine which we have gleaned from touring, tasting and reading about wine!

CHOOSING THE RIGHT WINE

Choosing the proper wine is actually a matter of individual taste. Any wine you like is the proper wine for you. The general rule of "white wine with white meat and red wine with red meat" need not be taken too seriously; however, there are certain marriages of food and wine which are pleasant to everyone:

Hors d'oeuvre: light dry white wine; rosé

Fish: dry white wine; sweet white wine

White Meat & Poultry: dry white wine; light red wine

Red Meat: full-bodied red wine

Cheese: Red wine is best with pungent cheese, but all wines (except
      sweet ones) are good with cheese

Sweet Dessert & Fruit: Sweet white wine; Champagne

A dry Champagne or rosé is good with all kinds of food and may be served before, during and after a meal. There are no rigid rules. Half the fun with wine is in exploring and experimenting.

THE CATEGORIES OF WINE

Generally speaking, there are four major categories—table wines; fortified wines, or wines to which brandy has been added to increase strength; apéritif or flavored wines; and sparkling wines.

Table Wines

These are, or should be, simply the juice of certain grapes, fermented (the process which turns the sugar in the juice into alcohol), clarified, aged for varying periods in tanks or barrels, and then bottled. These wines are usually relatively low in alcohol, from 9% to 14%. By their very definition, they are served at "table" along with food. Table wine is white, red, or pink, and all shades in between. It is primarily a question of how long the skins of the red or black grapes are allowed to stay in the vat when the wine is being made. All the coloring matter is in the skin of the grape. Leave the skins in long enough—you have red wine. Take them out sooner—rosé or pink wine. Don't leave them in at all—white wine. Some grapes are, of course, green or, as they are called, "white". There is no skin pigmentation. These grapes produce white wines only.

Fortified or Dessert Wines

Fortified simply means that after the normal fermentation of the grape sugar into alcohol has been completed, a strength of 14% give or take a degree, is the maximum. To go beyond this, brandy is added to bring these wines to around the 20% mark. Incidentally, when brandy is added during fermentation, fermentation ceases, some sugar is left unconverted, and you have a sweet drink like some ruby Ports or Muscatel. If you add the brandy after fermentation is completed, you can have a dry drink, such as the dry Sherries.

SHERRY, named after the city of Jerez in Spain, is the most famous of this great family of wines. It is made primarily from the Palomino grape. The principal types of Sherry are:

Fino, Manzanilla, Vino de Pasto—dry; serve cold.

Amontillado—moderately dry; chill.

Amoroso, Oloroso, and "Brown"—rich, sweet; serve at room temperature, though now often served "on the rocks."

Dry Sherry might come, more properly, under the heading of apéritif wine, that served before a meal.

Other fortified dessert wines are PORTS, MADEIRA, MALAGA, and MUSCATEL.

Apéritif Wines

The next group of wines are the apéritifs, or "flavored" wines. The best known is VERMOUTH. Vermouth is simply an infusion of wines with various herbs, roots, barks, etc.—the combination secret and known to the maker alone. Vermouth can be dry or sweet. Usually the dry is known as French and the sweet is Italian. The United States is a large producer of Vermouth. All Vermouths and their derivatives and all apéritifs are served cold.

Another group of flavored wines are the so-called "pop" or "mod" wines. Some, like Thunderbird and Wild Irish Rose, are relatively high in alcohol; the newer crop—Bali Hai, Boones' Apple, etc.—are quite low and flavored with pinapple, apple and who knows what else.

Sparkling Wines

Of course, the one that first comes to mind is CHAMPAGNE. Champagne is more than a wine—it's a way of life! Champagne is wine whose second fermentation is not completed—hence the bubbles in the bottle. The classic Champagne is made only by the Methode Champenoise, the contribution of a French cellar master-monk, Dom Perignon, at the end of the seventeenth century. His was basically a method of making practical the fermentation of wine, a second time, in the bottle. Such wines say on their labels: "Fermented in this bottle." There are other methods of making Champagne, but this is the most classic method.

The Champagnes of France are, of course, the original ones. All French Champagnes, except those marked Blanc de Blancs (white of whites—made from all-white grapes) are produced from a blend, containing wines made from red (Pinot Noir) grapes and white (Chardonnay) grapes. Pink champagne is simply a champagne made from some wine in which the red skins have been allowed to remain long enough to tint the mix.

Other countries have produced what they call "Champagne." The United States makes some very nice bubblies, though few, if any, use the Champagne grapes or methods.

Probably the next most important sparkling wine is Sparkling Burgundy. This is primarily an export to us.

The single greatest phenomenon in the bubbly world was the meteoric rise (and fall) of Cold Duck—a merger of red and white wines of no great distinction, carbonated.

HANDLING AND STORING WINE

Wine is a living liquid which continues to mature once it is bottled. Since it contains no preservatives, it will spoil if handled improperly. Wine should not be exposed to extreme temperatures, nor should it be subjected to shaking or joggling. Even the most modest wines will improve with a day's rest after purchase. Great wines, particularly the red ones, need several weeks' rest. Wines with cork stoppers must be stored on their sides. Wines to be aged should be laid in any dark, quiet corner at a constant temperature, ideally 50°F. Most people make do with part of a closet, stacking partitioned shipping cases on their sides with the flaps folded back.

PROPER TEMPERATURE FOR SERVING WINE

Red Wines: All but very young, light wines should be served at normal room temperature of 65°F.

White Wines: Champagne, Rosés: Chill before serving. As a rule, the sweeter the wine, the colder it should be. Avoid over-chilling as the wines lose much of their taste. One or two hours in the refrigerator will bring the wine to 40° or 50°F.; twenty minutes in an ice bucket will do the same thing.

SERVING

The correct service of wine adds greatly to the full enjoyment of each bottle. Red wine should be uncorked about one hour before the meal to allow it to "breathe." To open the wine, cut the tinfoil neatly below the lip of the bottle. Turn the point of the corkscrew all the way through the cork and pull it out. Wipe the mouth of the bottle with a napkin. Old red wines often have a deposit in the bottom of the bottle, consequently, careful handling is necessary to avoid circulating the deposit through the wine. Either pour the wine into a decanter, carefully leaving the deposit in the bottle, or serve it from a wine basket where it remains at an angle. Decanting will also help wines that have not had enough time to "breathe."

There is a Wine Ritual which makes the actual serving of the wine fun. It makes one's table a living part of the great history of wine, human beings, and conviviality:

1) The host pours a small amount in his glass first, so that he gets any stray bits of cork.
2) The host tastes the wine, to be certain the flavor is enjoyable, before serving the whole table. (Actually the wine should be tasted as soon as it is opened to ascertain whether or not it is good; this allows the host to open another bottle in time to let it "breathe" if the first bottle is bad.)
3) In pouring he fills the glasses approximately half full, leaving space for the release of the fine wine bouquet.
4) It is the host, rather than the hostess, who serves the wine and sees to it that glasses are replenished all during the meal.
5) After the first glass, it is acceptable to pass the wine bottle and let guests help themselves.

GLASSES

Any good glass can be used with fine wine, but a stemmed glass is ideal. Experts agree that one type of wine glass is perfect for all wines, including Champagne. It is long stemmed, tulip shaped, with the bowl the size of an orange (a six to eight ounce glass). The wine glass should be clear and thin without heavy ornamentation. The larger size also makes it possible to fill it only partially, one-half to two-thirds of the way, for full enjoyment of the fragrance and bouquet. Incidentally, the wine glass is always placed to the right of the water glass.

QUANTITIES

A general rule is that a bottle of wine serves four people. Quantities are deceptive, however, because it depends on what type of wine is in the bottle. "Bottle" usually means a fifth (25.6 ounces), and with Table Wines like Chablis or Burgundy, the fifth serves 4 to 5 guests. A fifth of Champagne will serve 5 to 6 guests. (A Jeroboam bottle is 4 fifths, a Magnum 2 fifths, a Tenth is ½ of a fifth, and a Split is ¼ of a fifth.) With the Dessert Wines like Sherry or Port, the fifth serves 8 guests.

FUN WITH WINE: WINE TASTING

Drinking is the only way to become familiar with wines, and wine tasting with friends can create an exciting evening. The best way to taste wine is with food, and one of the simplest and most satisfying of meals is wine accompanied by the two other basic foods that are products of fermentation—bread and cheese. Cheeses should be fairly mild (nothing sharper than a good Cheddar), and there should be several kinds. Crusty French bread or crackers complete the setting for a wine tasting party.

The wines should be as close together as possible—bottles of the same wine from two different producers, for instance. It is interesting when wines have been selected because there is a common ground for comparison between them, as for example, red or white wines from different regions, or wines from different districts of the same region. It is better to compare wines on the same level of greatness, because then it is possible to get a fair opinion about each one.

For a home party, five or six wines make an interesting tasting. There may hardly be less than four—and more than six may present some problem as far as space, service, glasses, and other details are concerned. For tasting purposes very little of each wine (no more than one or two ounces is poured into the glass. A regular bottle contains about 20 such servings. In most cases, therefore, half bottles are preferred. If food is served after the tasting, it is a good opportunity for the guests to have a second taste of the wines to see how they complement the food. In such cases wines are purchased by the bottle instead of the half-bottle.

The steps in tasting wine are:

1) Look at the wine in the glass, check its brightness, and compare the different shades—reds go from a brilliant ruby to a purple hue; whites go from a very pale yellow or greenish yellow to a rich, deep gold; rosés vary from a subdued pink to a lively, nearly red color.
2) Swirl the wine in the glass, thus allowing the wine to "breathe" and to make contact with the air to develop its bouquet.
3) Sniff the aroma, for smelling the wine in the glass is one of the greatest pleasures of wine tasting—it is a foretaste of the wine itself.
4) Sip the wine, but don't swallow it at first. Let the wine in your mouth; send it to the back of the mouth where the taste-buds are. (At this point, an expert

wine taster would know all there is to know about the wine being tasted and would not swallow it if there were many wines to taste.)

5) Swallow the wine and enjoy the multiple sensations from tasting and smelling the wine.

6) Concentrate on the aroma which lingers in the mouth, because a good wine leaves a lasting fragrance after being swallowed, and the greater the wine the longer this fragrance lasts.

7) The last and one of the most enjoyable steps is to talk about the wines which have been tasted. Indeed, exchanging opinions helps a great deal toward fixing impressions in one's own mind.

SUGGESTIONS IN CHART FORM
for Matching Wines to Foods

RED WINES

All red meats including Roasts, Steaks, Stews; Game, Duck, Goose; Veal and Cheese (White Wine and Rosé also acceptable)

BURGUNDY
MORE EXPENSIVE

La Tâche	Le Chambertin
Clos de Vougeot	Bonnes Mares
Richebourg	La Romanée
Musigny	

MEDIUM PRICED

Vosne-Romanée	Pommard
Aloxe-Corton	Beaune
Volnay	Gévrey-Chambertin

LESS EXPENSIVE

Mercurey	Fixin
Santenay	

BEAUJOLAIS

Not really a Burgundy, although allowed the name. It is not made from the Pinot Noir grape and it comes from its own area near, but not part of, the Côte d'Or. In addition to wines marked "Beaujolais," seek the better "Beaujolais Supérieur," "Beaujolais Villages," and ones with these "crus" names.

Chénas	Juliénas
Moulin à Vent	Côte de Brouilly
Morgon	Brouilly
Fleurie	Saint-Amour
Chiroubles	

BORDEAUX (CLARET)
Châteaux Wines
MORE EXPENSIVE

Château Lafite	Château Haut-Brion
Château Latour	Château Cheval Blanc
Château Margaux	Château Ausone
Château Mouton Rothschild	Château Pétrus

MEDIUM PRICED

Château La Mission Haut-Brion	Château Montrose
Château Gruaud-Larose	Château Lascombes
Château Canon	Château Pichon-Longueville
Château Palmer	Château Cos d'Estournel

ROSÉ WINES
MEDIUM PRICED

Château Meyney	Château Figeac
Château Talbot	Château Lynch-Bages
Château Pontet-Canet	Château Fourcas-Hosten

Petite Châteaux
LESS EXPENSIVE

Château Greysac	Château Plassans
Château Gressina	Château Pavillon Figeac
Château Cadillac	Château Ripeau

REGIONAL WINES
(St. Émilion, Médoc, St. Julien, Graves, St. Estèphe, Margaux, Bordeaux Supérieur.)

LESS EXPENSIVE
(From such shippers as B & G, Cruse, Calvet, Ginestet, Kressman, Johnston, Dourthe, Sichel, Tytel and others).

AMERICAN
California
MEDIUM PRICED

Pinot Noir—from the red Burgundy grape
Cabernet Sauvignon—from the red Bordeaux grape
Zinfandel—light, pleasant (no European counterpart)
Gamay—from the Beaujolais grape
Some to look for: Alamadén, Martini, Krug, Masson, Cresta Blanca, Korbel, Beaulieu, Buena Vista, Inglenook, Sebastiani, Heitz, Ridge, Freemark Abbey, Sterling, Chappelet, Sonoma, Simi, Wente, Martin Ray, Christian Brothers, Asti, Assumption Abbey, Ficklin (port); Gallo, Roma, Guild, Italian Swiss, Petri,

324 Wines

Cucamonga, East Side, Regina, etc., are producers of generic and popular wines, many under trade marks and trade names of their own.

Eastern
LESS EXPENSIVE

Various wines made from native American grapes (Concord, Deleware, etc.) French-American hybrids (Baco Noir, Chelois), and a few from true Vinifera grapes of Europe (Frank, Gold Seal). New York producers: Widmer, Taylor, Great Western, Gold Seal (Charle Fournier), Konstantin Frank, Bully Hill, Benmarl.

WHITE WINES

Fish, Shellfish, Poultry, Chicken, Turkey (Red Wine also acceptable), Ham, Veal (light Red Wine also acceptable).

BURGUNDY

MORE EXPENSIVE

Le Montrachet
(the greatest-scarce, expensive)
Batard-Montrachet
Chassagne-Montrachet

Chevalier-Montrachet
Corton-Charlemagne
Meursault
Corton Blanc

MEDIUM PRICED

Pouilly-Fuissé
(covers a multitude of wines—good and bad)

Chablis
Seek out premier crus with hyphenations
Chablis-Vaudésir
Chablis-Valmur, etc.

Look for such French shippers as Jadot, Drouhin, Latour, Ropiteau, Laguiche, Moreau, Chanson, Chauvenet, Piat, Calvert, B & G, Pic, Jaboulet-Verschères, or for such importers as Frederick Wildman; Browne-Vintners, Dreyfus-Ashby, Wile, Kobrand, House of Burgundy, M. Henri, Carillon, Austin Nichols, Peartree, Joseph Garneau, etc.

LOIRE
LESS EXPENSIVE

Muscadet—dry, inexpensive
Sancerre

Pouilly-Fumé
Vouvray

BORDEAUX
SWEET

MORE EXPENSIVE
(depending on vintage)
Château d'Y quem—the queen of the Sauternes—always scarce, always expensive

MEDIUM PRICED
Château Climens
Château Filhot
Château Suduiraut
Château Rayne-Vigneau

DRY
MEDIUM PRICED

Château Haut-Brion Blanc	Château Olivier
Château Carbonnieux	Château Couhins

There are many Petite Châteaux, as in Red Wines. Some are Châteaux Mouton Cadet Sec, Le Pape, Mercier, Timberlay. There are also regional wines blended by the great shipping houses simply called Graves, Sauternes, Barsac—and of late, Entre-Deux-Mers, Cadillac, Loupiac. These vary in sweet/dry.

RHÔNE
LESS EXPENSIVE

Hermitage Blanc	Also, Arbois and Provencal wines are
La Chapelle	worth trying.
Châteauneuf-du-Pape Blanc	

GERMAN
Rhine Wines—in brown bottles
MEDIUM PRICED

Schloss Vollrads	When marked Spätlese, Auslese, cost is
Schloss Johannisberg	higher.
Rüdesheimer—and hundreds of others.	

Moselle Wines—in green bottles
MEDIUM PRICED

Berncasteler Doktor	Wehlener Sonnenuhr
is the king here—scarse, expensive.	
Graacher Himmelreich	Ockfener Bockstein
Piesporter Goldtröpfchen	Miximir Grunhauser

ITALIAN
LESS EXPENSIVE

Orvieto	Verdicchio
Soave	White Chianti
Lugana	Corro

AMERICAN
LESS EXPENSIVE
VARIETALS

Pinot Chardonnay and Pinot Blanc—counterparts of French White Burgundy.
Semillon, Sauvignon—counterparts of French White Bordeaux
Chenin Blanc—Counterpart of French Vouvray
Riesling, Grey Riesling, Traminer, Gewürztraminer, Sylvaner—counterparts of German and Alsatian Wines
Generics: California Chablis, Sauterne, Rhine, etc., and Eastern wines: Niagara, Diamond, Delaware, and Scuppernong, etc.

Monopoles: Emerald Dry (Masson); Lake Country White (Taylor); Chablis Nature (Gold Seal).
See list of producers under Red Wines, American

CHAMPAGNES
Champagne goes with nearly anything, anytime.

FRENCH
Vintage—More expensive
Non-Vintage—Less expensive

Moët & Chandon (Dom Perignon is their top), Krug, Mumm (Lalow is their top), Piper-Heidsieck, Charles Heidsieck, Heidsieck Monopole, Roederer, Taittinger, Bollinger, Perrier-Jouët, Irroy, Laurent-Perrier, Pommery & Greno, Mercier, Ayala, Veuve Clicquot, Lanson. Other French sparkling wines: Sparkling Saumur, Sparkling Anjou, Kriter (a sparkling White Burgundy).

AMERICAN
California
MORE EXPENSIVE

Schramsberg—made by the Méthode Champenoise and using the approved grapes of Champagne. Korbel (Natur even drier than their Brut), Almadén, Weibel, Kornell, Masson, Beaulieu's B/V, Cresta Blanca, and others.

Eastern
MEDIUM PRICED

Taylor, Great Western, Gold Seal, Charles Fournier.

ROSÉ WINES
Salmon, Fish, Stews, some Casseroles, Steak on a summer's day, some rich Cheeses, Omelettes or Soufflés, Cold Cuts.

LESS EXPENSIVE
Tavel (Rhône), the best, and best known. Other popular Rosés from Anjou, Loire, Alsace, Provence. The United States offers good Rosés $1.50 to $2.50. Almadén's Grenache Rosé and Wente's Livermore Rosé are very popular, as is Gallo's Rosé. Italy's Rosés of Lake Garda are very good. Also Lancers and Mateus from Portugal.

DESSERT WINES
Fruit, Compotes, rich Cakes or Tarts, some dessert Cheeses.
Here is where your great Sauternes come in, also the sweet Barsacs; the "special" German Auslese, Spätlese, and Trockenbeerenauslese wines made of overripe grapes; Port, Marsala, Angelica, sweet Sherries, sweet Tokay, sweet Madeira (Boal or Malmsey), Germany's Sekt, and France's sweet demi-sec and sec Champagnes.

AFTER DINNER
Port (various types)
Cognac—a brandy distilled from grapes grown in the demarcated area of the

Charente, around the cities of Cognac and Jarnac.
(All other distilled grape wine is Brandy—not Cognac.)
Calvados—from apples (Normandy)
Marc—from pits and hulls of the grapes, distilled and aged—called Grappa in Italy.
Brandy—made wherever wine is made. California makes very large quantities.

LIQUEURS

Some distilled, some infusions, some secret formulae, some fruit (white) alcohols such as Kirsch, Framboise, Poire, Mirabelle. There are hundreds of kinds, types and brands. A few: Cointreau, Strega, Bénédictine, Chartreuse (green and yellow), Vandermint, Izarra, Galliano, Crême de Menthe, Drambuie, Grand Marnier, Amaretto.
Pernod, Berger, and Ricard are licorice-flavored, usually served as apéritifs.

FOOTNOTES ON WINE

There is more, much more, to say about wine. The interested reader can pursue his quest for information at the local bookstore or library. Once the wine virus gets into the veins, there is simply no cure. You will go on experimenting, reading, learning, tasting, talking.

One of the most interesting ways to learn more about wines is to take one of the many wine tours which are offered today. Our wine tour of France took us to two of the most famous wine growing regions in the world. Our learning experience was invaluable, but it also whetted our appetites to seek more information and to plan further trips. It seems that the more you know, the more there is to know! The Napa Valley in California provides one of the most interesting wine touring opportunities in the United States—one which we highly recommend, too!

We challenge you to take up the hobby or at least to learn enough about wine to enjoy it as one of life's great pleasures. As J. H. Voss said some two hundred years ago:

Who loves not woman, wine and song—
Remains a fool his whole life long.

Salud!

Jane and Glenn Johnston
Betty and Charley Davis

COFFEE PUNCH

1½ C. instant Yuban coffee
3 C. boiling water
1½ C. sugar
1 t. salt
3 T. vanilla
1¼ gal. milk
3 gal vanilla ice cream

Mix coffee in hot water. Add sugar, salt and vanilla. Chill. Immediately before serving, add ice cream which has been softened just enough to break up in the coffee mixture. It is best added in small amounts as it is served.

SERVES 40-45

Sustainers Committee

HOT APPLE PUNCH

1 (6 oz.) frozen lemonade
1 (6 oz.) can frozen orange juice
1 (46 oz.) can apple juice
5 C. water
3 sticks cinnamon
Orange slices
Lemon slices
Whole cloves

Simmer first 5 ingredients about 10 minutes. Stick cloves around orange and lemon slices and float on top of punch.

YIELD: 3 quarts

Patricia Carmack Ross
(Mrs. Kenneth L.)

HOT SPICED TEA

½ C. tea leaves
6 qts. boiling water
2 C. sugar
1 t. whole cloves
1 t. whole allspice
2 sticks cinnamon
⅔ C. lemon juice
1 C. orange juice

Add tea leaves to boiling water. Strain leaves off after tea is fairly strong. Add sugar. Add the spices which have been placed in a metal teaball for easy removal. Leave spices in tea for about 1 hour, then remove. Add juices. Serve hot. Leftover tea may be kept in refrigerator and reheated. Leftover spices may be used a second time for more tea.

YIELD: 40 cups

Vera Mitchell Garlough
(Mrs. Harry Thomas)

HOT BUTTERED RUM BATTER

2 lb. brown sugar
1¼ lb. real butter, melted
1 t. cinnamon
1 t. nutmeg
1 t. ground cloves
1 t. allspice
3 eggs

Mix all ingredients, adding eggs last and beat until smooth. Store in refrigerator. Allow mixture to come to room temperature before using. To serve, put 2 T. of batter into mug, add 1 jigger of rum and mix well; fill with boiling water. Will keep in refrigerator quite a while.

Sally Hilliard Shank
Tulsa, Oklahoma

COFFEE BRAZIL

1½ sq. sweet chocolate
1 C. water
½ C. sugar
¼ C. instant coffee
¼ t. salt
1 qt. milk
1 t. vanilla
½ C. whipped cream
¼ C. sugar

In saucepan combine first 5 ingredients and heat until chocolate melts. Cook for 3 minutes. Remove from heat. Stir in milk and vanilla. Top with sweetened whipped cream.

YIELD: 6 C.

Normand Dufilho Wilkinson
(Mrs. Jacques)

PARTY PUNCH
"An easy punch—more can be made as the crowd grows"

½ C. sugar
4 oz. brandy
1 lemon
1 lime
1 orange
1 (64 oz.) bottle Yago Sangría, chilled
(48 oz.) Sundrop for strong punch OR 64 oz. Sundrop for weak punch, chilled

One hour ahead, add sugar to brandy. Slice and deseed fruits, and add to brandy mixture. Chill. When ready to serve, mix Sangría with Sundrop. Add sliced fruit and crushed ice. Serve in a punch bowl with an ice ring made of frozen Sundrop with fresh strawberries inside. Note: If Sundrop is not available, Mountain Dew can be substituted.

True Sandlin Mann
(Mrs. Jack)

"THE" MILK PUNCH

1 fifth brandy
¼ C. white creme de menthe
¾ C. creme de cocoa
1½ C. simple syrup
Whole milk to make a gallon
   of milk
Nutmeg for garnish

(Make simple syrup by bringing to a boil 1½ C. sugar and 3 C. water.) Mix all ingredients and freeze. Serve with nutmeg.

Dorothy Turner Clendenen
(Mrs. Wade)

SUSTAINER'S BLOODY MARY

1 (46 oz.) can tomato juice
2 C. vodka
½ C. fresh lime juice
3½ T. Worcestershire sauce
Dash Tabasco
½ t. salt

YIELD: ½ gallon

Sustainers Committee

CLARET LEMONADE

½ lemonade
½ Claret wine

Wipe rim of tall glass with half lemon from which juice has been squeezed. Dip glass in granulated sugar. Put ice cubes in glass; half full with lemonade. Fill with Claret.

Cookbook Committee

BRANDY FREEZE

1½ oz. brandy
1 oz. dark Creme de Cacao
3 scoops vanilla ice cream
   (or enough to make thick)

Mix in blender and serve.

SERVES 1

Mrs. Robert A. Rowland
Austin, Texas

Substitution Chart

When the recipe calls for:	You can use:
1 T. cornstarch	2 T. all-purpose flour (for thickening)
1 whole egg	2 egg yolks plus 1 T. water
1 C. homogenized milk	1 C. skim milk plus 2 T. Butter OR 1/2 C. evaporated milk plus 1/2 C. water
1 oz. unsweetened chocolate	3 T. cocoa powder plus 1 T. butter
1 t. baking powder	1/2 t. cream of tartar plus 1/4 t. baking soda.
1 C. sifted cake flour	7/8 C. sifted all-purpose flour (7/8 C. is 1 C. less 2 T.)
1/2 C. butter	7 T. vegetable shortening
1 C. sour milk or buttermilk	1 T. white vinegar plus sweet milk to equal 1 C.
1 clove fresh garlic	1 t. garlic salt OR 1/8 t. garlic powder
2 t. minced onion	1 t. onion powder
1 T. chopped fresh chives	1 t. freeze-dried chives
1 t. dry leaf herb	1 T. chopped fresh herbs
1 C. dairy sour cream	1 T. lemon juice plus evaporated milk to make 1 C.

When the recipe calls for:	You start with:
5-1/2 C. cooked fine noodles	8 oz. pkg. fine noodles
4 C. sliced raw potatoes	4 medium-sized potatoes
2 - 1/2 C. sliced carrots	1 lb. raw carrots
4 C. shredded cabbage	1 small cabbage (1 lb.)
4 C. sliced apples	4 medium-size apples
4 C. shredded Swiss or Cheddar cheese	8 oz. piece Swiss or Cheddar cheese
4 C. chopped walnuts or pecans	1 lb. shelled walnuts or pecans

Measuring Equivalents

3 t. = 1 T.	12 T. = 3/4 C.	4 C. = 1 qt.
4 T. = 1/4 C.	16 T. = 1 C.	4 qts. = 1 gal.
5 1/3 T. = 1/3 C.	1 C. = 1/2 pt.	8 qts. = 1 pk.
8 T. = 1/2 C.	2 C. = 1 pt.	4 pks. = 1 bu.

28 saltine crackers, 14 square graham crackers, or 22 vanilla wafers	=	1 C. fine crumbs
1-1/2 slices bread	=	1 C. soft crumbs
1 slice bread	=	1/4 C. fine dry crumbs
1 stick or 1/4 lb. butter	=	1/2 C. butter
Juice of 1 lemon	=	3 T. lemon juice
Grated peel of 1 lemon	=	3 T. grated lemon peel
Juice of 1 orange	=	1/3 C. orange juice
Grated peel of 1 orange	=	2 t. grated orange peel
1 C. heavy cream	=	2 C. whipped cream
1 lb. American cheese, shredded	=	4 C. American cheese, shredded

Metric Tables

Measure	Equivalent	Metric (ML)
1 tablespoon	3 teaspoons	14.8 milliliters
2 tablespoons	1 ounce	29.6 milliliters
1 jigger	1 - 1/2 oz.	44.4 milliliters
1/4 cup	4 tablespoons	59.2 milliliters
1/3 cup	5 tablespoons plus 1 teaspoon	78.9 milliliters
1/2 cup	8 tablespoons	118.4 milliliters
1 cup	16 tablespoons	236.8 milliliters
1 pint	2 cups	473.6 milliliters
1 quart	4 cups	947.2 milliliters
1 liter	4 cups, plus 3 - 1/3 tablespoons	1,000.0 milliliters
1 ounce (dry)	2 tablespoons	28.35 grams
1 pound	16 ounces	453.59 grams
2.21 pounds	35.3 ounces	1.00 kilogram

Index

ACCOMPANIMENTS
  Baked Fruit Casserole, 297
  Barbecue Sauce, 302
  Blender Hollandaise Sauce, 299
  Cherry Sauce for Ham, 297
  Cranberry Jelly, 298
  Crisp, Crunchy Sweet Pickles, 301
  Curry Accompaniments, 302
  Green Tomato Pickle Relish, 301
  H & H Mayhaw Jelly, 298
  Hot Applesauce, 297
  Hot Mustard, 299
  Hot Sauce, 300
  Jalapeño Pepper Sauce, 313
  Mother's Chow Chow, 300
  Peach Conserve, 298
  Pickled Squash, 300
  Quick Brown Sauce, 299
  Quick, Easy, No-Soak Dill Pickles, 301
  Slang Jang, 302
  Spicy Broiled Grapefruit, 297
  Sweet and Sour Sauce, 299
All American Rice Casserole, 143
Ambrosia Cake, 253
Angel Food Mocha Torte, 263
Angel Salad, 63
Anita's 9 Layer Salad, 90
Anne Goddard's English Toffee, 267
APPETIZERS
  Antipasto, 10
  Appetizer Cheese Cake, 18
  Arkansas Hot Pepper Pecans, 10
  Artichoke Dip, 9
  Artichoke Nibbles, 9
  Avocado-Crab Dip, 23
  Barbequed Shrimp, 34
  Broccoli Turnovers, 11
  Canapés, 14
  Cantonese Egg Rolls, 13
  Caponata, 11
  Caviar Mold, 12
  Caviar Supreme, 12
  Chafing Dish Crabmeat, 23
  Cheese Mold, 17
  Cheese Squares, 15
  Cheese Stuffed Mushrooms, 27
  Cheese Wafers, 15
  Chicken Turnovers, 19
  Chili Cheese Dip, 19
  Chili Dip, 20
  Chili Sour Cream Biscuits, 21
  Chutney Roll, 18
  Cocktail Meatballs, 29
  Corned Beef Capers, 21
  Crab Ham Rolls, 24
  Crab Rangoon, 24
  Crabmeat Appetizers, 22
  Crabmeat and Broccoli Dip, 22
  Crabmeat Dip, 23
  Curried Chicken Dip, 19
  Deviled Ham Puffs, 25
  Dill Dip, 13
  Dilled Cocktail Meatballs, 305
  Easy Mushroom Hors d'Oeuvres, 31
  Elegant Cheese Dip, 16
  Empanadas, 25
  Eye of Round Roast and Buns, 26
  Fried Mushrooms, 28
  Gambas Al Ajillo, 36
  Gourmet Beef and Artichoke Dip, 26
  Guacamole, 27
  Harriette Briggs Ceviche, 22
  Hot Artichoke Dip, 9
  Hot Cheese Balls, 14
  Hot Clam Dip, 21
  Hot Gala Pepper Dip, 18
  Italian Oysters, 32
  Jalapeño Appetizer, 40
  Jalapeño Cheese Dip, 40
  Marinated Crab Claws, 24
  Marinated Shrimp and Onions, 36
  Marinated Vegetables, 305
  Miniature Quiches, 30
  Molded Caviar, 13
  Mushroom Canape Dip, 29
  Mushroom Won Tons, 28
  Mushrooms Stuffed with Snails, 30
  Oyster Roll, 31
  Oysters Ernie, 29
  Picadillo Dip, 20
  Pickled Curried Eggs, 40
  Roquefort Ring, 17
  Salmon Crêpe Hors d'Oeuvre, 33
  Salmon Mold, 32
  Sausage Cheese Mold, 16
  Sausage Pinwheels, 34
  Sausage Squares, 35
  Seafood Dip, 34
  Shrimp Cheese Balls, 35
  Shrimp Paté, 36
  Shrimp Remoulade Dip, 35
  Smoked Oyster Dip, 33
  Sour Cream Beef Mold, 26
  Sour Cream and Caviar Crêpes, 12
  Sour Cream Curry Dip, 33
  Spinach Dip, 38
  Spinach Fillos, 37
  Spinach Frittata, 37
  Steak Tidbits, 27
  Stuffed Grape Leaves, 38
  Stuffed Mushrooms, 31
  Stuffed Mushrooms, 312
  Summer Dip, 32
  Swedish Meatballs, 28
  Sweet and Sour Ham Balls, 39

APPETIZERS, continued
   Sweet and Sour Pork, 39
   Swiss Crabmeat Dip, 25
   Tapenade Orangerie, 38
   Turkey Appetizer Spread, 39
   Walnut Swiss Cheese Spread, 16
Apple Coffee Cake, 242
   Dessert, Crumble, 277
   Pie, Caramel, 286
   Pie, Sour Cream, 287
   Punch, Hot, 328
   Rum Cake, 253
Applesauce, Hot, 297
Apricot Balls, 269
   Bars, 269
   Dressing, 104
   Salad, 63
Arkansas Hot Pepper Pecans, 10
Arlyne Flanagan's Divinity, 266
Army's Blackberry Cobbler, 286
Artichoke Dip, 9
   Dip, Gourmet Beef and, 26
   Dip, Hot, 9
   Hearts and Brussels Sprouts, 209
   Hearts, Stuffed, 83
   Nibbles, 9
Asparagus Cheese Mold, 82
   Marinated, 82
   Sandwich, Hot, 249
Aspic, Chicken, 69
   Ring, 100
   Shrimp, 80
   with Shrimp Sauce, Tomato, 102
   Tomato, 101
Avocado-Crab Dip, 23
   Dressing, 104
   Guacamole, 27
   Jellied Guacamole Phillips, 83
   Oliva, 84
   Onion and Cucumber Salad, 84
   Salad Dressing, 104
   Salad, Mushroom, 83
   Soup, 43
Baked Crab and Shrimp, 152
Baked Crabmeat Potatoes, 217
Baked Duck in Orange Sauce, 191
Baked Eggs, 195
Baked Fish with Tomato Sauce, 167
Baked Fruit Casserole, 297
Baked Red Snapper in Creole Sauce, 169
Baked Rice, 220
Baked Savory Tomatoes, 225
Baked Tomato Vertis, 224
Baked Vegetables with Sour Cream, 226
Baklava, 270
Banana Daiquiri Hilton, 314
   Nut Cake, 254
   Split Cake, 254

Bananas Foster, 278
Barbecue Sauce, 302
Barbecued Fish, 310
Barbecued Ham, 135
Barbecued Shrimp, 34
Barley Casserole, 207
Basic Crêpe Batter, 233
Basic Curry for Seafood or Chicken, 233
Basic French Dressing, 105
Bass with Mushrooms and Almonds, 167
Bayley's West Indies Salad, 75
Beacon Hill Cookies, 269
Bean (s)
   Baked, Quick, 208
   Butter, Casserole, 208
   Green
      Horseradish, River Road, 214
      Piquant, 215
      Toni's Super, 214
      Williamsburg, 215
      Winter Salad, 99
   Monterrey, 311
   Soup, Navy, 43
   Soup, Pinto, 44
BEEF
   GROUND:
      Beef Enchiladas, 131
      California Casserole, 120
      Chili Pie, 133
      Delia's Barbecue Meat Loaves, 119
      Enchiladas, 132
      Flautas, 130
      Glorious Mess, 131
      Green Chili Enchiladas, 132
      Green Enchiladas, 132
      Hamburger Pie, 120
      Hot Tamales, 133
      Italian Casserole, 128
      Italian Spaghetti, 128
      Ivana's Basic Meat Sauce, 124
      Ivana's Italian Crêpes, 124
      Jeanne's Sloppy Joes, 116
      Knottie's Chili, 309
      Lasagna Casserole, 127
      Lazy Lasagna, 126
      Lu Lu's Lasagna, 125
      Manicotti, 126
      Meatballs, Cocktail, 29
         Dilled Cocktail, 305
         Klops, 119
         Swedish, 28
      Mexican Spaghetti Sauce, 129
      Old Fashioned Tamale Pie, 134
      Sopa, 129
      Stuffed Cabbage, 121
      Stuffed Peppers, 121
      Taco Filling, 130
      Tufoli Casserole, 127

BEEF, continued
  ROAST:
    Brisket and Rigatoni, 117
    Carbonnade a la Flamande, 115
    Eye of Round with Buns, 26
    Fillet with Green Peppercorns, 112
    Mold, Sour Cream, 26
    Muchacho con Comino, 113
    and Potato Salad in Bread
      Rounds, 71
    Pot Roast with Herbs, 116
    Pot Roast with Red Wine, 116
    Pot Roast Supreme, 115
    Rib Eye, 111
    Roast Peppered Rib Eye, 113
    Roast Beef Salad, 74
  SOUP:
    Beef-Sausage, 45
    Hamburger, 51
    Portuguese Soupas, 57
  STEAK:
    Filet Mignon with Chicken
      Livers, 307
    Flank, London Broil, 114
    Marinated, 112
    Oriental, 123
    Roll-ups with Noodles, 114
    Tidbits, 27
    Tournedos with Artichoke
      Bottoms and Sauce
      Bearnaise, 111
  STEWS:
    Bourguignon, 117
    Caldillo, 134
    Stew, 118
    Easy Oven, 117
    a la Francaise, 118
    Oriental, 123
    Stroganoff, 308
      Elegant, 308
    Sukiyaki, 122
      Easy-To-Do, 122
Beet Salad, 84
Bettie's Rice Salad, 96
BEVERAGES
  Banana Daiquiri Hilton, 314
  Brandy Freeze, 330
  Café Marrakech, 314
  Claret Lemonade, 330
  Coffee Brazil, 329
  Coffee Punch, 328
  Froylan's Margaritas, 314
  Hot Apple Punch, 328
  Hot Buttered Rum Batter, 329
  Hot Spiced Tea, 328
  Negroni, 314
  Party Punch, 329
  Sustainer's Bloody Mary, 330
  "The" Milk Punch, 330

Billie Butter's Chicken Tetrazzini, 183
Billie Butter's Shrimp and Scallops
  Gruyere, 157
Biscuits, Chili Sour Cream, 21
  Penny's Buttermilk, 234
Bisque of Hampton Crab, 48
  Tortoni, 264
Black Forest Torte, 263
Blackberry Cobbler, Army's, 286
  Cobbler, Easy, 285
Blender Hollandaise Sauce, 299
Blender Mayonnaise, 105
Blueberry Cheese Cake, 255
  Coffee Cake, 240
  Salad, 64
Bohemian Coffee Cake, 242
Boiled Custard, 313
Borscht, 45
Bourbon Bread, 244
Braided Coffee Cake, 243
Braised Red Cabbage, 211
Brandy Freeze, 330
Brandy Peaches, 281
Bread Pudding with Brandy Sauce, 277
BREADS
  Apple Coffee Cake, 242
  Basic Crêpe Batter, 233
  Blueberry Coffee Cake, 240
  Bohemian Coffee Cake, 242
  Bourbon Bread, 244
  Braided Coffee Cake, 243
  Caraway Cheese Gems, 234
  Cheesy French Bread, 235
  Cranberry Coffee Cake, 243
  Dallas Caddo Club Hush
    Puppies, 236
  Ethiopian Honey Bread, 244
  French Bread, 247
  Glass Mountain Coffee Cake, 241
  Melba Rounds, 236
  Mexican Corn Bread, 235
  Monkey Bread, 245
  My Mother's Bread, 248
  Nashville Egg Bread, 236
  Olive Bread, 238
  Onion Shortcake, 238
  Orange Nut Bread, 237
  Orange Prune Bread, 237
  Oven Buttered Cornsticks, 235
  Parmesan Wine Bread, 238
  Party Rolls, 245
  Pecan Sticky Buns, 241
  Penny's Buttermilk Biscuits, 234
  Polly's Pumpkin Bread, 239
  Quick Cheese Bread, 234
  Refrigerator Gingerbread
    Muffins, 241
  Rich Swoot Dough, 240
  Sour Cream Cornbread, 236
  Strawberry Nut Bread, 239

BREADS, continued
  Swedish Pancake Batter, 233
  Swedish Rye Bread Limpa, 246
  Two Hour Rolls, 246
  White Bread, 248
  Yorkshire Pudding, 312
  Zucchini Bread, 240
Breast of Chicken with Artichoke Hearts, 173
Brisket and Rigatoni, 117
Broccoli Chowder, 44
  Dip, Crabmeat and, 22
  Elizabeth's, 208
  Salad, 85
  Soufflé, 207
  Turnovers, 11
Broiled Shrimp Stuffed with Crabmeat, 164
Brownie Bon Bons, 270
Brownies, Good Rich, 271
  Mint-Flavored, 271
Brunch Casserole Supreme, 197
Brussels Sprouts, 209
  and Artichoke Hearts, 209
Buffet Crab, 149
Buffet Spinach Mold, 97
Butter Bean Casserole, 208
Butter Crisp Cookies, 271
Butter Pecan Cake, 255
Buttermilk Pound Cake, 260
Cabbage, Braised Red, 211
  Creole, 210
  Slaw, 96
  Stuffed, 121
Caesar Salad, 86
Café Marrakech, 314
Cajun Chicken Casserole, 185
CAKES
  Ambrosia, 253
  Angel Food Mocha Torte, 263
  Apple Rum, 253
  Banana Nut, 254
  Banana Split, 254
  Bisque Tortoni, 264
  Black Forest Torte, 263
  Blueberry Cheese, 255
  Butter Pecan, 255
  Buttermilk Pound, 260
  Caramel Fudge, 255
  Cherry Torte, 264
  Chocolate Applesauce, 256
  Chocolate Pound, 261
  Devil's Food, 256
  Fiesta, 257
  Greek Spice, 257
  Harvey Wallbanger, 258
  Hershey Bar, 258
  Jam, 258
  Lois Jackson's Lemon Cheese or Lane, 259

  Mrs. J. H. Laird's Pound, 262
  Orange Fluff, 260
  Persimmon, 260
  Plum, 259
  Prune, 262
  Rum Pound, 261
  Whiskey, 262
Caldillo, 134
California Casserole, 120
California Salad, 85
Canadian Cheese Soup, 46
Canapés, 14
CANDY
  Divinity, Arlyne Flanagan's, 266
  English Toffee, Anne Goddard's, 267
  Fudge, 267
  Orange or Grapefruit Sticks, 268
  Orange Pralines, 267
  Peppermint Crunch, 268
  Pralines, 268
  Tips, 266
Cantonese Egg Rolls, 13
Caponata, 11
Caramel Apple Pie, 286
Caramel Fudge Cake, 255
Caramel Icing, Mary Lewis's, 265
Caraway Cheese Gems, 234
Carbonnade a la Flamande, 115
Cardinal Chicken Salad, 70
Carolyn's Layered Vegetable Salad, 89
Carrot Casserole, 210
  Pennies, Copper, 86
Carrots with Almonds, 209
Casserole of Chicken, 188
Cauliflower and Shrimp Salad, 79
  Soup, 46
Caviar Crêpes, Sour Cream and, 12
  Mold, 12
  Molded, 13
  Supreme, 12
Celery Hearts, 210
Ceviche, Harriette Briggs, 22
Chafing Dish Crabmeat, 23
Charcoal Red Snapper Fillets, 168
Charley's Pimiento Cheese, 312
CHEESE
  Balls, Hot, 14
  Blintzes, 195
  Bread, Quick, 234
  Chili Con Queso, 198
  Chilies Rellenos, 198
  Chutney Roll, 18
  Dip, Chili, 20
  Dip, Elegant, 16
  Dip, Jalapeño, 40
  Enchiladas, 199
  Gems, Caraway, 234
  Grits, 200
  Hanaho Fondue, 200

338 Index

CHEESE, continued
  Hot Gala Pepper Dip, 18
  Mold, 17
  Mold, Sausage, 16
  Molded Bleu Cheese Salad, 74
  Pimiento, Charley's, 312
  Potatoes, 218
  Roquefort Ring, 17
  Soufflé, 197
  Soup, Canadian, 46
  Soup, Cold, 306
  Spread, Walnut Swiss, 16
  Squares, 15
  Stuffed Mushrooms, 27
  Swiss Fondue, 200
  Wafers, 15
  Welsh Rarebit, 204
Cheese Cake, Appetizer, 18
  Blueberry, 255
  Lemon, Lois Jackson's, 259
Cheesy French Bread, 235
Cherries Jubilee, 313
Cherry Sauce, 264
  Sauce for Ham, 297
  Salad, Sheri's, 64
  Torte, 264
CHICKEN
  With Artichoke Hearts, Breasts of, 173
  Aspic, 69
  Basic Curry for, 233
  Breasts with Bacon, 180
  Breasts Delight, 173
  Cacciatori, 177
  Casserole of, 188
    Cajun, 185
    Curried, 188
  Chinese, 179
  Coq au Vin, 178
  Coq au Vin Flambé, 178
  Corn Chowder, 46
  Dip, Curried, 19
  D'Wango, 187
  East-West, 174
  Enchiladas, 184
  French Style, 175
  Fruited, 176
  Garlic Baked, 173
  Gumbo, 47
  Hash, 186
  Josef, 310
  Lemon Barbecue, 177
  Louisiana, 177
  Moon Gate, 179
  N' Peppers, 190
  Noodle Soup, 48
  Pie, Old Fashioned, 182
  Salad, 70
    Cardinal, 70
    Cold Curried, 69

  Cranberry, 71
  Luncheon Sandwiches, 249
  Smoked, 72
  Sauce Piquante, 189
    with Shrimp, 176
  Soufflé, Cold, 187
  Soup, Chilled Sengalese, 56
    Cream of, 47
    Curry, 48
  Spaghetti, 181
  Spaghetti, Creamy, 181
  Spaghetti Sauce, 180
  Sweet and Sour, 180
  Swiss Enchiladas, 183
  Tetrazzini, Billie Butter's, 183
  Tomato, 185
  Tomato Crêpes, 184
  Turnovers, 19
  Two Sauce, 174
  and Wild Rice Casserole, 186
  in Wine, 175
Chili Cheese Dip, 19
  Con Queso, 198
  Dip, 20
  Knottie's, 309
  Pie, 133
  Sour Cream Biscuits, 21
Chilies Rellenos, 198
Chilled Pea Soup, 53
Chilled Sengalese Soup, 56
Chinese Chicken, 179
Chinese Spareribs, 138
Chinese Tuna Salad, 81
Chinese Vegetable Salad, 88
Chocolate Angel Strata, 288
  Applesauce Cake, 256
  Caramel Bars, 272
  Chess Pie, 290
  Filling, 263
  Cream Pie, 288
  Crinkle Cookies. Crews, 272
  Mousse Glück Quick, 280
  Pound Cake, 261
  Pound Cake Icing, 261
  Sauce, Sherried, 265
Chutney Roll, 18
Cinnamon Sticks, 272
Clam Dip, Hot, 21
Claret Lemonade, 330
Clay's Favorite Sweet Potatoes, 218
Cobbler, Army's Blackberry, 286
  Easy Blackberry, 285
Cocktail Meatballs, 29
Coffee Brazil, 329
Coffee Cakes (see BREADS)
Coffee Ice Cream Pie, 290
Coffee Punch, 328
Cold Cheese Soup, 306
Cold Chicken Soufflé, 187
Cold Curried Chicken Salad, 69

Cold Salmon Bisque, 54
Cold Shrimp Curry, 163
Cold Steak Salad, 73
Cole Slaw Dressing, 105
COOKIES
    Apricot Balls, 269
    Apricot Bars, 269
    Baklava, 270
    Beacon Hill, 269
    Brownie Bon Bons, 270
    Butter Crisp, 271
    Chocolate Caramel Bars, 272
    Cinnamon Sticks, 272
    Crews Chocolate Crinkle, 272
    Date Nut Tortes, 273
    Date Tarts, 273
    Fudge Squares, 270
    Good Rich Brownies, 271
    Jelly Ribbon, 274
    Luscious Lemon Bars, 274
    Mint-Flavored Brownies, 271
    Old Fashioned Soft Sugar, 276
    Pecan Slices, 275
    Praline, 274
    Ranger, 275
    Sand Tarts, 276
    Sausage, 276
Cool Cucumber Mousse, 87
Copper Carrot Pennies, 86
Coq au Vin, 178
Coq au Vin Flambé, 178
Coquille St. Jacques, 157
Coral Gables Fish, 170
Corn and Cheese Fondue, 211
    Indian Summer Vegetables, 227
    Peg Salad, 93
    Pudding, 211
Cornbread, Mexican, 235
    Sour Cream, 236
Cornsticks, Oven-Buttered, 235
Corned Beef Capers, 21
Cornish Game Hens, 192
CRABMEAT
    Appetizers, 22
    Bayley's West Indies Salad, 75
    Bisque of Hampton, 48
    and Broccoli Dip, 22
    Broiled Shrimp Stuffed with, 164
    Buffet, 149
    Casserole, 151
    Casserole, Kata's, 149
    Casserole, Overnight, 150
    Chafing Dish, 23
    Crab Claws, Marinated, 24
    with Curried Rice, 150
    Dip, 23
        Avocado, 23
        Swiss, 25
    Filling for Crêpes, 151
    Gumbo, 49

Ham Rolls, 24
Imperial, 149
Mor's Salad, 77
Potatoes, Baked, 217
Rangoon, 24
Sandwich, 249
Salad, Rice and, 75
and Shrimp, Baked, 152
and Shrimp, Melba, 152
Cranberry Coffee Cake, 243
    Jelly, 298
    Mold, Holiday, 64
    Salad, 65
Cream Cheese Frosting, 257
Cream Cheese Potato Salad
    Dressing, 105
Cream of Chicken Soup, 47
Cream Filling, 263
Cream of Pea Soup, 53
Creamy Chicken Spaghetti, 181
Creamy Dressing for Spinach
    Salad, 106
Creamy Icing, 262
Creole Cabbage, 210
Crêpes, Basic Recipe, 233
    Chicken Tomato, 184
    Crab Filling for, 151
    Ivana's Italian, 124
    Pie, Seafood, 165
    Salmon Hors d'Oeuvre, 33
    Sour Cream and Caviar, 12
    Suzette, 279
Crews Chocolate Crinkle Cookies, 272
Crisp, Crunchy Sweet Pickles, 301
Crockpot Quail with White Wine, 191
Crumble Apple Dessert, 277
Cucumber Dill Soup, 50
    Mousse, Cool, 87
    Salad, Avocado, Onion and, 84
    Salad, Danish, 88
    Salad, Lime, 87
    Soup, 49
Cucumbers, Sautéed, 311
    Sour Cream, 87
Curried Chicken Casserole, 188
Curried Chicken Dip, 19
Curried Chicken Salad, Cold, 69
Curried Eggs, Pickled, 40
Curried Rice, Crab with, 150
Curried Rice Salad, 94
Curried Rice Winston Salad, 96
Curry, Accompaniments, 302
    Basic for Seafood or Chicken, 233
    Chicken Soup, 48
    Cold Shrimp, 163
    Dip, Sour Cream, 33
    Indian Embassy, 163
Dallas Caddo Club Hush Puppies, 236
Danish Cucumber Salad, 88
Date Nut Tortes, 273

Date Tarts, 273
Dave Abbott's German Potato
    Salad, 306
Deep Dish Pizza Pie, 140
Delia's Barbecue Meat Loaves, 119
DESSERTS (Miscellaneous)
    Bananas Foster, 278
    Boiled Custard, 313
    Brandy Peaches, 281
    Bread Pudding with Brandy
        Sauce, 277
    Cherries Jubilee, 313
    Crêpes Suzette, 279
    Crumble Apple, 277
    Easy to Serve with Mexican
        Food, 278
    English Toffee, 278
    Fabulous Orange and Lemon, 279
    Fresh Fruit, 280
    Frozen, 281
    King's Pudding, 280
    Pashka, 281
    Quick Chocolate Mousse
        Glück, 280
    Raspberry Delight, 282
    Sherried Chocolate Sauce, 265
    Strawberries Romanoff, 284
    Strawberry Banana Trifle, 282
    Strawberry Topping, 265
    Swedish Dessert Waffles, 264
Deviled Oysters on Half Shell, 155
Deviled Ham Puffs, 25
Deviled Sea Food, 166
Devil's Food Cake, 256
Devil's Food Icing, 256
Dill Dip, 13
Dilled Cocktail Meatballs, 305
Divinity, Arlyne Flanagan's, 266
Dressing, Mashed Potato, 212
    for Turkey, 212
Duck, Holly Lawrence's Wild, 311
    in Orange Sauce, Baked, 191
Earlene's Chop-Chop, 230
East-West Chicken, 174
Easy Blackberry Cobbler, 285
Easy Desserts to Serve with
    Mexican Food, 278
Easy Mushroom Hor d'Oeuvres, 31
Easy Oven Stew, 117
Easy Pie Crust, 285
Easy-To-Do Sukiyaki, 122
Egg Bread, Nashville, 236
    Rolls, Cantonese, 13
Eggplant Caponata, 11
    Casserole, 213
    New Orleans, 213
    Ratatouille, 228
    Scalloped, 214
EGGS AND CHEESE
    Baked Eggs, 195

Brunch Casserole Supreme, 197
Cheese Blintzes, 195
Cheese Grits, 200
Cheese Soufflé, 197
Chili Con Queso, 198
Chili Rellenos, 198
Egg Casserole, 198
Eggs Country Place, 196
Enchiladas, 199
Fettuccine Rene, 199
Hanaho Fondue, 200
Italian Brunch, 201
Macaroni Loaf and Sauce, 204
Noodles Au Tim, 199
Paté Brisée, 201
Onion Pie, 202
Quiche Lorraine, 201
Spanish Eggs, 195
Spinach Ricotta Pie, 202
Swiss Fondue, 200
Tomato Quiche, 203
Welsh Rarebit, 204
Williamsburg Inn Fantasio
    Omelet, 196
Elegant Beef Stroganoff, 308
Elegant Cheese Dip, 16
Elizabeth's Broccoli, 208
Empanadas, 25
Enchiladas, 132
    Beef, 131
    Cheese, 199
    Chicken, 184
    Green, 132
    Green Chili, 132
English Pea Salad, 88
English Toffee Dessert, 278
Escargot and Potatoes, 153
Essie's Hot Open Faced Turkey
    Sandwich, 250
Ethiopian Honey Bread, 244
Etoufée, 159
Eye of Round Roast with Buns, 26
Fabulous Orange and Lemon
    Dessert, 279
Fettuccine René, 199
Fideo, 213
Fiesta Cake, 257
Filet of Beef with Green
    Peppercorns, 112
Filet Mignon with Chicken Livers, 307
Filet of Red Snapper Roquefort, 169
FISH
    Baked Red Snapper in Creole
        Sauce, 169
    Barbequed, 310
    Bass with Mushrooms and
        Almonds, 167
    Ceviche, Harriette Briggs, 22
    Charcoaled Red Snapper
        Fillets, 168

FISH, continued
  Coral Gables, 170
  Filet of Red Snapper
    Roquefort, 169
  Flounder Stuffed with Crab, 164
  Stuffed Salt Water, 168
  With Tomato Sauce, Baked, 167
Flaky Pastry, 284
Flaky Pastry with Sour Cream, 285
Flautas, 130
Flounder Stuffed with Crab, 164
French Bread, 247
  Bread, Cheesy, 235
French Dressing, Basic, 105
  Roquefort, 108
French Fried Shrimp, 159
French Onion Soup, 52
French Style Chicken, 175
Fresh Fruit Dessert, 280
Fried Deviled Oysters, 155
Fried Mushrooms, 28
Fried Zucchini, 227
Frosted Salad, 65
Froylan's Margaritas, 314
Frozen Dessert, 281
Frozen Fruit Salad, 66
Frozen Tomato Salad, 102
Fruit Casserole, Baked, 297
  Dessert, Fresh, 280
  Salad, Frozen, 66
  Salad, Mixed, 68
Fruited Chicken, 176
Fudge, 267
  Pie, 289
  Squares, 270
Gambas Al Ajillo, 36
GAME
  Cornish Game Hens, 192
  Duck, Baked in Orange Sauce, 191
  Duck, Holly Lawrence's Wild, 311
  Pheasant Madeira, 190
  Quail Cargill Style, 310
  Quail with White Wine,
    Crockpot, 191
  Venison Steak, 192
Garlic Baked Chicken, 173
Garlic Soup, 50
Gazpacho Andaluz, 50
Glass Mountain Coffee Cake, 241
Glazed Ham Loaf Ring, 135
Glorious Mess, 131
Good Rich Brownies, 271
Good Sauce for Shrimp, 106
Gourmet Beef and Artichoke Dip, 26
Gourmet Hominy Bake, 215
Grandmother's Kentucky Pie, 287
Grandmother's Pumpkin Pie, 293
Grapefruit Salad, 66
  Spicy Broiled, 297
  Sticks, Orange or, 268

Grasshopper Pie, 290
Greek Spice Cake, 257
Greek Salad, 91
Green Chili Enchiladas, 132
Green Enchiladas, 132
Green Goddess Dressing, 107
Green Tomato Pickle Relish, 301
Grilled Mushrooms and Cheese
  Sandwich, 250
Guacamole, 27
Gumbo, 55
  Chicken, 47
  Crab, 49
H & H Mayhaw Jelly, 298
Ham (See PORK)
Hamburger Pie, 120
Hamburger Soup, 51
Hanaho Fondue, 200
Harriette Briggs Ceviche, 22
Harvest Pie, 291
Harvey Wallbanger Cake, 258
Hershey Bar Cake, 258
Holiday Cranberry Mold, 64
Hollandaise Sauce, Blender, 299
Holly Lawrence's Wild Duck, 311
Hominy Bake, Gourmet, 215
Horseradish Ring, 89
Hot Apple Punch, 328
Hot Applesauce, 297
Hot Artichoke Dip, 9
Hot Asparagus Sandwich, 249
Hot Buttered Rum Batter, 329
Hot Cheese Balls, 14
Hot Clam Dip, 21
Hot Gala Pepper Dip, 18
Hot Mustard, 299
Hot Rum Sauce, 253
Hot Sauce, 300
Hot Spiced Tea, 328
Hot Tamales, 133
Hush Puppies, Dallas Caddo Club, 236
ICE CREAM
  Lemon, 283
  Lemon Sherbert, 283
  No-Cook, 283
  Milky Way, 284
  Strawberry, 284
ICINGS
  Caramel, Mary Lewis's, 265
  Cherry Sauce, 264
  Chocolate Filling, 263
  Chocolate Pound Cake, 261
  Cream Cheese Frosting, 257
  Cream Filling, 263
  Creamy, 262
  Devil's Food, 256
  Hot Rum Sauce, 253
  Lane Frosting, 259
  Lemon Cheese, 259

ICINGS, continued
Lemon Filling for Angel Food
  Cake, 265
Orange, 254
Orange Fluff, 260
Impossible Pie, 292
India Tuna Salad, 81
Indian Embassy Curry, 163
Indian Summer Vegetables, 227
Italian Brunch, 201
Italian Casserole, 128
Italian Oysters, 32
Italian Spaghetti, 128
Italian Tuna Soup, 59
Ivana's Basic Meat Sauce, 124
Ivana's Italian Crêpes, 124
Jalapeño Appetizer, 40
  Cheese Dip, 40
  Pepper Sauce, 313
  Spinach, 221
Jambalaya, 137
Jam Cake, 258
Jamoca Almond Fudge Pie, 291
Jeanne's Sloppy Joes, 116
Jellied Guacamole Phillips, 83
Jellied Waldorf Salad, 68
Jelly, Cranberry, 298
  H & H Mayhaw, 298
  Ribbon Cookies, 274
Joe Croxton's 1000 Island
  Dressing, 306
Kata's Crab Casserole, 149
King's Pudding, 280
Klops, 119
Knottie's Chili, 309
Korean Salad, 100
LAMB
  Mexican Style Leg of, 146
  Roast Leg of, 146
Lane Frosting, 259
Lasagna Casserole, 127
Lazy Lasagna, 126
Lemon Bar-B-Q Chicken, 177
  Bars, Luscious, 274
  Cheese Cake, Lois Jackson's, 259
  Cheese Icing, 259
  Dessert, Fabulous Orange
    and, 279
  Filling for Angel Food Cake, 265
  Ice Cream, 283
  Sherbert, 283
Lime Cucumber Salad, 87
  Dressing, 107
Lobster Thermidor, 153
Lois Jackson's Lemon Cheese Cake
  or Lane Cake, 259
London Broil Flank Steak, 114
Louisiana Chicken, 177
Lu-Lu's Lasagna, 125
Luscious Lemon Bars, 274

Macaroni Loaf and Sauce, 204
  Salad, 89
Mango Salad, 65
Manicotti, 126
Marinated Asparagus, 82
Marinated Crab Claws, 24
Marinated Garden Vegetables, 92
Marinated Shrimp, 76
Marinated Shrimp and Onions, 36
Marinated Steak, 112
Marinated Vegetables, 305
Marinated Vegetable Salad, 91
Mashed Potato Dressing, 212
Mayonnaise, Blender, 105
MEATS (See BEEF, LAMB, PORK,
  VEAL)
Melba Rounds, 236
MEN'S FARE
  Banana Daiquiri, 314
  Barbequed Fish, 310
  Beef Stroganoff, 308
  Boiled Custard, 313
  Cafe Marrakech, 314
  Charley's Pimiento Cheese, 312
  Cherries Jubilee, 313
  Chicken Josef, 310
  Cold Cheese Soup, 306
  Dave Abbott's German Potato
    Salad, 306
  Dilled Cocktail Meatballs, 305
  Elegant Beef Stroganoff, 308
  Froylan's Margaritas, 314
  Filet Mignon with Chicken
    Livers, 307
  Holly Lawrence's Wild Duck, 311
  Jalapeño Pepper Sauce, 313
  Joe Croxton's 1000 Island
    Dressing, 306
  Knottie's Chili, 309
  Marinated Vegetables, 305
  Monterrey Beans, 311
  Negroni, 314
  Portuguese Soup, 307
  Quail Cargill Style, 310
  Sautéed Cucumbers, 311
  Stuffed Mushrooms, 312
  Veal Scallopini, 309
  Yorkshire Pudding, 312
Mexican Corn Bread, 235
Mexican Salad, 93
Mexican Spaghetti Sauce, 129
Mexican Style Leg of Lamb, 146
Mexican Vegetables, 225
Milky Way Ice Cream, 284
Miniature Quiches, 30
Mint-Flavored Brownies, 271
Mississippi Mud Pie, 289
Mixed Fruit Salad, 68
Mixed Vegetable Salad, 94
Molded Bleu Cheese Salad, 74

Molded Caviar, 13
Molded Salmon Loaf, 76
Molded Vegetable Salad, 92
Molé Salad, 95
Monkey Bread, 245
Monterrey Beans, 311
Mor's Salad, 77
Mother's Chow Chow, 300
Mrs. J. H. Laird's Pound Cake, 262
Mrs. Paul Scott's Chicken Curry
    Soup, 48
Muchacho Roast Con Comino, 113
Muffins, Refrigerator Gingerbread, 241
Mushroom Avocado Salad, 83
    Canape Dip, 29
    Carrot, Tomato Casserole, 216
    Hors d'Oeuvres, Easy, 31
    Pie, 216
    Soup, 51
    Won-Tons, 28
Mushrooms, Cheese Stuffed, 27
    Fried, 28
    Scalloped, 217
    in Sour Cream, 217
    Stuffed, 31
    Stuffed, 312
    Stuffed with Snails, 30
    and Tomatoes, 216
Mustard, Hot, 299
    Mayonnaise, 230
    Sauce for Green Beans, 230
My Mother's Bread, 248
Nashville Egg Bread, 236
Navy Bean Soup, 43
Negroni, 314
New Orleans Eggplant, 213
No-Cook Ice Cream, 283
Noodles Au Tim, 199
Oatmeal Soup, 52
Old Fashioned Chess Pie, 287
Old Fashioned Chicken Pie, 182
Old Fashioned Soft Sugar
    Cookies, 276
Old Fashioned Tamale Pie, 134
Olive Bread, 238
Omelet, Williamsburg Inn
    Fantasio, 196
Onion Pie, 202
    Shortcake, 238
    Soup, 52
    Soup, French, 52
Orange Fluff Cake, 260
    Fluff Icing, 260
    Icing, 254
    Nut Bread, 237
    or Grapefruit Sticks, 268
    and Lemon Dessert,
        Fabulous, 279
    Pineapple Salad, 67
    Pralines, 268

Prune Bread, 237
Sauce, 230
Oriental Beef Stew, 123
Oriental Shrimp Salad, 79
Oriental Steak, 123
Oven Buttered Cornsticks, 235
Overnight Crab Casserole, 150
OYSTERS
    Bienville, 154
    Deviled on Half Shell, 155
    Dip, Smoked, 33
    Ernie, 29
    Fried Deviled, 155
    Italian, 32
    Pan Roast, 156
    Roll, 31
    Scalloped, 154
    Soup, Spinach, 59
    Stew, 53
Pancake Batter, Swedish, 233
Paprika Rice, 219
Parmesan Wine Bread, 238
Party Punch, 329
Party Rolls, 245
Party Squash, 222
Pashka, 281
PASTA
    Fettuccine René, 199
    Fideo, 213
    Macaroni Loaf and Sauce, 204
    Noodles au Tim, 199
PASTRY
    Easy Pie Crust, 285
    Flaky Pastry, 284
    Flaky Pastry with Sour Cream, 285
Paté Brisée, 201
Patsy's Layered Salad, 90
Pauline Langhorne's Dressing for
    Shrimp, 106
Pea Salad, English, 88
    Soup, Chilled, 53
    Soup, Cream of, 53
    Soup, Split, 55
Peach Conserve, 298
    Melba Ice Cream Pie, 292
Peaches, Brandy, 281
Pearline's Baked Tomatoes, 225
Pecan Slices, 275
    Sticky Buns, 241
Pecans, Arkansas Hot Pepper, 10
Peg Corn Salad, 93
Penny's Buttermilk Biscuits, 234
Peppermint Crunch Candy, 268
Peppers, Stuffed, 121
Persimmon Cake, 260
Pheasant Madeira, 190
Picadillo Dip, 20
Pickled Curried Eggs, 40
Pickled Pork, 139
Pickled Squash, 300

Pickles, Crisp Crunchy Sweet, 301
   Quick, Easy, No-Soak Dill, 301
PIES
   Caramel Apple, 286
   Chocolate Angel Strata, 288
   Chocolate Chess, 290
   Chocolate Cream, 288
   Coffee Ice Cream, 290
   Fudge, 289
   Grandmother's Kentucky, 287
   Grandmother's Pumpkin, 293
   Grasshopper, 290
   Harvest, 291
   Impossible, 292
   Jamoca Almond Fudge, 291
   Mississippi Mud, 289
   Old-Fashioned Chess, 287
   Peach Melba Ice Cream, 292
   Sour Cream Apple, 287
   Strawberry, 293
   Strawberry Custard, 293
   Strudle, 294
   White Christmas, 294
Pinto Bean Soup, 44
Piquant Green Beans, 215
Pizza, Deep Dish, 140
   Real Italian, 141
Plum Cake, 259
   Salad, Spiced Purple, 67
Polly's Pumpkin Bread, 239
Poppy Seed Dressing, 107
PORK
   All American Rice Casserole, 143
   Chinese Spareribs, 138
   Chops Jamaica, 140
   Deep Dish Pizza Pie, 140
   Ham Baked in Milk, 137
      Balls, Sweet and Sour, 39
      Barbequed, 135
      and Cheese Salad, 73
      Loaf Ring, Glazed, 135
      in Patty Shells, 136
      Puffs, Deviled, 25
      Rolls, Crab, 24
      Sandwiches, 249
      Savory Russian, 136
      Spiced Baked, 138
   Jambalaya, 137
   Pickled, 139
   Quick German Casserole, 141
   Real Italian Pizza, 141
   Rigatoni Florida, 142
   Roast with Sour Cream Sauce, 139
   Spaghetti Carbonara, 142
   Sweet and Sour, 39
Portuguese Soup, 307
Portuguese Soupas, 57
Potato Salad, 95
   Dave Abbott's German, 306
Potatoes, Baked Crabmeat, 217

Cheese, 218
Stuffed Baby New, 218
Vegetable Bake, 227
Pot Roast with Herbs, 116
   with Red Wine, 116
   Supreme, 115
POULTRY (See CHICKEN and TURKEY)
Praline Cookies, 274
Pralines, 268
Prune Cake, 262
Pumpkin Bread, Polly's, 239
Punch (See BEVERAGES)
Quail Cargill Style, 310
   with White Wine, Crockpot, 191
Quiche Lorraine, 201
   Miniature, 30
   Onion Pie, 202
   Spinach Ricotta Pie, 202
   Tomato, 203
Quick Baked Beans, 208
Quick Brown Sauce, 299
Quick Cheese Bread, 234
Quick Chocolate Mousse Glück, 280
Quick, Easy, No-Soak Dill Pickles, 301
Quick German Casserole, 141

R & K Vichyssoise, 54
Ranger Cookies, 275
Raspberry Delight, 282
Ratatouille, 228
Real Italian Pizza, 141
Red Snapper in Creole Sauce,
   Baked, 169
Refrigerator Gingerbread Muffins, 241
Regina's Herbed Squash
   Casserole, 223
Relish, Green Tomato Pickle, 301
   Chop-Chop, Earlene's, 230
   Chow Chow, Mother's, 300
Remoulade Sauce, 108
Ribeye Roast, 111
Rice Baked, 220
   Casserole, Wild, 219
   and Crabmeat Salad, 75
   Julia, 220
   Paprika, 219
   Pilaf, 219
   Salad, 94
   Salad, Bettie's, 96
   Salad, Curried, 94
   Salad, Curried Winston, 96
Rich Sweet Dough, 240
Rigatoni Florida, 142
River Road Green Beans
   Horseradish, 214
Roast Beef Salad, 74
Roast Leg of Lamb, 146
Roast Peppered Rib Eye of Beef, 113
Rolls, Party, 245
   Two-Hour, 246

Roquefort French Dressing, 108
  Ring, 17
  Salad Dressing, 108
Royal Zucchini Parmesan, 229
Rum Pound Cake, 261
SALADS
  DRESSINGS:
    Apricot, 104
    Avocado, 104
    Avocado Salad, 104
    Basic French, 105
    Blender Mayonnaise, 105
    Chicken Salad, 70
    Cole Slaw, 105
    Cream Cheese Potato Salad, 105
    Creamy for Spinach Salad, 106
    Good Sauce for Shrimp, 106
    Green Goddess, 107
    Joe Croxton's 1000 Island, 306
    Lime, 107
    Pauline Langhorne's for
      Shrimp, 106
    Poppy Seed, 107
    Remoulade Sauce, 108
    Roquefort French, 108
    Roquefort Salad, 108
  FRUIT:
    Angel, 63
    Apricot, 63
    Blueberry, 64
    Cranberry, 65
    Frosted, 65
    Frozen Fruit, 66
    Grapefruit, 66
    Holiday Cranberry Mold, 64
    Jellied Waldorf, 68
    Mango, 65
    Mixed Fruit, 68
    Molded Bleu Cheese, 74
    Orange Pineapple, 67
    Sheri's Cherry, 64
    Spiced Purple Plum, 67
    Summer Congealed, 67
  MEAT AND POULTRY:
    Beef and Potato in Bread
      Rounds, 71
    Cardinal Chicken, 70
    Chicken Aspic, 69
    Chicken Cranberry, 71
    Chicken, 70
    Cold Curried Chicken, 69
    Cold Steak, 73
    Ham and Cheese, 73
    Roast Beef, 74
    Smoked Chicken, 72
    Wheat Pilaf, 72
  SEAFOOD:
    Bayley's West Indies, 75
    Cauliflower and Shrimp, 79
    Chinese Tuna, 81

    India Tuna, 81
    Marinated Shrimp, 76
    Molded Salmon Loaf, 76
    Mor's, 77
    Oriental Shrimp, 79
    Rice and Crabmeat, 75
    Salmon Rice, 78
    Seafood Mold, 75
    Shrimp Aspic, 80
    Shrimp Supreme, 77
    Tossed Tuna, 80
    Tuna, 80
    Tuna or Chicken Bombay, 78
    Tuna Party Loaf, 79

  VEGETABLE:
    Anita's 9 Layer, 90
    Asparagus Cheese Mold, 82
    Aspic Ring, 100
    Avocado Oliva, 84
    Avocado, Onion and
      Cucumber, 84
    Beet, 84
    Bettie's Rice, 96
    Broccoli, 85
    Buffet Spinach Mold, 97
    Caesar, 86
    California, 85
    Carolyn's Layered Vegetable, 89
    Chinese Vegetable, 88
    Cool Cucumber Mousse, 87
    Copper Carrot Pennies, 86
    Curried Rice, 94
    Curried Rice Winston, 96
    Danish Cucumber, 88
    Dave Abbott's German Potato, 306
    English Pea, 88
    Frozen Tomato, 102
    Greek, 91
    Horseradish Ring, 89
    Jellied Guacamole Phillips, 83
    Korean, 100
    Lime Cucumber, 87
    Macaroni, 89
    Marinated Asparagus, 82
    Marinated Garden Vegetables, 92
    Marinated Vegetable, 91
    Mexican, 93
    Mixed Vegetable, 94
    Molded Vegetable, 92
    Molé, 95
    Mushroom Avocado, 83
    Patsy's Layered Salad, 90
    Peg Corn, 93
    Potato, 95
    Rice, 94
    Slaw, 96
    Sour Cream Cucumbers, 87
    Spinach and Avocado, 99
    Spinach and Mandarin Orange, 99

SALADS, continued
  VEGETABLE:
    Spinach Mold with Cucumber
      Sauce, 97
    Spinach Potato, 98
    Spinach, 98
    Squash, 101
    Stuffed Artichoke Hearts, 83
    Tomato Aspic, 101
    Tomato Aspic with Shrimp
      Sauce, 102
    Tomato Avocado Mold, 103
    Wilted Spinach, 98
    Winter, 99
SALMON
  Bisque, Cold, 54
  Crêpe Hors d'Oeuvre, 33
  Loaf, 158
  Loaf, Molded, 76
  Mold, 32
  Rice Salad, 78
Sand Tarts, 276
SANDWICHES
  Chicken Salad Luncheon, 249
  Crab, 249
  Essie's Hot Open Faced
    Turkey, 250
  Grilled Mushrooms and
    Cheese, 250
  Ham, 250
  Hot Asparagus, 249
Sauce Piquante, 189
SAUCES
  Barbeque, 302
  Blender Hollandaise, 299
  Cherry for Ham, 297
  Hot, 300
  Jalapeño Pepper, 313
  Mustard, for Green Beans, 230
  Orange, 230
  Quick Brown, 299
  Remoulade, 108
  Sherried Chocolate, 265
  for Shrimp, Good, 106
  Sweet and Sour, 299
Sausage Cheese Mold, 16
  Cookies, 276
  Pinwheels, 34
  Rice Casserole, All American, 143
  Squares, 35
Sautéed Cucumbers, 311
Savory Russian Ham, 136
Scalloped Eggplant, 214
Scalloped Mushrooms, 217
Scalloped Oysters, 154
Scalloped Tomatoes, Hearts of Palm
  and Artichoke Hearts, 224
Scallopini al Marsala, 144
SCALLOPS
  Coquille St. Jacques, 157

  Gruyere, Billie Butter's Shrimp
    and, 157
  Tetrazzini, 156
SEAFOOD (See CRAB, FISH,
    LOBSTER, OYSTERS,
    SALMON, SHRIMP and TUNA)
Seafood, Bisque, 56
  Crêpe Pie, 165
  Curry, Basic, 162
  Curry, Indian Embassy, 163
  Deviled, 166
  Dip, 34
  Mold, 75
  Newburg, 166
Sheri's Cherry Salad, 64
Sherried Chocolate Sauce, 265
SHRIMP
  Aspic, 80
  Baked Crab and, 152
  Barbequed, 34
  Bisque, 57
  Casserole, 161
  Cheese Balls, 35
  Creole, Super, 161
  Curry, Cold, 163
  Divine, 160
  Etoufée, 159
  French Fried, 159
  Gambas Al Ajillo, 36
  Grand Chenier, 158
  Marinated, 76
  Melba, Crab and, 152
  and Onions, Marinated, 36
  Orleans, 160
  Paté, 36
  Remoulade Dip, 35
  and Rice, Sylvia's, 160
  Salad, Cauliflower and, 79
  Salad, Oriental, 79
  Salad, Supreme, 77
  and Scallops Gruyere, Billie
    Butter's, 157
  Stuffed with Crabmeat,
    Broiled, 164
  Supreme, 164
Slang Jang, 302
Slaw, 96
Smoked Chicken Salad, 72
  Oyster Dip, 33
Sopa, 129
SOUPS
  Avocado, 43
  Beef-Sausage, 45
  Bisque of Hampton Crab, 48
  Borscht, 45
  Broccoli Chowder, 44
  Canadian Cheese, 46
  Cauliflower, 46
  Chicken-Corn Chowder, 46
  Chicken Curry, 48

SOUPS, continued
   Chicken Gumbo, 47
   Chicken Noodle, 48
   Chilled Pea, 53
   Chilled Sengalese, 56
   Cold Cheese, 306
   Cold Salmon Bisque, 54
   Crab Gumbo, 49
   Cream of Chicken, 47
   Cream of Pea, 53
   Cucumber, 49
   Cucumber Dill, 50
   French Onion, 52
   Garlic, 50
   Gazpacho Andaluz, 50
   Gumbo, 55
   Hamburger, 51
   Italian Tuna, 59
   Mushroom, 51
   Navy Bean, 43
   Oatmeal, 52
   Onion, 52
   Oyster Stew, 53
   Pinto Bean, 44
   Portugese, 307
   Portugese Soupas, 57
   R & K Vichyssoise, 54
   Seafood Bisque, 56
   Shrimp Bisque, 57
   Split Pea, 55
   Spinach-Oyster, 59
   Spring Garden, 58
   Squash, 58
   Vegetable, 60
   Venison, 60
   Zucchini, 58
Sour Cream and Caviar Crêpes, 12
Sour Cream Apple Pie, 287
Sour Cream Beef Mold, 26
Sour Cream Cornbread, 236
Sour Cream Cucumbers, 87
Sour Cream Curry Dip, 33
Spaghetti Carbonara, 142
Spanish Eggs, 195
Spiced Baked Ham, 138
Spiced Purple Plum Salad, 67
Spicy Broiled Grapefruit, 297
Spinach and Avocado Salad, 99
   Cups, 221
   Dip, 38
   Fillos, 37
   Frittata, 37
   Jalapeño, 221
   Korean Salad, 100
   and Mandarin Orange Salad, 99
   Mold, Buffet, 97
   Mold with Cucumber Sauce, 97
   and Oyster Soup, 59
   Potato Salad, 98
   Ricotta Pie, 202
   Salad, 98
   Salad, Wilted, 98
   Soufflé, 220
Split Pea Soup, 55
Spring Garden Soup, 58
Squash Bake, 222
   Baked Vegetables with Sour Cream, 226
   Casserole, Regina's Herbed, 223
   Mexican Vegetables, 225
   Party, 222
   Pepper Casserole, 223
   Pickled, 300
   Salad, 101
   Soup, 58
   Stuffed, 222
   Summer Vegetable Casserole, 226
Steak, Flank, London Broil, 114
   Marinated, 112
   Oriental, 123
   Roll-Ups with Noodles, 114
   Salad, Cold, 73
   Tidbits, 27
Strawberries Romanoff, 284
Strawberry Banana Trifle, 282
   Custard Pie, 293
   Ice Cream, 284
   Nut Bread, 239
   Pie, 293
   Topping, 265
Strudle, 294
Stuffed Artichoke Hearts, 83
Stuffed Baby New Potatoes, 218
Stuffed Cabbage, 121
Stuffed Grape Leaves, 38
Stuffed Mushrooms, 31
Stuffed Peppers, 121
Stuffed Salt Water Fish, 168
Stuffed Squash, 222
Sukiyaki, 122
Summer Congealed Salad, 67
Summer Dip, 32
Summer Vegetable Casserole, 226
Super Shrimp Creole, 161
Sustainer's Bloody Mary, 330
Swedish Dessert Waffles, 264
Swedish Meatballs, 28
Swedish Pancake Batter, 233
Swedish Rye Bread Limpa, 246
Sweet and Sour Ham Balls, 39
Sweet and Sour Pork, 39
Sweet and Sour Sauce, 299
Sweet Potatoes, Clay's Favorite, 218
Sweet-Sour Chicken, 180
Swiss Crabmeat Dip, 25
Swiss Enchiladas, 183
Swiss Fondue, 200
Sylvia's Shrimp and Rice, 160
Taco Filling, 130

Index

Tapenade Orangerie, 38
"The" Milk Punch, 330
Tips for Candymaking, 266
Toffee, Anne Goddard's English, 267
Tomato Aspic, 101
   Aspic Ring, 100
   Aspic with Shrimp Sauce, 102
   Avocado Mold, 103
   Chicken, 185
   Quiche, 203
   Salad, Frozen, 102
   Vertis, Baked, 224
Tomatoes, Baked Savory, 225
   Pearline's Baked, 225
   Scalloped, Hearts of Palm and Artichoke Hearts, 224
Toni's Super Green Beans, 214
Torte, Angel Food Mocha, 263
   Black Forest, 263
   Cherry, 264
Tossed Tuna Salad, 80
Tournedos with Artichoke Bottoms and Sauce Béarnaise, 111
Tufoli Casserole, 127
TUNA
   Cheese Casserole, 170
   Jalapeño Appetizer, 40
   Party Loaf, 79
   Salad, 80
   Salad, Bombay, 78
   Salad, Chinese, 81
   Salad, India, 81
   Salad, Tossed, 80
   Soup, Italian, 59
   Tapenade Orangerie, 38
TURKEY
   Appetizer Spread, 39
   Creme, 191
   and Oysters in Cream Sauce, 190
   Sandwich, Essie's Open Faced, 250
Two Hour Rolls, 246
Two Sauce Chicken, 174
VEAL
   Birds Garnished with Fresh Mushrooms and Artichoke Hearts, 145
   Cutlets Oscar, 144
   Orloff, 143
   Parmesan, 145
   Scallopini, 309
   Scallopini Al Marsala, 144
VEGETABLES
   Bake, 227
   Baked Crabmeat Potatoes, 217
   Baked Rice, 220
   Baked Savory Tomatoes, 225
   Baked Tomato Vertis, 224
   Barley Casserole, 207
   Braised Red Cabbage, 211
   Broccoli Soufflé, 207
   Brussels Sprouts, 209
   Brussels Sprouts and Artichoke Hearts, 209
   Butter Bean Casserole, 208
   Carrot Casserole, 210
   Carrots with Almonds, 209
   Casserole, Summer, 226
   Celery Hearts, 210
   Cheese Potatoes, 218
   Clay's Favorite Sweet Potatoes, 218
   Corn and Cheese Fondue, 211
   Corn Pudding, 211
   Creole Cabbage, 210
   Dressing for Turkey, 212
   Eggplant Casserole, 213
   Elizabeth's Broccoli, 208
   Fideo, 213
   Fried Zucchini, 227
   Gourmet Hominy Bake, 215
   Indian Summer, 227
   Jalapeño Spinach, 221
   Marinated, 305
   Marinated Garden, 92
   Mashed Potato Dressing, 212
   Mexican, 225
   Monterrey Beans, 311
   Mushroom, Carrot, Tomato Casserole, 216
   Mushroom Pie, 216
   Mushrooms in Sour Cream, 217
   Mushrooms and Tomatoes, 216
   New Orleans Eggplant, 213
   Paprika Rice, 219
   Party Squash, 222
   Pearline's Baked Tomatoes, 225
   Piquant Green Beans, 215
   Quick Baked Beans, 208
   Ratatouille, 228
   Regina's Herbed Squash Casserole, 223
   Rice Julia, 220
   Rice Pilaf, 219
   River Road Green Beans Horseradish, 214
   Royal Zucchini Parmesan, 229
   Sauces
      Earlene's Chop Chop, 230
      Mustard, for Green Beans, 230
      Mustard Mayonnaise, 230
      Orange, 230
   Sautéed Cucumbers, 311
   Scalloped Eggplant, 214
   Scalloped Mushrooms, 217
   Scalloped Tomatoes, Hearts of Palm and Artichoke Hearts, 224
   with Sour Cream, Baked, 226
   Spinach Cups, 221
   Spinach Soufflé, 220

VEGETABLES, continued
   Squash Bake, 222
   Squash-Pepper Casserole, 223
   Stuffed Baby New Potatoes, 218
   Stuffed Squash, 222
   Summer Vegetable Casserole, 226
   Toni's Super Green Beans, 214
   Wild Rice Casserole, 219
   Williamsburg Green Beans, 215
   Zucchini Casserole, 228
   Zucchini Soufflé, 229
Vegetable Soup, 60
Venison Soup, 60
   Steak, 192
Walnut Swiss Cheese Spread, 16
Welsh Rarebit, 204
Wheat Pilaf Salad, 72
Whiskey Cake, 262
White Bread, 248
White Christmas Pie, 294
Wild Rice Casserole, 219
Williamsburg Green Beans, 215

Williamsburg Inn Fantasio Omelet, 196
Wilted Spinach Salad, 98
WINES, 315
   Categories of, 317
   Choosing the Right, 317
   Footnotes on, 327
   Fun with: Tasting, 321
   Glasses, 320
   Handling and Storing, 319
   Proper Temperature for Serving, 319
   Quantities, 320
   Serving, 320
   Suggestions in Chart Form, 322
Winter Salad, 99
Yorkshire Pudding, 312
Zucchini
   Bread, 240
   Casserole, 228
   Fried, 227
   Royal Parmesan, 229
   Soufflé, 229
   Soup, 58

For additional copies of **The Bounty of East Texas** write:

JUNIOR LEAGUE OF LONGVIEW, INC.
P. O. Box 866
LONGVIEW, TEXAS 75606

The Bounty of East Texas at _____ **$9.95** per copy
plus postage and handling charges_____ **1.50** per copy
Texas residents - 5% sales tax _____ **.50** per copy

JUNIOR LEAGUE OF LONGVIEW, INC.
P. O. Box 866
LONGVIEW, TEXAS 75606

Please send me _____ copies of **The Bounty of East Texas** at _____ **$9.95** per copy
plus postage and handling charges _____ **1.50** per copy
Texas residents - 5% sales tax _____ **.50** per copy

Enclosed is my check or money order for $_____.
Make checks payable to THE BOUNTY OF EAST TEXAS.

NAME _____
STREET _____
CITY _____ STATE _____ ZIP _____

JUNIOR LEAGUE OF LONGVIEW, INC.
P. O. Box 866
LONGVIEW, TEXAS 75606

Please send me _____ copies of **The Bounty of East Texas** at _____ **$9.95** per copy
plus postage and handling charges _____ **1.50** per copy
Texas residents - 5% sales tax _____ **.50** per copy

Enclosed is my check or money order for $_____.
Make checks payable to THE BOUNTY OF EAST TEXAS.

NAME _____
STREET _____
CITY _____ STATE _____ ZIP _____

JUNIOR LEAGUE OF LONGVIEW, INC.
P. O. Box 866
LONGVIEW, TEXAS 75606

Please send me _____ copies of **The Bounty of East Texas** at _____ **$9.95** per copy
plus postage and handling charges _____ **1.50** per copy
Texas residents - 5% sales tax _____ **.50** per copy

Enclosed is my check or money order for $_____.
Make checks payable to THE BOUNTY OF EAST TEXAS.

NAME _____
STREET _____
CITY _____ STATE _____ ZIP _____